JETHRO TULL
Chronicles 1967-79

Laura Shenton

"It's all going so fast I cannot remember what I was doing last week."

- John Evan, *New Musical Express*, May 1970.

"There are some songs which you sit down and think 'I'll write a song' and they sometimes turn out okay. Then there are others which you just have to write, and they are the real songs, the ones which are going to last for you personally. And it's very important to please yourself and not your manager or record producer."

- Ian Anderson, *Disc And Music Echo*, November 1968.

JETHRO TULL
Chronicles 1967-79

Laura Shenton

WYMER PUBLISHING
Bedford, England

First published in Great Britain in 2022
by Wymer Publishing
www.wymerpublishing.co.uk
Tel: 01234 326691
Wymer Publishing is a trading name of Wymer (UK) Ltd

Copyright © Wymer Publishing.

ISBN: 978-1-912782-93-2

Edited by Jerry Bloom

The Author hereby asserts her rights to be identified
as the author of this work in accordance with sections
77 to 78 of the Copyright, Designs & Patents Act 1988.

All rights reserved. No part of this publication may be
reproduced or transmitted in any form or by any means,
electronic or mechanical, including photocopying, or any
information storage and retrieval system, without written
permission from the publisher.

This publication is sold subject to the condition that it shall not,
by way of trade or otherwise, be lent, re-sold, hired out or
otherwise circulated without the publishers prior consent in any
form of binding or cover other than that in which it is published
and without a similar condition including this condition
being imposed on the subsequent purchaser.

Every effort has been made to trace the copyright holders of the
photographs in this book but some were unreachable. We would
be grateful if the photographers concerned would contact us.

Design by Andy Bishop / 1016 Sarpsborg
Printed by Imago Group.

A catalogue record for this book is available from the British Library.

Roll Of Honour

Wymer Publishing duly acknowledges the following people who all put their faith in this publication by pre-ordering it:

Colin Altree
David Balca
Burr Beard
David Bethell
Rupert Bobrowicz
Stuart Brenner
Paul Burnett
Michael I Butler
Thomas Clifford
Gary R Cole
Martin Cope
Philip Cowdery
Andrew Cunningham
Troy DeAngelis
Paul Diana
Jon Dixon
Chris "Edward's Operation" Dixon
Rick Dodderidge
Ed Donnelly
Mike England
Alessandro Fagioli
David Flintham
Daniel A. Flynn
Alan Gasmer
Gary Goodson
Irvin Hansen
Michael Harwell
Paul Heiser
John Herman
Michael Herrington
Karen Hetherington
Douglas Hext
Paul Hooper
Michael Hurst
Ray Judd
James Kamberaj
Stephen Kracht
Bruno Laplante

Jimmy Lomas
Nik Magill
George Mann
Christopher McAdams
Jim Meale
Brian Miller
David Monks
Joel Murray
Libor Mysliveček
Alexandros Nalbanis
Ian Oxley
Kyle Parrish
Ronald Pease
Greg Peters
Trish Philbrook
Graham Pickett
Christine Ritchie
Nigel Sheppard
Charles Silver
Brian Slagel
George Smith
Eric Sweetwood
Kenneth Talbot
Tim Taylor
Paul Thompson
Martin Thompson
Mark Thundercliffe
Son Tuffnell
Howard Twiddle
Mikko Uusi-Oukari
Gregory Vick
Greg Walker
Stephen Waters
Graham Whitelaw
Laurence Withers
Brian Worth
Paul Wren
Mark Yates

Contents

Preface	**9**
Part One: 1967-71	**11**
Part Two: 1972-75	**83**
Part Three: 1976-79	**135**
Discography	**201**
Tour Dates	**215**

Preface

Although most consider that the seventies was the peak era for Jethro Tull, the late sixties were also a vital period for the band; it was during this period that group dynamics were established and every new line-up signified a stylistic change that would take Jethro Tull further towards their winning formula that shone through on later albums such as *Thick As A Brick* in 1972.

The scope of this book covers the years 1967 to 1979 in detail. It is certainly not the first book on Jethro Tull but the aim is to provide something that delves extensively into the history rather than something that offers an overview that sits in the context of a wider time period. Vintage gig reviews, quotes from band members that were printed at the time of the events, rare advertisements documenting how they were billed alongside their peers — it's all in here.

As author of this book I have no affiliation with Jethro Tull or with any of their associates and as such, an objective view on the history will feature here rather than one that sways towards a more recent, revisionist bias.

Preserving the detailed history of a band as influential as Jethro Tull is a vital endeavour because there will probably come a time where this information becomes harder to source due to being lost over time. Archiving matters and to many fans out there, so does the fascinating story of Jethro Tull and it is for those reasons that this book exists.

Part One: 1967-71

Born on the 10th August 1947, one Ian Anderson who had moved to Blackpool at the age of twelve started a band called The Blades. Named after M's club in Ian Fleming's *James Bond* novels, the band consisted of friends Michael Stephens on guitar with Jeffrey Hammond on bass, John Evans on piano and Paul Jackman on drums. They typically played blues music on the local club circuit. (Hammond would later go on to be known as Hammond-Hammond as a humorous nod towards the fact that his parents both had the same surname prior to being married).

In late 1963, The Blades played their first paid gig at Blackpool's Holy Family Youth Club. It was a youth club that John Evans attended, a Roman Catholic venue that used to hold a dance every Friday night. Over time The Blades' repertoire included songs such as 'Green Onions', 'Watermelon Man', 'Bo Diddley', The Rolling Stones' versions of 'Route 66' and 'Walking The Dog', The Pretty Things' 'Rosalyn', The Animals' 'Bright Lights, Big City' and Sonny Boy Williams' 'Fattening Frogs For Snakes'.

In early 1964, Paul Jackman was replaced by fourteen-year-old Barrie Barlow. Autumn 1965 saw Michael Stephens leave to be replaced by Jim Doolin (a trumpet and saxophone player) and Martin Skyrme (a tenor saxophone player). With this line-up, The Blades changed their name to the John Evan Band — with the "s" being dropped from Evans' name for phonetic effect. Evans' mother was a piano teacher who had already given him some lessons. A large reason as to why the band was named after him was that his mother paid for the band's van. They couldn't afford to pay her back so the least they felt they could do was name the band after her son.

Stephens left and new guitarists Chris Riley and Neil Smith were brought in. Hammond was replaced on bass by Bo Ward and later Glenn Cornick. A drummer by the name of Ritchie Dharma briefly took Barlow's place. Also, tenor saxophone player Neil Valentine and baritone sax player Tony Wilkinson were welcomed to the fold.

In May 1967, the band were given positive reviews for their performance on Granada TV's *Firstimers* talent show. Granada's entertainment producer, John Hamp, wrote in the *Radio Times*; "Jazz-blues, à la Georgie Fame, are presented by the seven-piece John Evan Band, from Blackpool. Again, it's an original number called 'Take The Easy Way' and the composer was bearded vocalist Ian Anderson. Most of the requests I get for auditions are from groups. These boys are certainly the best I have heard so far. And I think they stand a good chance of making the grade."

The same month, the *Blackpool Evening Gazette* commented; "A Blackpool group appears on Granada's new talent contest *Firstimers*, tonight. They are the John Evan Smash, a seven-man jazz blues group led by John Evan, of Warley Road, North Shore. *Firstimers* is a new three-month-long national talent contest produced by Granada. Groups will be given their first TV break in a nightly spot. At the end of three months a panel of judges will pick the winning act. The John Evan Smash will sing 'Take The Easy Way', written by Ian Anderson, of Devonshire Road, St Annes. The rest of the group is: Glenn Barnard (bass) of Kendal Avenue, Carleton; Neil Valentine (tenor sax) of Fallowfield; Neil Smith (guitar) of Bolton; Tony Wilkinson (baritone sax) of Norwood Road, St Annes; and Barry Barlow (drums) of King Street, Blackpool." (At some point in 1967, the band changed their name to the John Evan Smash. Based on the reports regarding their appearance on Granada TV, it is a strong possibility that it may have occurred in the May of that year. Also, note the swift change of line-up that must have occurred within a short space of time. The same Glenn Cornick was present though

— he sometimes went by the name of Glenn Barnard at this stage of his career).

Welsh band Amen Corner, fronted by Andy Fairweather Low won *Firstimers* with an old blues song 'Gin House Blues', first recorded in 1926 by Bessie Smith. Nevertheless, going on the show had given the John Evan Smash an important publicity boost. *Firstimers* ran from May 1967 to April 1968. Produced by Johnny Hamp, it was broadcast every weekday in the Granada region as a segment on the ten-minute magazine programme *On Air*, on at 4:50pm. Extended editions of *Firstimers* were broadcast on Wednesday nights. As one of the few British music programmes willing to engage with the more obscure and psychedelic side of pop, a total of over two-hundred editions were made.

A similar good fortune in such lexicon occurred when the John Evan Smash supported Ten Years After at a small gig in Manchester in mid-June 1967. It was there that they met Chris Wright — who at the time was a concert promoter. He was also active in the role of social secretary at Manchester University along with Terry Ellis. As part of managing Ten Years After, the duo operated under the recently named Ellis-Wright agency. Their names would go on to become a vital part of Jethro Tull's history.

When the group made the decision to move to London in 1967, Ian Anderson's father gave him a large old coat to help him through the winter. It was the same coat that would be making many on stage appearances at a later date (Anderson was quoted in *Record Mirror* in October 1968; "I started wearing it when we played a club last winter. It was very cold, so I found this coat and it's been with me ever since. Sometimes I don't feel like wearing it, but I suppose it has become a sort of trademark for us. Some people think we are always zany on stage but then we play to the audience. Other times we might feel belligerent, so we play accordingly.").

With financial struggles ongoing, the move to London was in a last bid attempt to make a living out of their music. By this point, they owed their parents and friends a considerable amount of money that had been put forward for equipment. It made sense for the group to move to London because amongst the financial struggles, they had gone as far as they possibly could playing in the north of England. Being highly aware of how they needed to make their operation sustainable, the thriving London blues scene seemed like a good option. With pubs and clubs running blues nights every night of the week, there was hope. Unfortunately though, with only three or four gigs booked before they made the move, the group split when they had nowhere to live and were struggling to pay for food. With the exception of Ian Anderson and Glenn Cornick the rest of the group decided to call it a day.

Cornick was possibly in a better position to stay in London because his parents had already moved there. Meanwhile Ian Anderson was living in Luton in a bedsit attic room. Barely getting by, he took a part time job at Luton's Ritz cinema as a cleaner (he was quoted in *Rolling Stone* in December 1970; "We'd boil potatoes one day and for two or three days afterwards you'd heat up a mixture of Irish stew and mashed potatoes that was cold and left over from the day before. Pease pudding — dip bread in it — it was vile.").

Determined not to give up music, Anderson and Cornick were eventually joined by guitarist Mick Abrahams and drummer Clive Bunker (the pair had played together as members of local blues band, McGregor's Engine). Together, they made a four-piece blues band. Anderson and Cornick had met Abrahams when gigging as the John Evan Band in Luton where even then, Abrahams had expressed an interest in joining the band.

It is possible that the move to London may have had an effect on the music. Anderson was quoted in *Disc And Music Echo* in November 1968; "We used to blow around at home — in Blackpool — and we worked out this version of Bach's eighth sonata with a swinging, hard jazzy sound. It was great. Then I came down to London last Christmas — I'd never been away from home before, it was just like the yokel hitting the city with all his belongings in a knotted hankie at the end of a stick — and I heard The Nice, who are onto the same classical thing. So we had to work out something different." It was largely the popularity of blues music in the late sixties that would help Jethro Tull come to prominence.

When the four-piece blues band consisting of Anderson, Abrahams, Cornick and Bunker began playing gigs in December 1967, they had yet to settle on a name for the band (this was advantageous in some ways because by going under different names they were able to get more bookings each week). The names included Navy Blue and Bag Of Blues. It was the name of Jethro Tull (an eighteenth-century agriculturalist and inventor of the horse-drawn seed drill) that stuck though.

Regarding the band's choice of name, Anderson was quoted in *New Musical Express* in November 1968; "Somebody in the agency was always making cracks about Jethro Tull because I looked a country sod." Represented by the Ellis-Wright agency (which would become Chrysalis in late 1969) by this point, they typically played two gigs each week which was just about enough to enable Anderson to live frugally. The other members of the band all had a place to stay at their respective parents' homes. In order to get more gigs, the agency was booking the band with clubs by telling the latter to expect a seven piece that included two sax players and an organ player, even though it was patently untrue. With a positive response from the venues that were pleased with the four-piece band as they presented, the band began to officially promote themselves as such. It was at their third gig at the Marquee where, upon having become more established as a live act and confident of their ability to get re-bookings, that the name of Jethro Tull stuck.

With a name, the band were able to get their first recording contract — kind of! It wasn't officially a record deal or really even a gentleman's agreement. MGM were already in possession of a demo tape that the band had sent in and being aware of their growing appeal at the Marquee, decided to put out a single. 'Sunshine Day' was recorded at London's CBS Studios in October 1967. Written by Mick Abrahams, it wasn't reflective of what Jethro Tull sounded like on stage, so much so that that particular song wasn't even part of their setlist! Equally, the B-side, 'Aeroplane', was an old John Evan Band track sans saxophones. Furthermore, the record label was inaccurately printed, referring to the band as Jethro Toe. Anderson was quoted in *Zigzag* in December 1969; "Yes, they made a mistake with the label — it was a mis-spelling on someone's part because we were in fact called Jethro Tull at the time. But we had only been together for about a week when we made that — it was one of the first things we ever did. We didn't actually have a record contract then, but I knew a producer through somebody else, and he'd asked us to make the record. In fact, it was rather a silly thing for us to have done — it was done as a laugh rather than being representative of our style at the time. We didn't play anything like that afterwards — it was just one of Mick's poppy kind of tunes."

In later years Glenn Cornick asserted that producer Derek Lawrence did it deliberately because he didn't like the name Jethro Tull. Released in February 1968, the record didn't sell very well at all, so much so that years later Anderson received a royalty cheque that totalled just a few pence. It did however, help Jethro Tull to get a residency spot playing at London's Marquee club. It was an excellent vehicle through which the band were able to elevate their profile.

Based on the latter, it is a strong likelihood that the following report from *Record Mirror* in February 1968 was something of an overstatement: "New British blues group, Jethro Tull, have signed a £50,000 contract with the Ellis-Wright Agency, and have also negotiated a five year recording deal with MGM records. Their first record, an original composition called 'Sunshine Day', is to be released on February 16th, on MGM in Britain, and on the Music Factory label in America. They also have an LP for release in the US in March. The group is at the Marquee on February 2nd and 9th, and at the Speakeasy on February 5th."

Still though, 'Sunshine Day' was reviewed in *Melody Maker* in the February; "Jethro was originally the man who invented the seed drill. This Mr Tull, misnamed on the label as Jethro Toe, is going down a storm with his group in London clubs with an unusual sound and approach. While not a hit, this West Coast flavoured tune will break the recording ice."

Across 1968, Jethro Tull would go on to play a total of twenty-two gigs at London's Marquee club. It was on 19th June 1967 that the John Evan Smash had first played there (with their second date there being on 4th August). Jethro Tull's residency at the Marquee began on the 2nd February 1968. Anderson's iconic appearance in the long old overcoat was extended as he attended the club with a Woolworth's carrier bag containing instruments, an alarm clock and a hot water bottle. Jethro Tull's last gig at the Marquee in 1968 took place on the 26th November. With *This Was* having been released two months prior, the band were welcomed with enthusiasm. The instrumental track recorded in 1968, 'One For John Gee', was done as a tribute to the club's manager who had been encouraging to the band from the start. The track was used as the B-side on the 'Song For Jeffrey' single.

It was just as well that the 'Sunshine Day' single didn't take off because it wasn't reflective of Jethro Tull at all, both in terms of the band's name as well as their trademark sound; 'Sunshine Day' features no flute. With Jethro Tull's overall image still being in its tentative stage, the late spring of 1968 saw managers Terry Ellis and Chris Wright suggesting that Mick Abrahams should be central to the band on his guitar — so much so that they suggested that Anderson give up playing the flute! The idea was informed by the fact that at the time, many blues fans were reluctant to embrace a band that had a wind instrument as the pinnacle of their sound. Jethro Tull's management were ultimately cautious that the band were just too strange to be commercially feasible. Abrahams was happy to embrace such logic — he was an avid blues fan who was keen to push for something more in the vein of something traditional. However, it was Anderson's stage presence of leaping about and playing the flute standing on one leg that helped to get the band so much valued attention from the press.

Anderson had begun playing the flute just before moving from Blackpool down to London. The way in which he had acquired the instrument was something of a coincidence. In order to raise some much-needed money at the time, he took an electric guitar to a shop in order to sell it for cash. The shop wouldn't take cash though. The best they could offer Anderson was a trade. So looking around the shop, and seeing a flute, he chose that on the basis that it was portable and compatible with the nomadic lifestyle he was living at the time. In the same vein, the speed at which Anderson taught himself to play the flute was considerably rapid. "I couldn't think of anything else

Granada TV Studios, May 3rd 1967.

WEDNESDAY: Jazz-blues, a la Georgie Fame, are presented by the seven-piece John Evan Band, from Blackpool. Again, it's an original number called "Take the Easy Way" and the composer was bearded vocalist Ian Anderson.

Most of the requests I get for auditions are from groups. These boys are certainly the best I have heard so far. And I think they stand a good chance of making the grade.

First Official Promo Picture, 1968.

JETHRO TULL

THE ELLIS-WRIGHT AGENCY LTD
CARRINGTON HOUSE
130 REGENT STREET
LONDON W.1.

Rolling Stone/December 27, 1969   PAGE 37

Stand Up!, Jethro Tull (Reprise 6360)
No, Jethro Tull is not just another English blues band. *This Was*, their first album, made some gestures in that direction, obligatory, in a way, for the time (summer of '68); in its differences it was intriguing even as it disappointed. Its inadequacies were unconventional; the essential problem seemed to be a style in search of a subject.

Bob Dylan once said that the English know how to pronounce "marvelous" better than Americans, but that they have a little trouble with "raunchy." *Stand Up!*, Jethro Tull's new album, has a fairly low raunch quotient, true to form, but it is quite marvelous. For one

Ian Anderson: low on raunch, but quite marvelous

thing, the band's orientation is more definite than before. With the removal of Rick Abrahams to form Blodwyn Pig, the musical tug-of-war which could be heard on the first album has here been effectively curtailed. Ian Anderson simply dominates the proceedings—doing all the writing and singing, and playing a potpourri of instruments. He revels a melodic gift on this album not ap-

parent on the earlier one, a fuller awareness of the coloristic possibilities of the flute, and a catholicity of taste.

Stand Up! has great textural interest, due, in part, to a more sophisticated recording technique, in part to the organ, mandolin, balalaika, etc., which Anderson plays to enrich each song. The band is able to work with different musical styles, but without a trace of the facile,

glib manipulation which strains for attention. I can hear ethnic influences throughout the album—a hint of Greek rhythms on the flute break of "We Used to Know" and in the body of "Four Thousand Mothers"—but they are too well assimilated to be easily pinpointed. "Bourree" has that unmistakable baroque swing, a suggestion of the traditional English round, some jazz interludes, and a straight-forward yet breathtaking bass solo before, it winds its way to completion. "Jeffrey Goes to Leicester Square" has a sense of the vague, charming disorganization of medieval music. "Look into the Sun," which finishes side one, is in its melodic twists and turns, a song of genuine poignance, with Martin Barre's guitar playing a model of lyricism and understatement.

On the second side, "We Used to Know" employs what could be called a fade-in, beginning softly and then building in volume, with Barre wah-wahing madly by the end. Only "Reasons for Waiting" is slightly marred, there being a superfluous string section.

As I've said, the album is not really funky; rather, it is a meticulously crafted work (no sterility implied) which deserves careful listening. At a time when many of the established stars are faltering, it is a particular pleasure to hear an important new voice. — BEN GERSON

Ian Anderson on flute

JETHRO TULL

thinking learning getting better

IT happens every time. Every year, the National Jazz and Blues Festival throws up one hugely successful group, previously more or less unheard of, except to the devotees down at the Marquee and other hip clubs, and thrusts them into the national limelight.

Last year, Ten Years After were the group who swept all before them. This time it was the turn of Jethro Tull, a four-piece outfit with their roots firmly in the blues, who came out of nowhere to become the stars of the Festival. Their version of "Cat Squirrel", theoretically the same as the Cream number, had the 20,000-odd congregation on their feet and cheering, while "Serenade to A Cuckoo" provoked incredulous gasps at the sheer joy and virtuosity of Ian Anderson's exuberant flute playing.

In fact, the whole band — Glenn Cornick, bass; Clive Bunker, drums; Mick Abrahams, guitar and Anderson, flute, mouth organ and vocals, were a powerful tonic to jaded ears, and judging by reactions of the audience and the business, they're well on the way to becoming one of the really big-name groups.

One of the strongest factors behind their success, is the intelligence and determination of Ian Anderson, a striking personality with a lot of good sense in his attitude to the pop scene.

Unlike a lot of people in new groups, he's thought a lot for himself about one thing of supreme importance—management, and just how valuable it is. Says Ian: "You get a lot of groups who suddenly find themselves having a bit of success. Everything starts working out fine, and they begin to resent having a manager who they think is milking them of their hard-earned cash, and cramping them artistically. So they try and get rid of him and want to do everything themselves.

"But it seems to me that there's about one group in a thousand who have the right sort of mind to deal with management, getting bookings and this sort of thing. They don't realise that to be a good manager you have to be just as creative, if not more so, but in a totally different way. The two jobs almost never mix.

"We—the group and Terry Ellis, our manager—realise this, and find that it works out beautifully. Sometimes it happens that he'll suggest something on the musical side, and sometimes one of the group will suggest something to do with our management. But we know that we couldn't do each other's jobs, and that's the way it ought to be.

VALUABLE

"It was the same when we made our album, which will be coming out soon. Terry produced it with us, with ideas exchanged all along the line, and we're all very pleased with the end result. The most valuable thing about making your record without outside interferance—apart from the obvious thing of being able to do it exactly as you want—is that you stand to fall entirely on your own efforts. You can't lump the blame on anyone else, and nobody else can take the credit if it works well.

"Apart from anything else, making your own record means you have to know about the technicalities involved. This is all very valuable knowledge and experience, realising what can and can't be done on record. As far as I'm concerned, the important thing in life is that you should keep on learning as much as you can the whole time.

"Like any other group, Jethro Tull have diabolically bad nights. We all get in a lousy mood and feel bad when it's all over — everything seems to be going wrong. But a lot of the other groups I've met just want to gloss over their failures and try to forget them as soon as possible. I'm not saying you have to brood over the bad nights, but we try and remember what went wrong, work out why it did, and take measures to stop it happening again. You've got to do that." R.S.

ROLLING STONE/APRIL 19,

Check one: ( ) All the above, ( ) Some of the above, ( ) None of the above . . . are Jethro Tull

Is it possible he really won't fight the Howard Johnson's purchase? Perhaps the best answer came during overtime at a Fillmore West basketball game last week. Graham was all over the court, exhausted but still going all out. Somebody suggested he should slow down: so what if he lost the game?

"Are you outa your fucking mind?" bellowed Graham. "Why play if you're gonna lose?" Fillmore West won the game by five points.

Jethro Tull & His Fabulous Tool

By BEN FONG-TORRES

According to the critics in England, Jethro Tull is the new super-duper group, the successor of Cream, "the most unusual group on the British scene."

According to its record company, Jethro Tull is a jazz-group that "often appears as old men—shaggy hair and beards powdered with white, lines of makeup on their faces . . ." And Jethro Tull, so the company's story goes, invented the plough and lived to write a book about it.

According to Ian Anderson, flutist and lead singer of the group, all of the above is not a silly milli-particle less than "absolute bullshit."

Jethro Tull, to take the most inconsequential inaccuracy first, was an 18th Century musician who invented the seed drill, made out of, among other things, an old organ pedal.

Today, Jethro Tull is a quartet of young men (all around 21 or 22) from North England (Blackpool and thereabouts) who combine guitar, drums, mouth harp and flute into a frenetic but rather primitive blues-rock sound. They have never appeared as "old men" in public (except in publicity stills and on their LP cover).

Formed a year ago, the band took a mere eight months to climb aboard the British charts. The boys did it by spending those eight months criss-crossing England and hitting "all the small clubs."

"We just played what we knew would be accepted," said Anderson. "In other worlds, just blues. They we started writing our own songs and shoving them in, and they were accepted, too."

An album *This Was*, comprised mostly of "accepted" original tunes plus one Roland Kirk composition, was put together. The band (there's Anderson; guitarist Mick Abrahams; bassist Glenn Cornick, and drummer Clive Bunker) donned the old-men getup for kicks, to complement the dogs on the proposed album cover photo. And Jethro Tull was ready to plough.

By then, the band's self-composed, lighter pieces, incorporating Anderson's flute, were being called jazz.

"People were all thinking we were like 30 years old, eccentric nut cases because I like to jump around the stage. So here we were 'old men playing jazz-rock.'"

Anderson, a quiet, Zappa-haired young man who owns two pairs of pocketless trousers and carries his valuables in a cord-strung leather pouch, swears that none of the group has any jazz background. Anderson knew Cornick in Blackpool, where the two played semi professionally for a short time. They roamed down to London with the intention of going professional. There they met drummer Clive Bunker, added a guitarist, and began looking for work.

Jethro Tull had what Anderson called "a six month period of natural growth, where we scrounged just enough to make a living." Still, the band moved fast, finding co-managers in Terry Ellis and Chris Wright (who also manage Ten Years After) and landing a spot in the Sunbury Jazz and Blues Festival. From there the critics took over. And while the group, Anderson says, established itself without the benefit of promotional splash in England, hype's slick menstruum has been preceding Jethro Tull at every point on its current American debut tour.

The band just may survive the publicity. When the rumblings about Jethro Tull being the "new wave of Jazz musicians" first cropped up, says Anderson, "we thought it was great fun. And I don't mind when people compare my flute playing with Roland Kirk's or a number of flutists. The only people it probably annoys are jazz musicians and jazz fans."

At any rate, Jethro Tull's inadvertant jazz will meet up with the real thing on the Fourth of July when the band appears at the Newport Jazz Festival. Among the other musicians slated to be there: Roland Kirk.

Jethro Tull was recently voted the #2 group in England (outdistancing such as the Stones), where their LP "Stand Up" and single "Living in the Past" reached the top of the charts and sold a ridiculously large number of records. Upstart Tull's "Stand Up" has already begun its advance on the U.S. . . . just released and charted with stars, bullets, and that stuff. Another example of Reprise's embarrassment of riches.

We need you too, Jethro Tull!

MELODY MAKER, February 14, 1970—Page 5

MARTIN BARRE

Jethro have a long way to go

DURING the summer of 1968 Jethro Tull, a strange group of musicians named after an agrarian pioneer, emerged out of the underground at Sunbury to become one of the top rock bands in the world.

Since that debut at the National Jazz and Blues Festival, Martin Barre has replaced guitarist Mick Abrahams in Jethro who have found commercial success with "Living In The Past," "Sweet Dream," their album "Stand Up" and their current single "Witch's Promise."

Jetho's Sunbury success overawed the band whose members disappeared to the safety of their own homes those eighteen months ago. It is a move they would like to repeat today. Martin Barre explained:

"We'll be spending six months of this year in America which is a thought that honestly depresses me. At the beginning of the year just to go over there was exciting and to play there was such a big thing — now I don't think any of us is looking forward to going over there.

"Everything starts to get on top of you, the way things have happened we've got no time to do anything ourselves and now our personal lives are suffering. I'm going through a stage of depression. We all want to buy houses where you can just sit down with your girl friend and be on your own. That's very important to me.

"We haven't stopped working this past year. It's like a conveyor belt thing, making records, going through America, it's endless but we haven't the time to get off the conveyor belt. Our schedule is so tight.

"I don't think our personalities have changed because you try and retain some part of you that's still sane. Things more personal to us are becoming more important but it's frustrating when you don't have time to do things on your own.

"What I'd really like to do at the moment is just to play in Britain because it's my home, it's nothing patriotic or anything, it's just that I'd like to do a concert tour and be able to go home every night."

Playing is still important to the members of Jethro—Clive Bunker, Glenn Cornick, Ian Anderson and Barre—and they've retained their enthusiasm for it as they wish to develop as musicians.

"We're very basic musicians but we are improving technique-wise and as long as Ian keeps writing as he is now, I can't forsee anything but improvement. We still enjoy playing very much. Our individual techniques have improved and we're now feeling the need to play fresh things.

"That's why I think we'll stay together for some time because apart from Ian I don't think any of us are capable of doing anything individually but we are improving together. Maybe in a couple of years' time when I'm more of a reasonable musician I'd like to play with other people and do something different but we've got a lot of different things to do as far as Jethro is concerned.

"We haven't gone half as far as we can go, you can only be as big as your music is good and we've got a long way to go as Jethro Tull yet."

Perhaps the main criticism of Jethro's music is that the sound of Ian's flute is too dominating. Martin was talking during a break in the recording of the group's third album "Benefit" which he says reflects their current use of the flute.

"We have got away from the sound of the flute and haven't used it a lot on the album. In fact Ian's playing more guitar than flute, we're only using the flute when we feel that a song needs the atmosphere of the flute.

"Some of the instruments we're playing now are difficult to use on stage especially in the big auditoriums. You can just about get away with a piano but it's difficult to get a good sound. I also play mandolin and flute and Ian plays the piano but generally on stage it's down to the guitars."

For Jethro it's still down to their individual brand of music, produced under high pressure during this, their most successful year. It's a long way from Sunbury.

ROYSTON ELDRIDGE

to do to avoid getting in a rut," he told *Disc And Music Echo* in June 1969. "I'd already taken three different courses at school and college in order not to become pigeon-holed, and the formation of the group just sort-of-happened. At the time I couldn't play any instruments. I began learning the flute immediately, and I only learned how to play guitar six months ago."

It's fascinating to consider that when looking back at the band's legacy, one of the first things that springs to mind about Jethro Tull is the strong musicianship that brought to life albums full of instrumental variety and songs with complex uses of key and time signatures. And yet, at the start of their tenure, their musical ability was commented upon as if it was something of a limitation. In fairness though, this is something that Anderson himself was candid about at the time in terms of how he was self-taught and only recently so prior to having the beginnings of his commercial success. *Disc And Music Echo* reported in June 1969; "Working life is a compromise between him lying in bed all morning enjoying twentieth century freedom and his managers Chris Wright and Terry Ellis organising business projects for six months hence. Composing life is a compromise between the flights of fancy that he would like to be able to record, and his own technical limitations; and also a compromise between the sound effect he would like and the limitations of his fellow musicians in the band."

On 29th June 1968, Tull were the support act for Pink Floyd when they played a free rock festival at London's Hyde Park. By August, although they weren't at the top of the bill, the Sunbury Jazz and Blues festival (organised by the Marquee club in association with the National Jazz Federation) did wonders for Jethro Tull because their performance was met with a positive reception by the audience, the press and importantly, record companies. The festival was the first time that Tull played to a large audience. A lot of the audience had already seen them perform at smaller venues and overall, the band were met with enthusiasm (Anderson was quoted in *Beat Instrumental* in February 1970; "At Sunbury we saw that all the little clubs — which seemed to add up to nothing very much — meant something altogether.").

Beat Instrumental commented in October 1968; "It happens every time. Every year, the National Jazz and Blues Festival throws up one hugely successful group, previously more or less unheard of, except to the devotees down at the Marquee and other hip clubs, and thrusts them into the national limelight. Last year, Ten Years After were the group who swept all before them. This time it was the turn of Jethro Tull, a four-piece outfit with their roots firmly in the blues, who came out of nowhere to become the stars of the festival. Their version of 'Cat's Squirrel', theoretically the same as the Cream number, had the 20,000-odd congregation on their feet and cheering, while 'Serenade To A Cuckoo' provoked incredulous gasps at the sheer joy and virtuosity of Ian Anderson's exuberant flute playing. In fact, the whole band — Glenn Cornick, bass; Clive Bunker, drums; Mick Abrahams, guitar and Anderson, flute, mouth organ and vocals, were a powerful tonic to jaded ears, and judging by reactions of the audience and the business, they're well on the way to becoming one of the really big-name groups. One of the strongest factors behind their success is the intelligence and determination of Ian Anderson, a striking personality with a lot of good sense in his attitude to the pop scene. Unlike a lot of people in new groups, he's thought a lot for himself about one thing of supreme importance — management, and just how valuable it is."

To which Anderson was quoted; "You get a lot of groups who suddenly find themselves having a bit of success. Everything starts working out fine, and they begin to resent having a manager who they think is milking them of their hard-earned cash and cramping them artistically. So they try and get rid of him and want to do everything themselves. But it seems to me that there's about one group in a thousand who have the right sort of mind to deal with management, getting bookings and this sort of thing. They don't realise that to be a good manager you have to be just as creative, if not more so, but in a totally different way. The two jobs almost never mix. We — the group and Terry Ellis, our manager — realise this, and find that it works out beautifully. Sometimes it happens that he'll suggest something on the musical side, and sometimes one of the group will suggest something to do with our management. But we know that we couldn't do each other's jobs, and that's the way it ought to be. It was the same when we made our album, which will be coming out soon. Terry produced it with us, with ideas exchanged all along the line, and we're all very pleased with the end result. The most valuable thing about making your record without outside interference — apart from the obvious thing of being able to do it exactly as you want — is that you stand to fall entirely on your own efforts. You can't lump the blame on anyone else, and nobody else can take the credit if it works well. Apart from anything else, making your own record means you have to know about the technicalities involved. This is all very valuable knowledge and experience, realising what can and can't be done on record. As far as I'm concerned, the important thing in life is that you should keep on learning as much as you can the whole time."

In August 1968, *Melody Maker* were in agreement that Jethro Tull were the stars of the show. They insinuated that it might have been somewhat overwhelming for Anderson as they reported that "most groups who play in the blues idiom present their music pretty seriously but at the recent National Jazz and Blues Festival, at Sunbury, the hit group on the Sunday evening was Jethro Tull who received a tremendous ovation for their set that featured the singing, flute and harmonica playing of Ian Anderson. In a long overcoat and sporting a wild mop of hair, Ian came over like a cross between Charlie Chaplin and the Wild Man of the Pampas and the audience loved it. Yet the success of the group at Sunbury overawed them and they hightailed it out of town. It took several phone calls to find Ian Anderson. Finally the group's manager, Terry Ellis, tracked him down to Blackpool and it was from there that Ian spoke to *Melody Maker*."

"I don't mind people laughing at me but what happened at Sunbury wasn't deliberate although if they hadn't cheered we might not have felt happy at all," explained Anderson. "I don't like this thing of standing around and trying to outplay everybody. We don't plan things out. We just go on and see what happens. You just keep it loose. If people go away happy, feeling like they've had something for their money then we're happy."

Regarding his flute playing, Anderson explained; "Somebody said to me, 'It's all very well, but it's just like Roland Kirk,' but there are only two ways of playing the flute, you either sing or you don't although what I play doesn't have the musical content of Kirk. But it's still the blues. I think it's the blues as much as B.B. King is the blues. Where do you draw the line? Where do you put the label? It's blues basically but we don't end up doing what everybody expects. And we don't need to make excuses for it."

Performing his flute solos stood on one leg, Anderson's scruffy appearance and eccentric stage presence was attention grabbing and importantly, memorable. So much so that it would be a while before the band's appearance wasn't a major subject in the music press. *Record Mirror* commented in October 1968; "The original Jethro Tull was a major force in the pioneering of agricultural improvement during the early eighteenth century. The present Jethro Tull is one of the most exciting of today's new groups. Because of the connotations of the original Jethro Tull, it is not surprising that the group appear on stage looking like four agricultural workers."

To which Anderson was quoted; "Just because we have long hair, people associate us with drugs. We get guys in the street coming up to us and asking for "a charge". The thing is we don't know what they mean, so we pretend to know what it is about although we don't want to. I'm trying to find a flat. I can ring and arrange everything but when I go to see the people they say the place has gone just because I have long hair. If people talk to us for a few moments they realise that we are really human and normal. I don't agree with people taking drugs or stimulants. They should be themselves without having to resort to those sort of things. In fact I don't even drink."

In June 1969, it was asserted in *Disc And Music Echo*; "Here with a message to all dubious parents who are still of the opinion that every hairy and strangely attired pop group is steeped in untold evils and definitely not to be admired by your teenage son or daughter, it's time you changed your ideas! For underneath the mass of hair that covers Jethro Tull, are four highly intelligent musicians, well educated, with as high a set of morals as you could wish for. Leader of the group is twenty-two-year-old Ian Anderson, former grammar schoolboy and art student whose original intention, he supposes, was to become a teacher of mathematics. Outwardly a very serious person, he is now totally steeped in his music and continually excited by the technical discoveries it has to offer. He is more worried that he still cannot write music, than that the group has been turned down by TV companies as 'not suitable for family viewing'."

Anderson added; "We're all very pleased to be able to appear on programmes like *Top Of The Pops*. It's all part of show business, and we're part of show business too. There's really no logical reason why we should have our hair long and dress the way we do. I grew my hair long simply because I like it better that way, and I dress the way I do because I feel comfortable — but if we are all agreeable, there's no earthly reason why in six months time we couldn't all have short back and sides and be wearing suits! You don't have to have long hair to play "progressive" music."

Ironically, Anderson's appearance was something of a practical habit rather than something that had specifically been thought up as a costume. He was used to wearing his coat a lot of the time as someone who had not long before gone to bed cold and hungry.

Having signed a record deal with Island Records, Jethro Tull recorded the first album at Sound Techniques in London between June and August 1968. Although Jamaican based Englishman Chris Blackwell's label had started out to cater for the vibrant music scene in the West Indies, he relocated to England in 1962 and although initially targeting the West Indian immigrant communities, by the mid-sixties he was signing up several British blues and folk bands, such as Traffic and Spooky Tooth. Alongside Jethro Tull, he soon added the likes of Free, Quintessence, Fairport Convention and King Crimson to the roster.

Tull's debut album, *This Was*, was released in the UK on 25th October 1968. It got to number ten in the UK (it received generous radio airplay from John Peel that helped give the album a boost).

This Was didn't get an American release until February 1969, by which time Jethro Tull were touring there and nurturing a small but enthusiastic following. The journalist writing in *Record Mirror* in October 1968 urged that; "If you are looking for real excitement in pop music, make a point of seeing Jethro Tull. Listen to their debut album on Island called *This Was*. It contains some of the group's stage highlights like 'Serenade To A Cuckoo' and 'Dharma For One'. If you can't get to see the group — get to buy the LP. It's the next best thing."

Under the heading of "Jethro Tull LP Sets Fans On Fire", *Record Mirror* reviewed *This Was* in November 1968; "Here it is folks — the hit debut album from Jethro Tull (already roaring in our charts). This is the group which set the audience on fire at the Sunbury Jazz and Blues festival and has been doing similar things to audiences ever since. From the opening number to the last track, the LP is full of excitement and emotion. It starts off with 'My Sunday Feeling' which has Ian Anderson on flute and vocal and a fine solo from guitarist Mick Abrahams. Ian alternates between flute and harmonica on the LP and comes across very well on these instruments and, of course, his stirring vocals. Basically a blues band, Jethro Tull has certainly been influenced by jazz music — especially on the Roland Kirk number 'Serenade To A Cuckoo'. This is one of the highlights on the album and features Ian doing his Kirk-influenced flute bit. Starting off with Ian playing straight-sounding flute it then goes into his vocalised flute sound. Another highlight is Clive Bunker's feature — 'Dharma For One'. It opens with a fast Eastern-type flavour for the tune and then Clive does his drum display — don't let anyone tell you pop drummers are all that inferior to jazz drummers. Not all of the LP is raving gear. Try 'Some Day The Sun Won't Shine For You'. This is a sort of Terry/McGhee thing with just Ian and Mick performing. A really pretty song. Go out and buy this record, then you will see why it entered our charts at twenty-three in the first week. Thoroughly recommended."

It was reviewed in *Disc And Music Echo* the same month; "Jethro Tull, we remember from our history books, was the man who invented the seed drill and somehow revolutionised the whole system of British agriculture about three-hundred years ago. There are some jolly exciting moments, too, on the first LP by the group of that name, *This Was*, plus brilliant flute, hard rhythms and strong songs. Live, Jethro Tull are one of our finest groups, but are somehow not quite together enough yet to be classed as great on record. When they get themselves together more, we feel Jethro Tull will take a lot of beating." The reviewer gave the album two stars out of a possible four.

This Was had also been reviewed in *New Musical Express* the month of release; "This LP sounds good and has a lot of humour about it, too. On the cover are four of the oldest-looking guys in pop, surrounded by eleven dogs in a forest. Open the cover and there's a picture of the weirdos playing two guitars, drums and a flute, but Ian Anderson also plays mouth organ, claghorn, piano, takes seven composing credits and sings quite well. Mick Abrahams is on guitars and sings, too (he also wrote a very good number in 'Move On Alone', and arranged the traditional 'Cat's Squirrel'). Glenn Cornick plays bass guitar and Clive Bunker is on drums. They play jazz really, in a soft, appealing way, and have a bit of fun on the side with tone patterns and singing. And who is Jethro Tull? The sleeve note says he and Terry Ellis produced the record after recording engineer Victor Gamm showed them what levers to pull."

Melody Maker opined in November 1968; "The eagerly awaited debut album by the group which was the sensation of the Sunbury Festival is no disappointment. Drawing on a variety of inspirations, the four-man group contrive to be just about the most exciting new thing to happen to the British scene, pop and blues."

And in *Beat Instrumental* in December 1968; "It's a great pity that the flamingo-like antics of Ian Anderson cannot be pictured with this LP. It sums up the great humour and enjoyment Jethro Tull instil in their music. With the band now near total acceptance, it's pleasing to see them emerge as individuals with a lot of talent on record, as well as their vital live shows. Anderson blows a fine flute, with Mick Abrahams proving himself one of the best of the new guitarists. Their 'Someday The Sun Won't Shine For You' sums up their music — alive and honest. I'm glad the public see that too."

The idea for the title of *This Was* came from Anderson's hopes that even at the time of making the album, the music on it would not be reflective of what his overall aspirations for the band were. He explained to *Melody Maker* in August; "We don't want people to think we are just a twelve-bar blues band. We've tried to get an underlying feel to the tunes to tie them together. It's about three months since some of the tracks were recorded. All the time we are trying to catch up, get new ideas across. That's why some groups worry when they are called progressive. Two of the tunes, 'Cat's Squirrel' and 'Serenade To A Cuckoo', we worried about putting on the album because they were someone else's but we do play them on stage and people like them, they go down well, so we put them on."

Three months later in the same publication he commented; "The whole Blues scene, with a capital B, is a bit dated now. Eighteen months ago people went to see a blues group and thought of themselves as being very different from those going to see Arthur Brown or the Nice. Now it's all the same scene. You can put us, the Nice, Aynsley Dunbar and an out-and-out pop group on the bill and the same people will come to see us all."

'Move On Alone' utilised the talents of David Palmer (now known as Dee Palmer — reference is made to "David" and "he/his" in this book only for historic purposes). Palmer didn't officially join Jethro Tull until later down the line. When he was asked to do an arrangement for a Tull album, he was already familiar with the band having heard them at Sunbury. Palmer was keen to take on the job because he believed in Tull's potential for putting folk music on the map.

Upon first working with Jethro Tull, Palmer played lots of Quincy Jones arrangements to them in order to demonstrate what was possible. Although Tull had started out playing twelve-bar blues, Anderson told *Disc And Music Echo* in June 1969; "You can't go on playing that forever. The only reason for its popularity was its basic simplicity. Even the most unmusical person can understand the blues. The blues thing played itself out, and all those groups with no ideas of their own have fallen by the wayside. Luckily we managed to come up with a few ideas — I somehow managed to start writing."

A number of the songs on *This Was* are based on blues progressions: 'My Sunday Feeling', 'Some Day The Sun Won't Shine For You', 'Beggar's Farm', and 'It's Breaking Me Up'. As it happens, 'Some Day The Sun Won't Shine For You' has a similar arrangement to that of Big Bill Broonzy's blues standard, 'Key To The Highway'. According to the album's liner notes, 'Cat's Squirrel' was included on *This Was* "because people like it". The track was written by Doctor Ross and had been covered by many British blues bands in the sixties, just one of whom was Cream. Abrahams would later go on to use the song with his band, Blodwyn Pig.

So why would anyone play music that they didn't feel was best reflective of their creative aspirations overall? Well, it is possible that in the late sixties, it made commercial sense to do so. *Disc And Music Echo* said in November 1968; "After all the self-conscious trends in music in the past ten years or so, everyone is going back to the blues: the musicians, the fans and the clubs. In the past year the blues has become big business — in this country, at least. When a year ago a blues group would have been lucky to get a maximum of fifty people into a club to hear them, today it's a matter of standing room only and the giants of the modern British blues scene can do no wrong... It certainly is a boom — the blues have caused more groups to be started than any other form of music for years. And with so many people about making music, it can't be at all bad, can it? Which are the up-and-coming names to watch? To call Jethro Tull an "up-and-coming group" may seem a bit of an anachronism, considering their album *This Was* is the hit of the month and anyone who sees them talks about nothing else for days afterwards. Jethro Tull are on their own; the greater mass of the rest of the country's new blues bands seem to fall into two camps: the blues "establishment", led almost exclusively by ex-members of John Mayall's Bluesbreakers, and the breakaways who are simply young guys who dig the blues and have decided to do something about playing their own."

It comes across that in some ways, perhaps Anderson saw the content on *This Was* as something of a means to an end. He was quoted in *New Musical Express* in November 1968; "Everything we do, consciously or not, is show business. A lot of people pretend the show business thing doesn't exist. They say, 'Look, we are down-to-earth honest real people.' I don't think there is an honest person in show business. Every time you go in front of an audience you become an act but because people have seen you do something for a matter of six months and they have liked it, to go on doing it for another six months to a year if it doesn't mean much to you, personally, is bad. Everything we have done, if not musically good, has been very honest. Basically the album was a bad album, but above all it was honest."

It was reported in the *Croydon Advertiser* in October 1968; "For those who have been sufficiently interested to ask 'Whither pop?' part of the answer lay in Olympop, the pop concert staged at the Fairfield Hall on Sunday 29th Sept. Compèred by Britain's new top DJ John Peel, it featured what, for want of a label, I must call progressive pop. Naturally it could not possibly show every direction in which pop music is progressing, but it did give a good indication of the way in which some of the best new names in this field are thinking, and how they are using their individual talents. For the real enthusiasts all this is very serious."

"The Fairfield audience held no screamers (although one couple in the stalls had a silent freak-out during a Brian Auger solo) and applause came only at the end of each song. The real noise came from the stage, and the result on Sunday was something of a marathon — nearly four hours of mind-blowing, ear-shattering music, accompanied by cohorts of lights and cameras filming the whole proceedings in glorious BBC Two colour. Apart from a late start there were virtually no hitches. Some pop stars have gained bad reputations, but on Sunday the professionalism of all the performers was never in doubt — not only do they all play their instruments, they also play them very well. I should also mention that on this occasion they were playing free of charge, since the concert was in aid of the British Olympic Appeals Fund."

"The evening began with Jethro Tull who, on quieter reflection, seem to have been one of the best groups of the night. They're a four-man blues group with a farmyard image — apt, since they have chosen the name of an agricultural equipment inventor for their title. Their excellent drummer, for instance, wears a squashed, manure-coloured felt hat and a dead-pan expression; and their lead singer is an incredibly-dressed exhibitionist who looks like a tramp with his long wild hair and shapeless calf-length overcoat, a picture he encourages by constant scratching of his person during other people's solos. He plays wild harmonica and Roland Kirk-influenced flute, moving

Less than two weeks after Mick Abrahams had left the band, Tull was invited to perform on The Rolling Stones' ambitious *Rock and Roll Circus*. Filmed over two days at Rediffusion Studios, Wembley — 11th-12th December 1968 — Tony Iommi from the Birmingham band Earth stepped in.

With the exception of Anderson's vocals, Tull's performance of 'A Song For Jeffrey' was mimed. Following this brief dalliance Iommi went back to his own band that soon morphed into Black Sabbath.

his legs around like a demented pantomime horse, while his mouth is apparently pivoted on the microphone. The resultant music is loud, clear and disciplined blues. My only complaint is that I couldn't hear a word during the up-tempo numbers, but I am not at all sure whether this is really important." Other bands who performed at the show included Ecleton, the Alan Price Set, Spooky Tooth, the Nice, Julie Driscoll and the Brian Auger Trinity.

And in *Melody Maker* in October 1968; "Jethro Tull recorded for BBC TV's *Colour Me Pop* at the Fairfield Hall, Croydon, recently when they appeared in concert with Julie Driscoll and Alan Price. The show is likely to be screened on Saturday, November 2nd. The group will also be appearing on *Time For Blackburn's* new nationally networked TV show at 7 o'clock on Thursday, October 24th. The group are currently in Denmark promoting their new album *This Was*. The album will be released in America in November, and the group will be touring the States for two months commencing January 1st. Jethro Tull appears at the Albert Hall on October 15th on a special charity show for Czechs stranded in this country." (the latter comment was made in reference to events that followed the Russian invasion of Czechoslovakia on 21st August 1968).

With Anderson clearly being the dominant member of the band by this point, it wasn't long after that Mick Abrahams left. The result was that the end of 1968 saw Jethro Tull go through two quickly assembled line-ups, one of which involved a pre-Black Sabbath Tony Iommi contribute guitar for a week and the other of which welcomed former Nice guitarist David O'List into the fold.

Considering that both were in Jethro Tull for such a short period, it is phenomenal that any footage of either exists but luckily, Tony Iommi's brief stint in Jethro Tull was captured on film when Tull performed on The Rolling Stones' *Rock 'n' Roll Circus* TV show. Fortunately for Jethro Tull, by December 1968, Martin Barre was welcomed to the band in what would be a significant partnership in Tull's tenure. (Tony Iommi was never an official member of Jethro Tull. He was brought in to play when needed, particularly for The Rolling Stones' TV show. Iommi had other commitments at the time with his band Earth — later to be named Black Sabbath — and wasn't available to join Jethro Tull full time. Endearingly though, in later years, Iommi stipulated that he learnt a lot from working with Jethro Tull with particular regards to the fact that they were organised and raring to start work in the morning).

The Rolling Stones' *Rock 'n' Roll Circus* also featured Eric Clapton, The Who and Taj Mahal, as well as John Lennon and Yoko Ono. Some of the acts played live and others mimed to a backing track. Jethro Tull performed 'A Song For Jeffrey', all of which was mimed with the exception of Anderson's vocals. The footage wasn't broadcast though because Mick Jagger wasn't happy with The Rolling Stones' performance.

Of Jethro Tull's appearance on the show, Anderson was quoted in *Record Mirror* in January 1969; "I think it was a good idea initially, but it was badly produced and badly run. I felt it was just thrown together. With a little more time and planning it would have been much better... It's all set in a circus arena. It starts with everyone coming on playing. Then the Stones introduce all their guests. We were going to play three numbers originally, but due to time commitments we only did one. It was 'Song For Jeffrey'. The Stones picked all their guests, like: Eric Clapton, Marianne Faithful, John Lennon and Yoko Ono, Keith Moon, Pete Townshend, etc. Although I'm a great admirer of the Stones, they're poor musicians. They played on their show and were awful — they couldn't get together at all. I was disappointed with them musically because they are my idols. You could find any other five musicians who are better than them. Mick Jagger has really mastered the sort of thing he does, but Brian Jones just can't play. The group's timing is all messed-up. But in spite of this, the Stones have a great presence and can communicate to their listeners. To sum them up in two words — they're delightfully bad. The sort of music I listen to is records by people like Ornette Coleman, Roland Kirk, and a few more modern jazz players. But you have to *really* listen to find out what they are doing. When it comes to listening to a Rolling Stones record, it makes me feel that everything is all right and I am home and there is no trouble anywhere."

Despite the success of their debut album, all had not been well. With the tensions in the band being what they were, Ian Anderson was actually the first person who could have left. The idea of having a flute player in the band had already been debated before. Jethro Tull's material that was dominated by flute suggested otherwise though. 'Serenade To A Cuckoo' was well received. It did however, result in a good few years of Anderson having to clarify that he didn't want to emulate or be compared to the song's composer, Roland Kirk.

Anderson, speaking to *Zigzag* in December 1969 said; "I was accused in one of the articles Leonard Feather wrote on the Newport Festival as being a second-rate Roland Kirk. It's extraordinary that somebody like Feather, who's known as a critic of some acclaim, anyways, can be so easily duped by sounds to think that I'm trying to be a second-rate Kirk. I mean, there's no comparison between Roland Kirk and me. I don't know how old he is, but I'm only twenty-one. I've only been playing flute for eighteen months. Technically, there's no comparison whatsoever. Sound wise, there is a similarity. Roland Kirk does it because he's a person who understands the instrument to fantastic degree. I do it because it's the one sound that I can make on a flute which will blend with a guitar; a strident noisy sound. I have to do it; it's a matter of coming across."

It was often the case that Anderson's flute playing was compared to that of Roland Kirk's. "People kept saying it to me so I went to hear Kirk and found I was already making a similar noise," Anderson explained to *Melody Maker* in November 1968. "I stopped listening again but I suppose something has rubbed off on me. I started out as a singer and when the others were playing I found I was just gazing round the lofty halls. I thought I'd like to be playing something and moving around too, so I got hold of the flute and harmonica and bluffed my way through. The great thing is to pick up something and mess about with it, it helps new ideas to come up. That's why I am now playing about on mandolin — it gives you a whole new approach. I don't really play the flute — what I do is what I would do if I was singing or playing the guitar. And I can only play in four keys. Anyway, all flutes sound the same to an audience whether it is marvellous or a joke."

A key factor that determined Mick Abrahams' departure from Jethro Tull was that he didn't want to gig as extensively as the rest of the group. When the suggestion of touring America was put forward, Abrahams was adamant that he didn't want to do it. Abrahams' influence on Jethro Tull's sound was strongly blues orientated, as is evident on tracks such as 'Cat Squirrel'. With plans for an American tour and a second album though, it was only a matter of time before Jethro Tull's music would take a different direction.

Meanwhile, Abrahams went on to form his own band, Blodwyn Pig. It was reported in *Melody Maker* on 21st December 1968; "Guitarist Mick Abrahams has left Jethro Tull and will form his own group after disagreements over musical policy. Terry Ellis, manager of Jethro Tull, told *Melody Maker*, 'For some time, Mick has disagreed with the basic policies, both musically and otherwise, of Jethro Tull'."

Anderson told *Record Mirror* in January 1969; "The main reason was a conflict of musical ideas. He wanted to continue playing the same sort of things we have been doing. And the rest of us wanted to progress and try new material. Presumably, Mick will form his own group."

And the same month Anderson was quoted in *Beat Instrumental*; "We weren't really getting anything new, musically. Mick and I were finding it harder and harder to get anything worked out."

In the same publication Terry Ellis explained that the band's line-up change was due to "major policy differences. The group is definitely going in a certain direction. Not just as musicians, but in every way. They do have an image as entertainers. The group want to put on a show so that people go home feeling as if they've had their money's worth. Mick didn't agree with this as a policy, and he's getting his own band going on a more exclusively musical basis. The break was a sad thing for everybody, especially so as things had gone so well in the past; but it was really inevitable. They had to go their separate ways for everyone's good."

Although history perhaps has it that the first album line-up lacked a cohesiveness in their working rapport, it is possible that over time such narrative may have been somewhat magnified — in the sense that when the album was made, everyone involved plausibly brought something to the table.

Regarding the rest of the band, Anderson told *Melody Maker* in November 1968; "Everybody goes their own way. There is no big get-together scene. It's all give and take. Some of my ideas are in the drum solo on the album and some of the drummer's ideas are in the melody of the tune. At the right moment it works out."

However, Mick Abrahams also appeared on the Tull single 'Love Story', released 29th November 1968. It got to number twenty-nine in the UK where it spent eight weeks on the chart. On the B-side was 'A Christmas Song'. It was reviewed in *Top Pops* in December 1968; "A very exciting disc from the four strange looking lads who are kicking up a storm album-wise. The rather repetitive lyric is set to a mostly storming beat but there are some nicely contrasting breaks involving guitar with yer actual wah-wah pedal and fuzz box, flute and bongos. A well-arranged disc which deserves a lot of success."

And in *Record Mirror* in December 1968; "What with having a hit album and all that, plus a very big following around the club circuit — well, why not a single for this capable and inventive group? This is tough on guitar sounds, lighter on vocal line and there's a directness about the song that I found worthwhile. Might miss, but commended. Flip: Indian and other sounds all mixed up but nice. Chart possibility."

Whilst the first release incorrectly named the band Jethro Toe, this release mistakenly credited both songs to Ian Henderson!

Before 'Love Story' was even in the charts, Jethro Tull taped a performance of it for *Top Of The Pops* in hopeful preparation. Anderson was quoted in *Disc And Music Echo* in February 1969; "Before we went on the guy from *Top Of The Pops* was saying, 'I'm not having that long-haired dirty band on my show,' but when we'd done it he liked the song so much he said he'd like to use it. Which would make it all worthwhile — even makes it worth losing a night's sleep, because we had to go straight off to a date in Birmingham after the show. But I don't mind at all, because it's *Top Of The Pops*, which means exposure to people who may have bought the single but have never seen us play —

most of them probably don't even *know* we had a top five album! We really need that exposure, and so do groups like The Nice and the Family. Engelbert and Malcolm Roberts and Dusty don't need it, because they've been seen so many times before. The Marmalade don't need it either, after being at the top for five weeks!"

Mick Abrahams' departure created new challenges. Anderson was interviewed in mid-December by *Beat Instrumental*. It was published in January 1969; "The first thing we have to do is work out some new numbers. After a year of playing the same stuff, I'm a bit worried of playing our Christmas thing down at the Marquee. They have known us right from the beginning, and they'll be expecting something different. The amount of time we've got to work things out is ridiculously small. From now we've only got three days off before we go to America on January 24th — and that's Christmas. I think I'll go up and see my mum for those days."

Equally though, a change of line-up would go on to create an opportunity for working on new ideas. Regarding the plans for Jethro Tull's second LP, Terry Ellis was quoted in the same feature; "It's got to be a different sort of album from *This Was*. Too many groups try and repeat a successful formula, but it's usually disastrous. At first, underground groups sell records on the strength of their live appearances. People have seen them at the clubs and want to take home forty-five minutes of the stage sound they've just heard. But you have to change for the second one, so we're making it more of a studio production record — the single, 'Love Story', was a step in the direction the LP will be taking."

It's just as well that Jethro Tull had made a conscious decision to move away from blues music. The fickle nature of the music industry was such that an ability to move with it was imperative and as it happened, the blues boom wasn't set to last for much longer. It was asserted in *New Musical Express* in January 1969; "When the present blues boom fades away, Jethro Tull will still be around — that is if their musical integrity hasn't broken them up and sent them off in search of other things. They are like that — honest to themselves and their followers, young, demanding, raw — and it shows in the music they produce."

Besides, it was certainly the case that Anderson wasn't what some might call a typical blues musician. On the blues standards front, he told *Record Mirror* in January 1969; "It can be a bit embarrassing at times. People come up to me and ask for a certain number and I have to plead ignorance. The main reason why I don't know many numbers is because I don't listen to many things — I base my playing on my emotions."

Mick Taylor was considered as a possible candidate but he declined as he was happy to remain with John Mayall's Bluesbreakers. Auditions were held over a period of three days to find Abrahams' replacement. The majority of candidates were not suitable in terms of their technical ability and the few who were came with preconceived ideas about the style of music that they wanted to play.

When Martin Barre attended the audition, he didn't promote himself very well at all; he forgot to bring a guitar lead with him and when he started playing, he was so nervous that he kept stopping — a deer in the headlights. Sent away with the rest of the unsuccessful candidates, a few days later Barre got in touch with the band and asked if he could have another opportunity to show them what he could do. His request was granted as a suitable candidate still hadn't been found. Turning up to audition at Anderson's bedsit, Barre brought with him an electric guitar but no amplifier and no guitar lead. Consequently, when he started to play, Anderson couldn't hear much of what he was doing, even when he knelt with his head to the floor to try and hear it. All the same, with tour commitments already on the cards and with Barre's enthusiasm being what it was, he got the job.

It seems that the auditions process presented the band with a lot of interesting characters to choose from as Anderson explained to *Record Mirror* in January 1969; "We auditioned loads of people, but none of them fitted. Some of them didn't have much of a clue. There was one guy who came early and stayed almost all day. After each new guitarist had gone he would start playing again. He really wanted the job but it was a bit sad really. Then we had another guy who you could almost call a professional auditioner. He came in and tried to take everyone over, saying 'let's do so and so'. The trouble was, we didn't know the numbers he was playing, apart from the fact they were rock 'n' roll things. After he had finished, he said 'must go now — I've got another audition to go to.' The following day when I woke up the audition seemed just like a bad dream. One of the troubles with most British blues guitarists is that they seem to have come from rock 'n' roll through out-and-out pop to blues, and have taken the easy way out. In the main, they play in a very tight style. Not many of them have a natural looseness in their playing."

Martin Barre had previously been a member of Penny Peep Show, a blues band that had made a contribution as a backing band during recording sessions at the Marquee Studios in Wardour Street. Impressed by their unique and innovative approach, Barre had first seen Jethro Tull when they played at the National Jazz And Blues festival at Sunbury.

Melody Maker announced on 4th January 1969; "Guitarist Martin Barre is to join Jethro Tull, and not David O'List, ex-Nice, as we planned last week. Barre, aged twenty-two, has been working with the Gethsemane group. His first appearance with them was on Monday 30th December at the

Welcome Martin Barre, who convinced Tull to employ him following a second audition without an amplifier!

Backstage in 1969. (left to right): Martin Barre, Ian Anderson, Clive Bunker and Glenn Cornick.

Winter Gardens, Penzance."

With a successful year to their name, Jethro Tull remained a humble band. Anderson talking to *Beat Instrumental* in October 1968 said; "Like any other group, Jethro Tull have diabolically bad nights. We all get in a lousy mood and feel bad when it's all over — everything seems to be going wrong. But a lot of the other groups I've met just want to gloss over their failures and try to forget them as soon as possible. I'm not saying you have to brood over the bad nights, but we try and remember what went wrong, work out why it did, and take measures to stop it happening again. You've got to do that."

The *New Musical Express* journalist who interviewed Anderson in November 1968 said of him as a person; "I liked Ian, the sense he made and his personal attitude to life. We walked together to Leicester Square Tube where Ian, on parting, asked when the article would be appearing so he could tell his Mum to get a copy. Jethro Tull are human."

Anderson was quoted in the same feature; "My idea when I left school was that I would never get anywhere, would have no money and people would dislike me. So if anything good does happen, I can say yes, I hoped that would happen, but I didn't expect it. That's why I am not jumping up in the air about the album. It certainly won't mean anything six months from now."

"I often wonder about the whole "star" bit," he explained to *Disc And Music Echo* in November 1968. "You read all these articles about people who say 'popular success hasn't changed *me*' and then go on to say how much it *has* changed them! Entertainment is where it's at — I feel it's more important to get up onstage and entertain the people who've paid to see you than it is to play good music. To refuse to admit this, which a lot of groups do, is not owning up to yourself — it's all "show business" whether you like it or not. There's a lot of good in the mystique of the star bit, but so many groups are trying to finish with it, that all the romance and mystique has gone out of that as well — just like sex."

With new guitarist Barre on board, Tull set off for their first tour of America, in which they would be playing as a support band. Conditions weren't pleasant though. They didn't play many dates and as a result, they weren't able to live comfortably. No glamour, no parties, just a lot of time spent in run-down hotel rooms. They couldn't afford to go out much socially. With Abrahams gone, Anderson had pretty much fallen into the role of leader but it wasn't to the detriment of group morale, or indeed, Jethro Tull's image overall.

As Anderson told *Hit Parader* in October 1969; "I am spokesman for the group only because I am more articulate. It's just very, very difficult to talk to people, particularly when they're journalists. Nowadays there's such a tendency to be drawn into rather elevated issues, getting into discussions about politics and sex. It's very easy for people to be drawn into these discussions and say their own little bit. By my doing the talking, we just don't talk about it all. The whole thing is a lot of rubbish. I don't believe I have any responsibility to the kids to preach any feelings I have on these sort of subjects. I don't know anything about them. I know nothing about war or politics or anything else."

As arduous as it was to tour America, it made sense to do so. The decision to go was based on how positively Jethro Tull had been received there thus far. Anderson said in *Beat Instrumental* in January 1969; "We're off to America for two and a half months, doing much the same circuit that Ten Years After did the first time they went over — the Fillmores and that sort of thing. The reaction over there has been pretty good up to now. The album has been getting a lot of airtime, along with the Beatles and the Stones, and it should be good for us."

The band knew it and so did the music press. In the same feature, the journalist hypothesised: "Jethro Tull would appear to be the sort of group that America is growing to love, and it wouldn't be at all surprising to hear in a couple of months' time that Jethro Tull are breaking attendance records, selling millions of discs, and getting even better recognition than they have had over here."

And of course, touring in America was an excellent opportunity to sell more records there. *New Musical Express* reported in January 1969; "Jethro Tull — who enter the NME Chart this week with 'Love Story' — open a two-month US tour at New York Fillmore East on January 24th. During its American visit, the group will begin work on its second album — the first, *This Was*, appeared in the NME LP Chart for seven weeks at the end of last year and re-enters it this week at number fourteen. Co-manager Terry Ellis flew to Los Angeles this week for talks with the Warner-Reprise label, which has signed a contract with the group for the distribution of its discs in America and Canada. The deal is said to carry a guarantee of 250,000 dollars."

Before setting off for America, Jethro Tull's chart presence in the UK was looking pretty healthy too. "The week before they leave for their first, two month long tour of America — Jethro Tull show every sign of becoming a singles chart name, too, as their 'Love Story' bubbles hopefully under the thirty. Whether it actually makes it is, as they say, in the lap of the gods (and you, the record-buying public)," reported *Disc And Music Echo* in February 1969.

The band's fleeting attitude towards the singles market was evident from Anderson's comments in the same feature; "It's such a shame that no one bothers about getting down to making good singles. People go on about what a drag the singles chart is but look at the LP chart — it's a gas!

Which is wrong, because it's the responsibility of everyone concerned with making progressive music to make good, catchy commercial singles which appeal to thirteen-year-old girls. It can be done. Canned Heat did it, with a beautiful song which also happened to be pure blues. And we've done it to a certain extent, even though our single isn't particularly good. If people bothered about it a bit though, we'd have a good singles chart rather than all these decadent ballad singers in our midst!"

Later in the year Anderson reinforced his view; "The chart scene is really important. You mustn't just bow out of it. I used to think it didn't matter about the rubbish in the charts but it's not the fault of the kids who buy the records. If someone brings out a good single, it will get the plays and the kids will buy it. Okay, so you have to compromise, but it's going to do some good in the long run. Eventually it will get the underground on TV. It will need a difference in attitude but if groups of sufficient name and standing put out good singles it will work. I'd like to see people like the Family, the Nice and John Peel — Peel could do a lot."

The success of 'Love Story' was such that for a while, Jethro Tull took a more positive approach to making singles. Anderson told *New Musical Express* in May 1969; "Two months ago my attitude was that singles were nasty tasteless things and that everything in the singles chart was rubbish, but that is very narrow minded. Why should we decry the tastes of millions and leave others to change it? We ought to be going out to try and change it ourselves... If it gets people interested in the music then I think the time has come to look at the singles chart for what it is and do something about it."

By 1969, Jethro Tull were gaining more acceptance. Anderson told *New Musical Express* in February 1969; "At one time it used to be that people would look the other way because maybe they think you carry disease or you might inflict on them a mighty blow with a switch blade. It is nice now that people do come up and are not afraid to talk, to say hello and ask what you had for breakfast and what size socks you wear. Even the girls — six months ago it was predominantly boys. Girls would not come up and talk. It is nice to see that there are now some reasonable girls getting in on the underground thing. I don't mean the ones in long fur coats with wide trousers and smoking that stuff. Not that sort of girl, but plain ordinary girls working in shops and offices, typists and secretaries — they come and see the group and seem to like the music."

In some ways, perhaps playing to American audiences was something of an acid test for whether or not a band could be accepted. Anderson reflected upon the first US tour soon after it was completed; "I like playing in the States but I'd hate to play there all the time. They seem more grateful and they show it more. Everyone goes down a bomb in America. If you're an English group and you don't get a standing ovation there, you won't get one anywhere." Swings and roundabouts though perhaps.

Anderson put the English phenomenon into context; "Most of the places we played we got standing ovations. But giving an English group a standing ovation has become something of a convention over there and it all gets a bit silly going back for an encore, then going back again and again. There are dozens of English groups travelling round America getting standing ovations but it doesn't mean as much as groups would like us to believe... In England they just throw a bottle if they don't like you and clap if they do. There is not really a lot of difference between American and British audiences. If you are British you have got a lot in your favour over there but the flood of English groups going to America is doing a lot of harm... English groups have got power mad. They whizz in to a place, take all the drugs and the groupies and whizz off leaving the wrong impression of what English groups are really like. The groupie scene? Yeah they are really sad people. I got very frightened and very annoyed because they represent to me all that is bad about the so-called underground."

As soon as they were back from America, Jethro Tull went to London's Morgan Studio in April 1969 to record their second album. The 'Living In The Past' single was already high in the UK singles chart — it was actually the first song that Barre recorded with Jethro Tull. It peaked at number three in the UK and was performed as part of the band's debut appearance on *Top Of The Pops*. The 'Living In The Past' single was recorded in the US across three different studios in New York, Los Angeles and San Francisco. The writing of 'Living In The Past' was done with a deliberate intention. Anderson was quoted in *Top Pops* in July 1969; "It was decided we would make a bid for chart fame or whatever. So I sat down in a hotel bedroom in America and wrote an A-side which I thought would make the top ten with the right exposure and everything has worked out to plan."

As much as Jethro Tull had something of an on/off relationship with the singles chart — sometimes they embraced it and other times they were cynical towards it — their musical originality always shone through. Regarding 'Living In The Past', Anderson explained to *New Musical Express* in May 1969; "It's in 5/4 time which means you can't dance to it unless you've got two and a half feet."

But he defended the value of the song to *Record Mirror*; "This is a single, not a token single. It is an attempt to get into the charts without blatant commerciality. If people are going to buy singles,

1969, Amsterdam.

we're hoping they'll buy ours. I realise the underground is still about and that underground groups sell LPs and not singles, yet these restrictions will be compromised in time. Classifications, like people, exist. Most people think of the underground as hairy and far out, so some sort of compromise will have to be made. This is not a commercial single for the sake of it. A lot of thought went into it and I think it's a good one. It makes me happy to think we've done it; it's an honest single."

New Musical Express commented; "If the potential that is so enormous is channelled in the right directions then pop has in Ian Anderson, the exuberant impish leader of Jethro Tull, the makings of an entertainer and personality to join the realms of the so-called superstars. Unlike some who are electric on stage but a damp squib off, or vice versa, Ian has the capabilities to excite in either medium. A capacity audience at London's Royal Albert on Thursday last week (8th May) for the group's tour with Ten Years After will vouch for the potential of Ian's incredible stage showmanship, not the least entertaining of which is the deadpan line in blunt humour he employs to link each number. ('This one's by Bach; I couldn't have wrote it. It's just ripe for prostitution on the penny whistle.' and 'This one's called 'Martin's Tune Again'. I should explain that Martin wrote a tune that was crappy so he had to write another one.'). But it is Ian's stage antics that make Jethro Tull such a visually exciting, as well as musically stimulating, group to experience. The old floor-length overcoat had given way to what looked like a doublet and hose for the Albert Hall concert with Ian prancing around like the devil himself on legs as nimble as Rudolf Nureyev's, wild hair flowing behind him. One minute he was there arm arched over flute, foot bent like a ballet dancer on the opposite knee; the next skipping cross stage on one foot, the other raised in the air."

Released in the autumn of that year, the second album *Stand Up* showcased Barre's guitar talents. Not only that, but the quality of the songs on the album made it clear that the whole band were playing well together. As the newest member of Jethro Tull, Barre was often the butt of some of the band's jokes. The fact that he was nervous at times anyway probably added to the amusement of the situation. In a state of nervous clumsiness, he would sometimes frantically scramble to plug the lead into his guitar when up on stage. Still though, there was no denying his abilities as a musician and what he brought to the band's sound overall.

Barre told *New Musical Express* in November 1969; "I was really frightened at first when I joined Jethro Tull. I thought I was an average or maybe slightly above average musician but I soon learned my shortcomings and it was pretty shattering. I discovered that I had been sitting back for the previous two years. At first with Jethro Tull I really had to force myself to play well. It took me a long time to get any confidence in myself." To which Glenn Cornick added; "The sixth or seventh gig Martin played was the Fillmore East. We had been used to things getting bigger but it completely overawed us and Martin had only been with us for ten days. After the kind of places he had been playing it must have been really mind-shattering."

A busy touring schedule was such that *Stand Up* was released a little later than first anticipated. Anderson: "Our new album comes out round about the beginning of June. We were supposed to finish it off last night, but we only did two songs. I wrote quite a lot when we were in the States. It was that and lack of sleep which made me ill, I think. I collapsed a couple of times and we missed the last gig in the States because I was bad. It happened again in the TV studios in Paris. I thought I'd got lung cancer and TB, but it was just exhaustion."

Commercially, *Stand Up* did better than *This Was*; it got to number one in the UK. Importantly though, it meant something vital for Jethro Tull in terms of their working dynamics. It signified the creative responsibility of Ian Anderson in terms of the writing and general organising of the group in the studio. 'Bourée' was initially credited to Ian Anderson but in actual fact, as the latter has keenly stipulated himself, it is a melody by J.S. Bach ('Bourée' is the Fifth Movement of Suite in E minor, BWV 996) that was a popular choice of tune for many classical guitarists to play. To play it on the flute was an unusual idea but it certainly added to the uniqueness of Jethro Tull's sound.

With the exception of 'Bourée' (which was the only track recorded at London's Olympic Sound Studio), all of the material on the album was written by Ian Anderson. *Stand Up* also featured the inclusion of a David Palmer string arrangement; it was a first for the band on the track, 'Reasons For Waiting'. A graduate of the Royal Academy of Music and a theatrical conductor, Palmer had previously done the horn arrangements on *This Was*. He would go on to make a significant contribution to Jethro Tull.

The album art for *Stand Up* includes a photo insert of the band that unfolds in the style of a pop-up book. A painter and wood sculptor by the name of James Grashow was invited by Ellis and Anderson to design the cover. Grashow was studying his craft in New York when he was offered the job. At the time, he had never heard of Jethro Tull. He had been recommended for the job by a school friend who knew Ellis. The artist had already worked on magazines but working on *Stand Up* was to be his first project with album art. It took him around two or three months to finish the whole thing. After the album was released, quite a few people got in touch with Grashow to ask him what the meaning was behind the fact that he had depicted Ian Anderson as having eleven digits rather than ten. Grashow has always been adamant that is was simply a mistake on his part.

1969, Amsterdam.

Regarding the pop-up element, Anderson told *New Musical Express* in June 1969; "It's taken the artist a great deal of time to achieve and it'll probably fall to bits after ten minutes. The LP itself is a good one. There are no virtuosos, no ten-minute-long solos and no improvisation unless necessary. It is difficult to resist all that sometimes in the current fad of jamming."

In August he told *Beat Instrumental*; "Yes, we're pleased with the album. It shows where we are, musically. We've avoided the current temptation to go in for marathon solos and involvements — improvisation is kept well down. If it adds something — fine. If not, forget it... We're lucky in that we've evolved a style which is hard to copy. Just so long as we keep doing our own material, we should avoid the mimics and build ourselves a long-term career."

Stand Up was reviewed in *Beat Instrumental* in September 1969; "All the titles on Jethro Tull's second album were written by Ian Anderson and his stamp is on the whole production with his unmistakable voice and a lot of flute, with Glenn Cornick on bass and Clive Bunker on drums etc., Jethro Tull can build up excitement to a climax as on 'Nothing Is Easy', move along at an easy shuffle with 'Bourée', or keep it quiet and beaty like 'Look Into The Sun', or break out with fast bongos and mandolin on 'Fat Man'. This is a good representation of what Jethro Tull do and do very well, whereas other groups might try it and fail to hang together, but they have not broken through new ground here."

It was reviewed in *Disc And Music Echo* in August; "In rock music, there are two kinds of groups: the live bands and the record bands. Beatles are a perfect example of the latter, and to a lesser extent so are the Byrds. And there are an awful lot of bands, too, which fall into the first category — bands which no one should ever miss the chance of seeing live but on records you can take them or leave them. Good examples are Chambers Brothers, Led Zeppelin — and, apparently, Jethro Tull. In fact the most impressive thing about the whole album is the sleeve, with the most beautiful wood-cuts of the band and (of course — see the title!) pop-out, cut-out figures of the group inside the double-gatefold sleeve, a la children's picture books. Obviously it cost someone a large packet, but just as obviously it will sell an awful lot of copies since Jethro are a very popular band — and deservedly so, because they *are* a live gas. It's a shame that with so many albums which are musically far more interesting, more will choose to spend their money on this than look around for the best. *Stand Up* is by no means a bad album, but it could be, certainly, one whole lot better."

It was also reviewed in *Melody Maker* the same month; "Jethro Tull is not just a flute player. While the scarecrow figure of Ian Anderson hitching up his leg on telly or at your local blues festival is the focal point, an album reveals a cohesive unit at work. Glenn Cornick on bass, Martin Barre on guitar and Clive Bunker on drums all make a heavy contribution to the sound of Jethro, one of the most distinctive on the group scene. Recently, in the *Melody Maker*, respected jazz writer Leonard Feather referred to Anderson offering 'a second-rate imitation of Roland Kirk'. Feather was understandably in a poor temper at the wrecking of the Newport Jazz Festival by the local louts. Because Anderson plays flute and frequently adopts the breathy effect Roland features, he is thus dismissed. But there aren't that many flute players around and comparing him to Tubby Hayes or Frank Wess would be just as unfair and pointless. Ian has technique and feeling. His style is probably derivative but that isn't so unusual even in the highest echelons of jazz. Ian has written all the songs which are extremely varied in mood and treatment. 'A New Day Yesterday' is three four jazz, 'Bounce' (sic) has classical overtones and 'Fat Man' has the air of a lunatic country folk dance. He has a blunt, unpretentious vocal style. He is not a genius. But he has a genius for utilising his skills and talents in a manner that is entertaining and valid. This is sturdy music, occasionally a little rough. Sometimes the rhythm section doesn't swing as much as it should, but Jethro are standing up — and saying something."

And in *Rolling Stone* in December '69; "No, Jethro Tull is not just another English blues band. *This Was*, their first album, made some gestures in that direction, obligatory, in a way, for the time (summer of '68); in its differences it was intriguing even as it disappointed. Its inadequacies were unconventional; the essential problem seemed to be a style in search of a subject. Bob Dylan once said that the English know how to pronounce 'marvellous' better than Americans, but that they have a little trouble with 'raunchy'. *Stand Up*, Jethro Tull's new album, has a fairly low raunch quotient, true to form, but it is quite marvellous. For one thing, the band's orientation is more definite than before. With the removal of Mick Abrahams to form Blodwyn Pig, the musical tug-of-war which could be heard on the first album has here been effectively curtailed. Ian Anderson simply dominates the proceedings — doing all the writing and singing and playing a potpourri of instruments. He reveals a melodic gift on this album not apparent on the earlier one, a fuller awareness of the coloristic possibilities of the flute, and a catholicity of taste."

"*Stand Up* has great textural interest, due, in part, to a more sophisticated recording technique, in part to the organ, mandolin, balalaika, etc., which Anderson plays to enrich each song. The band is able to work with different musical styles, but without a trace of the facile, glib manipulation which strains for attention. I can hear ethnic influences throughout the album — a hint of Greek rhythms on the flute break of 'We Used To Know' and in the body of 'For A Thousand Mothers' —

but they are too well assimilated to be easily pinpointed. 'Bourée' has that unmistakable baroque swing, a suggestion of the traditional English round, some jazz interludes, and a straight-forward yet breathtaking bass solo before it winds its way to completion. 'Jeffrey Goes To Leicester Square' has a sense of the vague, charming disorganisation of medieval music. 'Look Into The Sun', which finishes side one, is in its melodic twists and turns, a song of genuine poignance, with Martin Barre's guitar playing a model of lyricism and understatement. On the second side, 'We Used To Know' employs what could be called a fade-in, beginning softly and then building in volume, with Barre wah-wahing madly by the end. Only 'Reasons For Waiting' is slightly marred, there being a superfluous string section. As I've said, the album is not really funky; rather, it is a meticulously crafted work (no sterility implied) which deserves careful listening. At a time when many of the established stars are faltering, it is a particular pleasure to hear an important new voice."

So how were band dynamics going by the summer of '69? Well, according to Anderson who was quoted in *Melody Maker* in July 1969; "I first met Glenn at a Civil Service dance in Blackpool. He worked for the Ministry of Pensions at the time and wore a tweed jacket and horn-rimmed glasses, cavalry twill trousers and stuff. He had pretty short hair. We were listening to the group and we both thought they were terrible, that we could do better. So we decided to form a group. Glenn used to drink all the time and go out to the pubs with all his mates. I couldn't stomach that, not being a drinking man, so I got him away from all that and began to play him lots of good records and showed him a lot of the material I'd written. He became enthusiastic and we decided to come down to London."

"While we were still getting fixed up in Blackpool, ready to make the trip, we met Mick (Abrahams) and Clive. So Glenn and I went down to Luton and spent a month there practising with them. Glenn hasn't changed at all in the slightest in the last two years. He's generally always happy and enthusiastic about things. He does get angry with people who laugh at him in the street, but generally he's very even tempered. He doesn't get upset easily, but whenever he does it's only for a few minutes, then he just shrugs his shoulders and carries on. He plays better in the studio than on stage. On stage he gets involved in the spirit of the overall sound but in the studio he spends ages getting everything just right."

"The four of us don't mix socially and we don't talk to each other too much. When there are four people in a group, virtually living together and travelling together, there has to be a great deal of tolerance. If we have a night off the last thing we would do would be to get together. We all find our own separate existence outside the group. As far as the others are concerned I don't dig beneath the surface and try to find out what they are really like inside. We're just tolerant of each other."

"Clive is a bit of a mystery man. He comes from a large family and has about seven brothers or something. And they're all identical. If the brothers come to a gig we can't tell which is which, even his mother looks like him. I think he used to be a mechanic on cars. He always used to practice on his own. He had no records to listen to and he learnt through trial and error. What is good about his drumming is his own."

"Martin was an architectural student of some sort. He was at college, involved in playing and things. He's quite old, you see, twenty-two. Then he went to Italy and bummed around because he didn't want to be an architect. In order to live he had to play with some groups over there but after a few months he joined a band in England. I think we did a gig with him and asked him to come and do an audition when Mick left. He came along but forgot to bring his guitar leads, so we took on someone else instead. But he phoned the next day and we gave him an audition and took him on. Martin is a born loser. He trips over things, gets tea over his shirts and gets electric shocks from door handles."

The summer of '69 saw Jethro Tull perform at a number of festivals including the California Pop festival, the Miami Jazz festival and the Fillmore East. It was reported in *Beat Instrumental* in August 1969 that "early signs are that Jethro Tull is doing great business in the States."

Anderson was quoted in *Record Mirror* in August 1969; "At the Miami Jazz Festival, we topped the bill over people like Roland Kirk and Gerry Mulligan. At least fifty per cent of the audience were straight and middle-aged and we were a bit worried. The night before, Booker T. and the M.G.'s topped the bill and half the audience walked out. When it came to our spot to close the last night we thought we wouldn't stand a chance. But we went on and I made a few jokes about the music and they sat there and lapped it up. We won through because we entertained on a musical level. The programme ran late but when we finished a lot of the middle-aged people were standing up and gave us a great ovation. It gives one a fantastic feeling to know you've done well."

An eccentric stage presence wasn't necessarily a reflection of the man behind the antics. It was asserted in *Record Mirror* in October 1968; "On stage Ian Anderson appears the complete extrovert — but really he is a good showman. Offstage Ian is quiet and rather erudite. Don't let anyone think he is an absolute loon."

When journalist Richard Green interviewed Anderson for *New Musical Express* in September 1969, he found him to be "completely different to the kind of person I had imagined. Ten Years

After's organist Chick Churchill once described him as 'that bloke who stands on one leg and blows down a drainpipe' and, having seen the act, I formed the impression of Ian as being a bit of a wild man. On the contrary, I found him softly-spoken, quiet and extremely serious. During the half-hour we spent together, he rarely smiled, but looked straight at me as he answered my questions."

Speaking to *Melody Maker* in November 1968, Anderson said; "The romantic side of pop music is going away and I'm not sure it's a good thing. Today you are supposed to chat to the audience so they think: 'He's just an ordinary bloke, there's nothing special about him.' Of course, if you use your head a bit you can come across as interesting, from a character point of view. I feel the mystique of pop music is important, yet everybody is fighting to destroy it at the moment. Just as the hippies destroyed the romanticism in sex — which I think is a shame."

"I just allow the things inside me to come out in my music," was how he explained things to *Disc And Music Echo* in June 1969. "If I jump about on stage, it's completely spontaneous and unplanned. What will I be doing in ten years' time? Who knows? I may be writing music for listening, or on the other hand I might be the compère at the London Palladium. But whatever happens will be the best thing for me. The whole of life is a process of thought — learning about what you can do, and learning how far you can stretch your capabilities. And eventually understanding of what I'm doing is the one thing that gives me so much satisfaction I just want to jump about the room with joy. In fact if ever I went to see a psychiatrist I'm sure he'd find me a perfectly normal healthy individual with no evil complexes or hidden streaks."

The importance of working an audience was probably more of a priority than playing to be a musicians' musician. Anderson told *Melody Maker*; "Satisfaction is complementary between musician and audience. It may mean you have to compromise to get audience reaction, and at times it doesn't work, but an audience has come to see you and you must make out you are enjoying yourself even on the worst nights. It's a bad thing when groups are playing for themselves or believes the audience is not going to understand what they are playing. I always have the idea that these people have come to see us and paid money to do it — and I would be pretty sick if I had wasted five bob."

By mid-1969, Ian Anderson's stage outfit had changed, albeit somewhat beyond his control as a result of losing his overcoat in Chicago. Fortunately though, he was still in possession of the exact same trousers that he had worn for every gig during the previous eighteen months. "I've only had them washed twice," he relayed to *New Musical Express*. "They've actually gone rotten and you can poke your finger through the material. Every time I come off stage they are literally soaked, just like they've been in a bucket of water. And they smell incredibly. It drives everyone away... Basically I am a very clean person. I bathe and I wash my hair. It derives really from a desire to push things to their limits." And in *Beat Instrumental* in August 1969; "When you think how sweaty I get on stage, well, you can appreciate that they smell more than a little."

The Newport Jazz Festival in July 1969 was a success for Jethro Tull. On the same bill, Roland Kirk was pleased to meet Jethro Tull because with Anderson's flute work being frequently compared to his, it had raised his own commercial profile. Prior to doing the gig, there was some nervous reluctance though. Anderson was quoted in *Melody Maker* the previous month; "I'm a bit worried about it, I'm not really sure what they're trying to do. It will be very good, but I don't think you can mix it that far. Seeing us might upset the people who've come for Roland and Woody Herman and they might upset the people who've come for us and the other groups. It's good to bring old music and new music together, but I am a bit worried about it all."

Most gigs probably came with their own unique challenges. Martin Barre told *Beat Instrumental* in December 1969; "The trouble with America is that there is so much disorganisation. For example, the sound system is obviously the most important thing, but so often it's handled by a guy who just doesn't know anything about it. It's almost as if they are trying to kill off live music in the States. Some of those festivals, for instance, are terrible. A field filled with 50,000 kids — yet only a couple of thousand can honestly say they can hear or see anything. The distortion is awful — really you just can't distinguish between the different groups. But then I doubt if there is much discipline among American groups even. Be fair, the drugs thing is very big there. In our group, nobody touches them. But there it is the thing. There are very few really together groups — or at least that's my view. It just seems that they don't have the discipline to get together, work really hard and put the music first."

"One band that is together is Blood, Sweat and Tears. The Grateful Dead and Butterfield's band, too — but they are patchy. Jethro Tull does have discipline. Ian Anderson especially. When I joined, I was very sloppy. I thought I was an okay musician but I couldn't prove it. There's discipline in getting down to writing, and I don't seem to have that yet. But in terms of playing, we are together, and we do have discipline. Of course, it can be misunderstood. Because Ian has this fantastic concentration for music, people assume that he talks about nothing else all day. That's just not true. Come to that, people assume that the rest of us are like hermits, because Ian doesn't drink and doesn't get about much. In fact, we are just, well, normal."

"But in the States, it's so much emphasis on drugs. People talk about the violence there, but what frightened me, really frightened me, were the hippies, who after all are preaching peace. We went to one hall, a Fillmore I think, and I was shattered. All those kids and all of them seemed to be dazed, drugged. It was frightening — I know I just pushed myself into a corner. To be honest, I didn't see much in the way of violence. True, we had one nasty moment. We were driving a hire car in Los Angeles and got a bit confused on a motorway. In the back was a sealed bottle of whisky, which was mine. But there was an unsealed one — and it's an offence to have an open bottle in a car — and it was left by the previous person who had the car. Anyway, our long hair and so on — we were suspect. And they found some seeds. They assumed it was marijuana. In fact, they came off a hamburger bun. But we were guilty until we could prove our innocence, which is the opposite way round to Britain."

Jethro Tull had been invited to play at Woodstock but already frustrated at other festivals for having a chronic lack of organisation, they were informed by Ten Years After that Woodstock wasn't much different and so opted out of it. On 14th August — the day before Woodstock — Jethro Tull were at the Fillmore West in San Francisco. By this point they were already committed to perform in Houston and San Antonio. That said, Woodstock spanned the 15th, 16th and 17th of the month so if they felt strongly about it, Jethro Tull could have probably played there. It is also the case that Anderson was reluctant to do Woodstock due to not wanting to be associated with the hippie movement or at least, one particular kind of sound.

Regarding the whole hippie and underground thing, he was quoted in *New Musical Express* in June 1969; "The drugs and long hair aspects — it's all a bit dicey and something which fortunately I am not a part of, the drugs thing that is. If I did consciously attempt to do anything socially it would be through the songs. But I haven't yet approached that point where (a) I have anything constructive to say and (b) the means of putting it across. I haven't developed mentally enough to be able to do it."

It made sense that Anderson didn't want Jethro Tull to be pigeonholed with hippie music on the basis that by that point, Tull's music appealed to a fairly diverse audience. Anderson told *New Musical Express*; "I know from the gigs we have done in the past few weeks that there are new people in the audience, some older and some much younger. They usually go for the first time and laugh and don't know what's going on, but I would probably do the same at first. But it doesn't matter whether they like you or not — they are getting a chance to see you and make up their own minds. There's no question of pressure on them. I don't think anyone could accuse us of hyping our record. There was no lavish press reception and only one ad in the music papers. Then it was up to people to buy it if they liked it. I think we have come by our success fairly honestly without any pretensions of being aspiring pop stars. I am looking forward to the people who've bought the record coming along to the concerts when we get back."

It was asserted in *Top Pops* in July 1969; "There was a time when Jethro Tull were considered so underground that you could not see them, but times have changed and now the group lurk dangerously near the top of the charts with their highly commercial recording of 'Living In The Past'. Dangerously because in the strange stark land of hippiedom and the restless set it is considered that popular opinion is never the criterion of good taste and a hit single is likened unto a wart upon your ethnic image! Up until their hit single Jethro Tull have confined themselves within the bounds of good taste by making appearances in the album charts — where the likes of Des O'Connor fear to tread although it might be as well to remember that *South Pacific* and *The Sound Of Music* are this country's biggest album sellers — and an almost accidental appearance in the lower regions of the singles charts with 'Song For Jeffrey'."

Upon being asked whether success had resulted in a change to how Jethro Tull approach things, Anderson was quoted in the same feature; "No, because we are still working on songs that we put together many months ago and others from ideas we had long ago and now they've gelled into a song. As we become better known we get more freedom and not less. People are prepared to accept us on a wider range of music."

Being in Jethro Tull was more about the music than having trippy experiences. Anderson was quoted in *Rave* in November 1969; "I don't need to take drugs to freak out because I can do that quite naturally on stage — the release is there... I don't concern myself with recreations. There is always something to do — talking to people, gigging, travelling. The most annoying thing in the world is travelling five hours between gigs — wasting time reading trivial books. The only thing to do is to sit and think which is very uncomfortable in our van with our road managers..."

"Groupies frighten me because they're bonkers — must be screwed-up people to do that. Anyone who gets mixed up in that sex thing to that degree has to be out of their heads — it's not even physical. It's some kind of peculiar ego thing. These strange plays like *Oh! Calcutta!* just bore me. I'd probably throw bottles. It's very important that they are around and that the underground press should print their silly little four-letter words so that the public can profit by their mistakes. I'm learning."

"They're destroying all the good values. Sex is not underground anymore which is a shame. It has its dirty and warped aspects which are no longer underground. People expect that it is some kind of physical necessity. Love and romanticism have been killed off to make way for pornography. Sex is not just a schoolboy joke anymore, it has become something much less than that. The motives behind a more liberal attitude towards sex are fine but they don't work because of the people who are mouthing them. Everyone wants an instant revolution but revolutions are seldom successful and hardly ever successful immediately. It's important that they have their little revolutions and important that they shout because it has a gradual effect upon society but only over a long time. What these students are shouting about now is going to seem very unimportant to them when they are forty with kids."

When asked what money meant to him, Anderson was quoted in the same feature; "It means cigarettes, meals, rent, mandolin strings, plectrums, coffee and that's about it. Earning big money doesn't really concern me — playing to more and more people does. It will be nice to have some big money in a few years time because then I can go away and become a preacher or work in the Forestry Commission or whatever. I might even get married and then again I might not. It would be more important to me than most people. I might get married the day after we come back from America!"

Disc And Music Echo commented in August 1969; "Every year hundreds of British groups make the hectic slog across thousands of miles known as the American Continent. It means weeks of travelling, hard work, coming off stage to wring out their shirts, seeing places as far apart as Alabama and Chicago at a jog trot, living a world of perpetual rushing. They come back to Britain usually exhausted, mentally and physically washed out. Why then do they do it? Because "making it" in and to America is still the biggest achievement for a British group, both financially and emotionally. Jethro Tull have just returned from their second tour of America in seven months. They have literally stormed through America treading in the footsteps of the Beatles, Stones, Hendrix and the Cream. Like them, they have found ready acceptance of their music, massive crowds, and a magical response that is foremost the prerogative of American audiences. What *is* the magic British groups seem to put out to American audiences? And why is it that a British accent can almost guarantee instant success?"

Anderson retorted; "American audiences appoint you as their representative. To them — whether you like it or not — you are a group that stands for everything that's inside them. They think you're anti-police, anti-establishment, pro-love, pro-drugs (which we're not). You can't explain to them that the very reason you've got long hair is because you are conforming — to the pop image. I could stand up and say I didn't know anything or want to know anything about all that. That I'm just a professional entertainer trying to play music the best way I can, and it wouldn't make any difference. They still throw all kinds of stuff on the stage — it's incredible. This attitude is particularly American and yet every time I come back to Britain I can feel it growing here too. I believe America has changed a lot in the past two years. When the Beatles were at their height, people wanted artists who had mystique, who were untouchable. Real pop idols. Now they want to see an extension of themselves on stage. American youth is no longer involved in a kind of fantasy freedom. They've turned it into a bitter resistance against everything, which is frightening, more so as we've been appointed to represent that."

As much as being in demand in America was a commercial asset for Jethro Tull, it is likely that the whole thing was far from being sunshine and lollipops, as Anderson explained; "After the first couple of weeks you get nervous and irritable and wish you weren't there. Every hotel bedroom starts to look the same, and you lose all that lovely security you have at home. Getting any writing done is almost impossible unless you literally lock yourself away, which I had to do. Because you can't look round and see one familiar object. A kettle or a dirty cup that actually belongs to you. Sometimes I've been on my way to a gig in a black limousine and thought: 'Oh God, another place to play — I wish I was at home with mum' but then you actually get into the theatre and everything's got to be done. You have to talk to the promoter or an amp blows up, and when you step out on stage you're there, body and soul one-hundred percent, and you really wouldn't be anywhere else."

"And the one thing in favour of American audiences is that they do know how to be an audience. I suppose it comes from experience. But they know how to get into and out of a theatre, stand around looking "groovy". Unlike the British audiences who come out of the Albert Hall in London looking sneaky and as if they feel that they shouldn't have been there at all! Americans feel this rapport between the artist and themselves. They're part of you directly when you step out on stage. In America you have to talk to everyone in the street. This may sound nasty but it does get boring to have to treat everyone who comes up as an individual when you're used to treating them as an audience en masse. And there's this latest American saying about having a "rap". This means, as far as I can see, talking for fifteen minutes about a lot of meaningless rubbish that doesn't get either of you anywhere. People come up to you in Los Angeles or San Francisco and say 'Hey man, have you time for five minutes' rap?' and I find it all a bit mentally exhausting."

Equally though, it made sense to reach an American audience, as many British groups at the time were highly aware of. Touring in America seemed to be more about having a long-term promotional plan rather than one based on seeking to acquire immediate profits. Anderson told *Hit Parader* in October 1969; "The money's pretty important, I suppose, though I have yet to see much evidence of it. Most groups lose money coming to America. A lot of expenses you don't realise are expenses, until you see that nobody's going to pay for it except you. If you want profit, you can always try to find it in the half percent that's left. It's much more profitable for us at the moment to play in England. But it's even worse for American groups over there than it is for us here, because they cannot earn money, you know."

"That English money isn't worth much, really. The only thing an English tour is worth for an American group is selling that extra few thousand records, which is all it could mean to them. It's a sort of prestige thing, having tied up another country. Consider that selling thirty, forty-thousand records in England can get you into the top ten of albums; that amount means nothing in the States. American groups could do just as well by doing a little more work over here. An unknown American group in England couldn't earn much. The Iron Butterfly would be worth a hundred quid a night over there right now but they want to do it, and they're coming. They're doing a tour with us, in fact… Most English groups want to come to America; they have to, if they want to make any more than just a reasonable sort of living. You've got to be right at the top to make a lot of money in England. But England is still more important to me. The people, I understand them. I feel a sort of sympathy for the people where I can understand what makes them laugh, what they like and dislike about music. I don't say they're a better or worse audience, but I do know them. I don't like to offend people, and I do a lot of that over here in the States. It's a little bit upsetting not understanding people. I like it here, look forward to coming back, because it's a sort of a challenge."

"There isn't actually a lot of difference between American audiences and English ones when it comes down to playing in front of people. The only really obvious difference that I've come across is that people here seem to want to get away with things, which is a little bit disturbing to me. I've been used to playing to people who are neither super–conscious or aware, or in any way less conscious or aware, than they would be at any time during the day, doing whatever they do in the daytime. It's a little disturbing playing to people who are, to quote, turned on. It's difficult to know how to play to them. It's disturbing to know that they must to some extent imagine that I personally, and the other fellows in the band, are just the same as them, you know.

After an extensive touring schedule, it was necessary for time to be set aside for the next album to be made. Although some of the writing had been done on the road, it was clear that time was needed to focus just on being in the studio. It was reported in *Record Mirror* in August 1969; "This week, Jethro Tull go into the recording studios. The first objective is to make a single. Then they record their third album all in one go. So there won't be any gigs for three weeks by them."

Anderson commented; "I'm putting all the ideas which I got in the States into songs and then the songs into records. I don't believe what we are doing is a progression. My ideas haven't really changed over the past two years. What has happened is I'm better equipped to put them across. The third album is different to the other two simply because we have different matins at our disposal. It's the technique used in the studio and knowing the guys in the band better through working with them all the time that also makes the band sound different."

Everyone was in agreement that America would not have been the best place for Jethro Tull to record. Speaking to *Melody Maker* in September 1969, Anderson said; "There's too many live gigs. People don't understand what America means to groups to have to play there, even with six or seven months allocated, you have to play every day to cover the ground… We don't want to record in America. We've got good studios here."

Consequently, studio time in the UK had to be scheduled quite far in advance. "We had to plan the next album nearly two months ago, in terms of the amount of time we need, the engineer we want and any other people we want to work with. It's like meeting a deadline — it's not ideal but it's a job," Anderson explained to *New Musical Express* in September 1969.

He also told *Melody Maker* in December; "It's difficult to generalise about studios in America because I've only been to three of them, but those three were pretty rotten. There's no reason to try and spend twelve or fourteen hours of which you're going to have to spend at least four getting used to the studio and the engineer and how it works. Also in England the studio musicians are much better. I think it's probably because they're more in touch with playing their music and taking it seriously which tends to make for a better working relationship. You know, they're very difficult to work with, they're probably not as friendly as American studio musicians, but they produce a better end product if you can get through to them. They're all very "la-de-da" and sort of musically a bit snobbish, but if you can impress them with your personality you can tell them to shut up when you want them to shut up and get on with it when you want them to get on with it and they usually do."

As much as some of the writing had been done on the road, it seems that being back home was vital for Anderson to be able to get his ideas down in a way that was more certain and clarified: "I write more easily at home when I am surrounded by objects of personal value. I'm spending a week at home making the ideas that I got in America into a product. Nothing has been completed for nine weeks due to a continual round of hotels and aeroplanes. I want to spend more time and thought on writing. It's becoming more cerebral, not just spontaneous emotion. People might not notice any difference but I can as a musician."

Melody Maker reported in September 1969; "The new album will be wider instrumentally as far as the group are concerned. Martin Barre will be heard on flute, drummer Clive Bunker will probably use glockenspiel and various types of drums." Importantly though, the band had no intention to expand the instrumentation they used onstage. Anderson said, "There's the danger that if you play all these instruments on stage, people will say 'Yah boo, multi-instrumentalists'. We don't really play these instruments but we play the desired thing given time enough for rehearsal. I'd hate to add a piano or organ; I want to learn them anyway, and if we had a proper musician I'd have no reason to learn. We have a sufficiently large enough variety of things to use. The only things we can't play are the violins and cellos. Everything we play we have complete control over."

A lot of focus in 1969 had gone towards getting things right on stage — not necessarily to the detriment of what got done in the studio, but certainly to an extent that Jethro Tull's management had put a lot of thought into ensuring that things would run smoothly for the band on stage. Anderson explained; "The gigs get better all the time because if someone's promoting something on your behalf you have a lot more freedom to do things you've learned. You don't have to rely on a stagehand who doesn't understand pop music, the physical act of playing. You can do things yourself. That's why we're promoting the next tour — we know what's going to happen, there will be no major disasters like the curtain coming down when the stagehand thinks it should and things going wrong due to the management's inefficiency. You have to be aware of the effect on Joe Blogs in the audience if, halfway through a number, something goes wrong — the atmosphere's gone. We have to make sure that things don't go wrong."

There was a strong distinction between the working process on stage compared to the one in the studio. Anderson told *Disc And Music Echo* in November '69; "Our records and our stage act are still basically independent of each other, and likely to remain so. A stage act has to be visual as well as aural, and the chat I give the audience between the numbers is very important as well. I know a lot of people think my strange jiggings about on stage are still a terrible gimmick, but they're completely unrehearsed. I just seem to be motivated by the music — it's as if the music was holding me up. I'm quite honest about it — the music just takes over and gradually the movements become part and parcel of it. In fact I'm tending to write in physical terms now. It's almost as if I can hear things on the tapes which can be translated into music. Off stage I just can't do it. I've been asked by photographers to pose standing on one leg and I just fall over!"

On songwriting, Anderson was quoted in the same feature; "There's more to it than creating a tenth of an LP where each song is relative to the next. You can't afford to let anything escape you — it's all got to be pieced out absolutely accurately so you can say anything you want in three minutes, combining it with a catchy melody and rhythmic structure acceptable to public taste. It's really a question of combining your integrity with commercialism."

It's just as well that since they started, Jethro Tull had made a conscious effort to move away from blues music and more towards progressive rock, especially as the genre was gaining a lot of commercial momentum by that time. It was plausibly one of the many factors that benefited the band and ensured their longevity. *Melody Maker* reported in September 1969; "The *Melody Maker* Pop Poll results last week revealed a hefty swing to the progressively musical groups and singers although this was to be guessed at anyway looking back over the changes in the music scene of the past couple of years. One group who did well in both British and International sections of the poll were Jethro Tull. Their last single 'Living In The Past' was featured in both sections' singles placings and the group was voted second most popular British group and in the Brightest Hope ratings. It's certainly been a good year for the Tull. 'Living In The Past' having been a big hit and, perhaps more important, their second album *Stand Up* high in the album chart, the group look set for an even better twelve months ahead. They are currently working on a third album and a new single, 'Sweet Dream', is due out on October 3rd."

Prior to the release of 'Sweet Dream', Anderson said; "It's a good song, more in keeping with what people imagine us to be. It has a good guitar solo from Martin Barre, and judicious use of horns and strings. There's a very delicate blend of strings, horns, two electric guitars and a twelve-string guitar, all playing a tight pattern. It's nice to use extra instrumentation properly. The flute makes a brief appearance, but there is much more vocal."

On the way up. In 1969 Tull came second in the group category of *Melody Maker's* annual awards. The presentation ceremony was held at London's Waldorf Hotel on 17th September 1969.

The *Melody Maker*'s poll results for best group were:
1. The Beatles
2. Jethro Tull
3. The Rolling Stones
4. Fleetwood Mac
5. Cream
6. Pink Floyd
7. Family
8. Fairport Convention
9. The Who

Regarding the band's early following, Anderson commented; "It was your sort of long-haired sympathetic kind who were very much into the blues thing. We definitely came in at the right time when there was a big sort of return to the basic concepts of pop music, you know, blues and rock 'n' roll. It was refreshingly new and exciting after that excursion into the complicated, over-arranged so-called progressive pop thing of the *Sergeant Pepper* era, of which *Sergeant Pepper* was the only good thing. It was okay for us. We were learning to play music and blues is an idiom that is easy to feel rapport with. It is very simple to understand the feelings involved."

Following an isolated show in the Netherlands in early September, Tull's touring continued later the same month in Newcastle and the following night in Edinburgh. *New Musical Express* reported in October; "Said Ian Anderson, who regards Edinburgh, where he was educated, as his home town and was in the Scots capital on the second stop of Jethro Tull's seven-week British and Continental tour: 'We try to raise the level of musical understanding a teeny, teeny bit — we try to help the pop thing a little bit which is ruddy bad anyway — we play to our limits every night.' That was backstage at the Usher Hall. Out front Jethro, playing to a brimming-over house, promptly went out of their way to prove it. They surely helped educate a fanatical audience; they did something for pop in filling this expensive-to-rent hall for the first time in two or three years; and they did play to what seemed like their limits."

"The fans, softened up by Terry Reid and Savoy Brown, were all set up for the first barrage, the familiar 'Nothing Is Easy.' Hot, breathy Anderson flute and there was more where that came from. 'Play In Time' was out of a similar groove. Then a taste of something to come — the group's imminent single 'Sweet Dream'. A frenetic thing with too much vocal in it for me, but undoubtedly commercial in spite of what some people in the record industry have predicted. 'As long as it gets into *Top Of The Pops* we don't care what happens,' said Anderson. The remark brought a mini-Hampden roar. On to 'Fat Man', with Anderson picking up a mandolin and Martin Barre switching from guitar to flute and Glenn Cornick slinking off into the wings. 'He's a funny lad, Glenn,' quipped Anderson, the capacity house hanging on to his every word. 'We caught him listening to an Amen Corner LP the other night!' By now the audience (the ticket agency claimed they could have filled the hall twice over) were ripe for Clive Bunker's drawn out drum showcase. Altogether an out and out triumph, the likes of which hadn't been seen in Edinburgh for years. In a word, the audience was *Tullverised*."

New Musical Express also reported the same month; "Nowhere is the pop revolution that began under the title of 'Underground' more in evidence at present than on the current British concert tour of Jethro Tull. With the package format near death and the teenybopper groups sticking to their ballrooms for fear of going out to half-empty auditoriums, Jethro Tull has been packing in capacity houses at almost every stop. Yet, despite the amount of records they have sold in a relatively short existence, they remain a group at the head of a movement a large section of the press, public and music business thinks it can afford to ignore. London's Royal Albert Hall on Wednesday was the fourth stop of the tour and once again Jethro devotees were out in force — to such an extent that disappointed latecomers were touting for tickets in the street outside (something I haven't seen since the Cream's farewell concert at the same venue)."

When asked how the tour was going, Anderson was quoted in the same feature; "All right, well more than all right. It's been a sell out so far. It was a bit ropey the first night because we'd been recording. Tonight it ought to be better. I know Martin sounds better. He's learnt more about music in the past few months than he will all his life. I have as well. The group sounds better than the last time you heard us here. I don't think anyone is afraid anymore of failing to live up to a certain standard of playing. For myself, I feel more at home, more relaxed, than I did on the last British tour. I have got no worries about how we rank with other musicians or how our popularity rating compares with other groups. I have never enjoyed playing as much as I have in these past few days on tour."

Under the heading of "Flamboyant Ian Anderson — A Tonic To The Tour Scene!" *Disc And Music Echo* commented; "Jethro Tull were magnificent at the Royal Albert Hall last Wednesday (1st October). Their reputation filled the hall; their performance brought the thousands to their feet, stomping and shouting for more. The evening was one of fine music. My overall impression was that possibly Britain is at last moving towards a time when bands can embark on concert tours with confidence. They will draw large, discerning crowds who come to listen. This autumn we have already been blessed with successful concerts by Fairport Convention, Pentangle, Deep Purple, Ray Charles and Tom Paxton. For music lovers, this has been a good time to be alive. I am convinced the market is now there for gifted entertainers. Before Jethro Tull launched into their first song, 'Nothing Is Easy' off *Stand Up*, Ian Anderson stood and rambled hilariously into the mic. He apologised for all the talk, saying: 'Sorry about the chat, it's an ego thing — terrible thing — caught it in the States'."

"This was to be an anti-hard sell show. As soon as they started working, Anderson became really alive. He contorted himself into strange positions, his legs winding round each other like two mating snakes. His familiar breathy, talking flute stuttered a solo and then he swayed across the stage, knees bent, like a hippy Groucho Marx... Once again Ian's flute was featured. Between frenzied blasts he would leap back from the mic as if an electric shock had burnt his lips. A hand whipped the mangled mane of hair back from his eyes shining with wit and enthusiasm and then he would make another assault on the mic. You might feel that I was paying too much attention to Ian, but on stage he tends to have a hypnotic hold on his audience. But every member of the band had a chance to prove his worth. Glenn Cornick played through a nice bass solo, while Clive Bunker on drums had the stage to himself for over five minutes. Martin Barre is a fine guitarist. He is not on an ego trip. He plays with the group, rather than against it. However at certain times, noticeably during 'We Used To Know', his style really shone through. Throughout, the standard was high and they slipped easily from one mood to another. 'Fat Man' was played on flute, mandolin and drums. Their next single, which will be released on the new Chrysalis label, titled 'Sweet Dream', pounded along with a heavy stomping beat. To me it seemed pretty commercial, despite doubts in certain quarters."

Another journalist also reviewed this prestigious gig in the same publication: "At Jethro Tull's previous London concert in May, I thought them so entertaining that it would be the "kiss of death" for a heavy group in underground circles. Last Wednesday they returned to the Albert Hall with single and album successes behind them. Dead? No. Heavy? Slightly. Entertaining? Most certainly. But Tull's original fans seem very much in the minority, and replaced by a new and shorter haired audience. Ian Anderson gave us a lot of chat, took the mickey out of himself, was a bit nasty with the audience — and there was not enough music. But what music we did get is still some of the most entertaining and different around today. For 'Fat Man' drummer Clive Bunker had a mini-drum kit, Ian Anderson played mandolin, guitarist Martin Barre played a tin whistle, while bassist Glenn Cornick appeared in Edmund Ross-type South American gear and played maracas. All entertaining fun, but then the band seemed to lose interest in entertaining and the show ended with prolonged drum and guitar solos, chaos onstage, and an encore."

Glenn Cornick spoke of his venue preferences to *New Musical Express* in November 1969; "Concert halls are the only places where everybody gets a good deal — the public gets good music in comfortable conditions for a reasonable amount of money, the group has good playing conditions. You can get nostalgic about the good times but when you think of all the aggro — the stages too small to get the equipment on — having to change in corridors. Personally if I was going to see a group I would rather go to a concert than stand at the back of some sweaty club and just catch a glimpse of the guitarist's head."

Elsewhere, Anderson told *ZigZag* why he didn't miss the intimacy of playing in small club environments: "Those sort of atmospheres frighten the hell out of me. I went to a club the other night to see Roy Harper, and I thought about the time we played there and it was scary — to think we actually went on in a place so small, so claustrophobic, with people sitting so near. We did that at one point, but if we'd carried on playing in places like that we'd never have become musically what we are now, because it's very limiting in a small place; to play music demanding volume, feedback, sustained notes, and so on would become unmanageable, unbearable in that sort of atmosphere. Anyway, the intimacy that seems to be associated with that sort of place doesn't exist in my mind, because I feel a much more intimate atmosphere when we step out onstage at a concert hall holding from two to five thousand. When there's that many people, I find it much easier and more natural to talk to them."

"And "pricing" is not the right word really. It isn't a question of we want more money therefore we want bigger places; we want to play bigger places and play to more and more people at once — from their point of view as well as our own. We would never have time to play all the little places, and most people wouldn't see us at all. Our prices aren't outrageous — we don't charge any more than anybody else — we don't charge as much as we could charge. Really, the money is immaterial, so long as we're making a profit. I hate to owe money, and I'd hate to be in a position five years from now if I end up a schizophrenic or mentally unstable from doing this sort of thing as hard as we do, when I have no money. I want to have some money if I have nothing else. Money is important undeniably, although all it means to me at the moment is having food and sleep when I want to."

Tull had also received criticism from British fans for spending so much time touring the States, to which Martin Barre told *Beat Instrumental* in December 1969; "I don't see this criticism at all. There are maybe forty big dates we can do here and we want to do them. People say why don't we do the blues clubs now, but it's obvious why. We get a hit record and so we get a lot of new fans, maybe younger ones. So the clubs would get crowded out and the old Tull fans, remembering the group from the start, would have to suffer cramped conditions — and it'd be hard for us to work anyway. There are a lot more places to work in the States and we obviously can't do them all. I'd have thought we'd get more criticism from the States. We found recording a pretty difficult business in the States. It was very expensive and took us a long time — really we virtually ended up engineering the sessions for ourselves. Still, we did 'Living In The Past' there, in New York, and the flip in Los Angeles. Normally we're on eight track recordings. I think you need all that. The concept of getting a live sound in the studio isn't really relevant. But on the next album, we'll probably try a few in sixteen track. It may not work, but it's worth trying. Basically I'd say eight track is enough. When people talk of thirty-two track, well, I just don't see how you'd use it all."

Anderson was quoted in *Rave* in November 1969; "England is still enormously important to any group in terms of the world market. It is the trigger point from which so many things can be started. It is also a far healthier scene in England than America where almost any group can turn in an "underground" album. A great many of the completely unknown and very sub-standard British blues groups are flooding on to the American market with what is really just repetitive rubbish. It is becoming a flood in the States which can only really spoil it for better groups like the Nice and the Family."

Going to America was certainly not without its perks though. When touring there, Anderson went to see Elvis Presley perform: "I thought he was very good. He had the good sense to keep a sense of humour over his early rock and roll act and just kept the entertainment going. Listening to songs like 'Heartbreak Hotel' and 'Hound Dog' was a completely new experience for me — so was getting togged up in a tuxedo to go and see him. I looked very good but I think the green riding boots rather spoilt things — I had no black shoes."

By the end of 1969, band dynamics seemed healthy and professional. Anderson told *Disc And Music Echo* in November; "The reason for the rest of the band doing what they're doing is the love of an instrument. They want to improve themselves technically on that instrument, whereas I never played anything properly and I doubt I ever will. I don't want to be a super-flautist — I just enjoy being involved with music. I suppose I am the person who comes up with ideas for the group to play, but I always write with them in mind. I'm the one who's more capable of looking at the whole band objectively — because while the others are at home rehearsing I'm thinking about what we can do next. On stage the others probably do more than me. If you were to take one person out of the band and still have the music left — it would be me you'd remove. But replacing the band with other members wouldn't work. It's very difficult to find people who are musically compatible. We're not matey at all in our personal relationships. We're all very different people; we all accept this and we don't make any deliberate attempts to be chummy if we don't want to be. I don't imagine we would be friends at all if we weren't involved in the same business. The only thing we have in common is the music, and because of this moodies and bad tempers don't matter, whereas if we were more involved with each other personally that would make a hell of a lot of difference to our playing. We're just good companions. My personal friends are not involved with the music scene at all. I think it has to be like that. You have to have someone who will throw the whole thing into perspective."

Martin Barre added; "Obviously outside the group we all have different interests, but we do live together most of the time, especially on tour and in America and we are all good friends. But twenty-four hours a day of Jethro Tull would be very limiting. I find I want to do more and more things consciously outside the group, at the same time without having any intentions of leaving. If you can talk and play with other musicians outside the group you work with you will gather more ideas and become a more valuable asset to the group. In the short time I've been with the group I've learned more about what is good and bad in music than ever I did before. I'm much more enthusiastic than ever before. Although Ian does all the talking we do talk as well — it's just that he usually has it all worked out in his mind what he wants to say! And don't take too much notice of him saying he'll never play anything properly — I know he wants to be a really good musician. He wants to learn and play piano, because he knows it's difficult to do too much with a flute through two-thousand-watt amplification! Maybe our material ideas aren't the same, and maybe Clive and Glenn don't talk very much, but musically we're all the same, and that's what counts."

Having Ian Anderson as the spokesperson for the band wasn't problematic for the other members. It seems that it was helpful and convenient. As Martin Barre explained to *New Musical Express*; "I've done just two interviews since I've been in the group but none of us mind that. The kind of things Ian has to answer and talk about, all that analysis and comment, I wouldn't care to do that anyway... I cannot grasp being thought of as a personality — which I will never be. I am just a musician and I only relate Jethro Tull to music. Emotionally that sort of thing means as much to me as eating a boiled egg."

Glenn Cornick chipped in by saying; "I find it very difficult now to talk to people outside music. There are things the group does without thinking that other people think of as big things. People introduce you to their friends — this is so-and-so who you may have seen on *Top Of The Pops* — and it's like being in a zoo. Maybe they want a little of your supposed fame to rub off on them. Whatever it is, it is very embarrassing."

In response to the interviewer's comment that Ian Anderson seems to dominate Jethro Tull, Glenn Cornick was quoted in *Go* in April 1970; "Yes, he does. Why not? He writes good songs, and what's more, he's able to finish them, which is more than the others can say. Martin and I have both been working on songs for over a year, but we'll never get them done. Ian has the right direction of mind to sit down and write the beginning and end to a song."

Even Anderson himself didn't want to be a personality and was more interested in talking about the music. He was quoted in *Disc And Music Echo* in November 1969; "I would never use music as a means to an end to put my ideas across. I have strong social, political religious and moral views but I don't think the time is right to push them across. If ever I felt it necessary to tell people and discuss with them what I believe, I would do it in a medium outside my music. I wouldn't object to doing it on a TV talk show. At the moment I'm a musician and nothing else. Music becomes an impurity if clouded with messages."

Extreme fanaticism directed towards the band must have been uncomfortable at times. One reader's letter printed in *Disc And Music Echo* in November 1969 compared Jethro Tull to Jesus!: "Jesus Christ was similar in appearance to Jethro Tull, with his long hair, beard and gaily coloured clothes. He was looked upon as God's son, performing miracles. Everyone believed in him, but his clothes were never commented on. In the music world Ian Anderson, Glenn Cornick, Martin Barre and Clive Bunker are also performing miracles with their records and concert dates. Good luck Jethro Tull!"

After their relatively small tour of the UK, it was back to the States. Under the heading "Jethro Tull Tour — A "Stark" Raving Success", it was reported in *Music Now!* in December 1969; "A couple of weeks ago when Jethro Tull opened their third American tour, in the Bay City, Ian Anderson was suddenly confronted by an attention-getting device slightly beyond the power of his fluteful antics. It seems a young man, somewhat entranced by the natural rhythms of 'Bourée', took his clothes off and made his way up to the Fillmore West stage. There, with his back to the audience, he "did his thing" (but definitely out of rhythm). Anderson, seemingly oblivious to it all, continued with his playing until the end of the song, when the nudist exited. He then scratched his head, bewilderedly remarking, 'I could have sworn that guy had no clothes on'."

"The Jethro tour, by the way, equalled the force of the Stones' engagements, as each of the groups' gigs was pre-sold out before the day of the performance. Ian and friends will be cavorting in various dens of entertainment throughout America every night through to December 13th. A massive, ulcer-causing schedule to be sure, but one that the group's ever-growing legion of fans have demanded. In several cities, the Tull-Stones concerts are separated by only a few days and it's given members of the rock press time to evaluate and contrast the individualistic qualities of Jagger and Anderson — often to a remarkable degree of similarity."

Melody Maker reported in December; "On stage at the Santa Monica Civic Auditorium in Los Angeles (26th November) Jethro Tull was fantastic, garnering encore applause and a standing ovation. Anderson was in rare form and proved himself to be the most visual entertainer since Mick Jagger. However, while Jagger manages to play his sexuality for laughs, Anderson keeps everything dead serious."

New Musical Express reported on several of Tull's performances starting off with the Fillmore in New York; "With every seat full the theatre begins to regain its magic. With no high stage or orchestra pit to segregate the participants, and with the justifiably high-praised Joshua Light Show working excellently, the atmosphere is heavy and the effect a total involvement with the music. Fat Mattress had waved the flag and exited, leaving the stage to a boring and unoriginal American band called Grand Funk Railroad who nevertheless got a standing ovation and bore out Ian's feelings that a standing ovation USA style has to be viewed in perspective."

"Ian was in good form with the asides and witticisms when Jethro took the stage later at 10:15. Each line, move, or roll of eyeballs drew the desired response while Glenn Cornick, Martin Barre and Clive Bunker worked hard and tight behind to turn in one of the best sets I've seen them perform. New York rock fans pride themselves on their super awareness and it soon became obvious that the standing ovation at the Fillmore is treated as a kind of ritual. The group knows it will do an encore — it has to be pretty dire not to get asked — and the audience knows it too. But the game must be played to the rules, and with the required amount of stamping, shouting and clapping, so it is... The second set got underway at 2:45 — a normal time for the Fillmore. The second house was older than the first — which had been the last to sell out — and were also more Jethro conscious as opposed to being interested. Consequently, there was more reaction for Ian's patter, which is noticeably bluer than in Britain, and for the music. Again a strong act with the standing ovation procedure observed. At the end the audience gave signs of standing their ground in their demands for more until the exit music dispersed their appeals."

Of Tull's gig that took place at the University of Massachusetts: "Spooky Tooth and Johnny Winters had played and the audience was patiently waiting for Jethro. Ian changed hastily and tuned up his mandolin with Martin while Clive drew a skinhead on a blackboard and he and Glenn got engaged in a discussion about Vietnam, Nixon and the draft with a student guarding the classroom-come-dressing room door. The concert was in a large barn-like building normally used for basketball. A low wooden stage had been set up in the centre with seats all around. With 3,500 present, the show was a sell-out. For many of the young audience Jethro Tull was a new experience and the genuine, immediate way they responded to the band and Ian's banter made a telling contrast in retrospect with the hip, pseudo sophistication of the Fillmore crowd. The sound system was poor and the seating arrangement inadequate — Ian spent some time after pointing out to the student organisers how both could have been improved — but overall it was a greatly enjoyable show, as much for the way the audience responded as for the music."

The last gig the *NME* reported on took place at Boston Tea Party, a converted garage that could take an audience of up to 2,000 (Terry Ellis informed the journalist that the two dates there had been booked well in advance and would be the last small club appearance that Jethro Tull would be making); "The evening's show was a good one: the club was near to capacity despite the weather. The group went for an encore and got it from an ultra-responsive audience. Boston is a good place for rock."

The journalist took note of how touring was having an impact on health; "Ian got to bed at six in the morning, after getting into discussions with Terry, and woke the next day with a heavy cold. His is by far the most energy-sapping position in the group; not only working and moving the most on stage but also being Jethro's front man for interviews which, where the American underground papers are concerned, can be long and mentally tiring. Like the others he would come off stage each night with his clothes soaked in sweat, then have to change in an often-cold dressing room and go straight out into the night air — which is enough to tax even the toughest germ defences. He had been ill on both previous tours, once with tonsillitis."

"As he pointed out: 'Once you catch something it is difficult to get rid of it. You can't just stop and take a couple of days off to recover.' The four interviews lined up for him that afternoon didn't help to improve his condition… In the dressing room before that night's show Ian was shivering, his shoulders hunched together. The club was so crowded we had to go out into the street to reach the stage through a back door. Ian kept on his leather coat to keep warm and changed behind the stage. The chatting to the audience had to go, but it said much for the group that musically their act suffered very little. Between numbers, to those who knew, it was painfully evident that Ian was sick. Wednesday saw the start of the most arduous part of the eleven days. Five towns and eight shows in five days before the flight home, which all were counting off the days to. On the flight out from Logan Airport, Boston, for Kansas City, Glenn was saying that he in fact preferred the one-night gigs because they made the time go quicker. To him the travelling was not so much tiring as depressing. None of the group seemed concerned about the actual flying. I certainly was when we arrived at Kansas City just after dark in a blanket of snow, sleet and fog and landed only on the second attempt."

November saw Tull end '69 with a hit single, 'Sweet Dream'. It got to number seven in the UK. Even though Tull had two hit albums to their name, it was starting to look like they might carve their further success predominantly as a singles band. 'Sweet Dream' was reviewed in *Record Mirror* in October 1969; "Rushed round and hereby rush-reviewed. Currently on the wave of popularity, the group could be a commercial bet here, though there is an off-beat sameness here and there. Voice comes through well, and it builds well. Not absolutely sure, but should attract attention. Chart possibility."

It was reviewed in *New Musical Express* in the same month; "This is the single Island didn't want to issue because they didn't think it commercial enough. So here it is on Chrysalis, a new label run by Jethro's enterprising young management. This review is the third time I've heard the song, a composition by Ian Anderson, and I must admit that the first time — at Chrysalis — I wasn't immediately struck by its commercial possibilities either. The second time I heard it was on the Jethro Tull concert tour and then, seeing them doing it on stage, it began to make an impression. The third time I'm convinced that Jethro are going to do it again. The treatment is heavier than we've heard from them on single before and because of it the rhythm and lyrics take time to get through. So do the instrumental subtleties Jethro Tull excel at — and the fact that you'll get something out of it on each listen is why it will sell. Sadly, there's only the tiniest flicker of flute — towards the end — but it does feature strings prominently."

Although Jethro Tull's relationship with the singles chart was fleeting, most of their peers were in the same situation; whilst they may have preferred to do albums, it wasn't unusual for the likes of King Crimson, Spooky Tooth and Family to embrace the same approach. Advantageously for Jethro Tull, the content of their singles typically offered something that wasn't available on their albums.

Upon being asked if a hit single could be an embarrassment for a group like Jethro Tull,

Relaxing at the Albert Memorial in Kensington Gardens, London. The Memorial is directly opposite the Royal Albert Hall — a prestigious venue that Tull has performed at many times. Firstly in 1968 in an afternoon charity gig with several other bands. Tull jointly headlined with Ten Years After on 8th May 1969.

© Pictorial Press Ltd / Alamy Stock Photo

Anderson was quoted in *Rave* in November 1969; "It will only be an embarrassment if it seems that you have sold out. I think a lot of people thought that Peter Green had done that when he released 'Albatross' but there is no reason at all why you cannot make good commercial records which retain the musical integrity which you have. You just have to be careful not to say the wrong things to the right people. They are the people who up until now were represented by long hair, beards, sandals and art books under their arms. They were the first people to pay us the compliment of some attention. To us the three things of making albums, singles and doing live appearances are three very separate entities. You have to alter and change sounds even for those live numbers which you might put on an album. I write songs specifically to play on stage and then later I might re-present them for an album. I sat down in a hotel room in New York with the intention of writing a song for a hit single — something which would make the top ten. It was specifically written with that in mind and that is just how 'Living In The Past' turned out."

Anderson dismissed the notion that some fans accused Tull of selling out to commercialism. Speaking to *Zigzag* in December '69 he said; "Yes, that's quite possible — I've heard it from various sources, but all I can say is 'blow them', because out motives for playing music now are the same as they were a year ago — we simply have a better means of getting it across to people now. The people who liked us then, but don't now, were probably labouring under some misapprehension in the first place, or at least, weren't being honest with themselves as to why they liked us because we appeared to be underdogs or underground, whereas now we're obviously a pop group because we appeal to so many people. But our integrity remains intact in our own minds, and in the minds of a lot of others as well. Fleetwood Mac may have lost some followers, but those they've lost aren't nearly as important as those they've gained. That's why they and we do things like *Top Of The Pops* when we can, because it's important for us to get across to new people; to break this vicious circle which exists surrounding the tastes of the young public and what the producers of the programme are prepared to give them."

"It's a vicious circle because the producers give the kids what they think the kids want, and the kids only want what they want because that's all the producers give them. They have no chance to hear the so-called underground music forms because it isn't given the exposure on any broadcasts for the same reason. They probably can't afford to go into the local record shops, look through and buy albums — and so the singles market is important for them, as is *Top Of The Pops*, because by playing we give them the option or freedom of choice — if they like it, great, if they don't like it, then forget it. I've no objection to *Top Of The Pops* as an entertainment medium because it scores every time; it reaches a very, very wide cross section of the public and for this reason alone it's important for us to be on it — to get across to so many new people, who otherwise wouldn't hear about us. I hope that Family gets on *Top Of The Pops* because a lot of people should be able to listen to them and decide whether they like them or not."

In the grand scheme of things, it certainly seemed to be the case that Jethro Tull were keen to disassociate themselves from the underground scene. A reasonable decision overall on the basis that they couldn't relate to some of the more popular themes of the movement as they saw it. Anderson told *Record Mirror* in May 1969; "The underground is considered vulgar. Groups are crying because they can't get nudes on their LP covers. If and when they do get all the nudes they want, nudity will be so prevalent, it won't be noticed. The four-letter words are used so much in the States, they are getting to be commonplace. I think the cycle may have finally revolved completely with all the decency rallies sprouting up. Kids are realising they really don't want all this trouble. As the underground gets further out, it comes closer to change and to eventual compromise. I like watching these forces at work. It's even nice that people have a name like underground, but somehow in print, it looks odd."

And speaking to *New Musical Express* in June; "It's really nice to be on the inside. It's nice to be doing your little bit to improve the state of things. It's much better than just being underground and saying nasty things about *Top Of The Pops*."

'Sweet Dream' was the first Jethro Tull record to be released on the new Chrysalis label formed by managers Ellis and Wright. It was the result of a dispute between Island Records and Tull's Chrysalis management; Island didn't consider 'Sweet Dream' sufficiently commercial for release. The onus for its sales potential fell to Chrysalis, however, distribution remained with Island. Amongst the disagreement, the release of the single was brought forward from November to October 10th,

Chrysalis had planned for some time to launch its own label and in doing so, the agency took its other artists, Blodwyn Pig and Scottish band Clouds from Island to the new label. It wasn't long after touring with Tull in 1970 that Clouds broke up.

'Sweet Dream', was penned during the group's time in the States and recorded in early September. Terry Ellis said; "The new single is a heavy, rhythmic number, completely different from 'Living In The Past.' We feel it is the best record the group have made, and there is no disagreement over this. But Island doubt its acceptability as a single. On the other hand, we wish to continue the policy of releasing the best track available at any given time."

Anderson explained to *New Musical Express*; "Chris Blackwell (Island Records' boss) didn't think it was going to be a hit but having taken a lot of trouble over it — having written it for a single over a long period of time — we were determined to put it out. It was important this time to do something in a different vein. We had to write something a bit louder, with a more obvious beat, something more aggressive. Simply because to release anything else as easy-going as 'Living In The Past' anything more melodic sounding would have been presenting ourselves as something we're not. Kids who had only heard the singles might have come along to concerts and got a bit of a shock."

Talking to *Disc And Music Echo* in November, Anderson said; "Although our previous label thought the last two songs were okay, they were worried about this one. And I'm not clever enough yet to write a song that has immediate impact. The song isn't immediately catchy but it makes an impression after about five or six plays, and I don't think people will get bored with it so quickly. I've heard it a hundred times already and I still like it, which I couldn't say about 'Living In The Past'. It's heavy and strong and much more insistent — in fact on the whole more in keeping with what we do on stage. And it's the only single so far that we *do* play on stage."

In response to the fact that some people had accused Chrysalis management of using hype tactics, Anderson told *Zigzag* in December; "Well that is absolute rubbish because Chrysalis doesn't hype anybody. It's the most unhyping company there is — they're honest, like most people in the business these days. Most of the dicey managers and agents have disappeared because people realised and didn't want to work with them. The whole thing is now much better than people want to believe — they want to believe that groups are manipulated and are pawns in the games of management executives with cigars and briefcases. That's not true these days, except maybe in the case of a few old-school agencies and the bigger companies. When Chrysalis began, it was something like the group was at that stage — more or less a tentative experiment — and we all learnt together, with nobody demanding anything from anybody else. We tried things out, saw how they worked, changed them around and so on, until we arrived at the stage we are now, where Chrysalis is a fairly important business force on the scene and embodies recording, management, agency, publishing, record label — the whole thing."

So where were Jethro Tull at in terms of album aspirations by the end of 1969? Upon being asked if they were going to make another LP in the near future, Anderson was quoted in *Hit Parader* in October 1969; "We're doing it the first two weeks after we return to England. It'll be a little different. Our music has changed. I've written some more, that's all there is to it. It's not a conscious attempt to progress. Technically you progress, what you're capable of doing, your ability to write songs, arrange songs, progresses. The songs are just new songs, just a reflection of the times since I last wrote a bunch of songs. Now of course there'll be a change because Mick Abrahams isn't there any more. He's gone. He was getting a bit difficult to work with. Not in terms of musical aspirations — just in terms of business ideas, management ideas. Personality wise, there was always a bit of a clash. He didn't want to come to America; he didn't want to work seven nights a week; he didn't want to be a pop star, so he had to go."

"We got someone else — Martin Lancelot Barre. We picked somebody who could play pretty much in the style of the other guitarist because we didn't want it to be some sudden jump in terms of our overall sound. But he's a good person to work with, get along with. Coming into the group at this stage made him suddenly aware of the fact that he's got to work really hard, really do something to justify his being with the band. A good thing. It's nice to have people who are on their toes. The next album will have some of the things we're doing on stage now, probably half of them. There'll be a few more which are things we're not doing on stage — they'll be treated as a sort of recorded kind of music as opposed to the sort of thing we play. They'll be in the same sort of sound, but we'll get into production techniques more because we know more about it than we did. We can afford to take chances now, looking for the best way to achieve good recorded sound in terms of listening to stereo. But we also want to get as near to the style of the group on stage as we can. It takes months to find out, trial and error wise, what is the best sort of program. We'll be using eight-track for the next album; it gives a lot more freedom when it comes to stereo. Our first album was all done on four track, drums and bass and sometimes guitar always on the same track, which is terrible when it comes to a stereo mix."

It was reported in *Disc And Music Echo* in December 1969; "Jethro Tull had a lot of plans for 1970 — but most of them have been scrapped. Anyway, they are in the middle of recording a new album and there are plans for a single in January. The album should have been completed yesterday (Monday, December 22nd). There is a Scandinavian tour planned for next month; Germany is possible in February, and they return to the States after that."

To which Anderson commented; "There are also a couple of TV shows being fixed up, and another album — our fourth — will be out in August or September. But I don't really know anything about it — we let the people in the office do all the worrying. I just write tunes, sleep, wake up and write tunes. Of course, we'll be playing some dates in England."

The report concluded; "1969 was a good year for Jethro Tull so Ian really has got something to celebrate at Christmas."

Anderson: "Tuesday I'll be shopping for presents, Wednesday I'll blast up to Blackpool to see my parents and we'll just say 'hello' and exchange presents, and on Boxing Day, if there are any trains, I'll be coming back to London. I've got a lot of tunes to finish and quite a lot of work to do. Last Christmas Day we spent rehearsing."

As soon as 'Sweet Dream' had run its course in the charts, it was replaced in January 1970 by the double A-side single, 'The Witch's Promise'/'Teacher'. It got to number four in the UK. Tull's performance of 'The Witch's Promise' featured on *Top Of The Pops* in the same month. The single was the first Jethro Tull recording to feature John Evan (his first gig as an official member of Jethro Tull is most likely to have been at Nuremberg on 5th April 1970).

Regarding singles, Anderson was quoted in *Record Mirror* in January 1970; "They're not throw-aways by any means, but they were not specifically written for the singles market in mind as were our previous hits. 'The Witch's Promise' and 'Teacher' are really one fifth of an album! They are both tracks of over four minutes and we certainly will not be including them on our forthcoming album so this is the only time you will see these particular songs. In fact I'm certain that the people who buy our singles have been those that have bought the albums... But we haven't just thrown the singles away — we've had a lot of copies out in stereo and put in a colourful sleeve. It's not just to remind people that we are still around — the music means too much to me to do something like that."

'The Witch's Promise'/'Teacher' single was reviewed in *New Musical Express* in January 1970; "The new decade hasn't exactly got off to an inspiring start in the singles market, but the return of Jethro should help reverse the backward-looking charts. This new one, a double A-sider, could be a signpost to seventies singles in other ways besides the music — both sides, giving almost nine minutes of material, are in stereo and it's being sold in a colour sleeve. 'The Witch's Promise' is a Jethro I can't remember on record before. Slower and less rhythmic than previous singles, it is mainly a vehicle for the lyrics and distinctive vocals of Ian Anderson who, needless to say, wrote both sides. It opens in a short flute passage with a fine Martin Barre acoustic guitar taking over to subtly highlight Ian's vocal. Typical rhythmic Jethro breaks link the verses with piano and strings emerging effectively as it progresses. 'Teacher' is more the Jethro we know; more rhythmic; more a group number. A surprise is the use for the first time of organ, and it blends extremely well. I loved too the use of guitars, intricate and overlaid, and the compulsive riff pushing it along. Also the powering instrumental ending. 'Teacher' for me just gets the edge, but either way this could carry Jethro to their first number one."

Not long after the single's release, Jethro Tull's reluctance towards the singles market was evident. Anderson was quoted in *Beat Instrumental* in February 1970; "It's difficult to come up with anything that's representative of us that lasts only three minutes. You have to concoct a song for a single rather than coming up with one that means anything to you."

Regarding 'The Witch's Promise'/'Teacher' single, he said; "It's just a couple of tracks. There's no A or B side. There's a lot of pressure to follow up hits and people might say, 'Jethro Tull didn't have a hit,' but so what? They're just two songs we're putting out to bridge the gap before the next album. It would be nice if people are still playing them in six months' time, like an album."

Barre gave his opinion of the single to *Melody Maker* in the same month; "I really like the number. I was listening to someone's radio and they said: 'Hi there pop pickers, this could be number one.' Not being a pop picker I wouldn't know. But it would be unreal if we got a number one — great! Getting publicity for the single might have been difficult. When the record company had first taken 'The Witch's Promise'/'Teacher' single out to play to radio producers, many of them had refused it. Glenn Cornick told *New Musical Express* in February 1970; "They just turned round and laughed and didn't even want to keep it. If it got to the top twenty then they'd have to play it."

It would be flawed logic to assume that by 1970, Jethro Tull were an affluent band. In that regard, there was still plenty of work to do. Anderson told *Record Mirror* in January 1970; "I'm not even certain we have any money. I'm looking for a house at present but don't ask me where the money's coming from. I need a place where I can write in peace and not have to squeeze my composing in those few spare moments while we are on the road. No one really knows how much money we have but someone recently explained the tax situation to me and I nearly gave the whole thing up and went looking for a job digging the roads. After a thousand pounds money becomes meaningless and you hear about how you are playing a concert for so many tens of thousands of pounds but what you see of that is so small it's ridiculous. It's like playing for 75,000 cigarettes or 75,000 beans. The expense of touring in somewhere like America with the hotel bills and cost of transporting equipment is astronomical. In this business you either end up very rich like the Beatles and Stones or just about break even like Traffic and groups like us. Sometimes I wonder how anyone makes a living in this business. The only real criterion you can have is to do something which pleases you and incidentally pleases others. I genuinely like our music and I listen to it as much as to anything else. The real satisfaction and the thing which keeps you going is in pleasing yourself and as I consider I am quite hard to please so there is a good chance I may please others."

Previous experience of touring was such that the new year brought a somewhat revised approach to stagecraft. Martin Barre, speaking to *New Musical Express* in January 1970, said; "We have gone through a year of doing things in a certain format and now is the time to look at our mistakes and the reasons for our success. Ian has been doing his theatricals and being funny. We've stuck to playing obvious numbers the kids will know, and hoped that people will get good entertainment and good music… Maybe the kids want loud exciting music with drum and guitar solos but we have to do something we can enjoy every night. Once we get that it will convey itself to an audience anyway. We've all gone through a lot of changes as far as techniques go — from watching other bands and learning from mistakes. Now we have to find a way to use them."

He also talked about other aspects of Tull's music on stage: "It gets to a point where it is so loud you lose control of what you are playing. It becomes just a noise. Yet you have to play certain things loudly to fill out a large area of sound… It is physically impossible for Ian to keep on playing flute as much as he has done. It is a sincere part of Ian but he wants to get more into being a group. His problems are heavier than ours. I remember when I played flute: at the end of a number my head would be swimming. Often I'd actually fall over. It would be good for him to pick up guitar or piano, or play flute melodically and softly… The new album (*Benefit*) is more loose and relaxed. There are more tracks we are really pleased with. The first LP was very tense. I think you can tell the new one is different. Ian's going to play guitar now. He and I play together on 'Teacher'. We're going to have a month of rehearsing, then we'll probably use most of the new material on stage."

By 1970, in some ways, Jethro Tull were a different band in terms of how they saw themselves and wanted other people to see them. Glenn Cornick explained to *New Musical Express* in the February; "At the time we started to make it during the blues boom all the groups were going on with long faces making like they really had the blues. We went on playing blues but we were sending ourselves up — well maybe that's a bit too heavy but there was an element of humour about it; like we were laughing at ourselves for doing it. When we started we were playing all the standard blues things, 'Dust My Broom', 'Rock Me Baby', but we were not trying to prove anything. People were entertained by that."

As successful as 1968 and 1969 had been for Jethro Tull, they still had plenty to prove. Barre told *New Musical Express* in January 1970; "I'm afraid that people see us as a kind of joke band. They come along to see Ian because he is a bit freaky and funny and jumps about on stage. All of us are going to make it clear in the coming year that the music is the important thing. Our aim is to find what we're best at and take it to extremes. Led Zeppelin have taken their music to extremes and it is great. It is their music — rock and roll and heavy — and it belongs to them alone. Same with Joe Cocker; his band is very relaxed, very funky and different. Blood, Sweat and Tears again have got their own music. We are finding ours."

"Maybe people think that Ian's got it all sewn up being entertaining and visual, but that is not enough. We all have to be a part of what Ian does. On stage we need to be people rather than musicians standing there. We have no personalities on stage and we should have. You don't have to be flamboyant or say hilarious things. It is sufficient to be nice and pleasant and talk to the audience. Like Crosby, Stills, Nash and Young do. They are so informal to their audience it is great. It just brings the music closer. The other thing is that Ian can do more of what we do. You cannot fit into a band rhythmically with a flute. It's like having an electric guitar that plays only solos. It has worked in the studios, where we are playing much better. Before, we'd do the backing and Ian would put his flute and vocals on later. With him now playing on backing tracks it makes the group much more together. You see, we want people to judge us not by reading interviews and seeing us on TV but by coming to see us on stage." (At the time of this interview Barre had seen Led Zeppelin perform just a few days earlier).

When he was quoted in *Disc And Music Echo* in February 1970, Martin Barre was specific about what he considered to be points that the band could improve on: "Visually, Ian is going to have to calm down. I know he says what he does on stage is unrehearsed and just happens, but he's got it worked out in his mind. It's exhausting for me just standing there playing; for Ian every song must be like running the hundred yards flat-out, and if he carries on like that he'll never survive. Musically we realised at the end of the last British tour that our sound was not tight enough for our own satisfaction. We realised how much better it would be if we could augment the group with another guitarist. So on the next tour, and on our next LP *Benefit*, Ian will be playing lead guitar more often than flute. We want to improve all the time, and, besides, we're in the unfortunate position of not being able to stand still. The eyes of the world are on us; consequently everything we do has got to be that much better than the last. We're very open to criticism, and I personally will be glad when I've reached the position of being able to do just what I like — and hang the critics! Ian comes in for a lot of knocks, about having sold out, about putting showmanship before music and other things. But actually Ian is ten times more serious about his music and the music of the group than many of his contemporaries."

It is possible that the band had concerns that an intense touring schedule had put demands on them that took focus away from working on albums. Anderson told *Beat Instrumental* in February 1970; "In the past we've had to write ten songs in twenty hotel bedrooms in various countries — which isn't very good. The songs haven't been what they could have been. We need to record and play live, and it takes a long time to get where you can utilise your time properly and not waste it. We want to choose where we can play, not in front of monster crowds, but in good places in front of two to five thousand people, although I suppose there'll be festivals to do this summer. But they're not very satisfying for the musicians or the audience really. I think that by midsummer we'll have changed a lot musically. We should get a lot better through having time to rehearse. We just want to take it easy for a bit. We think we've been doing ourselves in rushing around entertaining other people and now we want a bit of time to enjoy ourselves while we still can."

Barre was quoted in *Melody Maker* that month; "We are still working on our next album. We have been a bit lazy I suppose. Some of the tracks are really ace. It will be called *Benefit* — for everybody's benefit I suppose… We are going to America twice this year and to the Continent for tours. We want to play in Britain and it depresses me that we can't play some of the smaller clubs. But that is up to our management, and we have the whole of this year planned out for us. It's frightening!"

There must have been times when the thought of touring America was overwhelming, as Barre explained to *Melody Maker* in February 1970; "We'll be spending six months of this year in America which is a thought that honestly depresses me. At the beginning of the year just to go over there was exciting and to play there was such a big thing — now I don't think any of us is looking forward to going over there. Everything starts to get on top of you, the way things have happened we've got no time to do anything ourselves and now our personal lives are suffering. I'm going through a stage of depression. We all want to buy houses where you can just sit down with your girlfriend and be on your own. That's very important to me. We haven't stopped working this past year. It's like a conveyor belt thing, making records, going through America, it's endless but we haven't the time to get off the conveyor belt. Our schedule is so tight. I don't think our personalities have changed because you try and retain some part of you that's still sane. Things more personal to us are becoming more important but it's frustrating when you don't have time to do things on your own. What I'd really like to do at the moment is just to play in Britain because it's my home, it's nothing patriotic or anything, it's just that I'd like to do a concert tour and be able to go home every night."

Despite Barre's reservations, the love for the music was clearly not diminished: "We're very basic musicians but we are improving technique-wise and as long as Ian keeps writing as he is now, I can't foresee anything but improvement. We still enjoy playing very much. Our individual techniques have improved and we're now feeling the need to play fresh things. That's why I think we'll stay together for some time because apart from Ian I don't think any of us are capable of doing anything individually but we are improving together. Maybe in a couple of years' time when I'm more of a reasonable musician I'd like to play with other people and do something different but we've got a lot of different things to do as far as Jethro is concerned. We haven't gone half as far as we can go, you can only be as big as your music is good and we've got a long way to go as Jethro Tull yet… We have got away from the sound of the flute and haven't used it a lot on the album. In fact Ian's playing more guitar than flute, we're only using the flute when we feel that a song needs the atmosphere of the flute. Some of the instruments we're playing now are difficult to use on stage especially in the big auditoriums. You can just about get away with a piano but it's difficult to get a good sound. I also play mandolin and flute and Ian plays the piano but generally on stage it's down to the guitars."

And in *Disc And Music Echo* in February 1970; "As far as I'm concerned I'm in Jethro Tull because I enjoy our music and I enjoy what we're doing. Money was a big thing at first but now I tend to take it for granted and it's lost its meaning. Money is not a reason for our doing anything — if I didn't enjoy what I was playing I would leave, and no amount of money could convince me otherwise."

When one journalist had the good fortune of being able to witness a recording session, they reported on the experience in *New Musical Express* in February 1970; "There can be few more boring occupations known to man than being a spectator in a recording studio. All you can do is sit impotently and marvel as the musicians enthuse their way through the umpteenth playback and devote most of an afternoon to perfecting in the simplest riff a dud note you gave up trying to spot hours ago. After spending two afternoons in the North London studio where Jethro Tull are working on *Benefit*, their third album, I began to doubt if anything of remote value could come out of such a slow and turgid process — let alone the five completed tracks played before I left that were sufficient to convince me a further invigorating blast of Jethro goodness is on the way."

"A longish beauty piece with the most maniacal flute and instrumental riff, a folksy track, and 'Play In Time', which they are already performing on stage, left strong impressions… In between takes of a shorter version of 'Teacher' for the American market, Ian — The Pop Star Mothers Would

Least Like Their Daughters To Marry — was finalising pick-up arrangements with tour manager Eric Brooks for his marriage the following Monday. He was a little self-conscious about admitting that he's moved from his £3 10s a week Kentish Town bedsitter to a temporary flat in more salubrious Belgravia — 'where a tin of beans costs eight bob'. Clive Bunker was unconsciously doing his Frank Zappa impression: newly grown beard and hair tied back. 'It's to hide his identity,' joked Martin Barre, explaining that while shopping in a supermarket with his mum, Clive had been the victim of a female fan attack between the dried fruit and the frozen veg."

Glenn Cornick was quoted in the same feature; "It's going to be a lot live-r than the first two. I felt the last one sounded like a group of session musicians performing various songs. It was pretty cold. This one will have more of a live feel."

In comparison to when Jethro Tull had just started out, they were now in a position to refuse gigs that they didn't consider to be a good fit. "Jethro Say 'No' To £10,000 Concert", ran the *Disc And Music Echo* headline in March 1970; "Jethro Tull have been offered the biggest fee ever for a British group to play at a British concert — the largest concert ever staged — but are likely to turn it down! Ian Anderson and his group have been offered £10,000 by Scottish impresario Harry Margolis to top the bill at Scotland's first pop festival, at Glasgow's 120,000 capacity Hampden Park football ground on D-Day, Saturday, June 6th. Others already approached for the festival include Marmalade and Tremeloes. But says Jethro's manager Terry Ellis: 'It's not a question of money. Of course we would like £10,000 but I don't think the group could hope to get itself over to an audience of this size. The largest place they have ever played was 70,000 and that was too big. On the next American tour we have stipulated venues of no more than 5,000 capacity.' But Margolis remains hopeful: 'This will be the first occasion ever that pop-starved Scotland has had its own big-name festival. I hope to have at least a dozen top names, from London, Scotland and America. The show will last from 1-7pm and I want to get the top in both pop and progressive music on the bill. Why was my offer to Jethro Tull so enormous? Simply because I think it would be worth it'."

Whilst Jethro Tull's popularity was growing, it wasn't all champagne and roses. The band's two concerts in Frankfurt in February 1970 fell foul to full-scale riots between fans and the police. It ended with five people being taken to hospital and damage totalling £5,000. Hundreds of teenagers had travelled long distances in the hope of being able to get hold of tickets even though the shows had sold out two weeks in advance. When two-thousand people were unable to get into the theatre, the riot started when they tried to find other ways of getting into the building. In the ruckus, more than a dozen fifteen-foot-high plate glass shop windows were smashed. German rock fans were often quite volatile at this time, and other bands experienced riots driven by a group of radicals who thought concerts should be free to access.

In many ways, keeping a sense of humour towards audiences was probably the way forward. Anderson's engagement with the audience was often comically sardonic. In April 1970, the journalist writing for *Go* noted that from the stage of New York's Fillmore East, Anderson told the audience, "It's a shame, really, the way this trend in pop music, or rock music, or whatever you'd call it, is going towards a rock-jazz fusion. All that this "jazz" is, is just over-long self-indulgent solos. Well, you know, we're no different from the rest because Clive's gonna do an over-long self-indulgent solo now…"

In May 1970, *Disc And Music Echo* reported that on 24th April at the Swing Auditorium in San Bernardino, there was chaos in the front row with some punters standing on seats and others yelling at them to get down. In response to this, Anderson was reported to have addressed the audience; "Some of you out there might like to see us, since you probably paid a ludicrous amount of money for tickets."

Just prior to the release of their third album, Tull were at a point of adopting a no singles policy. Anderson was quoted in *New Musical Express* in April 1970; "There won't be any more singles in the foreseeable future, it didn't really work. We sold a lot of copies of 'The Witch's Promise' for instance but not as many as we did of the last album. And we found that most of the singles were going to people who had already bought the albums and not, as we'd hoped, to the Edison Lighthouse buyers. I don't think it did us a lot of good because it wasn't like two different audiences; it overlapped. And we don't want to get caught up into thinking that we have to have hit singles, because it becomes a burden to remain alive in terms of chart success. Singles aren't indicative of your success to album buyers and most people but they are to radio producers."

Prior to the release of 'Inside' as a single, Anderson commented; "We would rather it didn't make the chart. It would be a bit embarrassing if it did and just got to number nineteen or something. We are definitely not going to release any more singles with a view to having chart success. We have had three top ten records but haven't had a number one. Maybe if we had a song we thought could make number one we might release it just for the egotistical feeling of being number one, but it would have nothing to do with our music. I am all in favour of the swing towards buying albums. I would rather buy an LP than singles. They are too much bother to put on; I never play singles."

"It doesn't mean we have turned our backs on the younger people we've gained through hit singles — and I recognise there are some — it means we feel there are now enough people interested and these are now the ones we will make the records for. We don't need to try and get across to any more."

Barre told *Beat Instrumental* in May 1970; "It's quite probable that we won't make another single. Although hit singles get you on to television, they didn't get us on to Radio One. So we didn't get across to new people. 'The Witch's Promise' was a dismal failure. It sold a lot in the first two weeks to our fans and then did nothing. They never played 'Teacher' on the radio, so I don't think it works putting singles out. We're not going to compromise and neither are the BBC, so that's the end of it. We wasted a week making a single, whereas it could have gone towards an LP. Albums are much better value anyway."

Besides, why focus on singles when there was so much to look forward to with a new album due out? Regarding the yet-to-be-released *Benefit*, Anderson, speaking to *New Musical Express* in April 1970 said; "I am pleased with my vocals. I enjoyed singing on this album because it was a lot easier. Like most people who sing because they are the only one in the group who can, I now write songs that are within my vocal ability: I know my limitations. I get credit for producing this one myself, and I enjoyed that side of it: the playing about with sounds. The guitar on 'To Cry You A Song' is, I think, a very good sound, and there are no effects on it. It came out the way Martin wanted it, clean and tight, and it pleases me we got it that way for him. That's important to me — that people are pleased with their own sound — as well as it fitting into the song. I play guitar on all the tracks and initially that was because I was writing songs in terms of guitar, which meant that Martin would have to learn the guitar piece and it became frustrating for him. It was okay when he first started because he wasn't so good then and it gave him the chance to play another person's ideas. On this album I thought it should be left to him what he wanted to play, just as Glenn and Clive are free to do what they like within the framework of a number written by me. Martin can do the same now, because I play the guitar part I've written for the song and that leaves him free to play as he wants over and above what I'm doing. He emerges much better than from the last album where he was playing half solos and half stuff I had to show him to play note for note. I think he's a lot happier, although Martin's very hard to please. He doesn't like most of what he plays."

Benefit was released in April 1970. With John Evan on piano, it gave the band the scope to expand their sound in that regard. Also for this album, Tull made use of unusual sound effects. In later years Ian Anderson expressed that it was perhaps something of an excessive decision but at the time, it was in keeping with what had already been done before by the Beatles. *Benefit* signified Jethro Tull's last flirtation with the blues. It got to number three in the UK and vitally, it really opened doors for the group in the US, reaching number eleven — their highest chart placing to date. Featuring the songs 'Sossity; You're A Woman' and 'Nothing Is Easy', *Benefit* was an important album for Jethro Tull's live setlist.

"Jethro Leaps — But Not Quite So High", ran the headline for the review of *Benefit* in *Disc And Music Echo* in April 1970; "This album doesn't advance by such a drastic leap as *Stand Up* did from *This Was*. It's more like the Jethro Tull we've seen and heard for the past year. It seems to be a remarkably long album, and shows what an exciting group this is. Exciting because they can have quite long guitar breaks and still retain a very tight and together sound. Martin Barre on lead guitar features well and more prominently, and Ian Anderson's breathy flute seems to have receded rather. All songs are by Ian and in places the lyrics are very weak — really cringing rhymes. There's the usual dedication to Ian's friend, Jeffrey, and one for his wife Jennie — 'Alive And Well And Living In'."

It was reviewed in *Beat Instrumental* in June; "Third album from the phenomenal Tull, and sure to be an immediate smash hit, *Benefit* is nevertheless a little disappointing. It's all Ian Anderson material here, good solid stuff, but the group seem to be relying a little too heavily on the same formula for success, and their overall sound isn't quite so fresh. Jethro are nevertheless a very together band, and *Benefit* includes some top standard playing on tracks like 'To Cry You A Song' and the nicely freaky 'Play In Time'."

In April 1970, Anderson gave *New Musical Express* an insight into each of the album's songs:

'With You There To Help Me': "The flute was recorded backwards and I've double-tracked the vocals in harmony — it adds a totally new perspective to the voice. We'll be doing this on stage."

'Nothing To Say': "This is one for the journalists — written from a growing dislike for American "rap" sessions where the underground writers come up and say, 'Well what do you want to talk about man?' I would rather talk about nothing."

'Alive And Well And Living In': "I must apologise for having a bad cold on this. This is a song for Jennie; it's a happy one. There are two things I write about — Jennie, and me, sometimes together."

As with several bands, Jethro Tull's popularity was enhanced by their performance at the massive Isle of Wight Festival of 1970. With many people getting in without paying, no exact attendance figure was gleaned but Guinness World Records estimated 600,000 to 700,000 people attended.

A new Jethro Tull L.P. for 8/6d?

Well, not exactly, but when J.T. came up with their two new sides we were reluctant to commit ourselves to naming an 'A' side, and it did seem a bit audacious to refer to these 8 minutes 45 seconds of joy as a single. So we have covered our embarrassment by treating the record as a mini-LP and releasing it in stereo in a sleeve with pretty colour pictures.

new Jethro
The Witch's Promise : Teacher

WIP 6077
in stereo on

Chrysalis

Released 16th Jan

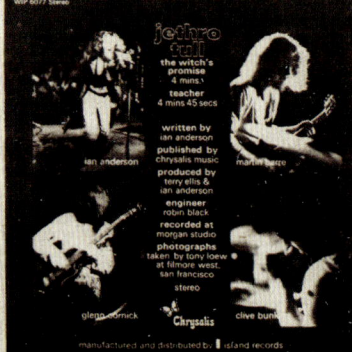

manufactured and distributed by island records

'Son': "This is a dialogue between father and son, who at the end of the song turns out to be thirty years old. I play acoustic guitar. It's an amusing one that brings back, as it does for me, all the personal experiences one's dad passes on."

'For Michael Collins, Jeffrey And Me': "Michael Collins was one of the astronauts, the one who stayed in the ship while the others went down to the moon. Jeffrey has a bird called Bananas! (Don't ask me what that has to do with it). I watched the moon shot on TV in America. It was nice watching it; I half wished I was there. It's one of those things — you think beforehand what a waste of money it is but when they are there and you're watching it is a great thing for mankind. Then when it's over you feel the same as before."

'To Cry You A Song': "Martin gets a really good, malleable sound here. I think it's his best guitar to date and it's also one of the stage numbers we can reproduce just like the record."

'A Time For Everything': "I wrote this on mandolin. It was some time ago in Malvern — Jennie and I went back there for our honeymoon — we played there and stayed in a hotel on the side of a hill. I went off on the hill to write the song. As luck would have it, it was one of the few occasions when I was pursued by fans. There I was, sitting down trying to take in the Donovan thing — trees and sunshine and nature — and there were half a dozen grubby little thirteen year olds thrusting fag packets at me for autographs."

'Inside': "You'll like this one: it's a sing-along and another mandolin track. We chose it as the single because while it's not typical of the other tracks — it's a nice pleasant happy little song — it doesn't imply any veering away from what we've done before."

'Play In Time': "This is about songs I like singing — like I was saying about writing about what I do. The fade-out is like a nightmare at a fairground."

'Sossity; You're A Woman': "I don't want to talk about the lyrics of this one. It's another stage number. We wanted to do an acoustic thing and Martin and I worked this one out in a hotel room in America."

Due to their busy schedule, it took Jethro Tull a while to complete the making of *Benefit*. Barre told *Melody Maker* in April 1970; "Two of the tracks we recorded nine months ago. Because of the work we've had to do it was a matter of recording a track here and a track there. In the end we had to cancel a concert tour of Germany to finish the album off. It's difficult to cancel out of a tour. Not because of the money but because it's important to us to play to new people. I enjoy playing on stage but it's hard to play again after being in the studios for a long time, you tend to feel nervous and unsure when you go back on stage. We're starting to record another album now because it'll probably take nine months again to complete it. The next album will probably be released around Christmas. Everything we record now will be for an album. There'll be no songs recorded especially for a single and in that way there'll be no pressure on us to have something completed for a single release. Singles and Radio One were a failure for us even though the last single reached number three. The idea of us putting out a single was for Radio One to play it a lot and for other people to buy it than those who already buy our records. But it was the same people who bought the album that were buying the single. 'The Witch's Promise' and 'Teacher' reached number three but it dropped that week which means that the young kids and the mums and dads who keep records in the charts weren't buying it."

Disc And Music Echo reported on 25th April 1970; "Shocked news reached Britain this week that Jethro Tull is now a quintet! Jethro left Britain last week for their latest American tour with no news of a change in the line-up. But on Monday (20th April), exclusive news reached *Disc* that John Evan, who fronted a pre-Jethro Tull band with Ian Anderson and Glenn Cornick, had joined the group on organ. John headed the John Evan Band with Ian, Glenn and Ian's close friend "Jeffrey" but two years ago decided to return to Blackpool and continue his art studies. Ian subsequently re-formed the band into the original Jethro Tull. John was featured on several tracks of the group's latest LP, *Benefit*. Jethro Tull's London office, Chrysalis, could not elaborate on the news on Monday, but did confirm John had joined the group as a regular member."

Anderson explained to *New Musical Express* in May 1970; "I wanted to feature piano more. I played on a couple of tracks on the album, but I thought it would be better to get somebody that could really play properly. So I asked John to come down and do the sessions and it worked out very well. He played on most of the tracks, and later we got around to thinking it would be nice to have it on stage as well, to give us the same sort of freedom we have in the studio — to play more varied and full music. We sort of suggested it to him and he thought it over and decided to leave the university.

After leaving Tull, Mick Abrahams continued to pursue his love for blues music with his own band Blodwyn Pig. Here he is performing at the Anson Rooms of Bristol University's Students Union on 10th June 1970. Also on the bill were blues rock band Ten Years After. Tickets cost 10 shillings with the entertainment running from 10pm to 2am.

So that's what happened."

Regarding John Evan's joining, Anderson said; "None of us had planned any interviews recently and nobody asked and it just didn't seem very important to make a big thing of it. The only way to do it would be to ring up the papers and say, 'Look, here's some exciting news.' That sounds a bit soft! So we thought we'd just wait till we played and people would hear about it, rather than making a big thing of it."

John Evan's recruitment expanded the band's creative scope. Anderson told *New Musical Express* in May; "There's a lot more variation musically, a lot more light and shade, and the piano particularly as opposed to the organ, which John plays as well. Most of it's piano and it's not very often you find pianos being played in loud groups. It's too difficult to amplify. But we've managed to overcome the problem. John plays a sort of grand piano and plays concert type things."

On why John Evan was brought in, Anderson was quoted in *Music Now!* in May 1970; "It was beginning to become a matter of doing much too much overdubbing. I mean, the songs were more complex, though still with our apparent simplicity which makes the whole thing more relevant to the people who don't deeply involve themselves in the actual music from a technical point of view. But nevertheless, our music is becoming more complicated, in terms of construction. It was pretty important at that point, as far as the recording was concerned, to be doing it in a way that still sounds live and immediate and not become a series of cut pieces of tape joined together in overdubs — all the time, every time. So after having played like that for about the first two tracks that we recorded for this album (*Benefit*), with me playing piano, I got to a point where I felt it was necessary to find someone else to do the piano."

"John was still at the university when I asked him to come and play on our sessions. John freed us so that the whole thing became more simple and direct — more spontaneous and with a live feel to it. We liked the final results and that's the way it worked really. I mean, at that point in time, I had sort of vague ideas about asking John to join the band, which I really didn't voice to anyone else. But that's the way I felt. I felt in playing on stage, we could do with somebody else to help. But had John not been available, I wouldn't have asked anyone else to do it. It's only because I know John. We've spent a lot of time together, living in the same place, all the time he's been at the university and I've been playing. It's only because of that that we asked anybody else into the band, really. Had he not been available, we'd still have been a four-piece group and I would have played piano."

1970 marked the year that Jethro Tull did their first major headlining tour of America. Naturally it was a big deal; being a support act came with less pressure. The stage set up was designed to accommodate the size of the venues that Jethro Tull were playing by mid-1970.

Barre told *Beat Instrumental* in May; "We're using smaller amps now, with a monster PA system with echo and everything. John Burns, who is a recording engineer, will be coming with us mixing on the PA. Some things need echo, things come up loud and go right down, so you need someone who's a musician who knows what it's all about to operate it. He's got a more difficult job than we have. We're getting a really tight spread-out sound now. Everything but bass will be going through the PA to get rid of that distortion you get with amps. It needs a lot of thought though, or else it's a dead loss. PAs are a weird thing."

The timing of the tour was fantastic — coinciding with the American release of *Benefit*.

Barre also dispelled concerns that Tull would be forgotten by British audiences; "If we get forgotten in the papers, it doesn't matter too much. The big thing is to see that our next concert tour sells out. If it doesn't, that's our fault."

Anderson also dismissed accusations of selling out to America; "It obviously hurts a lot when people think you have gone big time, but let me explain to those people who say 'Yaroo you have sold out because you can get more money in America'. In the States it has taken us six months of solid touring to reach the stage there that we reached here by playing round the tiny blues clubs. On the first tour we lost money, on the second we broke even and on the third we made a little. We are coming out a little ahead now but it's nothing like a big Led Zeppelin thing. So on this coming tour we hope we'll be at the stage we are at in England — headlining our own concerts, playing where and when we want to. We haven't really achieved very much in terms of financial gain from playing in America. We have from record sales, but not from gigs. This year we want to go and play there again and sell more records and play to more people but if everything works out well there won't be any need to keep going back all the time. You see, we've made enough to put deposits on houses — we still need mortgages — but beyond that nobody feels a need to build up vast sums of money. At this time that isn't so important as playing and enjoying making music in the way you want. That's why it hurts when people say we've sold out."

Focusing on America in 1970 was deliberate to help cement the band's popularity there. Thereafter, Jethro Tull wanted to choose where they would play. Anderson was quoted in *New Musical Express* in the May of that year; "England is the place we'll choose first. You see we aren't going to make much money playing in England; it is just bread and butter money to do the odd concert here so we might as well forget about the money and just play for the people where we like. At the moment we don't mind America but we want to play here because this is home and this is where we started. We all think it would be nice to go back and play the Marquee but that is impractical right now. But after this year, England will get more than its fair share."

Barre told *Beat Instrumental* in May 1970; "It'll be like starting again — musically — in the States. This time, apart from one or two numbers from *Stand Up*, everything will be new, and songs don't hit an audience when they hear them first time. But the album's coming out early there, so they should have got into them a bit. We're taking a bit of a risk, but it gets a drag doing the same numbers for a year. It takes about six months before you play a number really well. By that time you know the techniques that make it sound best. Instead of experimenting you just play the same solos every time. I got in the state where I'd come on stage, stick the lead into the hole, half volume for rhythm, full for solos. It was fun but there's more to it than that."

Even some of the quieter numbers from *Benefit* were included in the setlist. When performing 'Reasons For Waiting' Barre and Anderson switched instruments with Barre on flute and Anderson on acoustic guitar, the latter amplified through the PA system. Barre commented; "Ian starts off playing acoustic through a cabinet, with a very distant vocal. Then it builds up and I take over the guitar part and it starts hollering. It's very difficult to amplify an acoustic. I get the mic right in front of the sound box and play finger style, but you can get enough volume if you play quietly and carefully."

New Musical Express reported in May 1970; "Relying on equipment provided at each gig, the group has had to suffer through poor PA systems on previous US tours, often having to have speakers flown in from major cities at some cost. So beside the addition of John, they've now also got their own PA system — giving them eighty pieces of equipment to cart around the States. Tour manager Eric Brooks now needs four roadies to assist and the cost of the whole operation will take quite a chunk out of their earnings."

To which Anderson added; "It means that half the money we earn on every gig will be gone before we even get there. And when people say you have sold out they should at least think of all the trouble you have gone to, to make sure the sound is okay for those who've come to hear. You can get away with making excuses on stage about lousy gear, and you can get away with it to a certain extent, but it is eminently more satisfying for the audience and for us as musicians to know that the sound we are playing is the best we can make it."

The performance that took place at Long Beach on 19th April was reviewed in *Disc And Music Echo* in May 1970; "Well, it was one of those concerts (all too frequent of late) where the music and the stars were just fine, but the environment and the audience got all the reviews — unfavourable. Eric Burdon, backed by a fine group called War, preceded Tull, and exhorted the crowd to rush the stage, which they did, like dutiful lemmings. They never returned to their seats, so most of the main floor audience never saw Jethro Tull except for the occasional glimpse of the top of Ian Anderson's head. Fortunately the sound and vocals were undistorted, and even the softer things were audible over the audience rumble. The set roared off with 'Nothing Is Easy' and loped through 'With You There To Help Me' (featuring a long piano solo by John Evan which was very good and largely unappreciated), a nice acoustic Ian/Martin rendition of 'Sossity; You're A Woman' with a bit of 'Reasons For Waiting' in the middle, ending with a new arrangement of 'Dharma For One' that had Clive and Martin taking impressively good long solos, and doing more of the same for the encore."

"They had deliberately changed a few things since their last performance here. There were fancy sound effects during Ian's first flute solo, created by their sound man somewhere off stage — whirs and sputters and clicks, gasps and blasts. The noises seemed to come from Ian's throat, but he held the flute aloft and bugged his eyes as the sounds continued without him. Less leaping about this time, but it was still there in essence: the one-legged prance, the Groucho Marx boogie/lope, even a pirouette during John's piano bit. Ian was very much the ringmaster, alternately disdainful and sincere, taking it very seriously and with great good humour. There was more emphasis on the band as soloists. The five of them can create just about any musical mood, from flat-out relentless rock to delicate sweetness. After the concert, several arrests. Strange paranoia stories of kids handcuffed and dragged away, but it's all part of the concert ritual. The more busts, the more successful and talked about the concert, the larger the concert the more busts."

For John Evan, performing at this level was a new experience. He explained to *New Musical Express*; "At the start I had to do more or less what Ian told me to do but now I've been with them a while I am able to use ideas of my own. I found that I really did fit in well with them right from the start. No, I can't say that I've had any nerves at all — apart from the Long Beach Arena where there was a 15,000 audience and it was rather nerve-wracking for all of us. We've been getting varied receptions. They've all been very enthusiastic but in different ways — and the way they react depends on the size and the venue. There seems to be a critical size in audiences. At Long Beach there was a huge crowd in a restricted space and there was mass herding to the front so that people behind the first few rows got crushed and couldn't see. As far as we are concerned that is pretty worrying because the kids pay extortionate prices to get in — something like £2 or so — and we want to give them their money's worth."

And give them their money's worth he did! It was reported in *Down Beat* in June 1970; "At a recent concert in Long Beach, California, before 14,000 screaming, unisexed rock fans, Evan went into a leisurely introduction to a ballad with a generous quote from Beethoven's *Moonlight Sonata*. I wonder how many of those present were conscious of the interpolative tribute. Evan prefers piano to organ, which is itself significant: he's not interested in the power he can muster. What he has to say is strictly musical, and that kind of honesty from a musician — whether the genre be jazz or rock — is refreshing these days."

It seems that Evan was humble about the whole thing though, as he told *Disc And Music Echo* in June 1970; "American audiences are amazing. They applaud and applaud no matter how badly we play, with the result that almost every concert has been a bad one from our point of view. If only they'd criticise us. It's what we need most of all. The only consolation is that perhaps our music doesn't exhaust them completely, like so many "heavy" bands, and that when they get back home after the concert they think about it, and maybe decide that we weren't so good after all!"

On doing festivals in general, he commented; "The fact that you get so many people watching you at the same time, and the fact that you make more money than concerts, is far outweighed by the disadvantages — the hassles and so forth. What happens over there is that a few people think of Woodstock and think 'Wow, if we can get a quarter million kids we can make a stack of money.' They rent a field, put up a stage and think that's it but there are so many other things to think about, not least of which is the sound balance for groups."

It's fascinating to understand that being in a band perhaps wasn't Evan's first choice of occupation. "In some ways I have regretted joining the band, in that it has taken me out of an environment which I wanted as a career and into show business which I did not want," he explained to *Disc And Music Echo*. "I recorded *Benefit* as a session musician, spending two hours in the evening adding piano to their tapes, which I thought wouldn't do any harm, but then Ian kept phoning me, saying it was impossible for him to carry on with just four musicians as they couldn't get over on stage the way the music was evolving. I was eventually persuaded to join them with two thoughts — it would be better for me to sit at college for my degree with money behind me — and also I really believe Jethro would have broken up if I hadn't joined them. They felt they had reached their peak with the existing line-up and couldn't face the thought of retrogression. Initially I just felt as if I'd got a new job, collecting my wages every week. I imagine this sort of break must be totally different for a musician who has come up the hard way and for whom music is his life. But music will never be my life — I'm simply not a creative enough pianist for that. Technically I suppose I'm okay, but I have very few ideas."

Prior to joining Tull as an official member, Evan hadn't been active in practicing the piano for three years. So much so that he asked for a practice session to be organised in order that he could build up his skills again: "I phoned the manager from America asking him to find me a piano for a week — and he's been true to his word. I got home to find a studio with piano had been booked for me for seven days from 10am to 6pm — and there I'm stuck with all my old Beethoven and Debussy sheet music trying to get the real feel of the instrument again."

The performance that took place at the Santa Barbara Bowl on 22nd April was reviewed in *Disc And Music Echo* in May 1970. It was "outdoors, natural, without the Hollywood Bowl's moat or immensity. It was the coldest night Santa Barbara could remember (according to the promoter). It was the evening of the first quiet day after the Isla Vista student trouble and bank burning, and there were noticeably nervous expressions backstage. The promoter said he had to let a lot of people in free, afraid there might be trouble, you know. 'We lost a lot on this one,' he smiled tightly. The audience huddled close together, blanketed, some rubbing hands and arms in a warming ritual. Backstage was no better. Martin wasn't sure his fingers could function on the guitar strings, and while one or two members took solos the rest shivered behind the amplifiers. Around a hundred people drifted around backstage; one young man stumbled out front, as if to embrace Glenn or Clive, but he was hauled away. Much of the energy generated on stage went up into the night air instead of out to the audience (always a problem with outdoor evening rock concerts). The sound was perfect, a marvel of balance and clarity. Their own PA system travelled with them, also their own sound man. Despite the cold and the night, the audience demanded an encore. 'Since you were silly enough to ask for it, it will be a long one,' Ian said."

A couple of gigs booked at colleges had to be cancelled because of demonstrations. John Evan told *Disc And Music Echo* in June 1970; "The trouble with American kids is that none of them are average. They're all extremists of one kind or another — and all totally neurotic. The "love" people are all so forcibly peaceful that it scares me. Here, progress is a slow evolutionary process which is good and as it should be. In America they're trying to move the forces of progress unnaturally. I loathe the place and I'm not looking forward to going back again. But on the other hand I wouldn't have missed the last tour for the world. This is the main reason I'm looking forward so much to our autumn British tour. Audiences here are much more objective and you can sense if they don't like you or think you're not playing well."

With an intense touring schedule, it gave the group very little spare time and having to be creative in a hotel room was not easy. The discomforts of being away from home were not conducive to being a fruitful writing environment. Still though, not interested in indulging in the rock and roll lifestyle of sex and drugs, writing in a hotel room was often how Ian Anderson kept himself busy when not on the road or on stage.

It was on 9th June that Jethro Tull returned to the UK for some time off from touring in which they could really start working on their next album. By that point, their working dynamics for such process were comfortably established. Anderson was quoted in *Side One* in June 1970; "Thankfully, the whole thing seems just to be a natural kind of thing. I suppose we've found our feet within the rigors of touring, recording and living sparse private lives at home. We've found some kind of level on which to function in terms of coming up with new ideas and new ways of playing things. It does seem to go at a comfortable rate — comfortable within a rather hectic life that is! But, things do change slowly and naturally and that I *am* thankful for. It's not something which has to be forced so there's none of the frustration in playing something completely different."

"Things go smoothly and have gone that way since we started playing together. Hopefully, that situation will continue… I'm sort of like a foreman. In the studio I'm the one who tells people when it's time for a tea break, who occasionally does a little bit of ordering about. I sometimes shout into microphones and get the sounds together in a vague way, assisted by able engineers. I act in the capacity of producer but I don't think of myself as a producer — just as I don't think of producers as producers. The lot is superfluous! I have control but I don't think that I abuse that control. It's just a matter of getting things done at the right time — hustling people to work if there's a deadline — encouraging people to try new things if there's enough time to spare… There are always loopholes left for the individual to vary his musical contribution — even within the confines of the studio. In reality, I'm just the person who sorts things out and gathers things together and if I didn't do it someone else would! However, as you might have noticed, I am the one who talks the most, and therefore, it seems that I am the one best suited for the job."

Some of the tracks for what would be Jethro Tull's fourth album, *Aqualung*, had already been recorded by July 1970. John Evan was quoted that month in *New Musical Express*; "One is a spontaneous track ('Just Trying To Be') that took just twenty minutes to record and was done in one take. It's just Ian and I, with me playing celeste. There's another called 'My God' which is the only one we do on stage not recorded yet."

Glenn Cornick added, "To me it's the best thing we do on stage." On a later American tour in 1970, Jethro Tull's performance at New York's Carnegie Hall was recorded. It would later go on to form some of the content on the album, *Living In The Past*. That particular concert was a charity performance. Jethro Tull had been asked to do it by a drug rehabilitation centre. By July 1970, Jethro Tull were sharing the bill with the likes of Jimi Hendrix, B.B. King and Johnny Winter when they played to a crowd of 200,000 at the Atlanta Pop Festival in Georgia.

Being back on the road was a mixed experience for the band. They were doing well but it was certainly hard work. John Evan told *Record Mirror* in July 1970; "Being in a successful group is like being in the army. You have to be some place at all times. At first it was very uncomfortable, but now I'm getting used to it. You lose a lot of freedom and it breaks up old casual friendships with an invisible barrier. People I used to pass the time of day with seem to think of me as somewhat aloof, now. A superstar or something. They think I think that's what I am, so I've lost a lot of the ease and we don't get to talk about the same old things anymore. It takes a certain kind of person to stay with pop music, and although I'm really enjoying the whole thing I'll not be making a career of it."

Under the heading of "Jethro Tull Are Five, But Is Lead Singer Ian Sick?" it was reported in *Record Mirror* in July 1970; "Despite collapsing with a mysterious stomach complaint during the transmission of a European television show, Jethro Tull front man Ian Anderson made a speedy recovery to be able to make a massive world-wide tour. Tomorrow (Friday) he leaves with the group for a six-week, coast-to-coast personal appearance schedule. Currently one of the biggest money-spinning groups in the States, Jethro Tull returned from their last visit there only three weeks ago. Following America, they go to Japan from August 14th to August 25th, appearing in a music festival tied in with Expo '70. And while in that part of the world, the group move on to Australia and New Zealand for the first time. This virtual non-stop touring has cut down on the time available for recording, but their album *Benefit* is selling high into the charts in Sweden, Germany and other continental countries as well as in Britain and the States. However, it is unlikely that there will be any further single or album from the group before the end of September."

In August 1970, Jethro Tull played to one of their largest audiences thus far at the Isle of Wight festival. In September 1970, *Melody Maker* reported; "Jethro Tull start a twelve-day tour of Britain on September 23rd. It is their first British tour since the beginning of 1969, and the first with the new five-man line-up including new pianist John Evan. They will be supported by Procol Harum, who will be playing virtually their only British dates this year, and Tir Na Nog, a folk duo from

Ireland. The tour includes three midnight shows in Birmingham, Glasgow and Manchester."

On being back to touring in Britain, Anderson told *Disc And Music Echo*; "It was in such sharp contrast to America in that there, people come to concerts with fears of anxiety and foreboding. They almost expect violence to occur, the result simply of the environmental situation of the concert — security men patrolling everywhere, armed police — it's very inflammable. But in England everything is much more peaceable, yet the reception has been every bit as good as America. I had a really strong feeling of being back home. The audiences have felt relaxed with us and we've felt very rewarded. We did wonder about the tour before it started. It was possible people might have forgotten about us. In the future we definitely want to play more in Britain, not necessarily on tours, but just regular concerts round the country."

On 3rd October 1970, *New Musical Express* reported; "A total of 4,000 packed into a smoky, sweaty Birmingham Town Hall on Friday to see Jethro Tull, the third date of their current twelve city tour. They came — in two separate performances, one starting at midnight — to see the band, whose stature and reputation has increased so much since they last toured Britain a full year ago, but mostly to see the incredible Ian Anderson. There was no anti-climax. Tull got a tremendous reception from both houses and deserved every bit of it. The performance — a delicate blend of old and new material — had a stormy beginning with 'Nothing Is Easy' and continued through the contrasting calm and power of 'My God' to the final crescendo of 'For My Friend Jeffrey' (sic) and 'We Used To Know'."

"They played as if they had just come off a long, relaxing holiday, rather than straight from a punishing American tour. Glenn Cornick courted his bass like he was dancing a military two-step, Clive Bunker hammered his drums like they'd hear him in Newcastle, John Evan quietly wilted, and "Fattie" Martin Barre stood back and watched the antics with amusement. But Ian Anderson towered over them all — a seemingly tireless eccentric, prancing about the stage like a bee-stung dog. He leapt, cavorted, capered and danced like a marionette with its wires crossed, hurtling through every number with a pace which left the audience breathless. Yet such was his calm and wry intelligence and urbanity as he chatted to the audience in the odd pause between numbers that he almost made you believe his antics were normal. And because of his very dominance of personality, it was almost possible to forget not only his own musical genius, but the talent and highly polished dynamism of the group behind him. It was still Anderson's show. And at the climax of each performance, 2,000 fans leapt and danced in grotesque parody of the magic dancing Anderson — the pied piper of modern pop music." (Ian Anderson once referred to Martin Barre as "Fattie". A journalist picked up on it and for a while, the name stuck — much to all of their amusement).

With the title of the new album still to be announced, Anderson offered some information about it to *New Musical Express* in October; "Many of the songs will have a relationship with each other — they will be able to be taken on two levels… But it's not pretentious, at least I don't think it will sound pretentious when you hear it. It's not like the Kinks making their potted little statements about men in bowler hats. It will also be a little more humorous as an album. There's a song called 'The Pool' which is about Blackpool and the sort of thing Ringo might sing. And then there are still the personal songs about me, like 'Wond'ring Aloud', which is a love song."

In the same feature, the journalist relayed the conversation that took place between himself and Anderson, who played him some of the material from what would be on the new album; "Switching on the tape to play me a track called 'The Passenger', Ian rummaged through a pile of songbooks to find and read the lyrics. 'You see, this one is about a man on a train but it can also be seen as drawing analogies between a passenger on a train and a passenger through life'."

Based on Anderson's description of the song, it seems most plausible that 'The Passenger' was the working title for the song that came to be well known as 'Locomotive Breath'. Of the yet to be revealed *Aqualung* album, Anderson said; "Because we like the songs and enjoyed making it, it seems a bit silly to say it, but if the next album sold only two-hundred copies and those two-hundred people were still playing that record in five years' time that would really knock me out. That is what I really want to do — to play music that people will remember. Music that will still have the same feel in the years to come and not just be the biggest thing of its particular year."

By December '70 and with another tour of the US under their belts, Tull would undergo another line-up change. This time it saw Glenn Cornick leave the band. When Cornick's departure was officially announced in *New Musical Express* on 12th December 1970, Martin Barre was quoted as having called it "an amicable split with nothing personal behind it." Terry Ellis was quoted in the same report; "Glenn is now having a short holiday and, after Christmas, he will be working with friends to form a new group."

Retrospectively, conflicting accounts exist regarding Cornick's departure from the band. Cornick said in later years that he was sacked but other accounts insist that he was invited to leave by the band's management and given full support to continue with his music career outside of it. Either way, he went on to form his own band, Wild Turkey. It is plausible that Cornick wanted to go at a slower pace and that leaving Jethro Tull was perhaps the way forward in that regard. He had

Symbolically, Glenn Cornick is barely in shot. His tenure with the band ended in 1970, with Jeffrey Hammond-Hammond replacing him.

John Evan "returned" to the fold in 1970 with the band becoming a quintet in the process.
(left to right): Martin Barre, Clive Bunker, Jeffrey Hammond-Hammond, Ian Anderson and John Evan.

told *New Musical Express* in February 1970; "I am getting sick of going on tours, which I think all of us are, but if you don't play to the public you start losing your audience. So you have to work out a balance. The bad aspects, the hotels and continual travelling, are compensated by the good aspects, the playing before an audience."

Cornick was replaced by Jeffrey Hammond-Hammond, another old time friend who had been in the John Evan Band. When he joined Tull, music hadn't been a part of his life for a good few years. He was a good fit though because he got on with the band and they had already experienced a working rapport together. Hammond-Hammond fitted into the picture because like the other band members, he wasn't a musicians' musician who could play jazz and blues standards and jam with anybody. A vital ingredient of being in Jethro Tull was an ability to bring ideas to the table for the band's own music.

Anderson explained to *Record Mirror* in August 1969; "I like light and shade and tone colours in music. You don't need to prove you can play fast if you know you can do it. Technique shouldn't be used for technique's sake. We try to make each song have an identity of its own."

And he told *Hit Parader* in October 1969; "I've listened to some jazz, but never really taken it in, because it always is way beyond me technically. I can't think chords that fast, and I can't play the changes like those people do. They move with the chords so quickly, they know every note on the instrument. Whatever I play, it's because I'm making the most of what I know. I'd rather be tasteful than fantastic and clever. I don't mind when people call our music "jazz rock". If that's the way they see it, fair enough. People can call it whatever they want to call it. The only thing that would worry me is if they say it was badly played. I'm anxious to please mostly. Basically I like to please people. I know I can't please everyone, but it's important to me to try. I sort of compromise between pleasing myself and pleasing the people, because I know I couldn't do either one perfectly. If there's something I do that I don't really like doing very much, but I know the people like it, I don't mind being swayed by that. I don't think that's a bad thing. I have enough of a sort of total power, when I want to, to last me. I don't have to be able to play everything I want to play."

Hammond-Hammond's first studio recordings were for the album that would be the band's fourth. When Tull went into the studio over the Christmas holidays in 1970, it was the first time they had recorded anything in six months. Anderson told *Disc And Music Echo* in February 1971; "When Glenn Cornick left we had to find a replacement pretty quickly. Certainly if we had, had the time to spend holding auditions we would have found a more accomplished guitarist than Jeffrey — let's face it, he is pretty green — but I wanted to give him a job. I'd bought him a guitar for his birthday last year, simply because I couldn't think of anything else to get him, and then when Glenn left I asked Jeffrey if he could get it together to join us. I wanted to give him something to pull himself together. He'd been a bit weird in the past. He went through a long phase of not talking to anyone and just going for long walks and hiding in shop doorways to "sort it all out". I gave him a job painting the house while Jennie and I were away in America and things like that. But actually, though he's had very little experience, he has a very good feeling for music. His first gig was in the studio where we spent a week and a half on the new album. Then there were four days rehearsal before the European tour. Not only was that the first time he'd ever played a guitar through an amplifier, but it was the first time he'd been to Europe, the first time he'd been on an aeroplane even. He was very quiet at first and would wear very dark airman's goggles on stage so that he couldn't see anybody. He'd blush scarlet when I introduced him, but now he's getting much better. He even spoke into a tape recorder for some radio programme the other day which was amazing!"

New Musical Express reported in January 1971; "Despite its avowed intention of issuing only albums in future, Jethro Tull has a new single scheduled for January 15th release by Chrysalis — titled 'Lick Your Fingers Clean', it was penned by Ian Anderson. It is the group's first single since 'The Witch's Promise' which came out early last year and climbed to number three in the hit parade. Commented Jethro's manager Terry Ellis: 'We said we would not release any more singles because it seemed then like a complete waste of time. After all, 'The Witch's Promise' was number three in the chart, and yet it was only being played by Radio One every other day on average. I was really upset at the time, because when that happens you find that you completely lose faith in the medium. It is always difficult to get radio plays on a single, but you work on the assumption that if you are fortunate enough to make the chart you will then get your share. But after a while, you realise that you simply can't hold out against the BBC, because that in a way is opting out of your responsibility to the public. Ian has written this new song and it's a really fantastic single — we're all very excited about it'."

In January 1971, journalist Nick Logan wrote in *New Musical Express* of his observations from joining Jethro Tull on tour; "The Hamburg gig was the 2,000-seater Musikhalle theatre, sold out two weeks in advance, a Sunday afternoon show. I had half expected riot scenes but was told by the German promoter that the ugly happenings of a few months ago had now cooled off. Promoters had met agitators and explained that their actions up until then had only served to stir interest in the concerts involved and that if they wanted ticket prices to come down their best course of action would be to boycott the halls. After the show, a success for both groups, the record company had laid on a meal at the hotel for the entire JT entourage, who were also called upon to perform for a Berlin film crew, having to be filmed repeating their arrival at the hotel and then eating in the restaurant. John Evan, who punctuates periods of silence with outbursts of lunacy, managed to enliven the proceedings by falling off his chair during the meal, then disappearing under the table, while the waggish filmmakers prepared a surprise in the form of a live crayfish which came crawling across the table when Ian unsuspectingly lifted the lid off the platter. Gales of hearty Germanic laughter. Not that it's all fun and gaiety dear reader. Ian's wife Jennie had to go home ill during the time I was there and the group's sound engineer John Burns told me that he will be reluctantly leaving Jethro after the next British tour because the pace of his year with the band is taking a telling effect on his nerves and stomach."

The following month, journalist Royston Eldridge reported in *Sounds* on his observations of the tour: "Jethro started their tour in Scandinavia at the beginning of January and when I saw them in Germany they had been on the road for nearly a month. Life on tour for a band like Jethro is a strange existence; they live and work in an insulated, self-contained world that is seldom touched by anything outside of its immediate confine. Apart from the army, Clive Bunker commented on the way back from a concert in Munster, groups are the most tightly knit units of people. It's easy to understand what he meant after three days on tour with them. Their lives are administered and arranged with an almost military precision which leaves the group only to concern themselves with playing."

"In Germany, Jethro and Tir Na Nog, who played every concert with them, were accompanied by manager Terry Ellis, English tour manager Eric Brooks, two German tour managers, sound engineer John Burns and three English road managers. This cocooned environment affects the music: there's more depth and greater sensitivity in the songs — off their forthcoming album — which Jethro now include in their stage act. Ian Anderson is playing less flute and more acoustic guitar and his songs in general are quieter. There are still heavy parts in the new songs. Clive Bunker does his drum solo in the middle of 'Cross-Eyed Mary', but the music is full of contrast. And instead of finishing with a powerful climactic song, Jethro end their act on a soft note ('Wind-Up') which baffled some of the audience, expecting a pounding finale. It's doing the unexpected that makes Jethro such an entertaining and enterprising band though. The changes in their music have kept pace with their rise in stature and that's all you can ask of any musicians. They are progressing at a time when "progressive" means anything but that. Jethro now communicate and come across to their audience on two equal levels: there is still the strange visual attraction and humour of Ian Anderson, which was the group's original strength, but this is now balanced by a music that is better than ever."

Esteemed journalist Chris Welch also spent some time on the tour. He reported in *Melody Maker* the same month; "At the theatre in Milan the road managers struggled to get their equipment working with ancient electrical systems and ludicrous red tape. 'They are such idiots here,' said a Scots roadie. 'I've never met such idiots in my life!' The crowds at each concert proved to be like football fans. Noisy, excitable, they reacted to simple guitar choruses by Tir Na Nog as if a goal had been scored. Said Ian at one point, 'Milan 3 — Jethro Tull 1.' Police who entered the theatre in Milan with the obligatory steel helmets and wire mesh grills were greeted with boos and jeers. One felt, how stupid to jeer, and how stupid to wear steel helmets at a pop concert. A kind of rage at the current mania for official and unofficial violence gripped the stomach. It's the same phenomena witnessed in Holland, France or Germany."

"Let's hope it doesn't happen in England. But make no mistake, we are stupid enough to let it happen. Only apathy saves us from anarchy. Jethro are playing at the peak of their ability. Their act is now thoroughly musical, featuring the talents of brilliant pianist John Evan. John plays a beautiful piano duet with Ian on flute, which ranges from classical to blues and jazz influences. The group like to perform pieces which involve various members "laying out" and this emphasises their use and control of dynamics. Tull are not a loud or gimmicky band. They are singularly entertaining, original and highly advanced in their understanding of various musical devices. Ian is as amusing a musician who has ever set flute to lip and guitar to plectrum. The chants of 'Jethro!' proved that his visual comedy and audible musicianship can communicate with the people of any nationality. And apart from his minstrel-like appeal, and one-legged genius, there is also the rounded, mature brilliance of drummer Clive Bunker, and the solid guitar work of Martin Barre. New bassist, Jeffrey Hammond-Hammond, proved something of a mystery, playing straight bass and saying nowt. The phlegmatic control of Jeffrey was in marked contrast to the ever-raving activity of our Italian chums."

The journalist who wrote for *Beat Instrumental* in February 1971 found that Jethro Tull were too busy to give an interview. Better still perhaps, the situation provided said journalist with the opportunity to observe a recording session for the album that was still in progress at the time: "Somewhere in London stands a black-painted church building with its innards ripped out and carefully replaced with all that modern interior decorating can offer. Inside this sinister abode lies the womb of Island Records — its recording studios. Somewhere inside studio one the week before Christmas were Jethro Tull and somewhere in their various heads lay an unborn LP. Just as photographers are awarded gold statuettes for taking pictures of Jackie Onassis in her most intimate moments (or for climbing trees in the gardens of Buckingham Palace to complete a magazine's "Royal Scrapbook"), I did the equivalent in rock journalism by going to the recording studios with a notebook and pen concealed in my hand, disguised as a reporter."

"The security guard at Island is a very nice man who smokes a pipe and combs his hair in the door window when he thinks no one is watching. He sees all the groups come and go and assured me that Jethro Tull were nice lads. Warmed by this information I went up into the control room of studio one and met lead guitarist Martin Barre who told me that Ian would be along in a minute and gave me a seat. Then Barre and Jeffrey Hammond-Hammond — the renewed bass guitarist — went into the studios and hand-patted a ball of paper to each other."

"It was with this relaxed vision of a row of soundproofing screens and a paper ball rising and falling behind it that Ian Anderson entered. He came in gripping a small bag and without so much as a hi or hello went straight to the piano, set his bag down, and proceeded to tap out a tune. This to me was an acted-out example of the difference between a musician and a pop star. This is a scene which should be repeated before every top-of-the-pop-eyed middle-aged father to whom the pop musician is merely juvenile showbiz at its worst. He's the stork in a dressing gown and the tired-eyed face behind the control room dials at midnight. When you've spent ten hours a day in the studios creating music there's every reason to want to leap around when your newborn baby is presented live to the masses. Ian Anderson, superstar-and-bard, is Jethro Tull. He came to me looking very tired and intense to explain why the group weren't giving any interviews. Only a few weeks before the band had returned from a tour of the States and after each having a short holiday it was back into the recording studios to work on their fourth LP. A tired face says more than words and visible dedication doesn't need to seek excuses so we each compared our tight schedules and deadlines before apologising goodbyes."

The feature continued: "My return visit the next day — made in the hopes of meeting manager Terry Ellis who arranges their conversations — was again in vain, but about an hour's wait outside the studio provided me with an insight into the corporate personality of J. Tull. I came in as pianist John Evan was working over a catchy intro, which provided my head with continuous piped music for the next two weeks. Anderson remained in the control room and guided them into sets of two takes at a time after which the boys came up to listen to the playback. Then it was back into the studio for a further two takes. Anderson counts them in with a 'One, two, two two, three four...' He then comments on each take and the band is constantly following his advice as they play. Evan has to go slower. Someone made a boob. Someone admits to making a boob. 'One, two, two two, three four...' Then it's out beneath the red light and into the control room."

"A tape machine screeches backwards through its four-take history. The second one's better than the third. The fourth one's better than the first. Turn up the bass. Play a little slower John. Out beneath the red light and back to the instruments. 'One, two, two two, three four...' Anderson sings over a track from his position in the control room. The heavy doors give the sound a sort of singing-in-the-bathroom quality. One, two, two two, three four.' On my third and last attempt to interview the band four days later the same track was spinning through the tape machine watched by critical ears... My last visit to the studios was on the day before Christmas Eve and Ian Anderson was the only group member not holidaying at that time. Alone except for a technician, he mixed tapes of the preceding week's work to send on as a master tape to New York."

Anderson explained to *New Musical Express* in March 1971; "During the first week of rehearsals (for *Aqualung*) I must have rewritten several songs that were not going right, and even scrapped some and started new ones."

Aqualung was a long time in the making: between one-hundred-and-fifty to two-hundred hours worth of studio work was done. Before recording even started, three days were spent at Ian Anderson's Hampstead home where the band talked among themselves about how they would work with the songs. In rehearsals, various ideas were tested, with suggestions being made by all the band. It wasn't long after the release of *Benefit* that the recording process was started on for *Aqualung*. However, most of the early material for the album was re-done when Tull returned from their tour in America and changed studios. This changing and improving of tracks carried on throughout the process of making *Aqualung*, with three tracks being re-recorded after the band's January-February European tour. The reason for this is the extent to which the tracks evolved from having been played on stage. Towards the end of the sessions, as recording time was running out, it wasn't unusual for the band to be working in the studio from midnight through to 10am.

Released in March 1971, *Aqualung* gave Jethro Tull a significant boost in their commercial success. It showcased Anderson's writing talents in a more serious light as he boldly took on the controversial subject matter of God and religion. With a line-up that supported an enticing blend of rock and folk music, it was, for many, the album that signified Tull's arrival into the seventies that would see them making a landmark album for each year of that decade thereon. The LP signified a new direction for the band in the sense that it had a theme. Anderson wanted to get away from writing songs about the typical pop song subjects — love, feeling blue, feeling lonely etc. In wanting to avoid the trite and meaningless clichés, he endeavoured to write about what he saw as real problems that he himself could relate to. The aim was to create something that had a sense of truth to it in terms of how he saw the world at the time.

Anderson told *Disc And Music Echo* in February 1971; "The first thing on any album is to make the songs relate musically, and it just so happens that on this one, five or six of the songs relate to my ideas about God. It's a very personal thing, not intended to rouse people to riot, although the feelings behind it are a little unhappy."

In the same feature, Anderson was quoted as describing 'My God' as "a blues — a lament for God. Really within myself I'm referring back to the kind of ideas of God and religion with which I was brought up. In the context which I knew it, God is a highly personal thing, a feeling of righteousness and goodness. I don't look to God to help me in times of trouble. Luckily my parents let me choose my own way with religion. They sent me to Sunday school when I was young but I rebelled after the first visit and I was never forced back. I think my parents are the exception though, and there is so much religion today forced onto children simply by virtue of their parents' race or creed — and that in itself is inherently wrong."

"It's just this feeling that has come out in me," he continued. "In some of the songs there are only references to it, but others are more explicit. Like everybody else I see a lot of people with a lot of different religions, and whereas I respect their beliefs, I don't respect the reasons whereby they came to them. There is still this "bogeyman" aspect about God which is terribly wrong. Religion should still be taught in schools, but for its historical value, not as indoctrination. To hell with morning services and assemblies. What do they mean to school kids? I wouldn't want to take people away from God. In fact I don't think you can get any further away from God than we are today. We were at the Vatican in Rome a few weeks back and I just could not believe it. If they only spent money on people who need it, rather than spend it on their own buildings, but the album's a very personal thing — two or three of the songs are just me with an acoustic guitar — and as such it's bound to offend a few people I suppose. Melodically and lyrically the songs are much better than on previous albums. Now we're right back to the basic simple group sounds. Some of the songs are actually quite commercial — not deliberately so. I've even heard the cleaners at the recording studio singing one, so it must be catchy!"

Such was the significance of the album's lyrics, *Aqualung* was the first Jethro Tull LP to be released with them included as part of the album art. The lyrics to the title track are credited to Anderson's then wife, Jennie. The idea for the whole album was originally inspired by her. Wanting to be a photographer, she had taken photos of the run-down parts of London, many of which featured (as they were called at the time) tramps. Although the lyrics were actually written by Ian Anderson, he wanted to give Jennie a credit because the imagery of them was inspired by her photos. "It's about a rather pathetic character, someone socially degraded," was how he saw it at the time. "There's something marvellous about that situation. I would like to see the concept of God put into that sort of situation."

Anderson offered some insight into each of the songs on *Aqualung* for *Disc And Music Echo*:

'Cross-Eyed Mary': "A song about another form of low-life, but more humorous. It's about a schoolgirl prostitute but not in such coarse terms. She goes with dirty old men because she's doing them a favour, giving people what they want because it makes them happy. It's a fun kind of song."

'Cheap Day Return': "About a day I went to visit my father in hospital in Blackpool. I caught a train at nine, spent four hours travelling, four hours with my father, and four hours to get back again. It was a long song mainly concerned with the railway journey, but the section on the record is about visiting my father. It's a true song."

'Mother Goose': "Completely untrue, it's nonsense. It's the same sort of abstract ideas as 'Cross-Eyed Mary', imagery of a hundred schoolgirls all crying; it's full of surrealism. It's amusing."

'Wond'ring Aloud': "A bit of personal nonsense, it's a love song. It's difficult to write love songs if you write songs a lot; love is a separate, personal thing. But this is the most satisfying thing I've made a record of. It's well-played and sung quite well. It's a pretty song."

'Up To Me': "A song about selfishness."

'My God': "This is a blues for God, in the way of a lament. So many religions operate as a social service instead of a spiritual one."

'Hymn 43': "A blues for Jesus, about the gory, glory seekers who use his name as an excuse for a lot of unsavoury things. You know, 'Hey Dad, it's not my fault — the missionaries lied'."

'Slipstream': "A song about dying. It doesn't mean it's the end of the world, but it hints at a life hereafter. There's a line in it, 'And you paddle right out of the mess.' It's brief and to the point, lyrically and musically."

'Locomotive Breath': "Another song about dying, but it's not so serious as 'Slipstream'. It's an analogy of the unending train journey of life, you can't stop, you've got to stagger on. But it's not that serious. All of the songs have an element of humour, and sometimes pure silliness."

'Wind-Up': "A bit deeper, open to interpretation. It's fairly obvious what it's about."

Anderson concluded by saying; "To me it's a well-balanced album, musically. Technically it's better, there is better sound quality and better performances. There's an anti-climactic feeling to a lot of the songs, which I think is good. It should leave you wanting more, instead of ending on rave-up guitar solos and piano arpeggios. I hope it's an album people will want to hear again and again."

He told *New Musical Express*; "I'm not out to convert people. I'm just having a go at the people who mislead me, but it is not a concept album as such, not in the same way as *Tommy*. It doesn't tell a story, doesn't have any profound link between tracks, although there are statements made of a very personal nature. But they are not absolute truths."

As was noticed by many at the time, the Aqualung figure on the album's cover art was not too different in appearance to Anderson's own onstage persona at the beginning of Jethro Tull's tenure. This was no coincidence. The artist who was commissioned to do the album art referred to photos of Anderson whilst he was drawing the character for the front cover.

A consequence of this was that some people made the assumption that the songs on *Aqualung* were autobiographical. They weren't though. They were an accumulation of Anderson's imagination and observations of other people he had seen in large cities whilst on his travels. Anderson was quoted in *Circus* in August 1971; "Aqualung is a character that we invented, although he is sort of a consummate character of people I have known and have been aware of. He represents the tramp figure, the hobo, the very lowest part of society. He is considered to be degenerate morally, and very decadent, a kind of scum of the earth. And taking that figure, what I'm trying to do is to point out that to my personalised view of religion and the god complex. I believe that God exists within that character just as much as within the Pope. I believe that all human beings are alike in as much as they have a capacity for goodness. What you have to do is try to recognise it within yourself and try to be a good person, whatever that means, since we all have different standards."

For the writing of *Aqualung*, Anderson put a lot of thought into how the songs would come across on stage. The recording process wasn't an entirely smooth one. Due to the fact that some of the songs had already been played on stage and had worked well in such context, when it came to putting them down in the studio, a lot of adjustments had to be made so that the songs would sound good on record. Whilst the quieter sections translated well from stage to studio, the other sections were more technically demanding to arrange.

Anderson made the backing track for 'Locomotive Breath' by singing along to a hi-hat accompaniment. Everything else was recorded on top of that. He played the electric guitar on 'Locomotive Breath' because on the day of recording the song in the studio, Martin Barre couldn't get the sound across that Anderson had in mind. The final track includes input from both of them, some of which is overdubbed.

Aqualung did well commercially. It got to number four in the UK and number seven in the US. It stayed in the American charts for over a year. Not only that, but it was the first Jethro Tull album to get into the top ten there and selling over a million copies, it was awarded a gold disc by the Recording Industry Association of America in July 1971. It was reviewed in *Record Mirror* in March 1971; "*Aqualung* is undoubtedly Jethro Tull's most significant album to date and although comparisons are often odious to the artist concerned, the highest compliment I feel able to offer is that in significance it rates with Townshend's *Tommy*. The mind behind this latest electronic alert is, of course, Ian Anderson who in his infinite wisdom presents his character Aqualung as humanity's most common denominator 'snot running down his nose, drying in the hot sun — poor old sod' — like some super-dirty old man within whom there is as much God as anyone else! On the side of the album for which he reserves his most pointed attacks upon orthodox religions, the Pope comes in for a few kicks in the divine rear as do all those other gods which you 'wind up on Sunday' or use only their names as a final refuge in death. The glory, glory seekers are not going to find much comfort in the gospel according to Tull. And if all this sounds a bit too heavy, be not dismayed for there is the secret ingredient which adds lightness and brightness in the Tull repertoire — humour both black and white. There is some clever use of the Mellotron on 'Cross-Eyed Mary', some refined guitar from Anderson on 'Cheap Day Return', and deft bursts of electrical inspiration from new recruit Jeffrey Hammond ('A Song For Jeffrey') — remember him? — the inevitable but tasteful warblings on flute from Ian, but more of a revelation is his acoustic guitar work."

The album was reviewed in *Disc And Music Echo* in March 1971; "Ian Anderson and Jethro Tull succeed in making you want to hear their new album, *Aqualung*, more than once, because a lot of tracks leave you in mid-air, they end when you are expecting more, and that makes quite a change in these days of heavy, blasting sounds. The title track is full of surprises with some violent riffs, soft sections, frequent tempo changes, and Anderson's voice sounding like he's on the phone in one part. 'Cross-Eyed Mary' is also unpredictable, it starts fairly gently but builds up powerfully. And the chord patterns ignore all rules, wandering all over the place. 'Cheap Day Return' is one of the tracks that leaves you holding your breath. It's very short, under two minutes, just Ian and Jeffrey on guitars, and you really want it to last longer. 'Wond'ring Aloud' has the same effect, folking guitars strumming in 6/8 with string accompaniment which is hardly noticeable at first. It lets you drop after only forty-five seconds. Jeffrey's laughter is featured at the beginning and end of 'Up To Me' which has a good solo from Martin Barre. 'Mother Goose' is another basically folk thing but with a bit of sinister heaviness. 'My God' is rather sinister as well, especially with a chorus of "monks" chanting in the middle. The monks are eight Ian Andersons, courtesy of the wonders of multi-tracking. 'Hymn 43' is the only track with a really obvious ending. 'Locomotive Breath' is one of the more powerful numbers with Steve Cropper playing lead. The album ends with 'Wind-Up', the song about the 'brain-washing' school-system, and it's surprisingly a bit Elton John-ish. It's enough to say that this is Jethro's finest album." (A quick correction note here: It wasn't Steve Cropper who played the extra electric guitar on 'Locomotive Breath', it was Ian Anderson!).

It was reviewed in *Sounds* in April 1971; "There are two qualities in particular that make this album Jethro's finest: taste and variety, neither of which were present in such abundance in their work before. The material ranges from gentle love songs — 'Wond'ring Aloud' — to the percussive rock cuts like 'Locomotive Breath' with others in between like 'Mother Goose', an old English flavoured song, cutely phrased and unusually delivered. Even in 'Locomotive Breath' and 'Wind-Up', the other heavy track, there's light and shade with John Evan's piano introductions providing a contrast to what follows. Produced by Ian Anderson, who wrote all the selections with the exception of the title track lyrics written by his wife, and manager Terry Ellis, the whole album has been handled tastefully. David Palmer's orchestrations on 'Wond'ring Aloud' and 'Slipstream'; Martin Barre's guitar licks on 'My God'; Anderson's flute fills and the varying echoey effects on 'Aqualung' are all interesting but never intrude. Anderson's acoustic guitar work is another revelation: he has no pretensions of greatness in this department, but he does the job admirably and the five members of the group are a very solid unit now. From the packaging to the music it contains, this album is a complete work and this is from a group who were considered basically a live act. They improve every time out."

And in *Friendz* in May 1971; "There was a time when Jethro Tull could do no wrong. They were novel and a good name to slip in when referring to "progressive bands". They made music which was both creative and entertaining, and were dominated by a lead singer who also played the flute and, on stage, wore an old overcoat, perpetually raised one leg in the air like a giant, hairy, lame hen, and made dry, amusing, irreverent announcements between numbers. And they became very, very popular. And then there came a time when they could do nothing right. They had become sterile, they were just a backing group for Ian Anderson whose songs were tedious and stereotyped, they were only interested in making money, they had sold out to the States, the frolics had taken over from the music. And as if to redress the balance again, along comes *Aqualung* which will probably be very successful for them and also maintains high aesthetic standards. One side is called 'Aqualung', although only a couple of songs seem to relate in any way to the old man in question, and the other 'My God', although only the first two and last tracks emphasise the distortions and illusions which surround the contemporary pantomime of religion, and the fact that Anderson's God 'is not the kind you have to wind up on Sundays'. The instrumental work has considerable strength and symmetry, with Anderson playing rather more acoustic guitar than flute, though what remains retains its distinctive qualities. 'Aqualung' is undoubtedly the most perfectly rounded track, making skilful use of climaxes, menacing when he himself appears to be, with sympathy conveyed through subtle shifts of work, voice and tempo. It includes an exceptional and savoury guitar solo from Martin Barre who also cuts across 'Cross-Eyed Mary' and 'My God' with a choice sense of drama to complement the commendable lyrics. Elsewhere — 'Cheap Day Return', 'Mother Goose', 'Wond'ring Aloud' — there is the indication Anderson may have been listening to too much Paul Simon, often employing the same tone, phrasing and elements — you'll see what I mean. Nevertheless *Aqualung* is a striking, honest and compassionate piece of work which deserves most, if not all, of the attention it will receive. I still have a few reservations, but they probably won't last another listen."

And in *Rolling Stone* in July 1971; "Dating from at least the Electric Prunes' 'Mass In D Minor', rock and religion have evinced an unlikely affinity for each other. Eric Clapton, Peter Green, Jeremy

Spencer, Peter Townsend, John Lennon, George Harrison (and let us not forget the Reverend Richard Penniman) have all at some point dedicated themselves and their music to God in his myriad varieties. On the heels of *Tommy* and *Jesus Christ Superstar*, Jethro Tull's Ian Anderson joins this heady list. Tull is one of our most serious and intelligent groups, and Anderson's choice of subject for *Aqualung* — the distinction between religion and God — is witness to that. Further, Tull has a musical sophistication to match its thematic ambitions. Where *This Was*, their first album, was aimless and disorganised, *Stand Up*, with its dabbling in ethnic and classical forms, was eclectic in the best sense. Out of that experimentation was forged in *Benefit* a sound which finally provided the band with a concrete identity. Once a group has arrived at a coherent style, the next logical step is a concept album, and it is on the shoals of concepts that many a band runs to ground. Often such albums lack the hint of self-irony, which is basic to great rock and roll, and therefore come off sounding pompous. Ultimately an album like *Tommy*, for example, must stand or fall on its quality as a collection of songs; the thematic gloss is absolutely secondary. *Aqualung* is the album's lead character and is so named for his rheumy cough. Side one consists of a series of seedy vignettes drawn from modern secular English life, while the printed lyrics are cast in gothic lettering to emphasize the album's liturgical basis. The title song depicts the beggar in all his shabbiness and lechery. 'Aqualung' is actually three songs; as the different moods of the narrator unfold, the music changes accordingly. The initial melodic statement sung in a harsh, surly voice is ugly and plodding; it then shades into something milder and more sympathetic, then into something which rocks a little more. Another of society's dregs, cross-eyed Mary the slut, of the song of the same name, is the object of Aqualung's attentions. Anderson sounds equally disapproving here. 'Mother Goose' is the kind of song that Anderson writes best. As in 'Sossity' on *Benefit*, he uncannily captures the feel of a real Elizabethan madrigal (a consort of recorders here helps it get across). It's a song about a Hampstead fair and is filled with descriptive detail which is at once archaic and up to date. Lyrics and melody mutually accomplish the same purpose, for both express the continuity of English life."

The review continued; "Side two, subtitled 'My God', deals more explicitly with religion. The nub of the issue is Christian hypocrisy, how people manipulate notions of God for their own ends. There is some rather obvious talk of plastic crucifixes, Blakean allusions to locking 'Him in His golden cage,' and invective; 'The bloody Church of England...' Beneath the accusatory tone is a moving musical theme. Again, the structure is constantly shifting. There are stately hymnal changes, a jazzy flute break, a pomp-and-circumstantial motif which, when inverted, assumes a more chromatic, modern queasiness. The gamut of religious experience is encompassed in this song. 'Wind-Up' winds up the album and embodies most of the album's difficulties. While Anderson is adept at conceiving a musical approximation of an idea, his lyrics are overly intentional, ponderous, and didactic. It would be possible to ignore the lyrics, as lyrics can usually be ignored, except that Anderson sings them so melodramatically. Nor is his theatricality appropriate to the ideas or words. The over-enthusiastic delivery is probably meant to compensate for his inherent vocal limitations, but the original problem is Anderson's choice of subject. At a time when the more arcane varieties of religious experience are trumpeted far and wide, and atheism and agnosticism still more than hold their own, it is difficult for the modern temper to get worked up over good old-fashioned Christian hypocrisy. When Anderson sufferingly sings — 'So I asked this God a question and by way of firm reply...' — there is something depressingly anticlimactic about it all. There is a lot of misplaced emotion on this record. Thus, despite the fine musicianship and often brilliant structural organisation of songs, this album is not elevated, but undermined by its seriousness."

With *Aqualung* to their name, how did Jethro Tull compare to their musical peers? According to one journalist who wrote for *New Musical Express* in March 1971; "Jethro are today what you might term second generation progressives, the third generation being the Sabbaths, the Deep Purples, the Curved Airs. They are at a potential danger period where a drop in enthusiasm or loss of purpose and direction could see them into an abyss. Changes in personnel, however, have helped the band keep evolving."

Anderson was quoted in the same feature; "We might not be as popular as some groups because we don't have a definite style but we have been playing now for three years and are at the stage where we are not a new group anymore. We can be thought of as an established group like Mayall or The Who. And I think to a large extent the reason we are still around and evolving is that we have never tied ourselves down to using one style of music, like Mayall's band has never been tied down. He's mainly never tied himself down to musicians, but we've had changes as well, and I think that that is one of the things that has kept us going and kept us enthusiastic."

Tull's performance at the Gaumont State Theatre on 26th February was reviewed in *New Musical Express* the following month; "Within a society which is sometimes prone to exonerate pretentiousness and false piety, Jethro Tull have retained the criterion that entertaining an audience is the all-important maxim of their visual presentation. Amid a flurry of arms, elbows, hair, grimaces, knees and the compulsory pointed toe, Ian Anderson has created an onstage imagery which has firmly placed him among rock's leading front men. However, he hasn't let his maniacal pose transgress into Frankenstein proportions, for with an astute and level head he has reached the point where he can now send himself up to an acceptable point, yet never overstep the fine line which would result in people laughing at him as opposed to laughing with him."

"On Friday night, at the Gaumont State mausoleum in downtown Kilburn, Jethro gave an object lesson in stagecraft; my personal observations being that absolutely nothing is left to chance to the extent that careful timing plays a most integral part in their diverse performance. Though for the time being they still choose to envelope virtually everything with brash, vaudevillian humour, this could in time prove to be a distraction instead of a valid asset. But such has been their universal acceptance that I'm sure the group must be aware of the direction in which they will choose to project themselves. From the minute Ian entered stage left bathed in dramatic blue lighting for an acoustic guitar intro to 'My God', the tension started to build, prior to the rest of the group stealthily creeping to their instruments to join him halfway through the song, adding to the drama. From then on in, the continuity was tight and constructive with spotlighting, exits and entrances sustaining the impact and transfixing the spectators' attention."

"Next, they offered the title track from their soon-to-be-released album, 'Aqualung', which featured a double-tempo rock interlude and spoke well of future excursions in this vein. Since the addition of John Evan on organ and piano, the group's visual aspects have broadened with Mr Evan wandering aimlessly around the stage in a large, white baggy suit looking akin to Harpo Marx. Yet it must be said that during his many solo passages, most notable being 'With You There To Help Me', he overshadowed Ian during intricate interweaving solo passages. Yet another new album cut, 'Cross-Eyed Mary', became a vehicle for the percussive talents of Clive Bunker, a much-underrated musician who in both his backing and solo capacity has a great deal to offer, though seated at the back he is quite innocently upstaged by his cohorts. 'Nothing Is Easy' was well received by virtue of its familiarity and also in that it was the last number."

"As expected, an encore was called for and following a respectable time lapse they re-appeared to premier another one of Ian's cynical God-rock compositions 'Wind-Up'. An extended number, it was memorable for its interlude which gave Martin Barre ample opportunity to display his very personal guitar technique with just Clive in support. Again, this was most indicative of the high individual talents which Jethro encompasses. Newcomer, the near-mythical Jeffrey Hammond-Hammond on bass appears to be an introverted character and seemed to content himself with acting as a musical linkman within the context of the group — no more, no less. As 'Wind-Up' approached its conclusion, the members of the group quietly vacated the stage one-by-one until Ian was left to deliver the musical punchline, prior to waving goodnight and loping off into the wings to sustained applause."

The same event was reported on rather differently in *Disc And Music Echo*; "Roll up! Roll up! The circus comes to town! With that articulate and stage raving ringmaster Ian Anderson keeping under control John Evan, virtuoso pianist and loveable wandering clown in the baggy white suit, Jeffrey, the enigmatic silent stooge — oh! yes and Jethro Tull one of the most exciting bands on the scene. The feeling of the big top was there at Kilburn State Gaumont in London last week. Ian Anderson wandered on the darkened stage first and played acoustic guitar and sang. Then crash, surprise! The lights go on and there are the rest of the band. I thought we were off into another exciting evening, with Martin Barre's guitar interweaving with the Anderson-style flute as the basis of the individual sound. The famed Jeffrey does not appear to be as new to the bass game as was thought, but he does lack a certain drive that Glenn Cornick gave. But the evening slowed badly when Jethro Tull gave way to shows of individual virtuosity in which each member had a long solo and good as they were, don't do much for an evening with Jethro Tull. John Evan, much changed from his Isle of Wight appearance, where he was nervous and shy, wore a baggy white suit, and stumbled around stage reminiscent of a Bonzo. Ian Anderson finished the evening as he began, solo. He finished song, music and show with a halting few notes on the guitar, and the voice fading away. A very clever, surprise finish."

Aqualung would be Clive Bunker's last Tull album. He had become fed up with touring and wanted to settle down with his girlfriend and start a family. With his focus elsewhere, Anderson maintained that Bunker paid less interest and contributed less towards *Aqualung* than he did with earlier albums. By May 1971, he was out of the band. Things must have changed rapidly as Bunker told *Melody Maker* in March; "I love being one of the band. The songs are always interesting. Sometimes you have a good swear, but you never lose interest. Ian gets a basic idea and we all work out our own parts. In 'Song For Jeffrey' Ian thought of the drum parts — and it really worked out well… There's a lot of time in our arrangements where I don't play at all. Then I let it all out in the solo. I don't always know if it will come off. I like to keep a good rumble going! My solo is bits of excitement and bits of technical phrasing. I've got to work towards that excitement, and there are lots of stops and starts. I enjoy doing the solo and there is always the occasional night when something new comes out. If I go on saying, 'Oh, I'm fed up with this', something good comes out. If I go on feeling confident, it doesn't always work. At the Isle of Wight last year, I was really nervous. But the solo worked out well. I don't like doing solos on LPs. For recording, you've go to play as straight as possible. That was the mistake I made on our first album. Ringo is one of the best recording drummers. His timing is brilliant."

New Musical Express reported on 19th June 1971; "Jethro Tull are working with a new drummer — Barrie Barlow, replacing Clive Bunker — on their current tour of America which last week played before a riot-torn audience in Denver, Colorado. No reason has been given for the switch and it is not known if Bunker was sacked or if he left of his own accord. A spokesman for Tull's British agency Chrysalis told NME: 'I do not have any information on this. Terry Ellis is in America and is staying on there a while.' Writes NME staffman Roy Carr, who formerly fronted a Blackpool-based group in which Barlow was a featured drummer: 'I regarded him at that time as without a doubt the finest drummer in the North West. He was obviously much respected by others who would come along to watch him play. I recall that at that time he never wanted to become a pro musician. He was happier working as a toolmaker.' Apparently Barlow was also formerly drummer with the John Evan Band, a Jethro Tull nucleus which also contained Ian Anderson and Glenn Cornick. He came to London with the band when it also contained Mick Abrahams — but returned to Blackpool after two days." The new drummer was soon dubbed Barriemore Barlow by Ian Anderson — the name stuck.

Meanwhile, *Melody Maker* reported on the US tour in June; "Ian Anderson fixed his frightening eyes on the first few rows at the Anaheim Convention Hall. They had been giving Jethro Tull a slow hand clap for a long gap between songs while the group tuned up. 'It's actually easier than you think to play out of tune. We are trying to tune up. So be a good audience and *belt up!*' He is a man with a rasping tongue and this turning on the crowd could easily have rebounded. By the end of the show, half an hour later, the 9,000 crowd was beaten into total submission. Encore demands were deafening, overwhelming. They stood on their seats to cheer their thanks to a group that had put on a masterly performance. And it seemed to clinch the growing success story of Jethro Tull in America. They are now gigantically popular. Jethro Tull are on a month-long tour of the States. On two successive nights they sold out the Los Angeles Forum (19,000 seats) and Anaheim (9,000). They have been working hard in America for eight tours — and now all the evidence is here. They have become Britain's hottest rock export. These eight tours in two and a half years have been pretty gruelling, but then Jethro is a phenomenally hard-working group which takes just three weeks holiday each summer. The fruits of their dedication are now ripening. From Salt Lake City to New Orleans, from San Diego to Oklahoma, this tour is clearly a milestone for them, pulling in huge crowds all the way. The estimated total audience being reached during the month is about 158,000."

In the same feature, the journalist went into more detail about Tull's performance style: "Their act lasts one and a half hours and centres on *Aqualung*, the innovative album about a lecherous old man who eyes little girls in the park. Combining that powerful storyline with some strong tunes, the group manages to present a fiercely exciting rock opera, perfectly blending the visual appeal of Anderson with some blisteringly atmospheric music. It's rather cold and heartless music, but how it drives! The musicians are well drilled to act as Ian's foil. They project themselves to varying degrees, the most animated being keyboards man John Evan, who must have seen rather too much of Leon Russell."

"On stage, things are careful and cleverly timed: Ian knows exactly how long to keep an audience waiting before he leaps out for solo acoustic guitar work on 'My God'. Soon after this, he is joined by the rest, blasting out a thundering wall of sound: Jeffrey Hammond-Hammond and Martin Barre, John Evan and Barriemore Barlow, a long-standing friend of Ian, who replaced Clive Bunker on drums at the start of this tour. Anderson is a self-taught flautist whose dexterity and speed on the instrument is quite amazing. He coaxes and caresses it, chants gibberish to it equivalent to scat singing, and really makes it work. That flute is a brilliantly original "trademark" for Jethro. 'With You There To Help Me' follows — after John Evan, an interesting pianist, who believes in physical contortions a la Jerry Lee Lewis. 'Sossity', with Ian on acoustic guitar and with piercing eyes: 'To Cry You A Song', a wild roaring song, giving Ian full reign for leaping and gesticulating about the stage like a man possessed; 'Aqualung', 'Cross-Eyed Mary', 'Nothing Is Easy', then an encore, 'Wind-Up'."

"Anderson leads this band with staggering power and musically he is pretty well backed up. The dazzling guitar work of Martin Barre is especially pungent, providing a powerful sound desperately needed by a group relying every moment on mind-blowing dynamics. At Anaheim, Barre did a solo during the encore that deserved recording, so flashy and note-perfect was it."

The journalist observed of the audience, "With a crowd of 19,000 at the Forum, Ian Anderson was disappointed at the lack of intimacy — but that's one of the penalties of big American crowds. Having come to a concert by a group they dig, thousands of the crowd seem inexplicably happy to roam the auditorium during the actual show. This wrecks any concentration, creates too much noise and scuffle and can give a wrong impression that they don't like the performance. That is not necessarily true. It is simply another peculiar American characteristic which prefers restlessness to concentration."

Anderson commented; "People in the front row rabbiting all the time destroyed my attention and enjoyment. It affects my concentration and it's such a big place that we can't see beyond that first row, we are playing into total blackness beyond the first row, like blowing into the night. It's very disconcerting."

Two days later, Tull were at the Berkley Community Centre, a city that had been slightly sceptical in the past. Perhaps because their work was at one time too extrovert for the many self-appointed "we know where it's at" types who tended to populate the place. But now, before 3,000 plus, Tull were in fantastic form and the reception recognised it. The show began with odd vibes, but Anderson's sledgehammer showmanship, perfect timing and remarkable talent for extricating the band from dodgy situations quickly got a mainly student crowd on their side. They loved his one-legged stance, vulgar jokes and raucous English humour.

Maybe at last British music and style was becoming fashionable in insular San Francisco, for an announcement of a forthcoming concert by Emerson, Lake and Palmer at the same venue received a huge ovation. Of course, there were predictable slogan-chanters in the audience. A report at the time said that one girl nodded her head throughout the show and uttered: "right on" all the time, which was irritating enough to put anyone right off.

But Ian Anderson coped very well with the hippies. San Francisco undoubtedly adopted Jethro Tull because they figured that the group's wild hair and observant songs proved Jethro were on their wavelength — pot smoking and committed.

Anderson retorted; "Those people think that because I look a wild-eyed madman on stage, we all smoke dope, and I'm a freak who's going to bash people over the head with my flute. I am sorry to disappoint them, but we are not a smoking band and, in fact, off that stage we are quiet, well-spoken gentlemen. People are unwilling to believe I can be one person on stage and a different person off."

But America's reputation as more dangerous than the UK appeared to be borne out during this tour. In July a masked gunman held Terry Ellis up in his hotel room on Hollywood's Sunset Strip. The gunman crept in through the hotel room door just as it had been opened, and threatened to shoot Ellis if he didn't give him some money. It was thought that the gunman assumed Ellis had the cash takings from Tull's sell-out concerts from two previous nights at the Forum and the Anaheim.

When Ellis insisted that he didn't have any money, the gunman sped out of the room and down the emergency stairs into a waiting car. Ellis was quoted, "It occurred to me later that he might have given up quickly because of my appearance. He may have thought he had the wrong man as manager because of my hairstyle and the fact that I'm younger than a lot of managers. And anyway, I never carry the group's money around with me in the States. Crazy things happen — like this!"

From gunmen to riots! Under the heading of "Jethro Tull Plays Amid Tear Gas", *Rolling Stone* reported in July 1971; "Ian Anderson wandered on stage at the outset of the June 10th school's-out Jethro Tull concert here at Red Rocks Amphitheatre with tears in his eyes. The other members of Tull were also weeping, not to mention gasping for breath, as was most of the 10,000-strong audience. Swaying, fingering an acoustic guitar, Anderson surveyed the crowd and the Denver police chopper hovering in the distance dispensing periodic charges of tear gas at the rear of the assembly. 'Welcome to World War Three,' he croaked, and the music began."

The music, much of it from Tull's new "spiritual" LP *Aqualung*, went on for the next hour and twenty minutes, and so did the tear gas dispensing. In the wake of the concert, twenty-eight persons, including four Denver policemen and three infants, were treated at area hospitals for injuries received in the disturbances. Dozens more — policemen, concert-goers, and would-be gate-crashers — were treated at the scene by a volunteer medical team. On charges ranging from drunkenness, weapons violations, and possession of narcotics, twenty persons, including three juveniles, were arrested. One car was destroyed by fire, and several other vehicles were reported damaged.

Concert promoter Barry Fey blamed the trouble in part on a throng of ticketless longhairs whom he claimed were lobbing around their own personal canisters of tear gas (purchasable at local drug stores). "Two or three fuckups fucked it up for everybody," he said in the aftermath of the riot, adding that he didn't intend to sponsor any more concerts at Red Rocks. To clinch the deal, Sam Feiner, director of Denver's Theatres-Arenas Division, said he wouldn't allow any more rock events at Red Rocks as a result of the disturbances.

Lt. Jerry Kennedy of the Denver Police department justified the zealous response of his fellow officers at the scene "The show was sold out and about 2,000 people showed up expecting to get in anyway. We gave them the side of a mountain that overlooks the amphitheatre and said they could watch the show there. About 1,500 of them took us up on it. Then some of them began to move through the crowd talking about charging over the wall. One guy had a bugle and started blowing it. When they reached the bottom of the hill, they started throwing rocks at the officers and knocked one off his horse. When another officer went to help the injured one, he was hit on the head with a rock — took five stitches to sew him up. We started spraying the tear gas from a helicopter when a crowd persisted in throwing rocks from an inaccessible point on the hillside. We figured gas beats clubs by a long shot anyway. 'If you don't like the game, get your ass out,' is the way we figured it with them. I got a faceful of gas myself. Fact is, about fifty of the officers didn't have masks and got exposed to the gas."

One of the crew recalled; "I was in the car with Tull, and at first the cops wouldn't let us in. Then we got a special escort. The real trouble started during Liv Taylor's set — all kids outside were chanting 'Fuck you' and 'No more gas.' Then Ian went on and cooled it all out. I've never seen such an incredible energy turnaround. He was playing 'My God', and all those religious numbers from the new album. John Evan was so fogged by the gas, he couldn't even see the piano, and the drummer was having trouble, too. But Ian was awesome. The fumes kept coming, and he kept playing like a motherfucker."

A performance that took place at the Berkeley Community Theatre on summer solstice eve was reported on in *Rolling Stone* in July; "The crowd goes ecstatic. Anderson himself goes all but berserk as he raves against 'the bloody Church of England', hopping about on one leg, grimacing, twitching, gasping, lurching along the apron of the stage, rolling his eyes, paradiddling his arms, feigning flinging snot from his nose, exchanging the guitar for a flute, gnawing on the flute like a baton, gibbering dementedly. The other members of Tull, laid back till now, come in on cue, louder than the last clap of doom. Anderson wiggles his ass at the crowd with a fey flip of the hips that leaves his out-flung wrist limp. John Evan, who resembles an unmade bed with hair spilling out the bolster, hammers maniacally away at the piano. The ferret-faced drummer, Barriemore Barlow, flails savagely at his traps. Martin Barre attacks his guitar as if it were the throat of his foulest enemy. Bassist Jeffrey Hammond-Hammond detonates rhythm lines like thunderclaps. Throughout the evening, Ian Anderson moves like a maniac dancer, emotes like an Actor's Studio dropout."

By October, when *New Musical Express* reported on the New York Madison Square Garden gig, it was evident that Tull had begun working on material for their next album: "Entering the darkened auditorium — blinking from the backstage lighting — a monstrous roar of recognition rings around the bowl, repeat performances greeting Anderson's opening to 'My God' and the band's subsequent arrival on stage. Once they are in their stride, I'm more impressed with their second number, a ten minute composition of varying moods and dynamics that on the new Jethro Tull album — the name of which is announced by Ian as *Thick As A Brick* — has the working title 'Poet And The Painter'."

"It's a good explanation of Anderson's "taking chances", and evidence of a much tighter and adventurous Jethro than that of *Aqualung* and *Benefit*. John Evan's organ playing has a prominent role in that direction, while Barrie Barlow's fleet-footed drum work and Jeffrey's bass perfunctorily kill any ideas that the pair of them got into the band purely for old times', and "old boys'", sake. Over some nifty and exhilarating fast-tempo ensemble playing, Martin Barre's guitar alternatively further fills the gaps or rings out stirringly above the flow. They go on, through 'Aqualung', 'With You There To Help Me' and into 'A New Day Yesterday', similar qualities as those mentioned on 'Poet And Painter' noticeable in the new arrangements of the old material. The roars of approval are more than deafening. As I stand on one side of the stage, the clamour appears to have powers that almost physically cause unbalance. Towards the end of the set, when they get into 'Cross-Eyed Mary' and Barrie's drum solo, a good deal of stroppiness begins to break out at the foot of the stage. They end in a flashing blur of hair and power rock and, when they return for an almost half-hour encore, a cordon of stewards and roadies have to fight away the grappling bodies and arms at the front of the stage."

Despite the positive review, Anderson was struggling with a throat infection, something that had compromised tour dates previously. "I've seen a specialist about it. Apparently I've got a crooked bone in my nose," he said at the time. "I was told that if I had an operation on it and had my tonsils out it would be okay, but it would mean a two month layoff that I'm not prepared to have. I'd rather go on and risk the odd bad gig... I have been ill on every tour. I mean, there is nothing basically wrong with me; I am fairly fit. It is just that it is very arduous being on the road and anything that goes wrong with you becomes magnified because you cannot rest up and take time to recover. Then it becomes a major catastrophe. An ordinary cold can build up to destroy you on stage. The very slightest throat infection, for me as a singer, can turn into laryngitis. If an ordinary guy twists his ankle on the tube he can take the day off to recover. But when 10,000 people have paid for tickets then you have got to go on and take that chance."

"We are basically a live band — that is what people know us for more than the albums, so the touring becomes a part of your life. When you are on tour you are not exactly enjoying it. I mean, you should be enjoying the playing, but you're not going round thinking 'Hey this tour thing is fantastic.' You're more likely to be thinking 'Hey only two weeks and we'll be home.' But the thing is, once you get home and have had a rest, you start getting restless and thinking 'Oh yeah, just two weeks and we can get back on the road again'."

Overall though, things were looking good. Anderson told the American press; "*Aqualung* has been number three in the Australian charts... 'Song For Jeffrey' has been number one in Argentina and number one in Persia and we haven't done the slightest thing to make the band popular in either of those countries. We've never had the time yet."

With his typical deadpan humour he added, "I suppose people in Persia must think 'Oh those

19th February 1971: Norwegian film actress Julie Ege holds the *Benefit* gold disc on behalf of Warner Reprise at the presentation at London's Dorchester Hotel.

    John Evan (front row, left): Ian Anderson (front row, right), and back row, (left to right): Martin Barre, Jeffrey Hammond-Hammond, and Clive Bunker.

    The same month as this presentation, Tull were at Island Studios recording *Aqualung*. Within three months Bunker decided that a more domestic lifestyle was preferred. His last shows were at Filmore East in New York on 5th May.

Anderson with Julie Ege at the Dorchester Hotel. Ege was a Penthouse Pet of May which landed her a role in 1969's *On Her Majesty's Secret Service* as Helen, the "Scandinavian girl". Ege is probably best remembered for her role in the 1971 comedy hit film *Up Pompeii* alongside Frankie Howerd.

buggers Tull, we've bought their records and they never come here'."

At the end of 1971, Jethro Tull had a hit with the single, 'Life Is A Long Song'. It was recorded during a session along with four other tracks just after Clive Bunker had left the band. The session was done as part of Barriemore Barlow's initiation. All of the tracks from that session were released as a maxi single.

Barlow's recruitment was significant as it marked the beginning of what would be a stable line-up for the next five years. With Anderson, Barre, Evan, Hammond-Hammond and Barlow on board, the stage was set for what would be a big year and a landmark album, *Thick As A Brick*.

The mileage of this line-up is not to be understated, for this was the one that would go on to make the iconic albums *A Passion Play* (1973), *War Child* (1974) and *Minstrel In The Gallery* (1975). Anderson told *New Musical Express* in October 1971; "The instrumental ability of the band as a unit is a lot higher than it has been in the past. We are all capable of playing music that Jethro Tull couldn't have played two years ago. Not because the musicians individually are any better, but because as a group now we play better together. What we are doing on the new album is a lot more pleasing than anything we've ever done before. It is more valid from a lot of viewpoints. A lot of that is because we are a lot more together as people."

Much of Jethro Tull's individuality comes from the fact that their music was such an intense mixture of folk, rock, and blues combined with so many surreal ideas and eccentric lyrics. In many ways, as much as people associate the flute with the band's sound, it is still a difficult kind of music to categorise on the basis that ultimately, it is so diverse. All the same, they achieved long term success across a number of albums that went gold and platinum in several countries. In juxtaposition to this, it was often the case that — particularly in their earlier days — Jethro Tull were a misunderstood band on account of their unusual image. The way they dressed and the uniqueness of their music was often commented upon and they attracted fans from a diversity of demographics — those involved with the underground hippie movement and all the drugs and promiscuity that came with that image as well as music fans who related more to what was in the mainstream and deemed as acceptable content for BBC's *Top Of The Pops*. Overall, Jethro Tull would go on to earn their place in popular music history by getting through to all kinds of fans and age groups with their music and lively stage presence.

JETHRO SENSATION! JOURNALIST ENJOYS NEW ALBUM

YES, WELL the rest appears to have done them a power of good.

Although I much enjoyed Guy Peeleart's impression of Ian Anderson in his "Rock Dreams" book — Anderson as an old geezer in a long overcoat sitting on a park bench with his eyes on a little girl — I didn't think it told the whole story.

Maybe in Peeleart's portrait he is merely old before his time, but I'd always thought of him as someone who vaguely remembered food rationing after the war — perhaps he was eight or ten. And he resented it. War babies — they were born in the blitz, and grew up in privation and the nascent Welfare State. They're the sort of people who tell you they lived through a war for you when you spill their drink in a pub, yet they probably weren't properly conscious until it was all over.

Anderson looks as if he knows a ration book when he sees one, and he doesn't want to be reminded.

Tull's new album ["War Child", to be released by Chrysalis within the next few weeks) deals with that kind of stuff. Tea cups clink and people mumble as sirens wail and bombs drop all over the title track. Ian Anderson's writing is sardonic and not without a tinge of bitterness, yet he manages to create an atmosphere both evocative and with perspective. I can't claim to have fully taken in, let alone savoured the nuances of the lyrics of "War Child", but it does seem relatively (and mercifully) free of the rampant propaganda of "Aqualung" and the arrant nonsense of "Passion Play".

What really wins me over is that musically it is vastly more interesting and enjoyable than either of those albums. Tull have long been an efficient band, and recently they've been directed into a series of exercises that I've found stultifyingly tedious. For once, I have not been alone, though it hasn't exactly harmed J. Tull's record sales. This one, in the words of Michael Flanders, is a jolly pleasing noise.

Anderson has the reputation of being the strictest kind of musical Fuehrer, in the past it has showed. On "War Child", either he has changed his methods and allowed the band much more say in arrangement and contribution in performance than before, or he has found a vast new fund of ideas and energy lying around somewhere.

The album does include a lot of what you might call Classic Tull — tricks of style in the arrangements, mannerisms of time and riff, the distinctive nose vocal of the leader which sometimes comes too close to Dave Cousins for comfort. Familiarity breeding what it does, mannerisms and tricks which sounded pretty neat a few years ago sound somewhat uninspired these days: occasionally on this album they become a severe irritant, but mostly they have been absorbed enough into different ideas, or imbued with fresh attack, or used sparingly enough to make them part of what's going on here rather than dredgings of what Did It last time.

After the blitz noises which introduce the first (and title) track, there is piano, violin and humming for a bit until the rhythm section kicks its way in and starts riffing. There is singing and there is riffing a-plenty, with some splendidly discordant piano towards the end, which again features explosions.

"Queen And Country" follows — and you can guess how patriotic that is — in which the band sound not unlike Steeleye Span with a beef injection (perhaps I should say an injection of beefiness into their playing) while strings and (I think) accordian warble with gusto.

"Ladies" starts quiet and acoustic, with neatly interjected handclaps and then strings, and finishes at full gallop. "Back Door Angels" is

perhaps the closest they get to stereotype Tull, but it features some excellent counterpoint sections for strings, organ, bass and guitar. "Sealion" has mannerisms that annoy me, and is fairly straightforward heavy metull.

Side two opens with more tea cups and humming, but no bombs, on "Skating Away On The Thin Ice Of A New Day". Precarious hope dawns and stuff like that. Anderson sounds very much like Roy Harper, starting out softly with voice and acoustic guitar and building to a frantic finish: it's an impressive track.

"Bungle In The Jungle" is almost martial in beat, and for some reason it reminds me of Cream under the hand of Felix Pappalardi — perhaps in the way they've used the drums and voice parts, with guitar punctuation. There is a string section which sounds quite mad.

"Only Solitaire" is a short, pretty piece for voice and acoustic guitars. The main feature of "The Third Hoorah" is something that sounds like an electric harpsichord, but which could quite easily be some kind of synthesised device, played with flying but very accurate fingers in a solo which chatters on behind two verses after its own feature as if the brakes couldn't stop it in time. Strings and accordian (again, I think) also put in a welcome appearance.

The final track is "Two Fingers" which I find somewhat throwaway, very stylised and not much fun. The album lasts for just over 38 minutes, should you wish to know.

I leave you with this thought, penned by Mr. Anderson and contained in "Two Fingers". He says: You'd better leave your underpants with someone you can trust."

How right he is too.

STEVE PEACOCK

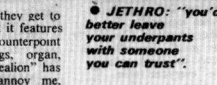

● JETHRO: "you'd better leave your underpants with someone you can trust".

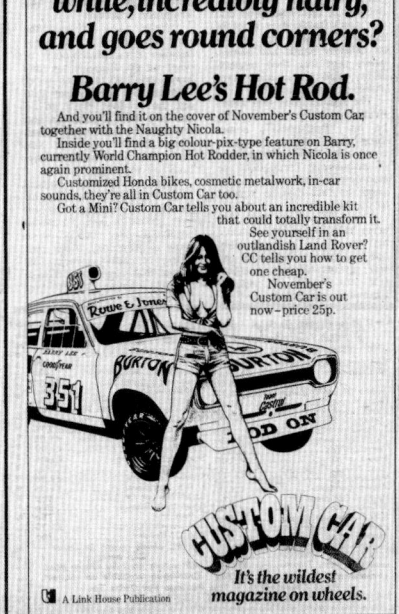

What's 14ft long, white, incredibly hairy, and goes round corners?

Barry Lee's Hot Rod.

And you'll find it on the cover of November's Custom Car, together with the Naughty Nicola.

Inside you'll find a big colour-pix-type feature on Barry, currently World Champion Hot Rodder, in which Nicola is once again prominent.

Customized Honda bikes, cosmetic metalwork, in-car sounds, they're all in Custom Car too.

Got a Mini? Custom Car tells you about an incredible kit that could totally transform it.

See yourself in an outlandish Land Rover? CC tells you how to get one cheap.

November's Custom Car is out now - price 25p.

It's the wildest magazine on wheels.

A Link House Publication

Performing at the Concertgebouw in Amsterdam, 12th February 1972. The second of two Dutch shows. Jeffrey Hammond-Hammond and Martin Barre sport the leading fashions of the day, which surely were regularly seen in any city at the time?

© Gijsbert Hanekroot / Alamy Stock Photo

Part Two: 1972-75

The early to mid-seventies were a vital time in Jethro Tull's tenure. From the beginning of 1972 through to the end of 1975, they would release four albums — *Thick As A Brick* (1972), *A Passion Play* (1973), *War Child* (1974) and *Minstrel In The Gallery* (1975) — each of which would go on to play a significant role in the band's legacy. Having formed in the late sixties, gone through multiple line-up changes and having established a strong musical identity by the time of *Aqualung*'s release in 1971, Jethro Tull had a lot of scope to take things further and indeed, that's exactly what they would do.

With Barriemore Barlow having joined in May '71, the band were at the beginning of what would be a long-term phase of stability. This line-up took advantage of their strong working rapport to create an ambitious album, *Thick As A Brick*. Despite his initial reluctances about being in the music industry when he had first joined Tull in January 1971, Jeffrey Hammond-Hammond was wholeheartedly on board by the time it came to making *Thick As A Brick*. Rehearsals for the album took place in the Rolling Stones' studio in Bermondsey. It was initially the case that the music wasn't going to be a single continuous piece. The band came up with individual segments and then elected to write short pieces of music to link everything together. Recording began in December 1971 at Morgan Studios in London.

With previous Jethro Tull albums, Ian Anderson had generally written the songs in advance but *Thick As A Brick* was much more spontaneous overall; a lot of it was actually written during the recording sessions. *Thick As A Brick* was built up day by day; Ian Anderson got up early each morning to prepare music for the rest of the band to work on in the afternoon. The lyrics were written first, with the music constructed to fit around them. Some sections were recorded in a single take with every band member putting ideas forward, including significant contributions from keyboard player, John Evan. For the recording, a minimum of fifteen different instruments were played by the band. Ergonomically, this exceeded what Tull had done on their four earlier studio albums and inevitably, it showcased the level of skill within the band by that point.

Some of this music had been played on stage prior to going into the recording studio. In November 1971, *Billboard* reported on their performance in New York; "At Madison Square Garden on October 18th where Jethro Tull appeared, attention focussed on Ian Anderson, lead vocal and flutist, for his mischievous antics that were sometimes playful, sometimes demoniac, but always full of craft and sorcery. The act began with a long song about evils of society and plastic religion — favourite themes for this British rock group. They did songs from their latest album, *Aqualung*, and some from one they plan to release this February, tentatively titled *Thick As A Brick*, British slang for numbskull. Tull's lyrics tend to have a fairytale quality about them, like medieval British legends. The music also borrowed some of the sounds of that period in their history, especially during John Evan's organ solos, but it was quite evident that the performance and sound was a style all their own." (On 18th November 1971, Jethro Tull finished the American leg of the *Aqualung* tour. They set to work on writing and recording *Thick As A Brick* straight away. They began another tour on 6th January 1972).

The *Thick As A Brick* era following 1971's *Aqualung*, cemented the band's identity; they were unique compared to other bands in that they had long left their blues influences and underground reputation behind. Not only that, but they still stood out in comparison to other groups who at the time were labelled as progressive. The line-up was clearly working happily together. Ian Anderson told *New Musical Express* in March 1973; "I'm the only original member left, but we are very much together as a group. When a group has existed a few years, one learns to tolerate other people. I don't believe in The Who's we-hate-each-other gimmick which they used in the beginning. I really think they are as together as a group as we are. The other members of the band aren't just musicians — they are friends."

Thick As A Brick was successful in both the UK and the US. It got to number five in the UK and quickly reached number one on the Billboard 200 chart in June 1972. Notably it didn't take long for the record to make a commercial impact. *Record World* reported in June 1972; "*Thick As A Brick*, the recently released album by Jethro Tull, has been certified gold by the RIAA, signifying sales of over one million dollars. *Aqualung* and *Benefit*, Jethro Tull's last two Reprise albums, were also certified gold."

Cash Box reviewed *Thick As A Brick* in May 1972; "The long awaited Jethro Tull album has finally arrived. Unlike the group's previous efforts, this time around, Ian Anderson has written an epic poem, if you will — so in actuality, *Thick As A Brick* contains a single song. Basically, the LP demonstrates the band's versatility as musicians capable of changing moods and timings in a moment's notice. Needless to say, this effort will follow *Aqualung* into the gold vaults."

Billboard reviewed it in the same month; "Ian Anderson and friends have a penchant for creating albums that delight, amaze and thoroughly entertain, *Thick As A Brick* being no exception. It is a suitable successor to the genius that was *Aqualung*, the wildly enigmatic imagery producing a spellbinding fascination. There are no individual songs as such, simply side one and two with no separation between the grooves."

Melody Maker reviewed the album in March 1972; "As the album is already brilliantly reviewed on the elaborately produced sleeve, there is hardly any point in adding our own comments. Ian Anderson's latest work consists of a poem wrapped in a newspaper. And a local newspaper of doubtful authenticity — the "St Cleve Chronicle" — I have heard informed observers remark: 'This is the silliest cover ever seen' — one can merely add that the joke at the expense of a local newspaper wears thin rather rapidly, but should not detract from the obvious amount of thought and work that has gone into the production of *Thick*. There are some twelve pages of painstaking material in the cod newspaper, which must have given Gerald "Little Milton" Bostock and Ian Anderson a lot of fun, and a considerable headache to the staff of Chrysalis, who spent a lot of time preparing the sleeve and photographs."

"But what of the music? It's a lot to take in a brief test run of the album. It needs time to absorb. Heard out of context of their highly visual stage act, it does not have such immediate appeal. But there is not quite the same doomy quality that *Aqualung* had; the ideas flow in super abundance, making me suspect this will receive similar if not greater acclaim. An intense level of performance is maintained throughout this long work, while not quite as battering as some of the extended works of, say, ELP. Ian's flute playing seems greatly improved. Not to say that it was below standard before, but he does seem to have taken care over increasing his ability on the instrument. Barriemore Barlow is a fine drummer who roars around his kit with lightning dexterity, and punches home the arrangements, while the Tull sound blossoms forth under the combined efforts of Martin Barre's reliable guitar and John Evan's excellent keyboard work. The band seem to be more co-operate now and each member pulls his weight most effectively. As the sleeve note says: 'Not blatantly commercial then, but a fine disc which although possessing many faults should do well enough.' We'd like to add that only time can Tull."

It was also reviewed in *Sounds* the same month; "One of the most disillusioning experiences of my musical life occurred when I saw Jethro Tull for the second time. It was three weeks after the first time, when I'd enjoyed them a lot — they were musically strong, and Ian Anderson had a fine stage presence, cracking lots of little comments and asides. I took it for a clever spontaneous performance. Then I saw them again, and everything was exactly the same — practically every note of the music (bar the goofs) and all the jokes and asides. I can't help feeling that someone who has his ad-libs rehearsed that carefully needs watching a little carefully, and I've been a little wary of Jethro Tull ever since, especially when I found successive albums breaking little new ground, and doing little more than refining down and adjusting slightly a concept stated on the first album."

"Ian Anderson has borrowed and created his own clichés, and stays with them — even on this new album. Apart from him, the band is completely changed from the first record, and there's no doubt that it's good — but limited, I think, by the Tull format. Martin Barre and John Evan especially come through with some fine playing, but they don't really break any new or particularly exciting ground; they get so far and seem to hit an undefined but quite recognisable wall of policy. I get the feeling that the band is being used as an effects box, as sidemen to a central idea that isn't really strong enough to justify its role."

"That central idea is Ian Anderson's new monster work *Thick As A Brick*, a long, related sequence of songs which reflects a bitter, cynical view of the world around him and the people who run it — businessmen, the church, schools... you know the things. That obviously is a vast over-simplification of the work, but I think Ian Anderson too is guilty of over-simplification — somehow *Thick As A Brick* sounds to me like a bit of an empty gesture, a hollow threat. There's nothing in there that hasn't been said before — though he does put it quite well — and I don't find much in there to jolt me, to catch my imagination. Maybe these things need saying over and over again, but does it really need a whole album to say it? I think not, but doubtless thousands will disagree."

Rolling Stone reviewed *Thick As A Brick* in June 1972; "For all its intricacy, the "theme" or poetry of *Thick As A Brick* is its least important aspect. Anderson's language (in *Aqualung* as well) is often wordy and ponderous, and its bitter condescension and breadth of denunciation can be unpleasant. What marks this album as a significant departure from other Jethro Tull work, and rock in general, is the organisation of all its music into one continuous track. Albums like *Sgt. Pepper* or *Tommy* were complete entities in themselves, but still chose to use songs as their basic components. While sections of *Thick As A Brick* are melodically distinct, they all inherently relate to each other. What connecting there is, is uncontrived and is often the occasion for some of the album's boldest playing. The lyrics, clever and dense as they are, are chiefly valuable as a premise for the music. The album's opening is sprightly, with Ian's flute poking in and out; a more introspective, minor key digression follows, then a stalking bass line, accompanied by horns and John Evan's excited Rick Wakeman-like organ. The relentless and mechanical gives way to something very stately and regal, as English as, yet less folksy than the opening passage. The piano plays arpeggios; Anderson overlays a jazzy flute. Some overdubbed guitar yammerings follow. Anderson takes to the violin and creates a whirling, macabre setting for the combative son's announcement, 'I've come down from the upper class…' As the other son begins to speak, the music becomes milder, then sunnier. A bell-like organ rings out behind a jig, performed in almost telegraphic rhythm. This, and its reprise on side two, is the album's most attractive section. An ominous heraldic organ shatters the calm, and the side ends with the electric guitar shrieking helplessly, like a wounded bird."

"Side two reintroduces side one's second statement. It merges into an energetic though hollow, unemphatic drum solo; then some free jazz, over which a set of lyrics is recited. A rather fine English folk melody emerges. Anderson's voice becomes more severe, a classical guitar is introduced, and the music takes an Iberian turn. A harpsichord plays as a guitar repeats the riff from George Harrison's 'Wah Wah'. The writing becomes very linear, with rapid harmonic shifts. This alternates with a vaulting melodic figure. Then a sudden whoosh, and we return to the closing theme of side one, now strongly reinforced by the organ, only to be momentarily interrupted by some expansive strings. As almost a postscript, the initial theme is recalled, and with it the sentiment, (the reviewer quoted the final lyrics on side two here). The members of Jethro Tull were hand-picked by Anderson (several are old school chums); no one, save Ian, remains from the original band. The playing, not surprisingly, is tight as a drum. Martin Barre's guitar and John Evan's keyboards especially shine, and Ian's singing is no longer abrasive. Whether or not *Thick As A Brick* is an isolated experiment, it is nice to know that someone in rock has ambitions beyond the four or five minute conventional track, and has the intelligence to carry out his intentions, in all their intricacy, with considerable grace."

New Musical Express also reviewed the album in March 1972 under the thought provoking title, "Brick — Is This Jethro's Tommy?"; "Ian Anderson's ultimate epic; with lyrics, allegedly, by one Gerald Bostock. And it's on lyrics that *Thick As A Brick* stands or falls. Personally it took me several listenings before I was able to make up my mind. I've finally decided I like it. Encased in a fine and well-designed sleeve (resembling a banal local newspaper), *Thick As A Brick* is an assault on the mediocrity and harshness of lower middle class existence in seventies Britain. The set opens with a quiet acoustic guitar passage from Anderson in alternating 3/4 and 4/4 time. Anderson sings the main refrain in couplets while the piece slowly builds with piano flourishes and the occasional powerful stab from the rest of the band. A clean guitar phrase from Barre leads into a short organ solo from John Evan. Building all the time, several machine gun riffs lead into the second major theme, preceded by a short flute break. 'The Poet And The Painter', although majestic, suffers a little from banal lyrics. A long, slightly rambling guitar solo follows and then guitar and organ swap phrases before leading into a long instrumental passage in which Evan has the spotlight all to himself. His organ work flaps a little, and resembles Sandy McPherson at times — no doubt intentionally. The piece turns into a 2/4 march — still building — in which organ states and flute answers. The final section of the first side is musically a folky jingle which develops into downright carnival music. At this point the whole *Brick* piece starts to get a little less strong lyrically but stronger musically. Side one ends with a three-beat pulse that is repeated, gradually mixing in echo, until the only thing left is the echo response."

"Side two opens in a similar way, then drops into an amazingly fast 6/8 passage, slightly reminiscent of ELP on 'Bitches Crystal'. This feeling is enhanced when new drummer Barriemore Barlow takes a solo that, for all its warmer production, resembles Carl Palmer's work. He finishes with overdubbed timpani. The drum solo introduces a free-blowing passage, interspersed by spoken words from Jeffrey Hammond-Hammond. Cacophonous, but it's probably intended to be. From now on the album degenerates. Lyrics and music get a bit boring, and the earlier inspiration seems to have died — although the arrangements and link-passages are still as exacting as ever. Shortly before the end an orchestra has about eight bars' worth of track then it's back to the original theme — both musically and lyrically — for the wind-up. Throughout the album Jethro play extremely well and very tightly, and it's obviously intended to be Jethro Tull's own stand-or-fall epic after the lines of *Tommy*. To Tullheads it will, of course, succeed; personally, I have some doubts."

New Musical Express also reappraised the album in July; "Most recent Tull album — ignoring the retrospective *Living In The Past* — is *Thick As A Brick*, which Ian obviously regards as Jethro's most important set to date. Musically and lyrically there is a definite lineage here with *Aqualung* — the points regarding America are again relevant. Yet whereas with *Aqualung* it was the lyrics that returned to a common idea, on *Brick* both lyrics and music have a linking theme. The degree of success varies enormously. In parts Anderson's lyrics can be eloquent and surreal, in others they border on the banal. In parts, musically, the use of light and shading is impressively effective, while elsewhere there's a total lack of subtlety, almost an overkill. Or worse, predictability. Listening to the album again this week, I felt too that I noticed a certain glibness about the music which I'm sure was never in Ian's head when he composed the piece. Then again there are passages like the poet and painter episode that hit just the right note of purity and poetry. It's on the lyrics, really, though, that *Brick* should be judged. Here, they're not as personalised as on, say, 'Wind-Up' from *Aqualung*, but at the same time they manage to encapsulate most of the feelings Anderson had been hinting at in earlier songs... the way that the life of the common man, whoever he may be — the one 'geared to the average rather than the exceptional' — is merely a tool in the hands of the same elitist group who, on the *Aqualung* set, elected God as the figurehead. Also the same elitist anonymous figures who govern and predestine the life of the common man, and worse still dismiss him with contempt as "thick as a brick", thereby stripping him of feeling."

It's possible that *Thick As A Brick* was released later than planned in the UK (and thus America) due to what was going on outside of the band's control. In the UK, the coal miners' strike began on 9th January 1972, and at that time three quarters of the electricity used in the UK was produced by coal-burning power stations. A state of emergency was declared on 9th February, and the miners voted to return to work on 25th February. There was an advert in *New Musical Express* on 26th February 1972 that stated, "*Thick As A Brick* now on sale" but the album was actually released on Friday 3rd March 1972. Essentially, it is plausible that the impact of the coal miners' strike may have caused a delay in the album's release.

Due to how it contains one continuous piece of music across both sides of the LP, many people regarded *Thick As A Brick* as a concept album. The lyrics were based on a poem by Ian Anderson's fictional young prodigy character by the name of Gerald Bostock. The idea behind the character was that he was almost like an exaggerated version of the young Ian Anderson (over the years, the age of the character has been quoted as being anything between eight and twelve years old). Intelligent beyond his years with the world at his feet, Bostock is at an impressionable stage in his life and trying to find his way in the world.

As Ian Anderson put it in an interview on Australian TV in July 1972; "In the case of *Thick As A Brick*, it started off from one line. The concept, or concepts, expressed in the music, or in the lyrics, is that everyone's right. And the necessity, I think, should be apparent for everyone to decide, to make their own judgment on things in their own way, regardless of age or experience, or even intelligence. We have at one end of the scale, the intellectual society, who are necessarily making judgments on people on the other end of the scale who may be thick as a brick — 'Your wise men don't know how it feels to be thick as a brick' — How the hell can they decide for the man in the street what he should want?"

As much as the idea was centred on the Gerald Bostock character, the lyrics are abstract enough that they had universal appeal, so much so that over the years, Anderson has been keen to advocate that it is not his place to clarify an exact and concrete meaning behind them, or indeed any of his lyrics. He has often advocated strongly against over analysing his music.

He was quoted in *Down Beat* in March 1976; "As soon as I begin to analyse my approach to playing music on stage, it then becomes a very deliberate and conscious dissemination of what I'm doing. And as soon as it becomes that, it immediately goes against the grain of the music I write and play. I don't sit down and say today I'm going to write a song that's going to be about this or that and then calculate a means of arriving at that end. Whatever I write — a forty second piece or a forty minute one — has always begun its life as a pure emotional feeling or observation. The act of building that into a finished recording is, of course, to a large extent, contrived, in as much as it's a conscious effort to derive a relationship between life and music and lyrics and put it into a sort of professionally embodied package and then sell it to the consumer and make money. All of that is a very conscious thing. I'm aware of all that, but I don't want to start getting any of that mixed up with the essence of what music is all about and the essence of what being a performer of music is all about."

The album art features a satirical impression of a local English newspaper. It contains all of the usual mundane and quirky sections that would be found in a real local newspaper — deaths and marriages, puzzles and advertisements. Upon telling manager and head of Chrysalis Records, Terry Ellis that he wanted to have a newspaper as part of the album art, Anderson was initially met with some reluctance. Ellis pointed out to Anderson that from the record company's point of view, it would be laborious and expensive to do. Anderson's argument was that if newspapers can be produced so quickly en masse on a day to day basis, then why wouldn't the record company be able to do it. Eventually, Anderson managed to get Ellis on board with the idea.

It wasn't expensive to create the content of the newspaper for *Thick As A Brick* because the band themselves contributed to it and had fun in doing so. In later years Anderson stipulated that it actually took the band longer to create the cover than it did to make the actual music for the album but all the same, they didn't have to get anybody else in to do the work. Anderson did just over half of it with Hammond-Hammond and Evan contributing a significant amount thereafter.

Chrysalis' Royston Eldridge helped with the layout — putting everything into columns and suchlike. He had previously worked as a music journalist for a local newspaper so the whole project was something that he was very much at home with. Chrysalis actually gave him a few weeks off from his usual duties in order that he could get the newspaper finished. The crossword puzzle in the middle was made by Hammond-Hammond. Some fans even took to sending their answers in to the band. There is also a dot-to-dot puzzle that once completed, shows a rude picture. At the time, Jethro Tull were very much influenced by the comedy style of Monty Python (in later years, Anderson stipulated that *Thick As A Brick* was intended to be a spoof album and tongue-in-cheek).

In the album's newspaper is a review from one Julian Stone-Mason BA, another fictional character through whom Anderson penned some interesting ideas: "One doubts at times the validity of what appears to be an expanding theme throughout the two continuous sides of this record but the result is at worst entertaining and at least aesthetically palatable. Poor, or perhaps naïve taste is responsible for some of the ugly changes of time signature and banal instrumental passages linking the main sections but ability in this direction should come with maturity."

When *Rolling Stone* reviewed *Thick As A Brick* in June 1972, there was much attention paid to the newspaper; "Written around a poem by St Cleve child prodigy Gerald Bostock, their music spins a delicate web of sensitive sounds: sometimes lilting, sometimes soaring to form a brilliant backdrop for the meaningful lyrics and improvisational techniques... ('One doubts at times the validity of what appears to be an expanding theme throughout the two continuous sides of this record but the result is at worst entertaining and at least aesthetically palatable') — Ian Anderson (a.k.a. Julian Stone-Mason BA) has not only slyly reviewed his own album, he's also supplied the newspaper which contains it. Like so much flounder, *Thick As A Brick* comes wrapped in the St Cleve's Chronicle, an apocryphal yet typical daily of Anderson's design. Played across the front page is the Gerald "Little Milton" Bostock scandal (the epithet refers to the author of *Paradise Lost*, not the soul singer). Eight-year-old Gerald is adjudged unfit to accept first prize from The Society for Literary Advancement and Gestation (SLAG) by virtue of the questionable contents of his epic poem, *Thick As A Brick*. Gerald is one of Ian Anderson's incarnations and ruses."

"Besides lyricist and impersonator, Anderson is also composer, arranger, singer, flutist, acoustic guitarist, violinist, saxophonist, trumpeter, satirist and overall composer. His adeptness at most of these functions, in particular, his ability to balance and fuse them, has created one of rock's most sophisticated and groundbreaking products. Most of the Chronicle's features display a dry, fatuous, very English sense of humour. Under the 'Deaths' column, there is the late Charles Stiff; and stories have titles along the lines of 'Mongrel Dog Soils Actor's Foot' and 'Non-Rabbit Missing' — Characters in, say, a page two story will turn up again on page five in equally ludicrous circumstances. It is all very clever, yet at first seemingly irrelevant. Page seven carries the words to *Thick As A Brick*. The writing is very dense and enigmatic, and the unidentified shifts in narrative voice compound the difficulty. The poem, as best I can make out, is a sweeping social critique, as pessimistic about poets, painters and the generally virtuous as it is condemnatory of politicians and other figures of authority. And what more perfectly encompasses or embodies the world Anderson aims to criticise than a daily newspaper? The paper in turn encompasses the poem. Furthermore, there are names in the poem which refer back to items in the newspaper. The poem "reviews" the newspaper, just as Stone-Mason reviewed the record. The entire package operates with the allusiveness of a Nabokov novel."

In March 1972, *New Musical Express* reported on Jethro Tull's tour plans; "In case you didn't know already, Jethro Tull are big business. About to undertake their biggest-ever British tour, the group have just returned from Europe, where they broke house records in Berlin, Frankfurt and Rome — the records having been previously held by the Stones and Zeppelin. The tour, which starts today (Thursday) and goes on until March 28th, will also be the first British gig for new Tullman, drummer Barrie Barlow. Barlow, who replaced Clive Bunker, has already done a couple of Jethro tours in America, where the band is now among the top half dozen rock attractions. On the British tour, Jethro will be playing almost every day, and the sell-out reports have already started rolling in. Portsmouth, Bristol, Birmingham, Newcastle, Norwich, Oxford, Manchester and Sheffield have all sold out at least two weeks in advance. The Albert Hall reports that it will be sold out within a day or so — the only tickets they have left are those for 60p. To tie in with the tour, Jethro this week release their cleverly advertised and much-awaited new album *Thick As A Brick*. Support group for the tour is the Irish folk duo Tir Na Nog, who played some of their earliest British dates on a Jethro tour. Since then they've added experience to their skill and have carved themselves a nice little reputation."

Melody Maker reported in March 1972; "Jethro Tull open their biggest ever British tour tonight at the Portsmouth Guildhall and already sell out signs are up outside halls up and down the country."

On tour, *Thick As A Brick* was a large scale performance. It was often played in its entirety. Solos and comedy sketches were added. A lot of skill and thought clearly went into the whole thing. So much so that with the earlier shows on the tour, Martin Barre recalled them as being a "terrible experience" due to the complexity of the music and the changes in time signatures.

New Musical Express reviewed the opening night's performance of the UK tour in March 1972; "Portsmouth Guildhall was packed to capacity on the opening night of Jethro Tull's current tour. With one or two minor reservations, the audience got its money's worth. The tour, Jethro's biggest ever in the UK, is also the first British tour for new drummer Barriemore Barlow, who replaced Clive Bunker shortly before the last US tour. Jethro are enormous in the US, of course, and the mistakes were the result of lack of acclimatisation with British audiences. US concerts are larger, seat more people, and therefore require more obvious stage presentation. English audiences are more subtle and on a couple of occasions Jethro seemed to have forgotten that. The show was fast, furious, skilful and colourful though. Anderson spreads the spotlight more than he used to, and each member of the group got a section — either musical or humorous — all to himself. 'A new Jethro', commented photographer Robert Ellis."

"Tull arrived on stage in peculiar fashion and proceeded to launch their new sociological/scatological epic, *Thick As A Brick*. A review of this appears on page ten this week, suffice for me to add the live performance is fast, technically perfect and even the hardest Tullheads in the front stalls were delighted and confused at the same time. Ian Anderson, dressed in black knee breeches and chequered coat tails, still catfoots around the stage like a combination of Max Wall and Mephisto. Almost vaudeville and almost high camp, but most of all pure Anderson (yes, he still stands on one leg). Martin Barre, dressed in a baggy suit of appalling hound's tooth, contributed careful guitar work with his usual diffidence, Jeffrey Hammond-Hammond, attired in revolting lime green tails, moved well with a curious jerky dancing motion, and played precision bass work throughout. Barlow drummed solidly and crisply, and his solo, which took place in the second half of the concert, was very fast and skilful — rather after the manner of Carl Palmer. John Evan, looning from piano (stage left) to organ (stage right) resembled a dissolute planter, with his crumpled white suit and his wild hair and beard and all. His looning was itself a put-on of Anderson's own unique movements, and on one occasion it got out of hand — so much so that Ian had to forcefully lead the raving Evan back to the organ stool and seat him upon it."

"There was a curious interlude between *Thick As A Brick* and the closing pieces. It was, I think, "humour", and it took the form of a comic dialogue between Hammond and Evan. It was well intentioned, but I personally didn't think it very funny. It didn't last long. Anderson was soon back, and he launched into 'Cross-Eyed Mary', which was received deliriously by the Tullheads. 'New Day Yesterday' followed, and finally 'Wind-Up'. All of these pieces were skilfully linked by taped voices, discussing the act, and the timing of these tapes, like the immaculate timing of the music itself plus other "effects", was a revelation."

"Off they went, and came back for the statutory encore. And this, in my opinion, was one place that Tull miscalculated. Prior to the last number, legions of fans had rushed the stage, obviously peaking in excitement. But the encore proved too long and too dynamically slow to retain this mass high. Martin Barre played a long and slightly un-worked-out guitar solo which left me cold (in contrast to his fine work earlier in the performance) and the whole thing was allowed to droop unnecessarily. But it was the first night of the tour, Jethro Tull are a highly professional and original band, and no doubt things will be adjusted."

In the same month, the comparison to The Who's rock opera was alluded to in *Melody Maker*. They reviewed the performance at length under the title of "Tull's *Tommy*?"; "One-legged pop flautist Ian Anderson caused a storm in the press world this week when he refused to comment on his latest "pop" recording, *Thick As A Brick*, or his recent concert at Portsmouth Guildhall described in many quarters as 'obscene', 'disgusting' and 'deafening'. From a telephone box, somewhere in Beckenham, his representative told a *Melody Maker* reporter on Sunday night: 'Ian doesn't want to talk about his concerts or the album until he has read the reviews' — Whitehall experts, China watchers and spokesmen said early this morning: 'This latest development will be viewed with some concern. Does it mean the end of the entente cordiale or is it a subterfuge to throw the Western alliance into confusion? These are the questions informed sources will be asking themselves — tomorrow afternoon. News At Ten, Catford, Monday.' So Jethro Tull won't talk eh? Never mind, this is nothing new in the "pop business". In 1932 the Canadian pop singer George Smith refused to speak to local radio stations for many weeks until he received an official apology for being described as 'that awful singer' during a broadcast discussion. Again, in the late fifties, rock balladeer Brian Barnes was notorious for his refusal to comment on his rare performances."

"But it remains a disquieting moment when the clamp-down of silence comes and we are left to blindly form our own opinions. Stumbling through the morass of conflicting evidence, I can only say that *Thick As A Brick* is a work that will receive as much acclaim as *Tommy*, and cause the trans-oceanic cables to hum with an excited chatter. The album work forms a major part of the new Tull stage act and is based on an impressive poem by one Gerald Bostock. It's one of those poems that fixes one with a penetrating gaze and snaps somewhat bitterly: 'I may make you feel but I can't make you think.' It goes on to say: 'I've come down from the upper class to mend your rotten ways.' Well you'll just have to read the poem, and fortunately it's all included in a massive sleeve note to the album, produced to read and look like a local newspaper. Whatever the interpretations placed upon Mr Bostock's lyrical flight, it has certainly inspired the men of Tull to new heights."

The feature continued; "The opening night of their first British tour in a year, at Portsmouth, was the best rehearsed and most cleverly executed show staged by a rock band. Their performance came somewhere between the musical excellence of Yes and the inventive audacity of the Mothers Of Invention. Many groups have tried a little stage "business", but few have succeeded in pulling it off so well. Even if their humour is not always hilarious in its written aspect, the natural humour of any Ian Anderson performance, and the perfect support he receives from Jeffrey Hammond-Hammond and John Evan, produces an impact that is quite unique. Their timing is superb and their ability to virtually play with an audience is quite fascinating. Near my seat in the back of the Guildhall, there were a few lads ready to shout the odd comment in their rustic simplicity. But even they were slightly stunned by the barrage of pre-recorded tapes, startling use of stage props, lights, and dynamics that in turn baffled, amused and finally delighted a crowd who responded by roaring great cheers of approval."

"My first impressions of the album were not enough to gain a full appreciation of *Brick*. And I still would prefer to hear them playing this massive work "live". At the concert they opened with a complete version of the *Brick* saga which lasted some forty-five minutes, with barely a pause. In fact Jethro were so ready to give us a mass of music, Ian was moved to apologise for the discomfort caused to patrons glued to their seats for a show that eventually lasted nearly three hours. 'It's a bit like Ben Hur,' he admitted solicitously."

"Despite the security clampdown, word has filtered through that the Tull men would prefer us not to reveal all the little dodges they get up to during the show, and as it would be rather like yelling 'Tony Perkins dun it', at a second house queue for *Psycho*, I shall merely say that I enjoyed the telephone, the tent and the men in white coats. And the playing was pretty good as well. New drummer (to Britain at any rate), Barriemore Barlow, proved a fast, accurate and hard-hitting percussionist, who played a dynamite solo and snap-locked on to the arrangements with great tenacity. The interplay between Ian and John Evan's educated piano and organ work was a source of great satisfaction, and stalwart Tullian, Martin Barre, while not a great soloist, lent just the right form of attack or subtlety, where needed. John's organ sometimes tended to be a bit over-loud, as did the whole band during their heavier moments."

"Still a wondrous sight in this age of modern marvels is that of Ian Anderson, dancing about the stage like some mad Austrian music master. He once told me his brother had ballet lessons and some of it rubbed off. I can well believe this when watching Mr Tull arch his body backwards, hair cascading over narrow shoulders, while his legs splay in many directions. He conducts his fellow musicians with mocking absurdity, and one of the funniest moments in the show came when John Evan, himself a strange galumphing figure, like the male lead in a Chekhov comedy, began a berserk imitation of his leader, only to be lead gently back to the organ and put firmly in his place. Amidst the clowning, as good as any vaudeville act in northern cabaret, Ian also plays a mean flute. It seemed to me his technique has been much improved, and that a considerable amount of practice has been put in. His melodic tone and ability to blow hard and soft on a difficult instrument has always been there. But some notably fast runs came through and some beautifully constructed phrasing that shows Ian ain't always fooling when it comes to fluting."

"It will be interesting to see the show again after a few days on the road have elapsed. Will they be able to sustain the comic interludes? Will they tighten up the "encore" which ran on too long at Portsmouth and gave us a surfeit of goodies? *Thick As A Brick* was a lot of music to take for an audience that had never heard any of it before. Its success was self-evident. The cheers were for all the effort the band had put into writing and playing the stuff, and not, as is often the case, for instantly recognisable material, easy to assimilate. The premiere of such a piece of craftsmanship is not an everyday occurrence, and Jethro Tull can be proud of their contribution to the arts and sciences of rock."

In April, *Record Mirror* reviewed the first of three performances that took place at the Royal Albert Hall; "It's nearly time for Jethro Tull's set on a dimly lit stage on Tuesday (21st March), and there are these five roadies all dressed in neat white Bogart macs and tartan caps, doing the last minute adjustments. Or could it be Jethro Tull? Confusion builds as similarly hairy individuals in identical garb slowly filter out from the various stage entrances until there are a round dozen on stage. The situation is resolved at length when seven of them fade back into the wings and the genuine Jethros hang their uniforms on a hat stand and launch straight into *Thick As A Brick*. Jethro Tull really don't miss a trick — even such mundanities, as their arrival on stage is handled with style, imagination and wit. They kept up the standard right through almost two hours of non-stop music interrupted only by some brief interludes of some Pythonesque Tull humour."

"While *Thick As A Brick* is slightly disappointing on record, it comes alive in the extended stage version, aided by Ian Anderson's masterly use of the stage and lightning switches from comedy to drama and back. Despite personnel changes over the years, Jethro Tull has always played superbly as a unit. But as usual, it was Anderson who stole the show musically as well as visually. His flute pumps along fiercely like none in pop did before him and his two solos during the new work were excellent: the first hovered and fluttered round the Albert Hall like a giant bird, the second was perfectly punctuated train rhythm. For good measure, the new theme was followed by 'A New Day Yesterday', an early Tull classic, and most of *Aqualung*. The latter particularly shows that if Anderson had not decided to lead a rock band, he could have made it as a solo acoustic singer-songwriter. Tull's absence from this country has prevented the group from attaining quite the reputation it deserves. Hopefully, their current month-long tour will change that. Obviously, the group still enjoys playing here, and Anderson admitted, 'This is the only country where we'd dare to try something new' — They get my vote for Best Concert of '72 so far, by a short head from Randy Newman."

Melody Maker also reviewed the same performance; "For some time, there have been threats by prominent groups that they will bring circus effects to their shows: clowns, elephants, jugglers and the Big Top. It's reassuring to find showbiz is alive in rock and that theatricality is never far away — but Jethro Tull prove that such excesses are totally unnecessary for them. Their own circus is all-human, totally man-made and all the better for that. The general misconception of the group as being one man in check pants standing on one leg playing a flute is quickly being wiped out, and musically they are coming up fast and strong as one of our most biting, creative units with a penchant for well-written, extended works."

"Ian Anderson is, of course, still cavorting around brilliantly, playing the Pied Piper, and Martin Barre still plays the fall guy in their unfunny attempts to be funny. But at London's Albert Hall last Tuesday, Anderson demonstrated again why Jethro's popularity is still building and why they are jamming concert halls with the converted throughout Britain. It's because they are a perfect blend of rock and showbiz. From the moment they came out disguised in white raincoats and flat caps and wandered about the stage, unrecognised by the audience, until they left two and a half hours later, very few eyes could have stopped focusing on their magnetic presence, their overwhelming drive."

"Their new album, *Thick As A Brick*, is attempting to become the tour de force that once was *Aqualung* alone. Ian is an underrated acoustic guitarist who opened the show in style, and his flute playing flows cleanly. Yet he should beware of over-long solos and of waiting for too long for the dynamics of guitars to bring back the pace. When the guitars do return, the boiling, fierce, peculiarly Tullian sound is remarkable — but several times, rather long flute solos could have been chopped down with effect. It was strange to find them ending with an *Aqualung* sequence. They run the risk of allowing that master work to eclipse other inventions, and it was odd that the forceful Anderson hadn't confidence to wind up with *Thick As A Brick*. He might regret not projecting his new work as a finale: ask Pete Townshend. But nothing can obscure the fact that Jethro Tull's creative energy is like a breath of air. Unpretentious and fun-loving, yet always playing extremely well, they have that rare ability to laugh at themselves. That alone is therapeutic for both musicians and audience."

Pretty much all the music papers had journalists attending this show. *Sounds* also reviewed it but far less favourably; "There was a due sense of occasion at the Royal Albert Hall when Jethro Tull played their monster piece *Thick As A Brick*. It was a full house, which is a tribute to the pulling power of a band which by now must rate pretty highly on the credit side of Britain's balance of payments. So it is with some sorrow and a little trepidation that I have to report that Jethro bored me rigid. From Ian Anderson's opening chords on acoustic guitar, a black cloud of depression lowered itself over the press box and did not lift until the end of the *Thick As A Brick* set, over an hour later. A quiet and restrained American gentleman, not noted for extreme or unfair judgements, shook his head doubtfully and muttered, 'very weird music'; a brash blonde lady exclaimed, less tactfully, 'utter crap!'; but from the floor and from the vast circular gallery above, the audience rose to its feet to cheer as one man."

"Even Ian Anderson himself, who must find standing ovations a bit old hat by now, was moved to a little speech as the applause finally died away through the sprouting mushrooms of the Albert's lofty dome: 'This is the only country where we could do a new piece like this straight off. In America they would jump all over us'. Now jump all over Jethro I don't want to do. It's pretty pointless when a lot of people have had a lot of fun. An Albert Hall-full of fans can't be wrong. I suspect that the audience loved them for the very same things I found excruciating: the precision of all the instrumental work, the control over light and shade in the texture of the music, the smartly-rehearsed ad-libbing and the slapstick gags, above all Ian Anderson's jabbering flute and prancing antics. I admired the perfectly-drilled changes when the band suddenly swoops from one section to the next, admired Barriemore Barlow's relentlessly paced drumming, Martin Barre's gutsy guitar work, John Evan's swelling, churchy organ piece. I marvelled at Ian Anderson's agility and the curious warbly sounds he conjured from the flute, raised a faint smile for the routine with the telephone, frowned at the rather tasteless parody of a television news bulletin (with the lightest of hearts, Vietnam still isn't funny)."

"No, the real give-away happened when Martin Barre (it was actually Jeffrey Hammond!) stepped forward to the mic to make another announcement-link, and described exactly how Tull were going to reach the next 'final orgasmic conclusion' — sorry mate, but the joke's on you; if you want to show everyone exactly how the music is put together, either you're guilty of demystification or of cynicism. You can't go around exposing how the machine works. That's what Tull came across as — a music machine, well-oiled and in perfect working order. The original inspiration — impossible to deny that it's there — has been gradually drained away in the search to perfect the show, just as happened to Townshend's *Tommy*. And the heaviest criticism is that, with all the perfectly rehearsed different sections, *Thick As A Brick* ended up sounding all alike."

After Tull's performance at London's Royal Albert Hall on 29th March, they took a short break before heading to Canada to perform in Montreal on 14th April. The following day, they were in the US to perform at Cornell University. They continued to tour the US with several visits to Canada in between until they went to New Zealand in early July, covering Australia and Japan in the same month. From mid-October up to the end of 1972, the band toured just in the US. Having toured there every year since 1969, Jethro Tull were generally welcomed back there by enthusiastic audiences.

In May 1972, *Cash Box* reviewed a performance that took place at New York's Nassau Coliseum that month; "Jethro Tull provided one of the most outrageous stage shows ever witnessed for about 30,000 people during two shows at the new arena — it was the last stop on their current tour. They had the audience with them all the way and eventually left amidst thunderous applause. With the PA system suspended from the ceiling so as to provide a better side view, the quintet first performed their Reprise LP, *Thick As A Brick*. The rendition included added instrumental detours as well as a reading of the news by Jeffrey Hammond-Hammond. This featured the group dressed in assorted costumes such as a rabbit and gorilla and provided for a short humorous break near the end of the song. To single out Ian Anderson's flute solo might be somewhat unfair as each member played exceptionally well, but he was simply incredible. Anderson is the only original member left but Jethro Tull exhibited why they are one of the best groups around."

"After *Brick*, and assorted duck calls and antics, 'Cross-Eyed Mary' followed and was a smashing success. The group also made effective use of tape to launch 'New Day Yesterday' and immediately afterwards, 'Aqualung'. Tull had now been on stage for two incredibly packed hours of fun and music. They left with the audience simply amazed yet calling for more. Obliging, 'Wind-Up' eventually did close the show. All that can be said is that Jethro Tull were simply unbelievable."

In the same month, *Billboard* reviewed a performance that took place at the same venue; "Both shows (Jethro Tull and Wild Turkey) at the Coliseum had been sold out in six hours, and one might have reasonably expected no small measure of tension in a crowd of those dimensions, particularly in view of the near-riot Jethro Tull had inspired at the Garden during their last tour. Yet Sunday's performance was marked by extraordinary courtesy on the part of the audience. The band didn't put them to sleep. Mixing music with pre-recorded tape and anarchic vaudeville, their set began with an hour and twenty minutes of *Thick As A Brick*, their latest and easily most ambitious Reprise album — which showed off the band's last year of development. The loose grouping of basic themes which forms the album was further expanded here, yet the band sustained an awesome intensity throughout the performance. There were customary extended solos, but it was clearly the ensemble playing that offered the most exciting music."

It should be pointed out that *Billboard*'s review indicated that Glenn Cornick's band had also sold out the large Coliseum, but in fact they were the support act to Black Sabbath.

In July 1972, *Cash Box* reported on a performance that took place at the Forum in LA; "Jethro Tull, as always, was an exciting, original and inventive group to both watch and hear. Tull's only contrast is the basic framework of its act and music. They have probably never performed a set the same way twice. Without ever resorting to the vulgar idiocies or negative machinations other groups thrive on, Tull manages to hold its audience visually captive with rather zany antics. The first piece Tull performed was *Thick As A Brick*. Ian Anderson was at his elfin best in this number, bounding all over and using his enchanted flute to emit sounds of its own. The group completed its set with four of its recognisable songs and were then forced into two encores. They are still one of the best."

"Bewildered By Jethro's Gorilla" so ran the *Melody Maker* headline the same month when it reported on performances in Japan: "Jethro Tull climaxed their world tour with a tremendous performance of *Thick As A Brick* in Tokyo last week. Despite an exhausting schedule of concerts that took them all the way from America to Australia, Tull sounded as fresh and committed as they did when *Brick* was premiered in England two months ago. Their humour and timing was just as sharp although guitarist Martin Barre later confirmed that the unexpected sound of English laughter from the audience had spurred them on. Most Tull fans will now be familiar with their opening routine. The group shuffle on stage in white raincoats and fumble with the equipment like plain clothes detectives. When the coats are thrown off, a roar of recognition goes up. Unfortunately at the Koseinenkin Hall, the sultry heat had put Martin's guitar out of tune, and some forty minutes of fumbling elapsed, while a hapless Jeffery Hammond-Hammond was forced to prolong stage antics scheduled to last only a few moments. It threatened to spoil the show, but when Ian Anderson appeared and murmured, 'So sorry we're late' all was forgiven."

"The theatre was ideal for Tull's presentation, in which good lighting and acoustics are vital. All tickets had sold out three weeks previously and the hip Japanese teenagers were obviously familiar with the music, although their general behaviour was polite and reserved. Rather like Dutch rock fans. The only shouts and oaths came from the contingent of American young people who live or are on vacation in Japan. The band seem to have tightened up considerably and playing particularly well were drummer Barriemore Barlow and Mr Barre on guitar. Their forte is the use of dynamics, and they are experts at contrasting volume levels between Ian's flute and acoustic guitar, and more violent organ and guitar sections. The arrangements were flawless, but a weak point seemed a tendency to repeat certain unison phrases over too many choruses. John Evan's organ tones were occasionally lacking in colour. But these are only minor criticisms of a beautifully conceived show that has few peers in rock. Apart from the lengthy *Brick* saga, other favourites include the powerful main title from *Aqualung*, and John Evan's bravura reading of the weather forecast."

"Guest appearances by various roadies in rabbit and gorilla suits made me laugh, even if the Japanese were slightly bewildered. Best moment — when the gorilla, who walked on after *Brick*, began taking flash photographs of the audience. Ian's facility on flute is now being matched by his increasingly enjoyable acoustic guitar work. He is still the central pivot of the band, but each player has a defined role, and Tull seem much more of a cohesive unit. Barry's drum solo was a highlight, featuring his fast, attacking style. And he showed a sense of humour too with a comic finale involving a specially rigged choke cymbal up front. When struck, after a great deal of posing in red underwear by Mr Barlow, it was mysteriously answered from the wings. Within seconds the rest of the group came dancing on stage in a lunatic ballet, bathed in flickering strobe light beating cymbals. It was pure pantomime that drew amazed cheers. Ian is now working on Tull's next album, and an entirely new stage act is being planned for next year. Jethro Tull are a band that never stop working to perfect and improve their show. And it explains why a band once resident at a Soho club can now tour the planet and delight fans from Los Angeles to Melbourne and Tokyo."

It wasn't just an array of costumes that went on the road with Jethro Tull. In July 1972, the *Sydney Morning Herald* reported that the band transported seventy-two pieces of equipment weighing more than 5000lbs that were insured for $45,000. In the same month, the same newspaper reported positively of Jethro Tull's live performance; "Leering, sneering, ranting, raving flautist Ian Anderson led his group, Jethro Tull, through a brilliantly sustained and successful rock concert at the Hordern Pavilion last night. Like a crazy Scottish rake, he conducted a madhouse of superb musical and theatrical performers. Anderson sometimes blew a fiendish flute. At other times he strummed a restful balladist's guitar. When he was not playing, he danced about the stage, conducting his four assistants with his twirling flute. He never let up, even though the group played continuously for two and a half hours. His right-hand man, Jeffrey Hammond-Hammond, played bass as if he was a cunning French baron. At the sudden increases in volume he would stride and strut, trailing his guitar lead. On odd occasions he turned into a pukka BBC radio announcer."

"Storming at intervals about the arena was John Evan, playing the part of a demented English aristocrat. When seated at his organ, or at the piano, he flailed his arms in wild response to Anderson. The whirlwind drummer, Barriemore Barlow, kept cool in the garb of a neck-to-knee swimming champion. At the end of his solo, he led the group in a hilarious chorus of crash-cymbals. The lead guitarist, Martin Barre, sought no greater status amid his peer group than that of a pink-cheeked yeoman. Jethro Tull were superb musically. Their numbers were beautifully controlled, despite frenzied spurts of adrenalin. Their riffs were almost classical in origin. But above all, Jethro Tull were superb theatrically. Their decadent dramatics dragged their evil electronics to great heights."

"Jethro Tull's performance derived from the theatre of the absurd, with frogmen and apes making unexpected entrances. The group took the foppish drama of The Who and the insane music of the early Pink Floyd to their logical conclusions. The audience obviously appreciated every delicate note, every sinister beat. They kept a stunned silence throughout the first number — a seventy-minute recital of *Thick As A Brick* — and were knocked out by the collection of older songs. Jethro Tull can be seen and heard at the Hordern Pavilion again tonight and tomorrow night — if there are any tickets left."

It was just a few months after the success of *Thick As A Brick* that the double LP, *Living In The Past* was released. A compilation album containing a wide range of Jethro Tull's earlier material, it included some of the band's early singles and live tracks. At the time of the album's release, a lot of it was material that hadn't been released in America before. With *Thick As A Brick* having been so successful there, it made sense to bring the US up to speed on Jethro Tull's previous output. One of the many strengths of *Living In The Past* is that it somewhat functioned as a "best of" album. When 'Living In The Past' (the single that had been released in May 1969 in the UK) was released in America in October 1972, it got to number eleven.

In February 1973, *Rolling Stone* reviewed *Living In The Past*. It's interesting to note the comparisons that were made between the band responsible for *Thick As A Brick* and the earlier line-up of Jethro Tull, as was featured on *Living In The Past;* "Who/what is (a) Jethro Tull? Like a pollster in an asylum, you'll probably get every conceivable answer, since Ian Anderson has yet to put the same cast of characters on two successive LPs. Although *Living In The Past* is no more than a hodgepodge of old English-only singles, EP sides, album tracks and a couple of live cuts, it answers the question fairly well, effectively telling the story of a band that's had as many faces and sounds as Medusa had snakes."

"When Anderson, Mick Abrahams, Glenn Cornick and Clive Bunker formed Jethro Tull in 1968, they were an extremely crude outfit that occasionally came on like an amplified Salvation Army band. *This Was*, though an uneven first release, was lit by frequent flashes of brilliance from Abrahams' guitar and Bunker's drums. 'A Song For Jeffrey' and 'Love Story' represent that segment of Tull's past here, and leave little doubt why the band was once the darling of the American underground. But though their combination of earthy, Muddy Waters-ish street blues and psychedelic pyrotechnics was the order of the day in the immediate post-Cream period, it didn't sit well with purist Abrahams; when the issue of musical direction finally came to a head, he was soon on his way to forming Blodwyn Pig."

"The addition of Martin Lancelot Barre plunged Tull deep into heavy rockdom, but hardly into the pit of directionless plodding inhabited by wah-wah wonders who shall remain nameless. Tull's songs became logically constructed, the playing was remarkably tight, and the lyrics were far more than words between jam sessions. They may have relied heavily on repeated riffs, but they were intricate, groin-rattling licks. The magnificent *Stand Up* was recorded with this Tull alignment, as were numbers like 'Driving Song' and 'Singing All Day'. The latter showcased the band's mellow side — not the contrived introspectiveness of an 'I'm Your Captain', but a touching expression of life's inner joys and sorrows."

"But Anderson, ever the perfectionist, felt the band's alignment was too restrictive, preventing the flute and the guitar from exploring their outermost capabilities. So enter an old school chum, John Evan, for the *Benefit* sessions, which worked out so well that Tull number three soon became a reality with his permanent addition. His rollicking piano and calliope-like organ fit in perfectly, allowing the band far more experimentation and versatility than ever before. Tull switched from soft, swaying ballads like 'Just Trying To Be' and 'Wond'ring Again' to hard rockers like 'Teacher' with an ease that defines imagination."

"*Living In The Past*'s two live cuts further demonstrate Tull number three's complexity and power. Evan showcases his virtuosity on 'By Kind Permission Of', weaving in and out of various classical, blues and neo-jazz themes, paced ever so gently by Anderson's haunting flute. 'Dharma For One' may be slightly restructured ('...which means it's a wee bit louder'), but it rocks out even more raucously than the original. Frequently, Anderson and Barre fly off on separate, simultaneous sorties, using the thumping, pounding backing of their fellows as an explosive launching pad. Was it any wonder why these guys were voted most promising new talent in a 1970 musician's poll?"

"But for all its potential, the band was in deep trouble, a schism rapidly forming within its ranks. Bunker and Cornick wanted to stick with solid riff-rock, while Evan and Anderson were dead set on a lighter, airier, less substantial sound. Cornick was the first to go, being replaced by another Anderson crony, Jeffrey Hammond-Hammond. The change affected Tull's sound drastically; *Aqualung*'s release saw the band's spirit and drive replaced by plodding efficiency and ho-hum competence. For many the album was a bitter disappointment: though it was Tull's first gold LP, it was frequently filed away after only a few listenings. Bunker's replacement by Barriemore Barlow completed Anderson's coup — he had handpicked his own group of sidemen, proficient but hardly a threat to his control over material."

"Their output (an EP and the epic *Thick As A Brick*) has been little more than amplified folkiedom and moralistic pop-rock — a pale shadow of their early work. Where once was a powerful English rock band appeared a pseudo-Socratic troubadour with an eclectic band of thespian yes-men. While it's an admittedly personal preference, I'd much rather have the dynamic 'Back To The Family' than a piece of heinous shlock like 'Up The 'Pool' or a work as emotionally vapid as *Thick As A Brick*. In his haste to avoid tuneless heaviness, Anderson seems to have forgotten that a little amplified talent was never a crime. Tull once had the talent; this new bunch I'm not so sure about. It sure hurts to lose an old friend, and if Tull doesn't get back on the right track soon. there's gonna be a lot more disappointed folks living in the past."

Not necessarily! *Billboard* reviewed *Living In The Past* in November 1972; "As graphically beautiful as this album package is, it is the music within that glows incandescently. As the title suggests, this album is an anthology of previously released material. Jethro Tull (under the ever-present tutelage of Ian Anderson) has woven a tapestry with fibres of melodic progressions and beguilingly provocative lyrics."

The Daily Reveille reported in October 1972 that "what appeared to be an English theatrical troupe or Queen of England's court jester invaded the Assembly Centre" in the form of Jethro Tull. It was considered that Jeffrey Hammond-Hammond garnered one of the biggest reactions from the crowd that night; when doing an impression of a news reporter, he told them that the band had just received a newsflash. Followed by this were stage effects in the form of a flash of light and a puff of smoke. The stagecraft and dynamism of the band's performance was such that, as the reporter concluded, "the encore, which was interspersed with the driving song 'Locomotive Breath' and a drawn-out lead guitar solo by Martin Barre lasted about half an hour and left the crowd satiated and no doubt, quite burned out." Jethro Tull were supported by Gentle Giant that night and whilst the reviewer spoke highly of their performance, he noted that the crowd didn't really engage until Jethro Tull were on stage.

In the same month, *The Philadelphia Inquirer* reported on the show that took place at Philadelphia's Spectrum the night before Halloween. To get into the spirit of things, some of the 19,500 capacity crowd attended in Halloween masks and costumes but the main attraction was Jethro Tull who were supported by Captain Beefheart And His Magic Band. Again it was noted that the crowd were evidently in attendance to see Jethro Tull. The journalist asserted that "it is the music, of course, that really counts. For those who ponder the fate of rock — fearing that the likes of Alice Cooper is leading the music on the path of self-destruction — there is more than a little consolation from Jethro Tull and a few other bands that remain dedicated to the task of keeping rock both entertaining and relevant. Not content with putting on a mere circus on the one hand or shoving messages down our throats with the other, Jethro Tull's music is among the most innovative being made today — several years after the arrival of this dynamic British band. Classical elements abound in the music, but it is never precious or pretentious. Jethro Tull never loses sight of the fact that this is a rock band. But it is a rock band unlike any other."

The Evening Bulletin reported that over their two-night sold-out engagement there, Jethro Tull had become the third rock group in history to play multiple capacity crowd shows at the Philadelphia Spectrum's 19,500 seat arena. The journalist advocated that by this point, Jethro Tull were comparable to the Rolling Stones, Chicago (both of whom had previously been met at the Spectrum with the same enthusiasm) and Neil Young. It was considered that "the secret behind Tull's ability to entertain and satisfy a large crowd every time out is twofold. First, the group's music, since it stems from the same compositional source, is related in a clearly evolutionary fashion. If you like old Tull music, you'll probably like new Tull music. Secondly — and this relates to fold number one as well — is the vise-like charisma of the group's singer and composer, Ian Anderson. The relationship between Anderson and the audience is fascinating. It seems as though a moderately large man is dominating almost 20,000 using only his mind and mouth as weapons. During the course of several numbers, Anderson stops singing or playing his unique brand of howling flute and just growls and roars at the audience, pawing at it menacingly with his voice and hands. The resulting screams of encouragement also sound a little like shouts of relief. Relief that Anderson is safely behind the spotlights and kept back from the audience by a deep moat. Tull's music is a rich, throaty blend of excellent tunes and forceful, intricate rhythms. On Tull's recent *Thick As A Brick* album, the group showed an interest in involved, waning and waxing numbers that run from single-instrument sections to full ensemble blasts. That was the bulk of the performance last night. Each number grew into the next, providing a musical river with shallows in some spots and fearsome vortexes in others."

It was reported in *New Musical Express* in November 1972; "Jethro Tull sold out Madison Square Garden. They appeared with Gentle Giant, who were unbearably gigantic, but certainly not gentle. Tull took forty minutes to set up, finally opening with forty minutes' worth of *Thick As A Brick*. We wanted to see them do 'Sympathy For The Devil' — or have Mott The Hoople come out and beat them up with a little ultraviolence. Drummer Barrie Barlow is a bit too repetitive on the high hats, mustering a lot of drill figures and exercises, not very exciting. He hangs onto a beat long enough to pull in his audience, and then, when he finally has them, changes to another tack. He did come out in his red long johns in an incredible change-clothes strip, flashing about like a dog in heat with a hydrant, soon followed by keyboard man, John Evan, attired first as a gorilla, and then as a big white rabbit. Bass player Jeffrey Hammond served as a BBC-type moderator, reading off the news from *Thick As A Brick*. Ian Anderson provided some flashy phallic flutings, and proved that he is, as ever, master of Jethro's destiny. The crazed audience couldn't get enough."

Melody Maker reported in the same month; "Although the American press has never treated Ian Anderson and his boys very well, Jethro Tull managed to sell out the huge Madison Square Garden once again, and played for an astounding two and a half hours to an ecstatic crowd. They began their set with 'a rather long number' from their last LP, *Thick As A Brick*, which lasted ninety minutes and was laced with extended soloing and rather bizarre dramatics. Mr Anderson introduced the second tune in his usual way, and Jethro Tull launched into a pastiche of hot hits from previous discs, including 'Locomotive Breath', 'Bourée' and 'Wind-Up'. Surprisingly enough, the band performed several numbers which have not yet been put on disc; they seemed to be quite diverse in nature, ranging from the very complicated melodic and rhythmic transitions which we've been used to from Tull to rather simple, three-chord riffs lifted straight out of The Who's repertoire."

"Their set was, for the most part, extremely tight and well-arranged, with notes always right in place even when Ian performed some unnatural acts upon the person of the guitarist, a gimmick which reeked of Bowieness. The rest of Jethro Tull is not to be overlooked, as they're fairly interesting characters as well. Jeffrey Hammond-Hammond is the only member of the band lacking a beard, and his stage manner also has much of the Don Van Vliet (Beefheart) to it, even to the bass playing. Whenever John Evan got out from behind his piano he acted like a mimic of Anderson, twirling around his hands and doing what has come to be known as the Ian Strut. Drummer Barrie Barlow played a twenty-minute solo which owed too much to Clive Bunker and Ginger Baker, in addition to being extraordinarily boring; his drumming during the rest of the show was flawless, so this tasteless display was a bit of a surprise. Martin Lancelot Barre (whose birthday it was the very day of the concert) played a fine rhythm guitar but fell apart during his half-hour solo, which consisted of techniques ripped-off of various modern masters (Pete Townshend, Jimmy Page, and Eric Clapton)."

Also in November 1972, *Record World* reported on Tull's performance at the Garden in New York; "Headlining the bill was the ever so phenomenal Jethro Tull! For myself, and many others there that evening, this was most definitely the concert of the year! For more than two hours of total stupification, Ian Anderson and company leaped around the stage in a frenzy of wild antics putting together, musically and theatrically, one of the most entertaining shows to be seen anywhere in a long time. Act one of this brilliant performance was *Thick As A Brick*, to be followed by 'Aqualung' more than an hour and a half later. The audience was ecstatically captivated. The group was extremely appreciative and gracious. Beautiful rapport. An evening to be remembered."

In December 1972, *Cash Box* also reviewed a performance that took place there; "Ian Anderson and company, affectionately known as Jethro Tull, returned to Madison Square Garden last week to destroy another one of their sell-out crowds with their fine music and zany stage antics. Performing *Thick As A Brick* in its entirety is a feat unto itself, but that was just for openers. Twirling his silver flute while leading his group through starts, stops and solos, Anderson proved once again that he is one of the most inventive showmen in the business. That's show business! Tull provides the audience with looking and listening pleasure, but the entire group pitches in, adding to the overall success of a concert that we could have watched all evening. Performing for almost two solid hours, Jethro Tull pulled material from all of their albums — and if the arrangements were the same as on their previous tour, the theatrics weren't. More and more groups are learning to combine theatre with music. But Jethro Tull, who have been leaders in the field since the very conception of the band, proved that they are master of both."

In the same month, *Billboard* gave their version of events; "Chrysalis Records' Jethro Tull conquered the inhabitants of the Garden in a performance excelling in music, comedy and drama. More than a mere rock group, Tull has fashioned itself into a totally absorbing theatrical rock experience. Drawing essentially from the music of *Aqualung* and *Thick As A Brick*, the UK group wove a web of delicate acoustical stylings (sic) with hard gut-grabbing rock and beautiful English folk melodies, as each "movement" of their extended works was greeted with hearty waves of recognition. Lead vocalist, writer and musician, Ian Anderson, impresses as a whirling dervish. The man's energy output is simply startling. Dressed in something out of a stray Dickens novel, Anderson lurched, lunged and minced about the stage, coddling his fellow players like a concerned mother hen brandishing his omnipresent flute as a majorette gone mad might. In fact, there is an intensity and interaction between each member of the fivesome, sparked by Anderson, that keeps the show flowing, dead centre tight, always alive and never boring. Near the end of the more than two-hour set, the Garden became the home of an English Music Hall Revue featuring the "Jethro Tull Players" in a series of sketches bordering on burlesque. The finale finds the five men suddenly disappearing in a burst of billowing white smoke filling the entire coliseum."

Even at the height of their success during the *Thick As A Brick* era, it was noted that Jethro Tull walked a fine line between being intriguing and being too over the top. "As a music producing unit,

Anderson offstage in Amsterdam, 12th February 1972.

Jethro Tull have always been one of the most misunderstood and underrated of bands — although their credentials as a dynamic stage act have rarely been called into question," was how *New Musical Express* saw it in July '72. "That very charismatic quality on stage is, in fact, the crux of the dilemma; the reason why, as far back as 1969, Jethro were recognising the difficulty of persuading critics and public not to regard them dismissively as — to quote Martin Barre — 'a joke band'. This kind of attitude tends to run thus: a band turns in a good, entertaining show, then from this particular process of thought it follows that the show must be an act. An act needs rehearsing. If it's rehearsed then it's mechanical. And if the show is mechanical, then the music must be too — to follow things to their (il)logical conclusion. While Ian Anderson's stage theatricals are in one respect Jethro's greatest asset, in a musical context they could also be said to be the band's greatest liability. All that to one side, truth is that Jethro Tull have always been a conscientious and dedicated band in the studio. They started with little enough knowledge of recording techniques, or of music too for that matter, relatively speaking, but set about mastering the arts of both aspects with a relentlessly inquisitive zeal."

At the time, the success of *Thick As A Brick* was something of a double-edged sword for Jethro Tull. Of course the success of the album had been fantastic for them in and of itself but the problems came when they were faced with the prospect of having to follow it up with something that could be considered equally as good. First of all, the band spent some time in Paris where they went to Château d'Hérouville to record. The venue appealed to them because Elton John had recently recorded one of his albums there (*Honky Château*). Unfortunately for Jethro Tull though, the recording studio wasn't what they were used to as it was less technically advanced than some of the others they had used before. The frustrations of this were such that after having recorded several backing tracks, they abandoned the project because they just weren't happy with the sound quality. Although Anderson later referred to the Château d'Hérouville as Château d'Isaster, some of the tracks worked on in those sessions would later make an appearance on *War Child* ('Solitaire' and 'Skating Away On The Thin Ice Of The New Day').

Upon returning to Britain, rather than recording the same musical ideas again, it made more sense to start afresh on recording some new ones. At this stage in their tenure, the band were confident that they could quickly get something conceptual done (as opposed to doing individual songs). As a result, *A Passion Play* didn't take long to write. It was demanding in terms of the long recording sessions that the band put in but overall, the album was made relatively quickly.

Anderson was quoted in *Circus Raves* in November 1974; "The things that appeared most calculated on my albums were figured out on the spot. For example, the 'Story Of The Hare' and the two pieces that surrounded it on the *Passion Play* were not carefully arranged and figured out. If you know music you'll realise that there are time sequences that cross themselves. It's appealing and interesting, but I could never have done it twice. I can never even remember lyrics to songs until I get on stage, and thank God I can remember them then."

For *A Passion Play*, Tull played a range of instruments as they moved further towards a progressive rock sound. Much of the album features dominating minor key variation. *A Passion Play* was the first Jethro Tull album to include a saxophone (played by Anderson) and an accordion and synthesiser (played by John Evan).

Notably, by the time Tull came to working on *A Passion Play* in March 1973, they were under pressure from Chrysalis to come up with the goods. Not only that but they were due to begin another tour of the US in the May. It was reported in *New Musical Express* in March 1973; "Although their current 1973 schedule allows for only two concerts in Britain this year, there are no signs of a let up in Jethro Tull's apparent ambition to take the title of The World's Most Travelled Rock Band. In between sessions at North London's Morgan Studios on the upcoming *Passion Play* album, Jethro recently completed a European tour playing to capacity houses all along the line. In Copenhagen they opened a new concert hall, and drew a sell-out crowd of 5,000 — the major part of their set, approximately one and a half hours, consisted of an improvised *Thick As A Brick*." Ian Anderson was quoted in the same feature; "I can't remember when I had my last day off. It must be well over one year ago. This year we're going to play three American tours — each one lasting four weeks. We're in the middle of a European tour, and we're going to the Far East and Down Under. So far we're not as big in Japan as we are in England and the States, but we got a very good reception in Japan the first time we played there, and we're going back this year. Anyway, I'm not interested in the markets, only in the music. Besides this hard programme, we have recording plans. We've already taped numbers for one and a half LPs to come after *Passion Play*, but I'm not sure whether we'll use this material. *Passion Play* was also recorded almost a year ago — but the music changed a lot after we taped it. So, after a few months, we decided to do the whole thing again. Thank God we're in a financial position where we are able to re-record, in spite of the high costs. That's why *Passion Play* has been a long time on the way."

With the hectic touring and the pressure to follow up *Thick As A Brick* with another good album, was there an extent of burnout going on? On 28th April 1973, *Sounds* ran the headline, "Jethro

Anderson onstage in Amsterdam, 12th February 1972.

Cancel Wembley Gigs (Doctor orders Ian to rest)."

"Jethro Tull have been forced to cancel both their Wembley concerts this weekend (April 28th and 29th). Chrysalis announced this week that Ian Anderson was suffering from nervous exhaustion and is under orders from his doctor to rest for at least two weeks. Tull have rescheduled both Wembley concerts and will now appear on Friday, June 22nd, and Saturday, June 23rd. Ticket holders for this Saturday's concert will now have their tickets honoured at the June 22nd concert, and holders for this Sunday will be able to get in on June 23rd. Ticket money will, however, be refunded if they are returned to whence they came."

"A spokesman from Chrysalis told *Sounds* that Tull had not taken a holiday for a year — they have been appearing continuously in countries all over the world, and in addition to live appearances they have been recording. In March the band finished their European tour, and since then they have been rehearsing their *Passion Play* stage show and recording a five-minute film which will be shown during the *Passion Play* stage show. Tull are scheduled to go to America at the beginning of May but they may miss the beginning of the tour unless Anderson has recovered. The band had hoped to take a holiday during June but they will now play Wembley instead."

Even before *A Passion Play* was premiered, they clearly needed a rest. Ian Anderson told *New Musical Express* in March 1973; "In 1974 we won't be touring as much as this year. We need a rest — a rest to create a new show totally different to most other presentations nowadays... I'm working almost twenty-four hours a day in Jethro Tull."

Tull toured the States from May to September 1973 (by September 1973, they would withdraw from touring until July 1974). During this period, they were supported by other acts on the Chrysalis label: Steeleye Span, Robin Trower and Livingstone Taylor. As well as being a long tour, it was peppered with technical challenges. On 5th May when the band played at Clemson, their equipment arrived so late that they had to do their soundcheck with the audience present and the actual performance didn't begin until 10pm. The following day's gig in North Carolina had to be cancelled due to a truck breaking down and causing untenable delays. Another date in Ohio had to be cancelled at the last minute because the stage there couldn't take the weight of the equipment.

It was reported in *Creem* in May 1973; "Tull concerts now are a real experience, and a unique one, for better or worse. Make no mistake: in terms of sheer professionalism, Jethro Tull are without peer. They stand out by never failing to deliver a full-scale show, complete with everything they know any kid would gladly pay his money to see: music, volume, costumes, theatrics, flashy solos, long sets, two encores. Jethro Tull are slick and disciplined; they work hard and they deliver. What they deliver is one of the most curious melanges on any stage. If their lyrics generally take a moralistic bent, the band themselves come on like total goofballs, and the contrast works nicely. All of them dress to the teeth, usually in Victorian waistcoats and tight pants, and from the instant Ian Anderson hits the stage he works the audience with all the masterful puppeteer mojo of the Merlin he often poses as. He whirls and whips in total spastic grace, creating a maelstrom around himself, flinging his fingers in the air as if hurling arcane incantations at the balcony. His eyes take on a satyr's gleam, get wild and pop from his head. He very effectively passes himself off as a madman reeling in riptide gales from unimaginable places. He exploits his flute exhaustively: baton, wand, sword, gun, phallus, club, virtuoso's magic axe. He twirls it like a cheerleader and stirs the audience to a frothing frenzy with it, then raises the ladle to his chops and puts the audience in a trance with an extended melodramatic solo."

"Jethro Tull are such solid entertainers that even if you can't stand the music, they're usually providing something for you to gawk at. A lot of it is real vaudeville: Barlow walks up to the mic during a pause, holds up a toy cymbal, raises a drumstick and hits it with an extravagant flourish. As he does so he rises on left tiptoes and arches his right leg out behind him like a cartoon Nureyev, rolling his eyes at the audience and mugging shamelessly. He gets cheers and an echoing cymbal shot which seems to come from nowhere and puts him into similarly exaggerated perplexity. He looks around, scratches his head and hits the cymbals again. Again the echo. Getting really worked up, he hits the cymbal again and again, faster and faster, the echoes coming at the same pace, and suddenly the rest of the band converges on him, each of them holding identical cymbal and stick and wildly bashing away."

"The audience eats it up. Costumes are utilised too, in a manner that's too calculated and too successful to be off the cuff. But what would you think if you saw a band stop an extended song in the middle to: Read a bogus "weather report", run through a bit where a band member walks to the microphone and begins to gesticulate and address the audience, while another member dressed as a gorilla stands behind him aping his every move, hop around the stage dressed as bunny rabbits, stop the music again, the silence broken by the ringing of a prop phone onstage which one band member answers: 'Hello? Oh yes, I'll see if he's here', then he turns to the audience, 'There's a call here for a Mr Mike Nelson.' So a roadie or somebody, dressed in full diving gear complete with fins, mask and aqualung, flaps on from stage left, picks up the phone, wordlessly mimics a brief conversation, then flaps back as the band tears into a particularly wild passage from *Brick* to wild cheers from the gallery. If that's your idea of entertainment, scarf up a ticket the next time Jethro Tull hit town. If you can get one, that is. It's a long way from my idea of rock 'n' roll, but then maybe that idea is dated. Or maybe this isn't rock 'n' roll and doesn't need to apologise for being something else either. Jethro Tull are going to be around for a while, will undoubtedly get even bigger than they are now, and their musical productions will become even more."

In May 1973, *The Evansville Press* reviewed the band's performance at Roberts Stadium under the headline of "Rock Concert Packs Stadium"; "Flute-playing Ian Anderson and Jethro Tull, writhing in an abundance of rock music, captivated an overflow audience last night at Roberts Stadium. The frisbees floated free and the marijuana smoke wafted in the coloured lights as the English group, in its first US concert for 1973, exploded onto the stage and began their brutal rendition of *Thick As A Brick*. It took nearly forty-five minutes for the sounds to finally die off from the title song of one of the group's albums. As expected, Anderson — with shoulder length curly hair and almost insane facial expressions — was the star of the show, with his flute wailing to the beat of the drums and the pounding of the two guitars. Anderson, dressed spryly in a pair of tight blue tights, knee boots, a silver belt and a plaid coat, used the flute as a baton to direct the band and skimmed over the stage as the music played. There was no doubt that he was in control and the degree of professionalism of the entire show — which is sometimes lacking in other performances here — made the high-ticket price seem worthwhile. The sound system for the concert was excellent and the timing of the lights precise. This was the second time that the Jethro Tull group has been in Evansville. The group was here nearly two years ago when its popularity was limited to a smaller, underground audience. Also appearing with Jethro Tull last night were Brewer And Shipley, who would have been enjoyable to hear in concert by themselves. Their mellow harmony on such songs as 'Tarkio Road' and 'One Toke Over the Line' provided a good down-home mood which was soon shattered by the driving sound of Jethro Tull."

In June, *RPM* reviewed a performance that took place in Toronto on 30th May; "Once again, Toronto had the pleasure of being host to one of Britain's finest super groups. The pleasure was in the likeness of The Jethro Tull Show, a complete audio/visual sensorium that comes this way but once a year. The opening act happened to be Brewer And Shipley, although by the time the concert was over it was hard to remember that they were really there. They did, however, get a roar of approval on their famous 'One Toke Over The Line'. Jethro Tull (an English agriculturalist/inventor who lived in the 1700s) comes in the form of five concert musicians, each member a star in his own right. Band leader and heartbeat of the quintet is singer, flautist, writer, dancer and genius extraordinaire, Ian Anderson, along with lead guitarist, Martin "Lancelot" Barre, comprise the only two originals of the band (sic)."

"John Evan is Tull's keyboard man, applying his expertise to piano, organ and the new field of synthesised sound, all at a time when keyboards are becoming an integral part of many bands, especially British. Jeffery Hammond-Hammond plays an amazing bass guitar and Barriemore Barlow makes up his fifth in the percussion department. This five man line-up combines all its individual energies into one explosive power unit. With hundreds of watts of electricity hissing through the suspended speakers, the crowd was ready to be freaked out. After a hypnotic opening to the *Passion Play*, a fantasy movie took those who wanted to go, into the fourth dimension."

"Unfortunately though, there were technical difficulties in the Toronto show and the second movie had to be canned, so some of the effect of the *Play* was lost. But in Ottawa (where general admission tickets caused nothing but aggravation for the young crowd), the show was complete and the audience received Tull's message more clearly: we're all part of the *Passion Play*. The *Passion Play* actually dominated the show as this is Jethro Tull's newest work following their previous composition, *Thick As A Brick*. *Passion* complements *Thick* as the second concept album to come from the group and supplies us with the answers to the queries we had about how Tull would top *Thick*. Both sides of the album were performed and at this point, avid fans are impatiently awaiting the release of the *Passion Play* album."

"The show supplied its own stage and technical apparatus including suspended lights that bathed the stage in colour and accented the band's colourful costumes. Sound equipment was excellent, simultaneously creating ear shattering but crystal clear sounds. Barre, playing his pet Gibson Les Paul, cranked out a powerful sound with no fancy attachments, while Barlow's three part drum solo was really unbeatable. He moved at super speed and pulled off a set that combined hard work and guts. Every member did his respective solo with great finesse. For their second number, an unexpected excerpt from *Thick As A Brick* led the way for a medley of other Tull favourites. The audience was enthralled but dismayed to find that 'Aqualung' would bring the show to an end. However, the band came back, and although the encore was pre-planned it probably wouldn't have been effective otherwise. Tull had by this time wound everyone up to such a state that 'Locomotive Breath', which incorporated into 'Wind-Up', blew the audience out totally. But then, Ian Anderson regretfully strummed his last chords and said goodbye, amid little applause and much sighing." The reviewer's claim that Barre was an original band member suggests he wasn't a fan.

On the 22nd and 23rd June 1973 the rearranged London dates took place. It meant that within days, the band had to be back in America to continue the tour that they were committed to there. *Melody Maker* reported at great length on the London shows under the title of "Crime Of Passion": "One and a half hours of solid good music by Jethro Tull at the Empire Pool, Wembley, would have been sufficient to send home many more contented fans. Instead, an over-long over-produced marathon seriously impaired their impact — and their reputation. The *Passion Play* which constituted the first part of the concert, and is the basis of their next album, was a disappointment. And time-wasting tactical errors like the back-projection spun out proceedings to such length that final items like 'My God' and 'Locomotive Breath' became a test of endurance for those glued by duty to the hard seating of the Pool, instead of a rewarding musical experience."

"As a fan of Jethro Tull, I had hoped not to fall into the general clamour of critical abuse that has been heaped on them in recent months. Tull are a band who always set themselves high levels of achievement. They spend such long hours in perfecting stage presentation, great chunks of arranged music, and volumes of words, that it seems almost churlish to raise a voice of protest and criticism. I'm sure Ian Anderson feels that too. During his greetings to the large and ecstatic audience, he bowed elaborately to the VIP enclosure (in which I was seated), and said, 'How are yer? Panel of judges. You always win in the end' — Come, come Ian, let's not squabble. Any band can overreach itself, make mistakes, err or commit acts of folly."

"Let it first be understood that my comments are made purely in the spirit of constructive criticism, and are no way intended as personal slights, insults or wrong-headed prejudiced, jaundiced, short-sighted, purblind, one-sided, superficial, illiberal, intolerant, warped, dogmatic hyper-criticism. Instead I come as Solomon would among the squabbling wives, and 'midst a clap of thunder and sheet lightning cry: 'Enough!' First of all it must be positively stated that the concert last Friday was a success as far as the vast majority of the audience was concerned. Long and loud were the cheers. Fans to the left and right of me were beating time with their hands, heads down and feet stomping. It was the first time they had seen Tull in well over a year, and they were determined to enjoy all that came before them."

"Reviewers of Tull concerts seem to spend a lot of time glancing at their watches, and I found myself checking out the time at frequent intervals. According to my Accurist (twenty-one jewels, anti-magnetic), it was 9pm when the screen came down and the dot started pulsating. But later I found my watch was fast, and after brief calculations, ascertained that it was in fact 9pm when the first bout of slow-hand clapping broke out, five minutes before the first flight of paper darts were stacked up and circling over the arena waiting for clearance. At 9pm the tone changed to a higher pitch, and quite a few people looked up at the screen to notice the dot had got larger. It occurred to me that this was one of Ian Anderson's little games with audiences, and it could have been more effective if the sequence had been shortened and if the house lights had been turned out. In a place as brightly lit and vast as the Empire Pool, attention cannot be focused on a distant grey screen for long."

"But it was a good time for meditation and a pause in the hurly-burly of life… But where are we — sitting on an intolerably hard seat waiting for Jethro Tull. Come on, lads, get it together for Chrissake. But lo — what was this? The dot was replaced by a frozen shot of a ballerina. Brilliantly this came to life, slowly, and gathering momentum, until the young lady leapt through a mirror. A stunning shot, and well worth the wait. By this time all the delay had been forgiven, and another brilliant stroke — Martin o' the guitar leapt on stage in a flash and puff of smoke followed by the rest of the band. Settle down chaps — it's all happening now — I thought. The *Passion Play* was about to be unleashed. The music seemed fast and powerful, Ian swapping 'midst that Tullian expertise at the lighting controls, from flute-with-band to acoustic guitar-unaccompanied out front. A new innovation — Ian played soprano sax with an attachment, with considerable facility, which added a new tonal dimension to the band sound. Jeffery Hammond-Hammond, their bass player, charged around the stage in suit and panama hat, in a kind of Monty Python-ish silly walk that seemed a parody of the natural movements of a musician inspired by his music."

"The piece continued unabated, and bearing in mind we haven't heard the album yet, seemed to take a considerable time to show any signs of cohesion. The structure had a kind of Elizabethan mode, with a plethora of changes that did not resolve into any satisfying or logical direction. The drums had to pound home each change and accent in pursuit of the main line and resulted in the group sounding like a circus band following the actions of a juggler. Hup — two, three, four! It began to occur to me that this was very poor music indeed. It was not that the complexity was daunting, simply that the musical structure was no longer a vehicle for self-expression. It was cold and unemotional. Not once during the evening did the music catch me in the pit of the stomach or cause hair to rise on the neck. Perhaps I was seeing Tull too soon after witnessing the glories of the Mahavishnu Orchestra."

"The lyrics or story of the *Passion Play* did not communicate one whit. At the end of the evening I had absolutely no idea what it was about. And I have sat and watched the Kabuki Theatre in Japan, where the actors howl and grunt in long-dead dialects, and their timeless plays of real passion shine with simplicity, that only the thickest brick could fail to understand. Part of the play was taken up with a movie, filmed in colour featuring members of the group and a ballet company. This fell flat at first, greeted with yells of 'no substitute', with which I was bound to agree, although a colleague who thought the whole show terrible, said the film was the best part, which at least shows how opinions can differ. It was beautifully photographed, but what did it mean, and what was the relevance to the play?"

"My feeling was if I had known we were about to attend a movie show, I would have chosen to see *Soylent Green* at the Empire, Leicester Square. The film portrayed various bees and newts prancing in some kind of provincial pantomime about a rabbit who had lost his spectacles. It was actually more pointless than Frank Zappa's *2000 Motels*. Thence we returned to Ian singing endless baffling lyrics, and a singular lack of good improvisation or real melody from the band. The ballerina popped back out of the mirror and the audience cheered in the baffling way that audiences cheer when their critical faculties are numbed by misplaced loyalty. At last now the *Passion Play* was out of the way, perhaps the band could afford to relax and start blowing."

"And Ian came on strongly with announcements that always entertain with their dry wit. To a heckler he touched his forelock and said: 'Yes sir, right away sir, what is it you want? *Thick As A Brick*? Right!' He told the audience they were looking really well and later said it was a pleasure to be back in Blackpool. When pianist John Evan did a run for the piano, featuring a neat forward roll on the way, Ian made me laugh aloud when he said: 'It's hard to believe he does this nearly every night' — Now the real Jethro Tull was going to stand up, and at 10:15pm came the first enjoyable moment. A brilliant flute solo by Ian on *Thick As A Brick*, as full of life, invention and joy as the *Passion Play* had been drear and lifeless. Ian's playing was pure quicksilver. A unison passage with bells was sheer delight. And the band rightly received an ovation for a drop of good playing. 'I really must apologise to the fellow who said 'get on with it'', said Ian, harking back to his previous put-down. It seemed a new spirit of instrumental creativity was infiltrating the group and then came the next highlight of Barriemore Barlow's exciting and entertaining drum solo. It followed a fairly predictable pattern in terms of construction, but he played a beautifully fast snare drum and the double bass drums thundered in the grand manner. The by-play with a choke cymbal at the front of the stage was funny, and the final freak out with every member of the group hitting cymbals and dancing in a strobe light was a knock out. Barrie finished his solo wreathed in smoke and next the band launched into 'Aqualung', notable for more excellent fills by Barrie, swirling round the kit and ending with a crack on the snare."

The feature concluded; "The band left the stage, to return for an encore, Ian introducing Martin as 'balding and diminutive', cueing him in for his guitar solo, not to mention a piano feature by the strangely strange John Evan. In his white suit and red tie he presents the appearance of a clumsy beach deckchair attendant, and plays curiously cold piano in a kind of perverse, classically-trained style, where the occasional introduction of "blue" or jazz notes sound almost quaint. There was more stage "business", with the famed telephone, which refused to ring, until the band had left the stage for good, when it rang twice and was symbolically unanswered. It was the signal for more yells and applause — but the house lights came up and the show was over. After the show I felt uncomfortable and filled with inner torment. The combination of hard planks and hot dogs can play havoc with the nether extremities. Also the music could take some of the blame. Arguments will rage long and loud over the merits of the show, but my final conclusion was that it should have been sub-edited and presented in a proper theatre for maximum effect and greater satisfaction. Before Jethro Tull jump through their next mirror — they should stop, and take a long cool look at themselves. The answer, my friends, is blowing in the flute."

The same performance was also reviewed in *New Musical Express* under the headline of "Jethro Tull, Where's The Passion Now?" and predominantly, the same complaints were expressed; "'God, they've changed a helluva lot,' I thought, sitting in the Wembley Stadium. But Ian Anderson was never content to stand still. Whatever comes out of his bag tonight there'd be no denying Tull's importance to rock music. They were the first underground outfit to make it, also playing an important part in building an image for Island Records. Right down to the final detail of their album sleeves Tull had been innovators. *Passion Play* started with a circle of white light projected onto a screen suspended behind the stage. As the circle grew larger, so did the volume of heartbeat which preceded the light. Strange eerie noises came out of the speakers, including what sounded like an Italian opera singer taking his morning gargle, and the circle finally enveloped the screen — at which point a lifeless ballerina appeared in its place. After a few minutes the ballerina was given motion and did a little dance before disappearing through a mirror."

"Enter one Jethro Tull amid smoke bombs and flashing lights. Anderson followed brandishing flute and the show had begun. What followed is difficult to describe because it's difficult to remember. Not one piece of music from *Passion Play* stayed in my head longer than a second after it was played. And this is the real criticism. It was just too much to take in one hearing, especially when one's concentration on the music was interrupted by another film sequence. This time there were two ballerinas and a whole lot of *Alice In Wonderland* animals. The story, I think, had something vaguely to do with the hare losing his spectacles. During the piece Anderson played flute, soprano sax, a sopranino and an acoustic guitar. He also whistled and sang. Much as I admire Tull for not repeating old material — and as much as I can marvel at the band's professionalism in delivering *Passion Play* — it didn't make much sense on one hearing. However, the audience, apart from one young man in front of me, who described the piece as 'rubbish' received *Passion Play* warmly."

"*Thick As A Brick* — the middle bit starting with the organ riff — made much more sense and showed Tull can reproduce their live sound onstage with no trouble. Yes, this was the madcap Anderson, dressed in tartan frock coat and knee-high boots. Okay — so his flute technique wouldn't stand up alongside Roland Kirk or Herbie Mann, but Anderson is communicating to a lot of people. He talks and barks like a dog into the flute. There's a hint of Bach and just a slice of 'Bourée'. Hammond-Hammond attempted that fabulous flowing bass line which Glenn Cornick played on the original but it didn't quite come off. Anderson cavorted like a demented leper, conducting the band with his foot, as *Thick As A Brick* came to its conclusion the audience sang along with him. The next song which began with a brief acoustic passage before developing into some real thunder and lightning, was presumably a new number not included on *Passion Play*. Martin Barre, who had previously hung back in the shadows of his speaker cabinets, started to move. He jumped around as if trying to deaden a fire. Barlow is left onstage for a drum solo. It was okay but, like the smoke bombs that followed, unnecessary. Jethro Tull don't need to resort to such clichés of modern day rock."

"No introduction is needed as the band break loose into 'Aqualung'. All of a sudden — what timing — the band stopped playing and crept over to a white telephone which has sat on stage all night. They cringed away from it and continue 'Aqualung'. But haven't we seen this before, Ian? The encore of 'Wind-Up'/'Locomotive Breath' is the best piece of the night. Evan started to loon, almost a parody of Anderson himself, and only just short of him in the eccentricity stakes. Anderson's voice is crystal clear and his spitting onto the stage when he comes to the line about schoolteachers grooming him for success conveys the bitterness which is such an essential part of his writing. Evan played beautiful piano and is clearly Tull's finest musician. Barre's solo was distorted and self-indulgent."

"Tull left the stage and the telephone started ringing again. Anderson returned to answer it and, after a few seconds' conversation, told the audience the call was for them. Truly a Tullian touch. So this was Tull's first British gig in over a year. For me, *Passion Play* failed musically and visually. What was that film about — other than just a surreal trick of its maker? Maybe the film and music will make more sense with the album's release. It would be nice to see Anderson writing an album of songs, rather than of extended pieces — in rock they rarely work. The stage patter was there but didn't seem so funny as it was a couple of years ago and Anderson's movements were a mite contrived. But it was good to see these five eccentrics back on home territory — personally though, I can't help but long for the days when Anderson flirted with Go-Go dancers and the thought of Jethro Tull getting into mixed media seemed laughable. Still, Ian Anderson couldn't really stand still."

Whilst the earlier reviews of *A Passion Play* largely informed what Jethro Tull would do next, as the tour went on the show was met with positive reviews. In September 1973, *Record World* reported; "New York — Madison Square Garden, jam packed with adoring fans, was treated once again this week to the brilliant theatrics and music of Jethro Tull. This New York appearance was contained in the third and last section of their American tour. The group recently announced an indefinite retirement from concert appearances, which according to their manager Terry Ellis, was partly due to the bad reviews on their show, *A Passion Play*. If true, there was absolutely nothing to confirm that in the reaction of the New York audience. *A Passion Play* is beyond the shadow of the doubt the group's best work to date. Ian Anderson has added abstract ballet movements to his own repertoire of antics and dance which he does throughout the rest of the show. And, one might add, with excellent results. The performance takes on an air of sophistication and grace with the addition of the visual medium created by the film and light show. Also performed were parts of last year's success, *Thick As A Brick* (minus the top hat and hare's costume). And previous to the fantastic and well-deserved encore, was the even earlier, 'Aqualung', which had the audience on their feet from the start."

A Passion Play was released in July 1973. The album art exudes a quirky element of realism whereby included in the original gatefold, there is an eight-page theatre programme from the fictitious Linwell Theatre. As with *Thick As A Brick*, the notes are amusing and describe the cast involved in the production — again, all fictional and portrayed by members of the band. Despite the fact that the contents of the theatre programme is fictional, notes are included that set the tone of the album in terms of its theme. They state:

First aid facilities in the theatre are given by Nurses Ltd. members who give their services voluntarily.

Patrons are requested not to smoke in the auditorium.

In accordance with the Linwell District Council's regulations and general conditions
(a) No obstructions, whether permanent or temporary, shall be allowed in any exit doors, exit ways (whether corridors or staircases), external passageways, gangways, foyers, lobbies or entrance halls.
(b) The safety curtain shall be lowered and raised at least once during the presence of the public at each performance.

Latecomers may be asked to wait until a suitable break in the performance.

The level of detail on the mock theatre programme was just as elaborate as how *A Passion Play* was performed on stage. It included the use of a film and was overall, strongly thematic. Sadly though, it was met with a lot of criticism, even from those who had spoken highly of *Thick As A Brick*.

Under the heading of "Tull: Enough Is Enough" Chris Welch was explicit in his dislike as he wrote in *Melody Maker* in July 1973; "It gives me no pleasure to report upon this recording. In fact I cannot recall an album by a British rock band that has given me more pain to endure. The real disappointment is that it marks, seemingly, the end of an era. After studying this album at great length, stewing my eyes out over the lyrics, reprinted on the inner sleeve, bending an ear to each nuance of the music, I am left with the feeling of never wanting to hear another British rock group album again. I don't want to hear arrangements, Moog synthesisers, electric guitars, or bloody clever lyrics for as long as the polar caps are frozen: if this is where ten years of "progression" have taken us then it's time to go backwards."

"Jethro Tull I have always enjoyed — with reservations. I liked Ian Anderson's restless attempts to try something new, to aim for perfection. I liked their humour, never exactly side-splitting, but dry and droll. Ian impressed me as a sincere and talented musician, as adept at playing the flute as he was at organising musicians to interpret his ideas. But gradually the basic truths of rock have been exorcised to the point where theirs becomes another kind of music; a desperate tortuous danse macabre where the listeners search for Tull's intentions, lost in a fog of bleating petulance and carefully maintained obscurity. I must admit chagrin at not finding the lengthy lyrics easy to interpret. Half a dozen readings gave me as many possible conclusions to be drawn. Perhaps they represent Ian Anderson's compassion for the human spirit buffeted by life's whims and fancies, jests and cruelties. If that's the case, then sobbing into a microphone won't help."

"And as the music is contrived to support the lyrics every beat of the way, the result is an endless, shifting conveyor-belt of chords; a unison beating of keyboards, guitars and drums, wholly lacking in melodic or rhythmic interest, and bereft of tonal quality. Part of the play is held up by an interlude entitled 'The Hare Who Lost His Spectacles', which sounds like Vic Feather reading Danny Kaye, and is the basis of the film shown at live concert versions of the play. There is no outstanding solo work by any of the musicians. Although Ian occasionally plays some soprano saxophone the bulk of the work is shared between John Evan's strangely foursquare keyboard style, Barriemore Barlow's flat sounding drums and the bass guitar."

"What is most depressing about *Passion Play* is the vast amount of work that has gone into its production. Aimed, I would think, at the American market, where size alone still seems to make some impression (and here I might be doing our American friends a grave injustice). It must have taken hours, months to conceive, write, rehearse and perform. Few bands could cope with the intricacies of the arrangement, but then few bands would want to. I repeat, it gives me no pleasure to fulfil the role of the "panel of judges" that Ian finds so distasteful. But all I can say is that music is a sacred trust, and for good or ill, that trust rests in the hands of musicians who today have greater technical and financial resources than ever before in the history of composing and performing. That musicians should want to utilise those resources is commendable and understandable. But please don't get lost in delusion and drama. Music must touch the soul. *A Passion Play* rattles with emptiness."

Notably, the bad review from Chris Welch was perhaps particularly hard for the band to take on the basis that in the concert programme that was issued for some performances of *A Passion Play*, specific reference was made to how Welch had placed the band's previous work in high regard; it was he who, upon having seen the premier of *Thick As A Brick*, had referred to it in *Melody Maker* as "the best rehearsed and most cleverly executed show" whilst asserting that the band's "ability to virtually play with an audience is quite fascinating" and that they "can be proud of their contribution to the arts and sciences of rock."

Despite the fact that the overriding narrative surrounding *A Passion Play* stipulates that it was poorly received by most at the time, that is simply not true. For whilst some of the most memorable reviews of it were perhaps the most scathing, the fact is that it was met with a positive reception in some of the less well-known accounts. For instance, a local paper reported on Jethro Tull's performance that took place at the Jenison Fieldhouse in East Lansing, Michigan in May 1973; "If you were one of those some 30,000 that could not get in to see Jethro Tull Tuesday night, all this reviewer can say is, 'you missed one hell of a show.' One hell of a show, unquestionably one of the best rock shows to hit campus in ages. The Jethro Tull concert was more than just a plain concert, it was one of those modern day rarities called a production. All 11,000 totally absorbed members of the audience were treated to much more than just music. They thrilled to Jethro Tull's own brand of theatre, film and acrobatics. This show was the complete show. Everything done to a turn. The music was superb, the films were well done and impressive, their stage antics were great fun and just the stage itself was incredibly impressive. The show began with a small light pulsating on a screen behind the stage. The light beat in time to a heartbeat and grew in size constantly until it nearly filled the screen. At that point the light switched into a photograph of a ballerina lying on her back, arms outstretched, eyes blank, as if she were dead and crucified. The ballerina then slowly rose and pirouetted her way around and through a mirror which signalled the start of the music. And what a start."

"The Tull congregation burst on stage in great clouds of smoke and began playing their incredibly complex and brilliant music. The ballerina appeared twice more. Once to signal the end of the first set of music, and again in a film called 'The Hare Who Lost His Spectacles'. Tull played nearly two and a half hours, mixing numbers in their repertoire into an almost continuous stream of music. Tull's musical blend was as basic as a one-two punch. They would lead with a hard-driving beat, then cut to a few bars of softer, more acoustic sound. What was possibly the best portion of music was the first set which consisted entirely of an original piece, soon to be released on a new album, entitled, *A Passion Play*. Group leader Ian Anderson had to be the high point in a superb evening. Anderson combines all of the intensity of a Calvinist minister, the graces of Vaslaw Nijinsky and the comedic ability of Emmet Kelley. He let loose with a fourteen-minute flute solo that left the audience standing and screaming for more. Barriemore Barlow, undoubtedly one of the best rock drummers today, also burst into a long solo at mid-show. Quite frankly, I haven't heard a drum solo like that since Krupa was recorded at Benny Goodman's 1937 Carnegie concert. Barre, Evan and Hammond-Hammond are also accomplished musicians. And great clowns. Just after Barlow's solo the group burst into a hysterical mock silent film routine." The reviewer noted that the acoustics of the venue were not to the advantage of the music but that overall, it didn't compromise the impact of Jethro Tull's performance. On this gig, they were supported by Brewer and Shipley who played for just twenty minutes prior.

Under the headline of "Tull: Can 72,000 fans be wrong?" it was reported in *Melody Maker* in August 1973; "I don't know how it is in England, but in this country the minute you get too big, too powerful, people start gunning for you. Therefore, it was with some caution that I approached Jethro Tull's *A Passion Play* performance here in Los Angeles. The advance critical word had not been good; oddly enough, though, it had been cautious. No diatribes about how this super-group had gone down the drain, only sad regret that his new log in Tull's book was not up to the high standards they had previously set for themselves. For audiences, the short-comings of *A Passion Play* didn't matter in terms of ticket sales. Over 72,000 fans plunked down their money in record time to see their favourite group perform. The Friday night concert I attended at the Los Angeles Forum had people almost seemingly hanging from the rafters, intent on receiving every nuance from the stage. It must be almost impossible for a group or artist to have any kind of critical evaluation from today's audience. Cheers filled the air, greeting everything from a throw-away kick to a major drum solo with the same enthusiasm. Ian Anderson had only to raise an eyebrow to bring the first ten rows to their feet. Why should he do more?"

"Any review of the concert *Passion Play* must rest with the work itself. Sad to say I found it almost impenetrable. Careful study of the lyrics did little to alleviate the confusion of the work itself. Granted, further study is warranted; there's no reason to assume it's possible, or even advantageous, to grasp a work in one gulp, but it does leave a concert audience floundering. A strong clue to the work itself must come through the film. Opening with the ballerina, prone, eyes closed in a dream-like state, she gives credence to the Jungian theory that all works of art are simply the creator's dream. If we take that tack, the non-plot and action of the work and the film become at least discernible. Her first and only words are, 'Something wonderful is going to happen', and we weave in and out of a real and fantasy world, courtesy of colour and black and white and the presence of a mirror. Clear separation of reality and fantasy is not the sole province of the mirror; for our ballerina moves from a theatrical stage to a garden setting with an ease that defies rational explanation and fulfils instead the dream-like quality of the whole."

The review continued; "Obviously in some sense out ballerina is being pursued by the ravages of success and the pressures of performing; the movie camera shot with a fish-eye lens to give the impression of rape is the give-away here. And the original Passion Plays were, of course, about the life and death of Jesus. Anderson has steadfastly refused to "explain" any of his works to his fans, which, perhaps (of course) is the right decision. For an audience it should hardly matter what the artist says, it's what the audience gets out of the work for themselves. When Jethro Tull went into 'Thick As A Brick' I breathed a sigh of relief and settled back to enjoy the rest of the concert. Anderson was in rare form, leaping about the stage with the precision of an athlete. His band is, of course, as fine a group of musicians as can be assembled and give them something melodic to play and there is no stopping them. I can only wonder how they enjoy playing *A Passion Play*. The audience was with Jethro Tull all the way; it would be impossible to read the reactions of 18,000 fans who shouted, clapped and screamed for more any other way. The overall evening was a colossal success and remarkably enough it was one of the only concerts at the Forum where the floor didn't turn into a battleground with lighted matches and sparklers being hurled to the ground in a furtive remake of World War One."

A performance that took place at the Kansas City Municipal Auditorium was reported on in the *Kansas City Star* in July 1973; "In what was undoubtedly the year's most smoothly executed rock concert, Jethro Tull played to a capacity crowd in the arena last night. The focal point of the performance was *A Passion Play*, the latest in Tull's string of masterful concept albums and concert pieces. Long before the houselights dimmed, a pulsing sound began to issue from the speakers, gradually increasing in intensity as a screen rolled down ominously at the back of the stage. As the audience was drawn further into a state of "willing suspension of disbelief," a white spot pulsed and grew into the film image of a ballerina. Simultaneously beautiful and grotesque, she rose and leapt, in a Dali-esque sequence, through a mirror as the group emerged from a cloud of smoke onstage."

"The musical quality of a Jethro Tull concert can almost be taken for granted. Under the direction of Ian Anderson, flautist-vocalist-composer, each instrument fills its own well-disciplined niche, without much room for jamming around. *A Passion Play* moved like a technically augmented operetta, an hour and a half of intriguing new music punctuated by slices of film, which, like the music, sprang from the conception and direction of Anderson. Perhaps the audience should have been provided with libretto, for the parable lost a bit of its impact because of the difficulties in projecting the subtleties of Anderson's lyrics through the echoing hall."

"Anderson, who has come to personify Jethro Tull, attacked the flute more ferociously than ever, lacing in some mad vocal licks. He even performed briefly on soprano saxophone, and from his Fagin-like stance put a few surprising touches on excerpts from *Aqualung* and *Thick As A Brick*. The real fascination of the evening lay in watching Jethro Tull play cat-and-mouse with their audience, keeping the suspense level high with professional precision. From time to time the music froze to a halt as the Tull members inspected a telephone stage right. Known to have occasioned strange happenings in the past, the "Tull-phone" was provocatively silent throughout the evening, though a spotlight often revealed it lurking suspiciously to the side. The tension finally broke as the phone shrilly sounded on the finishing note of the Tull encore, an extended version of 'Wind-Up'. Picking up the receiver, Anderson extended it toward his audience, smiling cryptically, 'It's for you'."

Despite the extent to which it was criticised overall, *A Passion Play* got to number one in the US. Equally though, it was only at number one there for a week. In later years, Anderson reasoned that the band's existing fans probably rushed out to buy it on the week of its release and then the bad reviews of it were such that the sales couldn't be sustained. The album did attain gold in the US though. In such regard, although at the time it was considered less of a success than Jethro Tull's previous albums, realistically, it is not the case that it failed chronically.

The album was given a positive review from *Record Mirror* in July 1973; "They've come a long way from their roots, and there are plenty who'd tell you Jethro should get back to a bit of simple funk. This is a long piece, often obscure and a little self-conscious, and any trace of R and B or even pop has gone. Jethro are doing English art-rock, and they can't hope to keep their vast following with such demanding music. Nevertheless, this is a much more enjoyable album than some critics have said. It may be smart but it does have a heart."

Billboard reviewed it in the same month; "One of this summer's more widespread pastimes for record buyers will undoubtedly be to try deciphering what the Tull passion play is all about. The LP gives every sign of becoming the most mysteriously worded gold album since *Sgt. Pepper*. Format of the album is a single disc with no separate cuts. But basically the sound is a little changed from *Thick As A Brick* and the songs can be easily lifted from the clever instrumental connecting sections. There's also a spoken fairytale with musical fills that work a lot better than the usual such efforts. Double fold jacket features more mystery — a dead ballerina and a fold-in program showing the group as the cast of a provincial British theatre. The group are currently touring and their entire show is the stage version of this album."

The *Reading Evening Post* considered in August 1973 that *A Passion Play* was "just random phrases incomprehensively linked together." Similarly, it was considered in the *Aberdeen Evening Express* in September 1973; "Jethro Tull, the group personified and fronted by the harum-scarum flute player who made a gimmick of standing on one leg while giving out with some of the best pop ever heard, have now come up with a very strange LP. Their record, *A Passion Play* is really an acquired taste. It opens with a medieval sounding jazz break and is followed by music akin to the atonal pieces of Mingus in the late fifties. This is, of course, full marks to Jethro Tull for daring to take pop far beyond the present spectrum. The only criticism is just where are they taking us? How many of us have heard of Mingus, Parker or Kerouak? For the current two million fans who bought the last album, this is a worthwhile addition to the collection. For first time listeners — play it very much by ear. Since writing this review, I hear Jethro Tull are quitting concerts, reputedly because of press criticism of their performances of *A Passion Play*. And that's a great pity. The group remain one of the best in the world and we can ill afford to lose them."

Of course, *A Passion Play* is an unusual album. When Jethro Tull got back to England and were under pressure to quickly put it together after not managing to make an album in France, Ian Anderson had an idea for a concept along the lines of what might happen to a person when they die and that rather than there being a heaven and hell, what if there were other levels of post-death options and experiences. The abstract nature of the idea and the verbal imagery of *A Passion Play* was deliberately designed to be quite open-ended.

As with *Thick As A Brick* and indeed many Jethro Tull albums, Anderson was keen not to spoon-feed the listener when it came to the meaning behind any particular set of lyrics. Retrospectively, Anderson noted that it was ironic that *A Passion Play* did so well in non-English speaking countries; if the complexity of the lyrics required a non-English-speaking person to work harder at listening to the album then surely they were the most likely to feel frustrated and confused with it.

It is important to consider that the negative media campaign against *A Passion Play* was plausibly more prevalent in the UK than elsewhere in the world. Not only did the album get to number one in the US and Canada but it also sold well in Germany and Norway.

In terms of the thought that was put into how *A Passion Play* would be performed on stage, on the LP, there is a pre-programmed piece of synthesiser music that fades out at the end of side one and then up again for the beginning of side two. This section of the album couldn't be played by the band on stage — by their own admission, the best they could have done with it would have been to do some sort of mime to it. Anderson felt that both of those options weren't in the spirit of what they were trying to convey.

As a result, he figured that it would make the most sense to stay true to including everything that is on the album on stage by playing visuals during the sections of pre-recorded music. The idea also appealed to the band ergonomically because it was a chance to pop off stage for a brief moment to have a drink and a smoke as required. For the visuals, the band made a film based around Jeffrey Hammond-Hammond's 'Story Of The Hare Who Lost His Spectacles'. The short film was expensive to make compared to the standards of the time. The project consisted of a whole day that included a three-person camera crew working with 35mm film, catering trucks, unions and mobile dressing room.

The segment surrounding 'The Story Of The Hare Who Lost His Spectacles' wasn't the only part of *A Passion Play* that was accompanied by a visual on stage. The stage show opened with a short mini movie that Anderson had shot with a high-speed camera. The footage was of a ballet dancer playing dead — as per the image on the album's cover art — and getting up in slow motion. Frames were cut from the footage and it was put back to normal speed as the dancer jumped through a mirror, running away through the other side and into the music as it were. In addition to this opening film, there was also a film sequence in the middle of the stage show and then towards the end as well. Anderson figured at the time that the project was worthwhile, even though it came with its technical challenges; the movie screen had to be lowered from above the stage and the film segments had to start exactly in time with the music. To take the whole thing on the road every night was no small undertaking.

All of the effort, expense and thought that had gone towards the stage performance of *A Passion Play* didn't protect it from being met with an overall hostile reception. In later years, Anderson considered that perhaps as soon as reviewers entered the auditorium, they may have already made up their minds that the music was something that they wouldn't like on the basis that with a mini movie at the beginning, the album was immediately presented as something that was going to be a little bit outside of the expected norm. In the same vein, the show didn't begin with an announcement that Jethro Tull were about to come on stage, the film simply started and nobody in the audience knew how long it would last before the band were to come on stage.

Ironically perhaps, the use of previously taped material was not exclusive to *A Passion Play*. After *Thick As A Brick* had been performed on stage, a tape was played. The band had recorded themselves having a mock backstage conversation referring to an idiot in the front row whilst making other humorous backstage-type comments (requesting towels and toilet roll). Still though, this was played at the end of Jethro Tull's performance of *Thick As A Brick* and the audience had the option of leaving the gig by that point. With *A Passion Play* though, the pre-recorded material was so integral to the show that if the audience didn't warm to it, it was inevitably going to have more of an influence on how they viewed the entire show.

Such was the hostility towards *A Passion Play* that rumours were in circulation that further tours wouldn't take place and that Jethro Tull were on pause for an indefinite period. In later years though, when asked about this phase in Jethro Tull's tenure, Anderson confirmed that it was a rumour that got out of hand due to a miscommunication between the band's PR people and the press. He was quoted in *Pop* in March 1974; "We've never considered splitting up. Rumours like this are made up by Sunday newspaper writers because they have nothing better to do that day. I can't imagine we'll split up in the near future, simply because we work so well together — each member complements the other... Even now I don't understand why the English music press had such a negative opinion of the album. Personally, I think *A Passion Play* is the most commercial record we've ever made. I've said before, but those who reviewed the album a couple of weeks after its release were much more favourable compared to those who had no time to absorb the work and wrote their reviews based only on a quick, cursory listen."

"*A Passion Play* is not the kind of record you can hear once and then whistle by heart. Fans don't normally jump around and dance and scream at our concerts — they usually sit down and pay attention to the music. However, I saw a lot of journalists milling around at our shows last year, generally chatting away to each other all the way through the show, and then they reported in the press afterwards that the concert was boring! Naturally, we have our off-days after five years on the road; nevertheless, we rehearsed for those shows well in advance, with some new jokes and features worked out, in order to make things a bit special. Even if I say so myself, I think we're the hardest-working band in the music business."

Without doubt, the retirement rumours were blown out of proportion. Anderson was quoted in the Australian *Go Set* in August 1974; "The retirement only lasted for the first weekend really. We split up on a Friday on the plane a reformed again on Monday after breakfast. When I phoned the others and said that we were going into the studio and that we should all go together. It was not really a retirement, we were back together as a group after a couple of weeks of rehearsing, and working on a whole lot of things, I mean different types of music. We spent a long time in the studio, doing about two and a half album's worth of music of various sorts from which we picked the obvious connected material. It was connected in the sense of what "they" refer to as a concept album. We stuck it all together and it will come out as the next group album called *War Child*."

For those who believed it to be entirely true that Jethro Tull were going to call it a day, the story was reported on with considerable bite. Such was the case in *New Musical Express* in August 1973; "In a shock announcement this week Jethro Tull joined the rapidly-swelling ranks of the "I quit" brigade. Tull manager Terry Ellis, in a statement describing the decision as an 'indefinite retirement' from gigs, appears to lump the blame squarely on the shoulders of the rock press and their 'critical abuse' of the band's work. With Jethro's *Passion Play* at number one in the US charts, the band have cancelled all gigs planned after September 29th — final date on the third section of their record-breaking American tour. Future Jethro activities will be centred around a movie to be made of a musical written by Ian Anderson."

Terry Ellis was quoted in the same feature; "The group have been working continuously for nearly six years, during which time their total recreation from concerts has not been more than one month. In particular, the effort they have put into preparing their concert appearances has been immense. The preparation of the music and production of *A Passion Play* began a year and a half ago and is, in their opinion, the best they have ever done. The abuse heaped upon the show by critics has been bitterly disappointing to the group and, illogical as it may be to identify the opinions of reviewers with those of the public, it has become increasingly difficult for the group to go on stage without worrying whether the audience are enjoying what they are playing. This has been a great burden and, in the circumstances — with the film already in the planning stages — the group thought it better to cancel all concert plans to concentrate on the film and to reconsider the situation after that."

In the same feature, it was reported that the band's US tour would continue and that the box office sales had been phenomenal. So much so that all 70,000 seats for four New York shows — two at the Nassau Coliseum and two at Madison Square Gardens — had sold out. In contrast, *A Passion Play* had dropped to number twenty-four in the UK, at least by the standards of the NME album chart where it had only ever got as high as number seventeen.

Anderson told *Melody Maker* in December 1974; "After so much work, when somebody wipes you out in one line it is as if they have hit you in the stomach after a full curry. I must be allowed to be hurt and sensitive. Of course I am going to go away for a week and sulk."

And in the *L.A. Times* in the same month; "The astoundingly negative criticism we received definitely affected us. I'd be less than human if my blood didn't boil when I read that some punk kid journalist — barely out of his nappies, no doubt — has written that our music is bad and unimaginative. That's terribly destructive criticism — and certainly unjustified. It hurt all of us a great deal."

The band's disappointment at how *A Passion Play* had been slated was not necessarily as a

A very happy-looking Jeffrey Hammond-Hammond. Ahoy, Rotterdam, 12th October 1974.

The arrival of the codpiece.

result of them having high expectations based on previous success. Anderson was quoted regarding Jethro Tull's earlier days in the same feature and it comes across that the same modest approach was embraced after a good few years at the top: "I don't think anybody had any real expectations from the band in those days. If anything, we figured we might become popular for a year or so, then we'd go back to playing the clubs. It's a source of constant amazement for me to wake up in the morning and realise I'm in some exotic part of the world, in an expensive hotel and doing okay. It's nice not to have any expectations. Even today, I live one hour at a time. If I had to worry about maintaining our current popularity, I would be very uncomfortable. I don't worry about gold records or selling out the Forum three nights in a row. I just think about making records that appeal to me. So far there's been a lucky coincidence that the songs I write are the songs people are listening to. I guess that just shows they have very good taste."

Although after *A Passion Play*, it looked on the surface that Tull had gone off the radar, they were in actual fact working on something new — *War Child*. The album's cover art features a reverse polarity image of Anderson superimposed over a cityscape in Melbourne. *War Child* was released in October 1974 — almost a year and a half after *A Passion Play*. Such was the uncertainty surrounding Jethro Tull after the slating of the latter that in order for the band to move on, it had been deemed necessary for them to do a press conference to explain what had happened and what their plans were going forwards.

In *Sounds* in January 1974, journalist Rob Mackie reported on Jethro Tull's press conference that took place in Montreux; "It is a Very Big Deal even as press conferences go. A good many journalists in Europe have been building up a store of questions to ask Jethro Tull for quite some time; and a good many rock photographers would have to struggle to find a more valuable subject to get in the viewfinder. Montreux and Jethro Tull — for it is their press conference — make an irresistible combination, and there's a general air of slightly nervous expectation, as if people are half-expecting Ian and Co. to make their appearance strolling upon the lake. There is a reason, other than the view, why the event is in Montreux."

"In 1971, Tull did a benefit concert in Zurich. The concert was a 13,000 sell-out and raised 50,000 francs — around £6,500. Today the cheque is being presented to Montreux's Mayor elect, to provide a special room, equipped with facilities for all kinds of music, within Montreux's youth centre. There's a further tie-in between the group and the city, for it was here that *A Passion Play* was evolved, during six months of rehearsals in an old brick factory. It seems that the group remained incognito without much difficulty — and indeed, sitting in a discotheque later in the day with Ian Anderson and John Evan, there's no glint of recognition, even when the DJ plays records by 'Jaytro Terl'."

"The band feels pretty much at home here, although Martin Barre admits that it's all a little too pretty, and after a while you begin to wish for some good old English grime again. The event even makes a short snippet on the TV news that night. The band is asked in French for their idea of what culture is. Ian looks slightly taken aback, but gives a sensible answer in English. John Evan joyously upstages him by emerging from the midst of the Tulls, looking uncharacteristically splendid in his Rod Stewart striped suit. Leaning confidentially towards the camera, removing his Meerschaum from his mouth, and with only the slightest trace of Blackpool in his cultured tones, he pronounces meaningfully, 'Le culture, c'est la vie'. It looked pretty funny in the middle of a news broadcast."

"After the TV guys and photographers have had their go, and after the official cheque-handing over ceremony ('From the group to you and the young people of Montreux. Don't spend it all at once'), it's down to the press conference proper: a pleasant surprise for those of us who had been getting used to the idea that the Tull entourage wouldn't be terribly downhearted if they never saw any of us lot again. Ian's last round of press interviews occurred about two and a half years ago. The conference was remarkably orderly and worthwhile, and provided an opportunity at last to hear Ian's views on the controversies surrounding *A Passion Play* and its reception by the press, as well as the band's future plans. Apart from being slightly baffled by one or two of the questions from the non-British section of the gathering — Was his role in the band the same as Pete Townshend's in The Who? Was his new look specially for the film? — Ian is expansive, lucid, relaxed and in very good humour."

According to *New Musical Express* in January 1974, Terry Ellis told the press conference; "We've asked you here to clear up the confusion that seems to have followed the group's decision to retire from concerts at the end of last year, to clear up any misunderstandings that the group might have split up."

According to the same feature, Anderson told the press; "I think Jethro have possibly been the hardest working live group over the last five years. Not just in America but all over the world. And we have to play large halls most of the time. When we had the opportunity to play England last year, we chose to do two shows at Wembley rather than play lots of smaller halls over the country. We did that so we could play the show we had been playing in America, using all the lights and a lot of equipment, and generally keeping the show up to the standard it was in America. Unfortunately that standard doesn't seem to have been well-received. The thing that annoyed me was that people seemed to dismiss it casually (*A Passion Play*) — whereas it was a record that took a lot of time to make and needed time to listen to. It didn't seem that critics were prepared to take that time. Personally I think the music on the last album was our best-written, best-conceived — and possibly our most commercial as well — but it maybe wasn't too easy to get into first time around. I do feel that music ought to require the same effort from the listener as it does from the musician who plays it."

"Obviously that's a very broad statement. It maybe doesn't apply to people who play funky music — when they just stand there and get it on, and the audience can reciprocate at the same level. But musicians who play more structured music, or lyrics with more depth — then that requires greater attention. In some cases it may be very good to explain it beforehand. But I rather like the idea of offering the individual the opportunity to read into things what they will — people listen in different states of consciousness and they will, whatever you say, make their own interpretations. I would far rather put the ball firmly in their court and say, right, we've done our bit — now, here you are. People seemed to object to the fact that they actually had to sit down and listen to it more than once, and to qualify the statements of their criticism — they seemed unwilling to do that to a large extent. They would rather dismiss it in a few words, which I do find unfair. It certainly doesn't reward me in any way whatsoever for months of work. It's not a very constructive criticism."

"Criticism ought first of all to be beneficial to the artist. Unfortunately, criticism tends to be aimed at the audience rather than the artist and, even more unfortunately, seems to have an effect on what the public might believe, might buy, or might come to see because very often they seem to have no other source to turn to other than what they might read in the papers... Criticism aimed at a specific piece of music is fine if it's constructive to the artist. I found nothing constructive in what I read, and I can only assume that it would have adversely affected public opinion if we'd have carried on this year doing odd tours in between making the movie. But there were other reasons, the biggest of those being that we've been working non-stop for five years, making records and playing tours, and for a couple of years now we have wanted the chance to do something different."

"There's no such thing as a wrong direction. There is only one direction you can take — because each album is a mirror image of how the band is thinking at the time... I would listen and discuss the thing endlessly, y'know. I would discuss it endlessly with Terry or with any of the people in the office — and they have every cause, for commercial reasons, to say, if warranted, 'Look, we're a bit worried about this...' I would listen to any critic who qualified the statements he made. But with *A Passion Play* there was more than usual adverse criticism which wasn't qualified, which simply exhibited the attitude: 'Well, okay, Tull have done their sort of epic *Thick As A Brick* thing. They've got that out of their system and we don't want to go through that again'."

"What those people don't know is that we made three sides of a double album during the time we were in Montreux, three sides of a double album which was just songs, y'know. But it didn't have this great amoebic surge, this growth thing that playing an extended piece has. I think *Passion Play* was so much better than *Thick As A Brick* in musical terms, lyrically and so on. But it's not an accessible album. I still don't think it warrants the kind of criticism that says, 'This is clearly not a good piece of music' or that it waffles, or that the lyrics are obscure or whatever. What pisses me off, is that the next album returns closer to songs, and everybody's going to think it was a calculated move on our part because of what happened to *Passion Play*."

The music for the *War Child* album was actually material that had been written for a feature film with a long synopsis penned by Ian Anderson. After three to five months of struggling to negotiate things in the lexicon of pre-production though (finding a director, leading actors, script writers etc.), it wasn't to be. In later years Anderson stipulated that the commercial mileage of the plot might have had its limitations as far as the big American film companies were concerned.

Although the project was given some interest from the film industry, an agreement couldn't be reached with the band on who would have control over casting, the choice of director and the final cut. The theme of the movie that wasn't to be — the *War Child* theme — wasn't too dissimilar to the theme of *A Passion Play* in how it explored ideas surrounding what might happen to a person when they die.

In later years Anderson surmised he wanted the film to be about the abstract nature of the afterlife regarding a young girl who was killed in a car crash (he also stipulated that a key reason as to why the movie idea was scrapped is that against his vision, American film industry bods wanted to contextualise the idea into something less abstract). As Anderson saw it, the film should have been set in a middling-sized town where the town council were divided between left and right wing movements. There weren't to be protagonists and antagonists though; the idea was to explore the interchangeable roles of good and evil.

Although as an album, *War Child* doesn't tell the story of the film that was never made, it still features scenes that were part of the original synopsis. The songs aren't linked and it is not a concept album. With the movie idea having been scrapped, it made more sense to leave the use of a story out of the equation altogether and instead to present the album as a collection of individual songs.

Anderson was quoted in *Down Beat* in March 1976; "Well, you see, *War Child* was done after first having taken a long time off the road. For six months, we didn't play concerts and *War Child* was like getting back together with the guys in the group after three months of not even seeing each other very much, then saying, 'Right, we have to start rehearsing a new album' — It was like entering a new phase of the group's existence. I enjoyed playing fairly simple, shortish pieces of music — a sort of renewing thing, another cycle. It was an enjoyable album to make, a very easy album to make. It had a good vibe to it. Then we had a single from it ('Bungle In The Jungle') which was a very catchy, sort of commercial sound as far as all the disc jockeys were concerned. So everyone sort of thought, well Jethro Tull is back playing it safe, doing something nice and inoffensive. For us, it was absolutely the right thing to do at the time, because that was the mood."

When *Rolling Stone* reviewed Jethro Tull's performance that took place at the Forum on 18th July 1973, the journalist noted that the crowd "politely listened to *Passion Play* and then became delirious when Tull finally played more familiar songs from *Thick As A Brick* and *Aqualung*." In the same review, an anonymous friend of the band was quoted as he said of Anderson, "I think he's got it out of his system now, all that complicated shit, and I think he'll get back to writing good tunes."

Anderson was quoted in the *L.A. Times* in December 1974; "When I listen to a piece of music, I always give it my full attention. The only musical trickery I use when I play or write are those which try to entice the audience into wanting to make that effort. I admit to doing that. I even admit to making a lot of music that people could not have possibly enjoyed."

War Child was also met with mixed reviews. Some saw it as another concept album whilst others weren't pleased that Jethro Tull had gone back to the format of doing an album containing individual songs. Anderson told the *L.A. Times* in December 1974; "My attitude has always been that we're a live concert group. Basically, the band sells records as souvenirs. The last couple of years, half our concerts have been taken up with a complete piece like *Thick As A Brick* or *Passion Play*. If we'd done another album like that we would have been in the absurd situation of performing it in its entirety and then having an hour left to play what? There would be no room to do justice to any of the other extended pieces. It's very painful to have to hack my work up into condensations. So we came back to working on a loose concept, but with individual songs in such a way that they would stand on their own. A year or two from now, we will be able to play parts of *War Child* and they're going to sound whole in themselves. It's important that our concerts are the best we can make them."

War Child was reviewed in *Rolling Stone* in December 1974; "Ian Anderson, the guru and master musician behind Jethro Tull, had a good thing going. Ian would play the pied piper with his flute, dance about and dangle a leg while his band ambled through snatches of convoluted but impressive jazz/rock jamming. Jethro Tull, which had begun life modestly as a group specialising in fluted pop with some classical pizzazz, became instead a didactic warhorse, the vehicle for Ian's obtuse sermons, a launching pad for ambitious messes of noodling like last year's *A Passion Play*. Such stuff didn't sell well. Even avid fans found *A Passion Play* boring. To recoup his losses, Anderson has now returned with *War Child*, an LP of relatively brief songs, some of them within the four-minute mark. Each handcrafted track comes chock-full of schmaltz, strings, tootie-fruitti sound effects and flute toots to boot, not to mention Anderson's warbling lyricism. British audiences have long had the good taste to avoid such pablum. Hopefully American listeners, hipped by *A Passion Play*, will follow suit. Remember: Tull rhymes with dull."

In October 1974, it was advised in *Sounds* that *War Child* is "vastly more interesting and enjoyable" than both *Aqualung* and *A Passion Play*. The reviewer continued to advocate of *War Child* that "the album does include a lot of what you might call Classic Tull — tricks of style in the arrangements, mannerism of time and riff, the distinctive nose vocal of the leader which sometimes comes too close to Dave Cousins for comfort. Familiarity breeding what it does, mannerisms and tricks which sounded pretty neat a few years ago sound somewhat uninspired these days. Occasionally on this album they become a severe irritant, but mostly they have been absorbed enough into different ideas, or imbued with fresh attack, or used sparingly enough to make them part of what's going on here rather than dredgings of what *did it* last time."

After the way in which *A Passion Play* was reviewed, particularly in the UK, some of the music press were undoubtedly cynical towards anything that Jethro Tull happened to release next. The headline for the *Sounds* review seems sarcastic as it states "Jethro Sensation! Journalist Enjoys New Album!"

Fortunately, negative reviews of *War Child* were in the minority. It was reviewed in *Cash Box* in October 1974; "The effusive and unending talents of Jethro Tull continue to pour north on the group's brand new Chrysalis LP, one that has a foreboding cover, but a wealth of captivating material sure to draw both die-hard Tull fans as well as those unfamiliar with the supergroup into the heart of the record. Particularly effective selections on this LP include 'Skating Away On The Thin Ice Of

The New Day', 'Bungle In The Jungle' and the thought provoking title track. Ian Anderson composed all the material here."

Circus Raves stated in November 1974 that "another LP of epic proportions and heartfelt sentiment, has become Ian's answer, his philosophy, to the dog-eat-dog world he suddenly realised he was caught in when the critics demolished the *Passion Play*."

In December 1974, the *Belfast Telegraph* described *War Child* as a "distinctive mixture of heavy music and lyrics with a message." As a side note, one of Tull's greatest admirers, Deep Purple's Ritchie Blackmore, cites *War Child* as his favourite Tull album.

War Child features the hit single 'Bungle In The Jungle'. The track had commercial appeal with its memorable melody and was something that people could dance to. It was given a lot of radio play. Anderson wasn't too pleased about the way in which it appealed to people; the cheerful way in which the song was embraced by the record-buying public was at odds with the meaning behind it regarding the cruelty of life in the concrete jungle.

In October 1974, *Broadcasting* reported on 'Bungle In The Jungle' by stating that the single was Jethro Tull's first top forty singles success in two years. A local DJ who was interviewed briefly advised that the success of the song was likely down to the fact that the band had supergroup status and had already kept fans interested with their output of albums over the years prior. 'Bungle In The Jungle' was Jethro Tull's biggest hit single in the US. *Cash Box* reviewed it in the same month; "Jethro Tull is back after much too long of a musical hiatus. But one listen to the new disc and the Tull sound is as fresh and vibrant as it always was. Ian Anderson's vocal is powerful and his flute playing enhances the arrangement as always. The lyric is in the haunting metaphorical imagist mood that Tull has always typified so well. This is going to put them back on the hit path in a hurry!"

War Child was given a boost via the release of 'Bungle In The Jungle'. It got to number two in the US and to number fourteen in the UK. Anderson was quoted in *Circus Raves* in November 1974; "We're all animals, competing, aggressive, out to win at the expense of others. And we have our codes, our rules and laws that we've invented which are convenient within the context that we operate. At this point in history the rules are one way. They change throughout the ages. But if aggression and competition is what everybody wants to do then I'll go along with it... The overall theme of *War Child* is that all of us have a very aggressive instinct which is something we're occasionally able to use for the betterment of ourselves. At other times, aggression at its worst is used as a very destructive element. When it's not at its worst it remains merely comical. I don't think that aggression is such an evil thing." Although the lyrics and themes on *War Child* still have their darker moments, the album was considered by many to be more accessible than *A Passion Play*.

On 25th July 1974, Jethro Tull performed at Adelaide Centennial Hall. It marked the start of their Australian tour that would continue through until 5th August in Sydney. After that, the band went straight on to New Zealand and then Japan where they wrapped things up in Tokyo at the end of August. Anderson was quoted in the Australian *Go Set* in August 1974; "It's really actually something of a relief to get back on the road, for all of us. Perhaps more so for the others than me because they went back after the last American tour with the intention of getting embroiled in domestic affairs, sorting themselves out you see. After being on the road for three years and having no permanent base for their wives, children and mopeds and the other encumbrances of life, they became a bit disillusioned with it after a month or two, whereas I went back with my suitcase, and opened it in a rented apartment."

"Having divorced myself, though not literally (yet), from my immediate new-found family ties, really being home wasn't that much different from being on the road, except that it meant working in the studio all the time. I was the one who, two days after the group had split, phoned the others up and said, 'Right, we've had our little rest, time to start up again.' But I think they were all anxious to get back on the road again. Me too. As soon as our recording schedule was through it was very nice to get back on the aeroplane again and do that sort of five musketeers thing, which is really nice. It's a very physical act, getting on the aeroplane going from A to B to C to D and back to A again. It's a very physical shifting of one's material body around and it takes place on stage in the same way, but there's a necessity for a physical performance, a physical expression of what essentially is just a pile of jumbled abstracts in the form of a loose verbal imagery and a cacophony of notes under which one attempts to discern some logical harmony and time signature. A very physical thing, I think that's what it's all about."

"You know after a while, after a few years of touring you begin to equate physical moving of yourself, the travelling with the sense of day to day progression of your life. The minute you stop still and stay in one place it really feels like you've lost all your impetus, stopped moving, stopped living almost. Travel becomes very necessary after a while and becomes addictive in a certain sense. You have to continue to play a constant reaffirmation of your worth as a human being, in the most elementary way — to discern once again who you are and what you're here for: We provide a public service. I suppose it's a bit like gas and electricity. I mean, we are our own natural resources."

The break from touring had probably helped Jethro Tull to come back to it with a renewed sense of enthusiasm. The tour programme for *War Child* stated that "the music benefits on a couple of fronts — first, because of the respite from constant touring, the group were able to take their time over recording. Second — the personnel have now been completely stable since *Thick As A Brick*."

A performance that took place in Melbourne was reported on in *The Age* in July 1974; "The theme of much of the group's material revolves around religion, working class struggles, and send-ups of upper class values. On religion the group sings of a God that doesn't have to be wound up on Sundays. Songwriter Ian Anderson says most of his songs reflect his own beliefs and experiences, but many come from the ideas of people around him. At Festival Hall last night the group performed a selection of the best songs from their first six albums, plus a few tracks from their latest, *War Child*. Although the new songs went down well with the capacity crowd, the best response came from early numbers: 'Aqualung', 'Cross-Eyed Mary', and 'Locomotive Breath'. Solos by Ian Anderson on flute, Martin Barre on guitar and John Evan on piano were all highlights. Throughout the concert, bass player Jeffrey Hammond-Hammond appeared as an uncoordinated puppet as he half strutted, half danced across the stage. John Evan, wide eyed as if in a trance, put his face through a series of contortions as they went through heavier instrumental numbers. Drummer Barriemore Barlow, wearing a basketball uniform and tights, was continually on hand during the lighter portions."

Under the headline of "Tull: Full Scale Return" it was reported in *Sounds* in September 1974; "In Los Angeles last weekend Ian Anderson gave the go-ahead for a full-scale return to concert appearances for Jethro Tull. Anderson was on his way back to the UK after a five-week tour of Australia, New Zealand and Japan. The tour had been arranged to allow the group to check out their own feelings about touring again. It is almost a year now since Tull announced their "indefinite retirement" from live appearances in September last year due to pressure of work, the restrictions of a constant touring schedule and not least the disappointment they felt after the strongly negative critical reaction to their *Passion Play* concert and album."

"In Los Angeles, Anderson announced that his mind had been made up to return to live work by the warmth of the audience reaction the group had encountered and their excitement at playing live again. Ian Anderson has confirmed that Tull will tour Britain and Europe this autumn and America in 1975. Chrysalis have booked some tentative dates, pending Anderson's approval, and further venues including a London date are being negotiated. Dates so far confirmed are: Edinburgh Usher Hall November 9th, Glasgow Apollo 11th, Birmingham Odeon 19th and 20th, and Manchester Opera House 22nd. Jethro Tull have a new album, *War Child*, set for release in October. recorded in Morgan Studios London, this is not the soundtrack of the film *War Child* on which the band have also been working but a new collection of ten songs by Ian Anderson including 'War Child', 'Queen And Country', 'Bungle In The Jungle', 'Third Hoorah'."

Many were keen to welcome Jethro Tull back to their stages. Regarding the dates that the group were due to perform at the Empire Theatre there, the *Liverpool Echo* remarked in September 1974 that "the last time they played here was to a capacity crowd at the Stadium, and they can expect the same response at the Empire. It will be good to see the group back in action following their voluntary retirement after the way *Passion Play* flopped."

In their review of *War Child* in November 1974, the *Liverpool Echo* considered that "this album marks Jethro's return to the scene. Ian Anderson has continued where he left off with *Passion Play* but he doesn't fall into the same trap. Basing their new stage show on this album, they are set to prove that they will be back to stay this time. 'War Child' is the outstanding track."

In October '74 rehearsals began in Rotterdam to prepare for their tour of Scandinavia. For the rest of the year, the band played various venues on the Continent as well as some in Britain — it was their first time performing in their home country in almost eighteen months. After their dates in Sweden and Denmark, it was time to wrap things up for the winter, during which time Anderson went to Montreux to begin work on what would be Tull's next album (The 9th November 1974 marked the beginning of the *War Child* tour. The European leg of the tour ended in Denmark on 5th December).

Even though the *War Child* film was abandoned, a small amount of what was going to be the film score had been recorded as demos for the prospective film. As a result, the *War Child* orchestral theme was often played while the audience came into the auditorium prior to seeing Jethro Tull play their gigs. At the time, the origin of the music wasn't explained to the audience.

In November 1974 *Melody Maker* journalist Chris Charlesworth reported on what he described as "Jethro Tull's triumphant comeback" in Edinburgh; "Rise Sir Ian of Flute, for thou hast indeed redeemed thyself. The critics have had their way, the Passion Play has been forgotten and Jethro Tull are back once again playing the kind of music that won them their hard-earned reputation as brilliant showmen and inventive instrumentalists. 'Tis now over a year since Tull shattered the rock world with their announcement that they would cease live performances because of the critical abuse heaped upon *Passion Play* and though some wags were overheard to suggest that tax problems may have also been a factor involved, no one seriously expected Jethro Tull to cease operations overnight. Now they're back, as we all predicted they would be, and the lay-off has certainly been

Ahoy, Rotterdam, 12th October 1974.

beneficial."

"Twelve months of heart-searching on the part of Ian Anderson has quelled his fury at the critics and enabled him to examine, in the cold light of day, just where Jethro went off the rails. Wisely, he's decided that the fans — in fact everybody — would prefer to hear more familiar music, shorter tunes and a little less soprano sax. You could call it putting the fun back into the band for that's the overall impression I came away with after their tour debut appearance in Edinburgh's Usher Hall on Saturday evening. Ian and his musicians were smiling and laughing which is a sure sign that all is now well. Their stage antics, totally unpredictable as always, were a model of professionalism and the music, I am happy to report, was for the most part a joy to hear."

"The show is a well-rehearsed piece of theatre as much as a rock concert. Like strange English eccentrics, the five members of Jethro Tull behave like possessed demons for a full two hours. Outlandish clothes, curious props and an attractive brunette clad not unlike a Bunny Girl are all produced from the conjuror's top hat that Anderson must consider to be his arena. Jeffrey Hammond-Hammond, in a black and white candy stripe outfit and matching bass guitar, leaps to and fro as if the floor beneath his feet were constructed from hot bricks, while Martin Barre, in a peculiar floral outfit that may have been borrowed from Elton John's elaborate wardrobe, joins him in these sorties, criss-crossing the stage and covering a remarkable distance during his two hour reign."

"At the keyboards, John Evan resembles an ice cream vendor in his ill-fitting white suit and baggy trousers held aloft with a wide leather belt, all of which accentuates his already portly demeanour. Attached to his Hammond organ is a small urinal into which he apparently relieves himself following his now accepted somersault routine. At the drums, Barriemore Barlow appears clad in red shorts over what seems to be a red body stocking. He resembles a featherweight boxer, but his percussion work on the double bass kit is anything but featherweight. The rhythms he pounded out on the bass drums, and his superfast snare work, lifted an otherwise routine drum solo into a technical achievement par excellence."

"But for all the action that surrounds him, Ian Anderson remains the supreme showman: a ringmaster whose flute substitutes for a whip and whose gestures put one in mind of a completely mad professor over-injected with vitamins or perhaps some less harmless drug. Like an American cheerleader, he rallies his musicians, whipping up tempos with circular movements of his right hand or balancing precariously on one leg while executing a delicate flute passage. His wispy beard, tights and codpiece give him the medieval air of a court jester, a role that I am certain he would not be loath to acknowledge."

"An added attraction is Miss Shona Learoyd whose duties as props handler makes that institution, the British roadie, redundant forever. Instead of a hairy, denim-clad member of the crew handing over instruments when required, Jethro now utilise this petite brunette, suitably costumed for this task. A definite aesthetic improvement. There is also a four-piece string section comprising three violins and a cellist. The four ladies concerned are clad in black and all wear identical platinum blonde wigs, making them look rather like oversize dolls. As Fanny open the bill, it doesn't take a degree to come to the conclusion that Ian Anderson has decided to surround himself with girls for his UK tour. That, coupled with a crack about David Bowie and rubber underwear, would seem to indicate that gay liberation exerts no influence within this band."

"The concert opens with a piece of orchestral music played through the lofty PA system and the arrival onstage of a tuxedo-clad conductor waving his arms around amid a profusion of dry ice. This lasts for some minutes before the restless audience, right on cue, begin to demonstrate their impatience. Two bright flashes burst and Messrs Hammond-Hammond and Barre appear through the smoke, dressed identically in flowing Japanese robes (which are later discarded) and play a doctored version of the riff from 'Aqualung'. But when the lights go up and Anderson is in view for the first time, the band switch into 'Wind-Up', thus setting the tone for the whole show which comprises mainly familiar pieces from the Tull repertoire. Jethro frequently slip in passages from one song into another, and throughout their concert I detected bits of the dreaded *Passion Play* here and there, and one reference to a rabbit who had lost his spectacles. 'Thick As A Brick' follows 'When I Was Young', and that moved into a very long rendering of 'My God'. It was during this piece that Ian chose to undertake a particularly lengthy solo on the flute designed primarily to demonstrate his skill on the instrument rather than actually play music. Though I was impressed by his speed, his ability to wheeze at the same time as he played and the various tricks he played with electronics, I became restless, perhaps because the flute isn't my favourite instrument but more likely because I'd much prefer to listen to the group instead of one man's virtuoso technique."

"John Evan followed Ian Anderson in the spotlight, playing a peculiar piano solo with classical overtones, which drew the odd shout of 'boring' from an audience who obviously felt the same way as myself. After an interlude which included some tomfoolery with a wooden dog called Brian and a moving tree, the whole band came back for 'Skating Away' and it was here that the music reached its highest peak with Anderson on acoustic, John Evan on accordion, Barriemore Barlow flitting between bongos and an elderly xylophone and Jeffrey Hammond-Hammond on stand-up bass (also painted in black and white stripes). The song just floated out into the hall with Anderson's voice at its most gentle. 'Wond'ring Aloud', taken at a similarly relaxed pace, preceded the first new song of the evening, 'Ladies', another quiet, simple piece that was chosen as the vehicle for Barlow's drum solo."

"A burst of flares and flashes signalled the arrival of 'War Child', a brash piece of loud, extrovert music containing none of the subtleties of the previous three pieces. During the breaks from vocal work, Anderson chose to balance a large balloon on his head, eventually bursting it at an appropriate moment. 'Bungle In The Jungle', the band's single, followed, a jolly rollocking item, and the concert ended with 'Aqualung', thus satisfying requests that had been levelled at the group all evening. They played this faultlessly. There is an encore that includes various pieces of Tull music all stitched together and the band leave the stage to the continuous, unanswered ringing of a telephone that has now become an accepted feature of their performances. Various other special attractions are promised for the shows at the Rainbow this week, but even without them I can happily report that the post-retirement Jethro Tull is well worth the price of your concert ticket."

Notably, Jethro Tull did two performances in Edinburgh — one on the Saturday and one on the Sunday. *Sounds* commented that "the scene hasn't been noticeably the richer for their absence and it was comforting to see two sell-out Edinburgh concerts." The journalist considered that whilst Jethro Tull's music hadn't progressed to an outstanding extent, the overall performance was as stellar as ever and that the visuals in terms of smoke and lighting and how the band used them had intensified compared to before. Sardonic humour intact, Anderson told the audience at one point, "On behalf of the musicians, the management and the Inland Revenue, it's good to be back. Welcome to another evening's light entertainment!"

In October 1974, *Sounds* had also reported that Tull's two dates for London's Rainbow — 14th and 15th November — had sold out so quickly that additional dates had been added to the schedule — 16th and 17th November. *Melody Maker* reported on one of the November performances. The reviewer noted that it was a sell-out and that the crowd were ecstatic as they witnessed a production of "brilliant theatricals" within a "breathtakingly long show" of two and a quarter hours that featured glittering costumers and props galore. Pan's People started the show. The reviewer concluded that "Jethro Tull are back on the road with an absolutely splendid show, a lesson in control, perfection and dynamics. Ian Anderson's contrived Charlie Chaplin-like pathos is a delight. Fanny also appeared. Stunningly lacking any style they relied on the overkill of volume but failed abysmally to communicate anything beyond sheer desperation. The real tragedy is that they wasted our time: Jethro need no support act."

Meanwhile the *Liverpool Echo* on 22nd November 1974 reported that; "A few thousand Jethro Tull fans turned up at Liverpool's Empire Theatre last night hoping that the criticism that greeted their last album — *A Passion Play* — hadn't killed off the spirit that has made them one of Britain's finest bands. They weren't disappointed. The music in the two-hour set was of the finest even by their own high standards, but what must have pleased the fans most was the performance of the group's leader and inspiration, Ian Anderson. Throughout the performance he twisted, contorted and forced his body into a hundred rapturous shapes, yet incredibly at the same time producing flawless and inspired music from flute, guitar and saxophone. The line-up of Barlow, Barre, Evan and Hammond-Hammond seems to be now more or less stable, and this reflects itself so favourably in their music."

On 25th November 1974 Tull played at Cardiff's Capitol theatre. The setlist played that night was reflective of the band's new material as well as the classics;

1. War Child Waltz/Classical Intro
2. Thick As A Brick
3. My God (including a flute solo with God Rest Ye Merry Gentlemen and Bourée followed by a piano solo)
4. Cross-Eyed Mary
5. (How Much Is) That Doggie In The Window? (Patti Page cover)
6. Skating Away On The Thin Ice Of The New Day
7. Wond'ring Aloud
8. Queen And Country
9. Ladies
10. Drum Solo
11. War Child
12. Sealion
13. Bungle In The Jungle
14. Aqualung

15. Back-Door Angels
16. Guitar Solo (including Minstrel In The Gallery)
17. Locomotive Breath
18. Hard-Headed English General (unreleased, a work-in-progress tour song)
19. Back-Door Angels (reprise)

The *Coventry Evening Telegraph* advocated on 11th December 1974 that "Jethro Tull's recent concerts, incorporating as much vaudeville as music, showed that the band were just about ready to come out of the shadows. *War Child* also shows an inventiveness much more acceptable than the ill-conceived *Passion Play* — there's a subtle introduction of strings and even accordion to create and atmosphere that relates to the theme of the album. Just the thing to re-establish the reputation of Anderson and friends."

The same month, *Melody Maker* commented that "Jethro Tull are at a new peak. All round the world their concerts sell out — and the new album *War Child* has repaired any damage that might have been caused by a year's convalescence from public view."

Even at this stage Tull shunned the typical rock star trappings. In response to the excessive demands made by other touring bands at the time (he didn't name them!), Anderson remarked; "We are not into contracts which say: thirty crates of Dom Pérignon. We pay for anything in our dressing rooms ourselves... It is becoming increasingly difficult to promote shows with the same standard as in the past. We have great tax burdens — but I'm not leaving the country, get that clear! But to continue what we are doing well — costs are rising all the time."

He was quoted in the *L.A. Times* in the same month; "I don't want to be enjoyed on a "rock star" level. It's too easy. That's why you find scuba divers and rabbits walking on stage during Tull concerts. That's why some Tull albums have no individual songs. Those things are meant to disturb people. They're meant to break up that predictable rock 'n' roll flow."

By the end of '74, Tull's working dynamics with each other seemed to be in good health. Anderson opined to *Melody Maker* of his opinion on the other band members:

John Evan: "There is nothing about John other than an unbelievably normal, boring sort of ex-university student, settled down with a wife and seven beagles. He is always wearing a white suit. He is into being super-normal, a quiet, pleasant guy. Says, 'Looks like rain today, figs are doing fine and cabbages are coming on okay.' When he comes out on stage he is exactly the way he is then, always. We have a saying which goes: four of us and the remains of John (he's always on his hands and knees). There is something about him which precludes his walking in a normal way. Not because he is drunk or anything. Somebody once gave him a duck. He carried it and took it everywhere with him. Somebody must have trodden on it because it had a broken leg. He put it in the bath for a swim but the water was boiling hot and it was swimming around in circles trying to get out. He is a danger to anything living or breathing around him."

Jeffrey Hammond-Hammond and Barriemore Barlow: "They cling to the other side of life and they are into reverting to domestic husband/father figures. They are very serious and passionate, domestic, responsible, caring human beings. Evan you might describe as schizoid. Barry enjoys life but when he comes back off the road, they are both very considerate of the other part of their lives which they have erected. They both have a conception of what life should be like off the road. They are very friendly, have similar musical tastes and I always think of them together. They think and feel music along the same lines. Whereas John and Martin and I don't have so much in common."

Martin Barre: "Tull's exceptionally gifted lead guitarist. Life for Martin is a mixture of fantasy and reality. He enjoys the fantasy more than the reality. He's at home with his big house — not that big, but fairly big — and big car and lives a fairly normal life, but when he gets that break on stage for his solo, it's something fantastic, and I can't resist watching him. He's amazing. I mean, for Martin, the ultimate would probably be having all of Pan's People in his living room, but once he'd got them there he'd be really nervous. He is a complicated guy in one sense but straight in another. For someone to shout fuck off to Martin on stage when he's in the middle of a solo is like somebody stealing my wallet or my woman."

By this point in their tenure, Jethro Tull's entire discography was substantial and worthy of extensive promotion. In January 1975, *Cash Box* reported that in the US, Warner Bros. would run an intensive promotional campaign of the band's eight albums released up to that point. Spanning six weeks across January and February, the campaign would utilise AM and FM radio spots, posters, TV advertising, in-store displays and contests. It was in the January that Jethro Tull reconvened at North Carolina's Civic Centre to start rehearsals for a tour of America. A flamenco style band by the name of Carmen would join them on the US leg. On March 13th, the tour concluded in Boston.

In January 1975, the *Kansas City Star* reported on Jethro Tull's gig at the Kemper Arena. The journalist considered that "presented as a conceptual whole on stage, *War Child* would have lent itself to oppressive dramatics, which Anderson and company wisely avoided, no doubt anticipating the same sort of critical barb which greeted *A Passion Play* in '73. Skilfully, interwoven with past material, songs from *War Child* received a lighter, though effective, treatment and the overall mood was a return to the happier entertainment of Tull's *Thick As A Brick* show in '72... Bursting on stage through the closing stanzas of 'Wind-Up', the group flashed briefly back to *Passion Play* and *Thick As A Brick*. The latter, Anderson quipped 'bought my mother a colour television set'."

Throughout the performance, quirky additions were included in the show to break up the intensity of the music — a maid appeared to dust off Anderson's guitar for 'Wond'ring Aloud', a large white rabbit bounded across stage during 'Skating Away On The Thin Ice Of The New Day' and a female ringmaster appeared with a ball to balance on Anderson's nose during 'Sealion'.

In February, *The Evening Bulletin* reported on the performance that took place at the Spectrum in Philadelphia. The journalist called it "one of the most entertaining and musically vital rock shows in quite some time" and urged that the band had "mounted a kitchen-sink extravaganza" that featured the female string players wearing silver wigs, extras in rabbit and zebra suits, stunning lighting effects and a stage set-up that included a catwalk and two platforms extending into the front section of seats.

It was considered that Anderson "seemed in better shape than at any point in his career, pirouetting, posturing and prevailing with choreographed exactitude and dramatic Elizabethan flourish. As a singer, he possesses a narrowly confined vocal range which he works to great advantage. His Scottish burr, now rather dilute, alternates between a hard edge and a lilting gentility with superb control. Tull's music exhibits a similar duality — on one hand there is the gut level, martial quality of the hard rock, offset by the soothing, pastoral air of the Anglo folk strains which sound from Anderson's acoustic guitar."

The journalist concluded that "the clockwork precision" of Anderson's "tightly arranged but improvisationally roomy compositions" were "vigorously maintained" by the rest of the band.

Cash Box reported in the same month; "The Forum, LA — After selling out a hard to believe five concerts at the mammoth Forum, Jethro Tull came out opening night and stunned the huge gathering of fans with their precision and highly developed sense of theatrics. Ian Anderson dashed madly about the stage waving his flute phallically and brilliantly portraying the mad musical wizard he so obviously is. It was a stellar performance and the fans screamed their appreciation every chance they got. Featuring a cross-section of their material and staying away from overdoing any one period of their recording history as they have been doing in recent tours while they performed *Thick As A Brick* and *Passion Play*, Tull paced the show brilliantly and performed nearly flawlessly."

"Their control of the very enthused crowd is merely another in a long line of achievements. Anderson, besides leading the music, performed the function of spokesman. With between-song patter that linked the music thematically and also was most entertaining and comedic, the scraggly looking lead singer/acoustical guitarist/flutist twisted the emotions of the crowd into whatever shape he desired. The band also shared Anderson's showmanship and performed on the grand scale so that even the fan in the furthest reaches of the arena could appreciate their onstage antics. Rabbits, zebras, and other figments of Anderson's fertile imagination also had their turns in the spotlight and added a surreal element amidst the thunder of the music. Songs included were virtually a Jethro Tull greatest hits collection. Favourites were 'Aqualung', 'My God', 'Thick As A Brick', 'Wond'ring Aloud', 'Bungle In The Jungle', 'War Child', 'Bourée' and their latest single release, 'Skating Away On The Thin Ice Of The New Day'. After tumultuous ovation which included literally thousands of flickering lights that set the Forum ablaze, they came back in a wave of glory to perform 'Locomotive Breath'. Beyond all doubt, Jethro Tull have redeemed themselves after being severely criticised for the self-indulgence of their last *Passion Play* tour. The fans at the Forum were thrilled to see them back on the stage and the legend that is Jethro Tull continues to grow and grow."

The two month US tour was intensive. It was made even more complex by the fact that the band had brought with them a string quartet consisting of four female musicians on three violins and one cello respectively. The quartet had their own solo spot but it was technically demanding for them to play so loud on stage. Anderson had sorted it so that all of the quartet's instruments were fitted with pick-ups in order that they could be heard through the amplifiers. Sonically it worked but the demands of the tour were such that the musicians were out of their depth compared to what they were used to doing performance-wise — they were from a classical music background and were more used to playing with orchestras.

As a result, it wasn't long before they were out of the picture. Due to the use of strings on the tour, David Palmer became more closely involved than he had been previously. He co-wrote the orchestral parts with Ian Anderson and was actively involved in the rehearsals with the string players in the run up to the tour. Palmer actually flew out to America for it. Once the string quartet had disbanded, Palmer was responsible for doing the string arrangements with a keyboard instrument.

From this point onwards, he was pretty much the sixth member of the band. Whilst many may have argued that the use of strings was not in-keeping with the style of rock music that Jethro Tull was sometimes associated with, Anderson was keen to utilise more acoustic instruments and to have them there as a contrast to the loud electric guitar, bass and drums.

For their next album, Tull would break their tradition of recording in London when they purchased a mobile studio. With the exception of the time they had spent recording in Paris, making an album outside of the UK would be a first for them. The idea of a mobile studio appealed because of the flexibility it would offer in terms of location. Also, they had been advised by their accountants that it would be a good idea because despite the costs of building a mobile studio, they would still save money overall by not having to pay studio bills.

As was the case for many bands at the time, being able to record in different countries was also advantageous as both America and Britain were out of bounds for tax reasons. *Minstrel In The Gallery* was the result. The album was recorded in the mobile studio in Monte Carlo because through a friend of a friend, the band found out that there was an old radio station that was available for use. It was empty with no equipment in it, which made it acoustically a good venue in which to record. Next to it was a car park in which the band's truck could stay. There were plenty of hotels nearby and with everything being priced at an out-of-season rate, it made economic sense.

It also offered the band a break from the mechanics of what they had grown used to by this point in terms of recording in studios in Britain. The title track on *Minstrel In The Gallery* was derived from the idea of a minstrel playing down to the gallery, as is evidenced on the photo that features on the back cover of the album. The theme of the gallery is continued on the album's front cover and is also apparent in the historic feel of much of the music within.

As it happened, the circumstances in which the album was recorded had a profound impact on the end result. Due to being in a holiday resort, it was often the case that some of the band got a bit lapse in turning up to sessions. Consequently, this left Ian Anderson to work on quite a lot of it on his own and there were some frustrations resulting from that.

Although *Minstrel In The Gallery* is musically impressive, it was felt at the time that the group were not as focussed and cohesive as they had been on previous albums. Anderson was part of the fun too though. They spent a lot of time playing badminton, so much so that for a period, they converted the studio into a court. With no net being available, they improvised by using a long piece of gaffer tape with newspaper slung over it to create a makeshift net. Barrie Barlow's wife had previously bought him a badminton set from Harrods as a present. It wasn't long before all the rackets got smashed up and the band had to buy him some new ones.

By the middle of 1975, Jethro Tull were very much at the top of their game. *Cash Box* reported in the May; "Jethro Tull's latest Chrysalis album, *War Child*, has sold over one million units, qualifying it for a Warner Bros. platinum record award. The platinum award comes on the heels of a resurgence of sales activity on the entire eight album Jethro Tull catalogue. All of the albums are RIAA gold award winners with *Aqualung*, *Thick As A Brick* and *Living In The Past* having previously attained platinum status." (It was in the spring of 1974 that the band collected platinum awards for the American sales of *Aqualung*, *Thick As A Brick* and *Living In The Past* — it was reported in *Billboard* in the March).

Once *Minstrel In The Gallery* was completed, Tull played a small number of shows in Germany and France in the June and July of 1975. After this, they performed in Vancouver on 24th July. A tour of the US (with sporadic dates in Canada) continued into the November. By 1975, with many tours to their name already, Jethro Tull were still going strong as a live band. During this tour, the support acts were The Sensational Alex Harvey Band, then Gary Wright and finally, UFO.

Released in September 1975, *Minstrel In The Gallery* was Tull's eighth studio album. It was certified gold in both the UK and the US. It reached number twenty in the UK and number seven in the US. The album also fared well in Norway, Denmark and Austria whereby it was in the top twenty in each country.

It was reviewed by *RPM*; "The Jethro Tull vocal material — Ian Anderson — moves a little to the left of front and centre for a pounding "out front" performance by a fine lot of musicians. John Evan's piano and organ, the drums of Barriemore Barlow, bass guitar and string bass of Jeffrey Hammond and Martin Barre's lead guitar, not to mention Anderson's acoustic guitar and flute, have an important say in this production. A beautiful showcasing of this instrumental beauty all lushed up with violins, and a cello. There's probably an incredibly large audience waiting to hang this latest Jethro Tull."

It was reviewed in *Cash Box* the same month; "Like all Tull material, *Minstrel In The Gallery* is a combination of music and thought. But what makes this Tull outing the sculpted musical work it is, is the fact that the music has the obvious upper hand. Ian Anderson's lyrical range shows more in the way of the extrovert while the inner moments benefit from bodily underpinnings. Musically the Tull backing unit is given room to stretch out and they make the most of it. *Minstrel In The Gallery* is the type of album that will hang from a mantelpiece when it's not being played."

Billboard opined; "One of the rare groups that holds its enthusiastic mass audience year after year turns in a new solid effort in its distinctive and familiar style. A highly energetic effort by writer/producer/leader Ian Anderson and company, more streamlined and less grandiose in concept than recent Tull releases. No shortage of hit single possibilities on the set and that Tull sound is displayed without undue clutter. Not that the lyrics are any more basic than before, it's just that Ian Anderson's twisty melodies and flute-guitar riffs are presented more directly." In the review, the best tracks were listed as being 'Minstrel In The Gallery', 'Black Satin Dancer', 'Baker Street Muse' and 'Requiem'.

Sounds also reviewed the album the month of its release; "A new Jethro Tull album is not the most exciting release in the world these days: not the type of record to force its way onto your turntable and remain embedded on your consciousness forever. With *Passion Play* and its schizoid time changes, Ian Anderson led his merry bunch of men through disjointed pastures, less melodic than those instantly recognisable tunes that earned the group their solid gold status. *War Child* was a step in the right direction; looking back to yesterday but leaning substantially on their "new direction"."

"In concert, *Passion Plays* were interspersed with quick trips down memory lane, Anderson performing old masterpieces with a disturbing mechanical vengeance. Older fans weaned on *Stand Up* and *Benefit*, coming of age with *Aqualung*, have easily grown disappointed and disillusioned over the last few Tull years. That's why *Minstrel In The Gallery* is such a pleasant surprise. Quite honestly, I was dreading listening to it, expecting to see yesterday's heroes (codpiece and all) parading through the speakers, a mere shadow of former glories. But Ian Anderson, and curiously enough the band, seem on top of the situation once again. It's their best album since *Thick As A Brick* yet closer in harmonic melodies and gentle emotions to songs like 'Jeffrey Goes To Leicester Square', 'Reasons For Waiting' or 'To Cry You A Song'."

"The album smoothly combines the best Tull elements, wrapping them around Anderson's voice with sensitivity and understanding of the material. Returning to softer melodies offset by coarse sounding rock, it's the perfect working man's guide to Jethro Tull. Drummer Barriemore Barlow has stopped thrashing about at random, sticking to a more hollow sounding use of percussion reminiscent of Clive Bunker's best work with the band. Martin Barre is still not a great guitarist — one suspects he never will quite make it — but as on *Aqualung*, the lead guitar work is unimaginative but more than adequate. Bassist Jeffrey Hammond-Hammond lays low while John Evan rises to the cause with some lovely and haunting acoustic piano playing that nicely compliments the softer side of Anderson."

"The biggest change, of course, is with Anderson himself, sounding surprisingly fresh and inspired. The title track is standard fare played well with good, bitter, satirical lyrics. 'Cold Wind To Valhalla' is perfect fireside stuff, decorated by hand-clap percussions and nice in-built tensions with flute and acoustic guitar. 'Black Satin Dancer' kicks off with an introductory flute tease before the piano wraps itself around the music, ending in a merry sort of jig. 'Requiem' is another acoustic piece that finds Anderson returning to his old throwaway phrasing. Most of side two is taken up by the album's finest moment: four songs carefully sewn together under the name 'Baker Street Muse'."

"Anderson has always had both a lyrical and musical flair for concepts but this one wears better than previous forty minute epics, edited down to a rousing sixteen minutes of lovely playing. A string section supplements the band, serving as connector between harder rock and soft late night listening. With much of Anderson's material, the urban life of London lends itself to the atmosphere, the writer proclaiming himself just another 'Baker Street Muse' with Indian restaurants that curry his brain. The piece is stuffed full of his wonderfully cynical "fuck you" attitude that made *Aqualung* so attractive. He's even back to the gutter on 'Crash-Barrier Waltzer', while 'Mother England Reverie' is another media put-down as well as a statement on that all-consuming ninety-eight percent tax. Ian Anderson is quite a clever lad, aware of his ability to remain above the rock rubble. 'We're getting a bit short on heroes lately', he sings earlier in 'Cold Wind To Valhalla'. With *Minstrel In The Gallery*, Ian Anderson regains his hero stance quite nicely."

The album was reviewed in *Rolling Stone* in November; "Chances are, most of you have long since forgotten the notion of Elizabethan boogie as an art form. Well, it's revived here on *Minstrel In The Gallery*, Jethro Tull's latest concept-as-afterthought entry in the fall record sweepstakes. The fact that Ian Anderson and the lads have once again plundered the British secular music tradition signifies little and delivers less. Anderson, still holding to a self-consciously bizarre musical stance, has difficulty maintaining the centre of attention with his mannered vocals, irrepressible flute and acoustic guitar. And although, accompanied only by his guitar, he introduces each hauntingly familiar refrain as a ballad — aided by intimate spoken intros and incidental studio background noises — the tunes are soon deluged by a wash of lugubrious string passages and the anachronisms of Jeffrey Hammond-Hammond's mechanical bass lines and Martin Barre's hysterical electric guitar montages."

"In addition, contrary to the LP's basic concept, the lyrics are instantly forgettable. In keeping with the times, Tull does get points for technical competence. Still, despite the diligence with which these gents execute the often clichéd arrangements, the most soulful moment on the album is a line from 'Baker Street Muse', sung in passing by Anderson as he leaves the studio. Finding the door locked, he screams: 'I can't get out!' That's roughly the same feeling that this listener got about midway through side one."

The *Aberdeen Evening Express* commented; "Jethro Tull will be back in the album charts in double quick time with this new LP — their best since *Aqualung*. It is dominated by Ian Anderson, but the group members are also in great fettle, emphasising that Tull are still one of the best rock bands around. Excellent."

And finally, from the *Reading Evening Post*; "There's only one way to listen to Jethro Tull and that's with total commitment. Ian Anderson's lyrics are as deep as the music is complex. It's not an exaggeration to say that each individual listener has his own individual interpretation. This album is a more mellow creation than Tull's previous barnstorming offerings, with more use of acoustic guitar. In fact it's almost beautiful in parts, an adjective one cannot often use in describing Jethro Tull's music. But Anderson isn't mellowing by any means. He's changing, sure, but he still wields a mean pen. His suite 'Baker Street Muse', all about the seamy side of London, paints accurate pictures of the capital as it picks up all the threads from the rest of the album and weaves them up into a bitter tirade. It's a piece in typical Anderson style and is guaranteed to create yet another gold album for the band."

Upon its release, Ian Anderson told *Melody Maker* about the personnel dynamics; "Right now I tend to be locked away from them because I'm writing material for the next album. At the moment, we don't have much to say. They're probably talking about me behind my back, wondering what I'm writing. I also have to be aware of writing something that they really want to play. There's no point in me writing something that isn't going to interest them at all... Ian Anderson is part of Jethro Tull, and Jethro Tull are a big part of Ian Anderson. That's all I do basically. I don't do anything other than Jethro Tull. I think that maybe the other guys have their more pertinent interests outside of the group, whereas I don't. The only thing I do is this group, which makes me more involved than they are. I do more than play on the record or play on stage. I have a wider involvement, like producing and mixing. Nonetheless, when we do get on stage, it's five people up there and I expect them to work as hard as I do and I expect them to play better than I do."

Regarding the other members' active involvement, Anderson commented; "They always can, if they want to. When Martin writes something, as he does about once every three years, the chances are I'll use it, because the chances are I'll like it. He wrote something about a year ago which I liked. If he wrote more I'd probably use more and I'd incorporate it into the songs I was writing. He doesn't do that much but when he does it, I'm pleased to have it. Presumably, if he wanted to write more, he would. He has every encouragement to do more, as do John and Jeffrey. At one time or another, they have all made writing contributions. They're just not terribly prolific, let's just put it that way, whereas I am... On *Passion Play* there was a track where the royalties were split up between everybody because we were all involved. It said on it 'by Jeffrey Hammond-Hammond, John Evan and Ian Anderson' in that order. On *Thick As A Brick* there were some bits that John Evan wrote, which I don't remember he got credited for but he certainly got paid for. On *Minstrel In The Gallery* there was a bit on the title track where Martin did a three minute instrumental, which Martin wrote and he is credited for that on the album and gets paid for it as a percentage of the total royalties from the album."

As much as over time, Anderson has expressed mixed feelings towards the working conditions of making *Minstrel In The Gallery*, he has also stipulated that it can't have been that bad as Jethro Tull would go on to make another album in such way. He also considered that with hindsight, the sound quality on *Minstrel In The Gallery* was one of the band's best up to that point.

Minstrel In The Gallery made strong use of the musical contrasts that Jethro Tull were known for by this point. Hard rocking moments blend with quieter acoustic ones to make for a diverse and immersive listening experience. Not only that, but it features both short and long songs — a happy balance between what fans may have been expecting from the band at the time. In particular, 'Grace' is only thirty-seven seconds long whilst 'Baker Street Muse' comes in at just over sixteen and a half minutes.

Regarding 'Grace', Anderson told *Down Beat* in March 1976; "My big private goal, my actual composing ideal, is just to write a thirty-second piece that just totally evokes something. Everyone will say, 'I know just what he means.' That's my sort of private thing. I don't get caught up in that too often, just once in a while. There's a song on *Minstrel In The Gallery* called 'Grace'. It's just a forty second piece. I literally woke up one morning and looked out the window and just sang words that perfectly evoked for me a feeling, and put it to a sort of quartet arrangement for strings. For me it evoked something that I think countless people will sort of share in and understand. The only twist is in the words... 'May I buy you' is so ambiguous, whether it applies merely to the $2.50 breakfast at the airport or the whole thing. I mean, we pay for all this in one way or another. That ambiguity is a consciously put-in thing, but it's not something that anybody will really pick up on, though some people obviously will. The last line doesn't even need to be there for most people. It's there as an extra twist, an amusement. It's there if you happen to feel, like I do, a certain cynicism about all your pleasures in life. Because I wake up some mornings and the sun is shining and the birds are twittering and I feel like going out and strangling the little bastards."

'Baker Street Muse' was written as a whole and put together as a mini concept piece consisting of contrasting sections of music; 'Pig-Me And The Whore', 'Nice Little Tune', 'Crash-Barrier Waltzer' and 'Mother England Reverie'. Anderson pointed out that the song relates to some of his experiences and the characters he observed whilst living in a rented mews cottage just off Baker Street as well as some of the people he observed when the band were recording the album in Monte Carlo. He told *Sounds* in September 1975; "It drives you crazy being somewhere like that for nearly two months. It made me sick getting up in the morning and watching all these people lying on the beach with their amazing vanity. Most of them are really ugly people, physically grotesque; the women are unattractive and the men are obscene. And they lie there in the sun getting a tan to go back home to the office and say, 'Look where I've been.' And they do nothing... I get very aggressive in that sort of situation because I've got a lot of things to do. Anyway, no doubt some of that aggression came out in what I was singing about."

With Anderson having done a lot of the work on *Minstrel In The Gallery* alone, it is understandable as to why some may have expected him to consider making a solo album not long after but he was keen to stipulate — even when asked about it in later years — that he couldn't do Jethro Tull without the others and that the band was his main focus. Regardless of who did what in the group, they were very much a unit with a convincing rapport. Besides, the title track on *Minstrel In The Gallery* is the only song on the album where another member of the band (Martin Barre) shares a writing credit with Anderson.

Co-writing credits were rare for Barre. Not just in terms of *Minstrel In The Gallery* but across Jethro Tull's entire discography. Barre's heavy guitar solos had been a key part of the live material on tour prior to the album being made. In this instance though, Barre's riff was such that it was used as part of a song on an album.

As a single 'Minstrel In The Gallery' placed at number seventy-nine in the US in October 1975. On the B-side is 'Summerday Sands'. *Cash Box* reviewed the single in August 1975; "It is a far better thing that Ian Anderson has done with 'Minstrel In The Gallery' as this 4:12 is a deft return to the density and meaty substance that characterised earlier works. Lots of heavy riffing effectively compliments Anderson's vocal posturing while his unobtrusive flute runs stab at the periphery. Tull is hot this time out."

The *Liverpool Echo* reviewed it the same month; "It's good to see Jethro Tull back in business again with a fine single — 'Minstrel In The Gallery'. And what a fine song it is as Tull immediately stamp their usual brand of chunky rock on an energy packed single."

By 1975, Tull had an established approach to live performances. "I've always been dead set against that sort of ridiculous encore syndrome that most groups, who should have known better, finally submit to," Anderson told *Melody Maker*. "You have a group like Procol Harum playing their own particular and peculiar home-grown music, their own niche in the music world, for an hour. Then they would go offstage and the audience would bring them back on. They are being brought back on the strength of the music they'd been playing for the last hour but they come back and play some third-hand rock and roll, simply because that's the easiest way to get the audience standing up, clapping their hands and breaking a few seats. That's a ridiculous situation. I've always firmly believed that the encore is part of the show. It's such a predictable thing. I'm not going to go back on and play rock and roll or somebody else's music for the encore. I'm going to play some more of what we do. It's just a part of the show to me, as it is for the audience, because they know that when you go offstage for the first time that you're going to come back again and play another half hour's worth."

"We do a half an hour encore because it seems a damn sight better than doing another five minutes and then going off and going through this ridiculous performance of being brought out again for another five minutes. There are groups who delight in doing four or five encores but that's bullshit. It's bullshit because everything is calculated in terms of saying that they'll save this song for the third encore and then they find themselves on a night where the audience isn't so heavy that they've left the best numbers for the third encore and the audience didn't bring them back. Presumably then they go back and play it in the dressing room... We come on and we say that we'll go through this absurd pantomime of the encore. We were going to play it anyway."

"The encore for us is the time we go offstage, freshen up, have a quick drink, half a ciggie and on again. It's more like an interval. After that half hour, that's about it. I want to finish it on a very brittle, anti-climactic note so that everyone is aware that this really is the end. We don't finish the encore trying to incite people to want more. We do it the other way. That's calculated if you like, but it's the opposite effect to going on to win applause and win success by playing rock and

Jai Alai Fronton Hall, Miami, 28th August 1975.
Stripes were definitely the fashion if you happened to be Jeffrey Hammond-Hammond.

Jai Alai Fronton Hall, Miami, 28th August 1975.

roll and saying, 'put your hands together' and all that rubbish. The audience can do that if they want, you don't have to tell them. I don't have to urge anybody to clap their hands. If they do it, then it's real. If they don't, then you haven't got into that rock-and-roll-Geno-Washington-let's-all-pretend-hard-enough-then-we-will-actually-have-a-good-time. The music has got to do it, not the tricks of showbiz, which is what a lot of people — us included but not as much as people think we do — employ. We're not really a showbiz group. I, at this point in time, am adamantly against this production sort of show."

Tull's performance on 27th October 1975 at the Milwaukee Arena was reviewed by journalist Dominic Jacques; "Anderson is a sorcerer — whirling, twirling and bounding across the stage. As he performs, a giant rabbit casually walks past him. Nothing unusual. No need to be alarmed. Giant rabbits show up at rock concerts all the time. Tull's theatrics work well because the band doesn't fall into the trap of taking itself too seriously. There is no pretence here. Anderson has been called 'the original madman' and 'the fool to this band of tarot card musicians' — in a profession full of fools and madmen, he is the real thing."

A local newspaper reported candidly on the performance at the Jenison Fieldhouse in October 1975. The journalist began by asserting that the band "is not a band for every taste. Some people loathe the band and say that leader Ian Anderson's songwriting skills are virtually nil. Others proclaim that the group's first album, *This Was*, is the only tasteful venture Tull has ever produced — thanks largely to the work of Mick Abrahams who left the band after that point to form the superb Blodwyn Pig. Even loyal followers of *Aqualung* found themselves in the dark after the mysteriously vacuous *Passion Play* was first released. And of course, there are always the loyal Tull fans, who have remained with Ian Anderson through the highs and lows of his career. Like the Moody Blues, Jethro Tull has a steadfast following too large to be called a cult and too small to be anything else of major importance."

Having made a balanced assessment of how people may have related to Tull by that point in their tenure, the journalist went on to say that "the concert was, in every way, spectacular" and that "those who find fault in Tull's present direction would hardly object to the material performed." The whole band was described as a strong unit and a range of songs were played from Jethro Tull's albums up to that point.

When a local newspaper reported on the gig at Kalamazoo Wings Stadium in October 1975, the journalist gave a glowing review of what the whole band contributed; "The other members of the band also gave their all. Barriemore Barlow exploded in a cloud of smoke with a drum solo that survived machinegun-like strobe lights. John Evan on piano had the audience in the palm of his hand. If he played classical his listeners mellowed with him but when he started to jam, they were right behind him. Jeffrey Hammond-Hammond played electric bass and bass fiddle, both of which matched his black and white striped suit. Between playing his instruments and duelling with the lead guitarist Martin Barre, Hammond-Hammond showed his talent for juggling. Martin Barre showed the same fast fingering on guitar that Ian Anderson did on flute. He blended into the music, not above it." It was also noted that whilst the Wings Stadium wasn't an ideal venue for a concert, Jethro Tull definitely gave it their best.

The *Harrow Midweek Observer And Gazette* in December '75 considered; "Rarely has a musician been so bitterly criticised as Ian Anderson when Jethro Tull's *Passion Play* was unleashed in spring 1973. Both the album and the stage show got an almost unanimous thumbs down from critics worldwide. Disheartened and disillusioned, Anderson and his hand-picked band retired hurt, tails between legs, and emerged just over a year later with an album light years away from *Passion Play*. Yet even today, Anderson, creator of at least two rock milestones, *Aqualung* and *Stand Up*, deems *Passion Play* his greatest achievement. He says it's gripping, emotional and moving and yet, because of either critical abuse hurled at *Passion Play* or the continual battle against becoming predictable, Anderson returned to songs and simplicity for *War Child*, *Passion Play*'s successor."

"*War Child* was good, better than its predecessor, and even gave the band a hit single in the States with 'Bungle In The Jungle', but it wasn't the sort of stuff to put the band back up there in the higher realms of the first division. *Minstrel In The Gallery*, Tull's new album, is. *Minstrel In The Gallery* follows where *Aqualung* left off four years ago. Anderson is again a singer/songwriter way on top of his form, and at least fifty percent of the record ranks alongside the band's former glories. An olde English rural atmosphere permeates the album, even the band's name conjures up visions of ploughmen and farmers trekking across great fields like something out of Hardy's Wessex. A group of 'strolling players' are introduced to the local dignitaries from the gallery. Smattered applause, a muffled cough and a whisper and the minstrels are away."

"Acoustic guitar and flute crisply interweave in attractive melody before Martin Barre's spiralling guitar adds meat and grit to the proceedings. Anderson's singing is as distinct as ever, though it's not so much the quality of his voice which strikes home, but rather his phrasing. In much the same way as Bob Dylan and Ian Hunter, Ian Anderson embellishes verses with delicate twists of the tongue, and well-timed pauses. Just listen to 'Requiem', possibly the best and certainly the most beautiful track on the album, where he unleashes a whole host of dainty ornate knick-knacks from his box of treats. 'One White Duck/010 = Nothing At All' and a couple of sections from the 'Baker Street Muse' suite, see Anderson again as the folkie, alone with an acoustic guitar, until refreshing strings drift finely across the lyrics. Tull are one of the few rock bands to use strings to good effect. It all started on *Aqualung*, developed through *Thick As A Brick* and has arrived in grand style on 'Baker Street Muse'. Whether he's cavorting around with Pan's People at The Rainbow, addressing the Royal Albert Hall in green tights and codpiece, busking outside the Marquee or sticking out another Tull album, you can't really ignore Ian Anderson. He's a star."

Late '75 saw Jethro Tull undergo their first line-up change since 1971. Jeffrey Hammond-Hammond reportedly returned to painting, which had always been his principal interest. Meanwhile Tull were recording in Switzerland with a young American bassist John Glascock.

It was reported that Tull were in the process of recording eighteen new Ian Anderson songs, from which the best ten or twelve would be selected for inclusion on a new album, planned for May release. Anderson said in Montreux that the songs were all about people from different walks of life — an ageing rock star, a housewife, an artist, and so on. "Some are sung in the first person, others in the third person," he explained.

In anticipation of what 1976 was set to look like for Tull, Anderson told *Melody Maker* in September '75; "I will give you, glibly, a prediction straight off. I would suggest that Jethro Tull, in the latter half of '76, will become a much more hugely popular group. I think that, by the time the next album comes out it will contain probably a number of songs which actually reach a lot of younger kids again. At the moment I am feeling very youthful and very energetic about pulling little birds and getting into fights. I'm very much into that. I'm very energetic, much more than I was a year ago, when I did a bit more sitting down and remained very calm about things. I'm a bit more up now. I don't know why. I don't really want to appeal to that younger audience but I think it'll happen. Just going by the songs I've been writing for the next album and the way it's going. People are actually going to think the next album really is good. People will think the next album will be really neat."

"The reason is that the songs, so far, will hit them long between the eyes. I'm getting better at doing that, although I don't do it all the time. It's not a style but I will employ it because I'm feeling a bit more like that than I have done for a year or so. The last time I was feeling super-energetic was around *Passion Play* time but then it took the form of a tremendous group thing. That's what happened. This time it's not like that. It's confined to the songs and the chords and the words and the group thing will be very carefully handled to assist that. I'm not going to let the group submerge it, the way it happened on *Passion Play*. The group will not submerge the essence of the songs, which are really simple. You will understand the words but you will also say, 'actually, that's quite neat' — I think it will be a good year. It'll probably appear to be the sort of music that is going to appeal more to fans that we don't have yet. It'll pick us up a lot more people who can identify with what I'm saying and what I'm doing and what I'm going to be like this time next year. I'm getting increasingly into very emotional things and I didn't used to be. It's difficult for me to figure out why. The songs will appear more directly emotional and will gain us the new fans. I think that the people who have been fans in the past will say that it's okay and say that we're back doing okay stuff again."

It was during the first half of the seventies that some of Tull's most iconic albums were made. Through this, with the addition of many live performances, the group cemented their identity; eccentric, innovative and unafraid to do something beyond the expected. Having embraced the wave of a multitude of highs and lows and generally coming out on top overall, the remaining half of the decade would see Jethro Tull go on to create some of their most memorable music yet.

February 1977, Hammersmith Odeon.

© Steve Emberton

Part Three: 1976-79

By 1976, Jethro Tull had a strong discography behind them. Consequently, the compilation album *M.U. — The Best Of Jethro Tull* was released (with M.U. standing for Musician's Union). As well as including a range of classic and well-known tracks, it featured the previously unreleased track, 'Rainbow Blues'. The album got to number forty-four in the UK and to number thirteen in the US.

With regard to the next studio album, the idea for *Too Old To Rock 'n' Roll: Too Young To Die* came about from how Anderson and David Palmer had been working on a stage musical about an ageing rockstar who suddenly comes back into fashion. The pair of them were hoping to get Adam Faith on board for the lead role but as was the case with the *War Child* movie, the project failed to materialise.

Released in the spring of 1976, *Too Old To Rock 'n' Roll: Too Young To Die* got to number twenty-five in the UK and to number fourteen in the US. It was the first of Jethro Tull's 1970's albums not to acquire gold status in America. The album signified bass player John Glascock's first with Jethro Tull.

The absence of Jeffrey Hammond-Hammond made a difference to the band's onstage appearance. Hammond-Hammond was a colourful and animated part of the live performances. His clothes had been self-designed but to signify the end of his time in Jethro Tull, he set fire to his famous zebra stripe outfit (it had matched his zebra-striped bass guitar and his zebra-striped electric six string guitar). As with his involvement in Jethro Tull, the iconic zebra stripes were no more.

In an interview with BBC Radio in 1979, Anderson told the story of how the band had pranked Hammond-Hammond on their last gig together; "He did this juggling act; and on the last night, Jeffrey's last gig with the group, substituted for the tennis balls was, I suppose about three pounds in weight of the real thing. Not actually the real thing. It wasn't real zebra — belongings. We actually managed to get something from a horse — squeezed something out anyway which looked like it — about two and a half pounds of steaming hot horse turd dropped out, and Jeffrey just about managed to get his hands apart in time, and this stuff lay all around him steaming in the spotlights. That was his farewell concert. Nice present from the lads, you know."

Whilst many bands would have struggled with the departure of such a prominent figure in their line-up, this wasn't the case for Tull. That said, it wasn't easy for them to find a new bass player. At that point the only two bass players that Ian Anderson had mainly played with were Hammond-Hammond and Glenn Cornick. When Hammond-Hammond left the band there were no immediate ideas as to who they should recruit. Fortunately, whilst touring America, they had worked with a group by the name of Carmen. Knowing that Carmen had split up, although they hadn't spoken to John Glascock much previously, Jethro Tull invited him to join them. In later years Anderson advocated that if it wasn't for the fact that Carmen had split up, he would have felt guilty inviting Glascock to join as he had no wish to take the bass player away from a group of musicians who were giving it their all to make their way up the ladder to success on their own.

Prior to being in Carmen, Glascock had played in a number of British recording bands including The Gods and Toe Fat (who were also to provide the nucleus of Uriah Heep). Glascock was quoted in *Rose-Morris International* in June 1976; "I believe I am the first extra singer that Jethro Tull has ever had. Up until now Ian did all the harmonies on the albums."

To which Martin Barre added; "It's good for the group because it brings Tull closer as a band. Up until now it's always been Ian. But now it'll be so much better for us having two guys singing — especially on TV things. It's going to be very good for us."

According to *Sounds* in January 1976, Jethro Tull were using the following equipment:

Ian Anderson:
Martin Acoustic guitars — models 045 CF, 042 CF, 230 CF
Artley & Conn Flute
Selmer Saxophone
Bermachelli Soprano Sax

Martin Barre:
Gibson Les Paul custom
Fender Broadcaster
Hayman Custom
Martin Acoustic
Yamaha Acoustic
Hi Watt 100 Amp
Hi-Watt 4 x 12 cabinets
H/H stereo echo units
Vox amp
Marshall tremelo amp
Marshall cabinet
Multi-phase custom built pedal

John Glascock:
Fender Precision bass
Fender Jazz bass
Yamaha acoustic
Martin bass bins
Martin bass horn
Crown amps
Martin pre-amp
Acoustic pre-amps

John Evan:
Hammond C3 organ
Leslie tone cabinets
Steinway grand piano
Country piano pick-up
Mini Moogs
Hohner accordions
Wurlitzer electric piano
Vako orchestra
Fender Rhodes key stage piano
Sound City electric piano
Hi-watt amps
Hi-watt cabinets
Audio masters

Barriemore Barlow:
Ludwig blue Vistalite
24 x 14 bass drum
22 x 14 bass drum
13 x 9 tom tom
14 x 10 tom tom
16 x 16 tom tom
18 x 16 tom tom
20 x 18 tom tom
14 x 10 Ludwig snare
Ludwig sticks Rose-Morris
Ludwig silver sparkle
Ludwig black super classic (mainly for recording)
Paiste cymbals
Evans Oilfield drum heads

Ludwig musser marimba
Premier marimba
Ludwig glockenspiel
Natal bongos
Indian tablas

John Glascock said in *Rose-Morris International* in June 1976; "I've got two Marshall stacks. I can use four one-hundred watt lead tops and three one-hundred watt bass tops with two two-by-fifteen Powercel reflex bins and two four-by-twelve Powercel cabinets. I use the four Powercels in the one cabinet. I was going to use two separate cabinets for the lead part of the sound but one is plenty for the volume I'm playing at. The two bass bins give it the bottom part. I'm driving the whole thing about three on each amp. On stage it sounds very good to me — and the guy on the board says it's giving a good sound out front through the PA."

In an advert for Marshall amps placed in *Melody Maker* in 1976, Martin Barre was quoted; "Of course I still get the odd attack of stage fright, but now I know one thing for sure. I sound a lot better now than I did then. I've been using Marshall a lot lately, because over the years Marshall gear has continued to improve and there are not many pieces of equipment you can say that about. These Marshalls really belt it out — with lots of top, a nice low frequency response and not too much middle. And that's without using boosters — because with Marshall you just plug in and it sounds good. What's more, it has a compatibility of reproduction both on stage and in the recording studio. And it sounds just the way I like it — drivey and heavy. Of course there's another basic advantage of using Marshall and lots of volume. It drowns out the sound of my knees."

Anderson told *Down Beat* in March 1976; "Everybody has room, every night. Room to move and room to breathe. It's very important that we are regularly changing little things, almost on a day-to-day level. Someone says, 'Can we change those twelve bars there?' or 'Let me do this and you do that.' It may be a change of one note in a set arrangement or it may be a loose discussion about some improvised piece of music. It happened last night. There was a change in about thirty-six bars that we just loosely discussed, and it was an improvised piece. It happened in the encore, towards the end."

Regarding how Jethro Tull worked as a group, Barriemore Barlow, speaking to *Rose-Morris International* in June 1976, said; "(Ian) still writes most of the stuff, and any writing we do is the instrumental pieces. We write those pieces for the simple reason that Ian needs to get offstage and have a beer, cigarette, and go to the bathroom. When we do something like that we write it completely as a group."

By the spring of 1976, fans wanted their Tull fix. Anderson was reluctant on how to best get it across though. In *Down Beat* in March, he explained; "We recently did some live filming and recording in Europe with a view to the possibility of the video disc becoming a commercial reality, within, conservatively, the next five years. It's already there and it already works; but I personally worry very much about video being a purchasable commodity, because it doesn't lend itself as readily to the more abstract quality of music. Music is the prime abstract art. Not my music, I'm not saying that. But music, in its finest form, is the abstract, and literature is the verbal reality, almost on a conversational level. Film, since the talkies, has been the totally accessible, very immediate, art form. It works immediately. It has to, because conventionally it's employed as a one act experience — you go to the movie, see it, and go home. Whereas with music, one has access to repeated performances — either live or through recordings. Music stands repetition. One gets more into it as a result of repetition if the music is worth anything at all. Particularly in England now, we've arrived at a media situation where the music is so instant — where it's designed to appeal only once. And I might not like it the first time. I would hope to be involved with music that will withstand repetition. I'm into repetition, and the musical formats that we deal with employ repetition." In March, Tull made TV appearances on *The Old Grey Whistle Test* and *Supersonic*.

So how was the creative mood after the release of *Minstrel In The Gallery*? According to Anderson: "*Minstrel In The Gallery* is much more intense, much more introverted, much more a solitude. It may again be seen as a totally sort of uncommercial thing. People may really not like it. And I shall be somewhat despondent and disappointed if people don't enjoy it. But finally, I have to do what I want to do. Otherwise, we have no possible excuse for getting together, me and the audience. We have no reason under the sun to even breathe the same air, unless it's the result of me saying I'm playing what I want to play because I actually have to cope with this and say it for whatever obscure or selfish set of personal reasons. So there exists a coincidence where other people derive some enjoyment or some emotional sort of reward from that. That's all it amounts to really, a coincidence, because I'm not terribly responsible when it comes to catering to what people want."

Regarding the conception of Tull's 1976 album, Anderson told BBC Radio in 1979; "Well the album came about at a time when Jethro Tull was rehearsing in Switzerland. We started work on an album which was just going to be a Jethro Tull album, but it seemed as though some of the songs were leading towards something, and what happened was that David Palmer and I started to evolve — as the album was taking place — another thing going on at the same time, in our spare time between rehearsals: another project which seemed destined to become some sort of stage musical. And gradually the attention of the group drifted from the album we were supposed to be working on to this newer project. We decided then to make that the new group album, instead of the songs which we were working on. Not because they were any better, but because it was something we got more involved with: it had an identity or a concept, to use the over-worked word."

Too Old To Rock 'n' Roll: Too Young To Die was in the making just before the emergence of punk rock and some of the musical simplicity that followed the genre. As it happened, the album was centred on the idea that fashions come around again every so often which, ironically perhaps, is what happened with punk long after. The focus on youth culture and the musical accessibility wasn't worlds away from what had been done with rock 'n' roll in the nineteen fifties. The hero of the story on the album clung to his old-fashioned music, dress and behaviour — only to find himself suddenly popular again as what is in vogue makes yet another shift.

The name of the hero of *Too Old To Rock 'n' Roll: Too Young To Die* is Ray Lomas. Anderson maintained that Ray Lomas is based on a real person. When they were putting a name to the character in the story of the album, Palmer and Anderson were sitting in a hotel in Montreux in Switzerland. They were watching the mountains out of the hotel window over breakfast whilst trying to think of a name. During such time, Palmer recalled an acquaintance of his by the name of Ray Lomas — who was in actual fact an old rocker. By then Lomas would have been in his thirties but he was still set on the old rock 'n' roll traditions of the Teddy Boy era. There was something about the name of Ray Lomas that stuck with Anderson. He considered that it simply sounded like the character that they had in mind. Rather than hunt around for a name that sounded like Ray Lomas, they chose to use his name. They even went so far as to check with the real Ray Lomas that it would be okay with him to do so, for which they were granted permission from the man himself.

Anderson told *Sounds*; "We'd gone off to Switzerland to rehearse and to write and arrange for the new album and while I was there — we'd already recorded the title song and the mixing of it renewed my involvement with that particular song, although it didn't have anything to do with the other songs we were preparing for the record. And David Palmer was with me and when we were talking about it he told me he knew this guy who was a friend of his who was in certain ways very much like the character in the song. And I thought it was a great name, and he had a wife called Ivy and a dog called Scout. And at some point we thought it would be really nice to write a sort of musical and stage theatrical thing around this character. Not in any way a nostalgic thing but just taking that song and expanding the song into a character and making a comment not about then but about now. Making a comment on today's fashion and style not just in terms of clothes and music but about basically the social behaviour of people and the way it's influenced by what happens to be the fashion of the moment, the way to be for young people."

Anderson was keen to assert that the character of Ray Lomas was not intended to be autobiographical. The title track of the album was written by Anderson and Palmer during their stay in Switzerland over the Christmas period. From the start, the intention was to create something theatrical that had the potential to be elaborately performed — a humorous turn from some of the cynicism portrayed on the previous album, *Minstrel In The Gallery*.

The story of *Too Old To Rock 'n' Roll: Too Young To Die* is depicted in the centrefold of the album sleeve in the form of a comic strip. When looking for someone to make the comic strip, the band first asked artists who worked for some of the daily newspapers at the time but they all turned out to be too busy. They finally found an artist who worked for one of the British boys' magazines (in 1979 Anderson told BBC Radio that it might have been *Wizard* or *Hotspur*). They gave the artist a little bit of a storyboard to follow but with a bit of licence to interpret it. It was never supposed to be a rigid, complete, meaningful story. The purpose was to get across the idea that whilst fashions may come and go, they usually come back again so there's no point in changing your clothes or behaviour — if you hang around for long enough you'll be back in fashion again. Anderson considered that to be the important statement to convey.

In the comic strip, Ray Lomas is portrayed as a disillusioned has-been who is upset by contemporary fashion. His alienation seems to be exacerbated in how his friends have managed to settle down in life. When Lomas applies to go on a TV quiz show, he is accepted and travels to London for it. Whilst there, he is rejected by someone who he takes a liking to. Upon arriving home, he seeks solace in riding his motorbike. A crash causes him to end up in hospital. Whilst there, the image that Lomas represents becomes fashionable again and upon leaving the hospital, the ageing rocker is once again popular. The strip ends with Lomas receiving an invite to make a "demo hit single" whereby the trailer for "Next week..." states "Ray Lomas becomes a pop star!"

Anderson told *Sounds*; "We did the story and I started to write songs to illustrate specific points in the story... In terms of the actual story thing I don't think it was ever important. I mean, you take something like the soundtrack for *South Pacific* or something away from the film and as music it doesn't in any way tell a story. No soundtrack I ever heard ever tells a story; it merely illustrates in song — not necessarily the particular high points of a story, but certain points where music is the right medium for that particular part of the story. And that indeed was the way we approached it. It's very orthodox in musical type of terms. I would hope that all the songs work as songs. And indeed that's the only way they need or should work on a record album. I've never really got behind the idea of a concept album thing. I always found it from the start, a redundant phrase when they said of *Sgt. Pepper* that it was a concept album. It was a bunch of songs certainly all of which didn't fit into a festive, circus frame of reference — in no way did they tell a story or anything. A few of them had a circus orchestra feel about them with people cheering in the background but no way could I see it as a concept album. Unless you're referring to the drug which induced that music — in which case most of my albums have been Löwenbräu albums!"

Despite everything that they had achieved by 1976, commercial support from those in a position of influence wasn't always a given for Jethro Tull. Anderson told *Melody Maker* in the May of that year: "I must confess I'm slightly put off by the fact that the 'Too Old To Rock 'n' Roll' song was completely refused as a single by the rock press and by BBC Radio. I hadn't realised just how difficult it is at the BBC these days to get plays... I don't think it's a question of getting back in vogue. It's a question of my perhaps naively believing that rock music does have a place, or should we say free enterprising rock music has. In other words, not being hyped by management or record companies, which my thing isn't. I hope that by appearing I've made it a little bit better than it might otherwise have been."

Speaking to *New Musical Express* in June he said; "The 'Too Old...' song, the title, was actually spawned in a moment of depression. At one point on an American tour I'd been really down after a duff gig that was probably my fault, and thought: I'm really past all this. Why should I be travelling another five-hundred miles to another town. Let me off at the roundabout. Whereas 'The Chequered Flag' is lyrically more like 'Bungle In The Jungle' (*War Child*). It's accepting the sort of hardness of life, and saying: Well, it's hell. But it's all worth it, getting out there and doing it."

The idea for 'Salamander' came to Anderson whilst he was wanting to create something different to what he had done before. He said in later years that the piece allowed him to play things that wouldn't be possible on regular concert E tuning and that the piece is played on a lot of open strings. The writing of the piece was also unique in that, untypically for a Jethro Tull acoustic song, Anderson and Barre worked on it together in the studio. 'Salamander' was recorded in Monte Carlo. In later years, Barre recalled that it was a difficult song to perform live due to how the guitar needed to be tuned differently. This is something that Anderson agreed on too.

Regarding 'Quizz Kid', Anderson commented; "I may wake up tomorrow and think this is rubbish. But tomorrow I'll write another song cause if I don't I'm not me."

The saxophone solo in 'From A Dead Beat To An Old Greaser' was played by David Palmer. Although at the time he was not a permanent member of the band, it marked his first appearance with them — as musician rather than arranger — on record. Modestly, Palmer told *Sounds* in January 1976; "If the group broke up today Ian could find unknown musicians and have them sounding like Jethro Tull in one month."

Martin Barre was quoted in *Rose-Morris International* in June 1976; "I used my old fifty watt amp on *Too Old To Rock 'n' Roll* simply because the one-hundred watt was too loud. The fifty watt has a good studio sound — really thick — but the one-hundreds will work out good too, once I get used to them. It's really strange because I still feel that tendency to play flat out, to use everything I've got and have it completely wide open — to use all the top, take all the bottom out, put all the middle in, and have the volume flat out. It's psychologically difficult for me to accept that you don't need all that; that you've got some to spare. My main problem is I've never had anything in reserve — I've always had to utilise everything the amp had to offer — and more — because I've had to boost it with pedals. But now I don't have to do this. I've got enough top and good response from all frequencies."

In response to the journalist's comment that *Too Old To Rock 'n' Roll: Too Young To Die* was more of a group album than any previous Jethro Tull ones, Anderson said; "The songs capture a lot of what the group is today. The group don't like to play that many solos. I don't either. I think that as you play longer and longer in a group, you've got to play together with more sympathy. But it's difficult to contemplate what the functions of the members of a group should be at this time. I've always worried that people equate the Jethro Tulls and Led Zeppelins and so on with that kind of six-year-old rock group heavy formula, where every song must have a guitar solo; where every song must have a flute or a harmonica or whatever; where it's sort of obligatory, following the lowest common denominator. So it worries me to have solos just for the sake of showing off. Today, there are so many good young guitarists and drummers around and it would be wrong for them to do what groups like us were doing six or seven years ago, drum solos and guitar solos and that. Nobody wants to sit through that anymore. You don't have to prove that you can play your instrument.

Performing 'Too Old To Rock 'n' Roll: Too Young To Die' on Supersonic, 27th March 1976.

Then, it was the day of the virtuoso musician. That seems to be rapidly disappearing. The best guitarists today in new groups are extremely integrated into what the group is playing. That would seem to be the criterion of what a good musician is about."

Too Old To Rock 'n' Roll: Too Young To Die was a return to the highly successful *Aqualung* format in that the ten songs telling the story of Ray Lomas are interconnected, and, as with *Aqualung*, the character on the album sleeve bears a close resemblance to Anderson. Anderson considered that it was important to be honest about the fact that, as he saw it, there was a certain amount of himself in any character created for the purpose of writing a story or a song around. He told BBC Radio in 1979; "There's something of you in there, and it's wrong perhaps to cover it up — so you slip a little bit of that in; or, in the case of *Aqualung*, the artist slipped a little bit of that in and made the *Aqualung* character look a bit like me. I'm sure (perhaps) that it helps sell records if the character on the front looks halfway familiar, but at the same time in invites that obvious criticism that the whole thing is literally and truthfully autobiographical, which is fairly far from the truth. I am not an old rocker. In fact up until that time I used to invariably wear leather jackets and tight trousers and pointed shoes simply because it wasn't in fashion. I share that emotion of wanting to avoid the current fashion, whatever it is. But in terms of the familiarity with or the love of old rock 'n' roll music, I can't pretend to any sort of nostalgia or interest in that sort of music. I've always hated rock 'n' roll; I've always hated Bill Haley and Elvis Presley and all that mob. I've always found it very boring — even when I was ten years old I found it very boring music. The same old thing, the same old words, the same old clichés. Within two or three years of rock 'n' roll being about, it became the music of clichés and uninventiveness and record production tricks and heavy-sell techniques on the part of publishers, record companies and all sorts of promo men. I've always disliked rock 'n' roll for that which it represents in terms of the Music Business (in capital letters)."

Nevertheless, Anderson was a fan of Adam Faith, a British rock singer of the early sixties. It wasn't widely well known at the time of its release that when *Too Old To Rock 'n' Roll* was written, Anderson had hoped that Faith might star in the stage version. It could be argued that there are echoes of Adam Faith's style on several of the tracks on the album. Anderson advocated in later years that it is plausible as to how it happened during the writing process of the album (and that it wasn't a bad thing if that was the case).

He asserted that of all the rock musicians of the era, he had always preferred Adam Faith because he found him to be a bit more rough and ready in his appearance — with more of an edge to him than Cliff Richard (even from the days before the latter got into religion, smart suits, and movies). Although Anderson had wanted to approach Adam Faith with the prospect of doing a stage show during the writing of *Too Old To Rock 'n' Roll: Too Young To Die*, by the time it came to recording the album, it became overtly apparent that Faith was too busy; not only was he in a West End show but he had also begun to tell the press that he was hoping to do less singing anyway — he had grown disenchanted with both the music business and indeed his own singing career.

Anderson speaking to *Sounds* in June '76 said; "I thought it'd be great to get Adam Faith to play the character because he's from that era, he's got the right sort of background, and also because he's an actor as well as a singer."

It didn't happen because Faith was already committed to rehearsing for a play, *City Sugar*. Anderson added; "So I thought well, that one's out, and I couldn't really see anyone else in that role. At that time I had around half a dozen songs for the group album and ten or twelve songs for this project and I decided that I'd either ditch it or do it myself."

New Musical Express reported in June 1976; "Ian Anderson claims the album was the result of a theatrical production he wrote, based on an actual person called Ray Lomas, and which he hoped to present on stage with Adam Faith taking the leading role. Faith was unavailable and once again Jethro Tull were presented with the structure for an album, the hand-me-downs of another independent idea of Anderson's. Any pointed lyrical association, he seems to infer, is merely coincidental. But certain songs fit him like a motorcycle jacket."

To which Anderson commented; "Well, I suppose they do. But if they fit me, they must also fit pretty well every other rock 'n' roll singer. They must fit everybody who's been going for five or six years. They must look on today's current output of the new generation of pop music with a certain disdain. With a certain kind of, disappointment really. Because I don't see any new Whos, Rolling Stones, or Led Zeppelins on the horizon."

With regards to Adam Faith being unavailable, Anderson explained to *Circus*; "Finally I thought, 'Well, let's go ahead and do this as a group piece rather than ditch the whole thing.' And obviously I didn't want to get personally involved in any kind of West End musical kind of deal, because that's strictly nasty business. By this time I'd very quickly and easily written all the material for this musical project, whereas the group stuff was in limbo. There was a lot of music there, but it was simple songs — some of them short, some of them long — that were a bit heavy. You know, a bit like *Minstrel In The Gallery*, but a bit more severe. And the new stuff, in contrast, was quite up and had a different feel. So I made the decision to go ahead with *Too Old To Rock 'n' Roll*. We were then left with a bunch of songs, some of which we didn't use on the record because they weren't convincing in the way we played them. And since they didn't fit into the original concept, the story had to be rehashed here and there, and of course hugely abbreviated. The point of the songs was never actually to tell the story — only to illustrate certain points… So that's really where the record is from. And where the cartoon strip is from, since it seemed necessary to finally point out that the songs did have some fundamental reason for being there. It's obviously sort of incomplete — and it is a bit, perhaps, finally unconvincing as a story. But obviously in the rush to get the thing out, to have it released to some standard that's okay, you have to make those kind of compromises."

"Tull — Not A Ray Of Light", ran the headline for Chris Welch's *Melody Maker* review of *Too Old To Rock 'n' Roll: Too Young To Die*; "Romanticising the working lad as a cult hero is a popular theme with rock musicians. They have oft flirted with, or observed at close hand, the heroic deeds of rocker, mod, beatnik or raver at some time in their own youth. And they have experienced the excitement of lust, thrills and adventure as rock stars, not to mention the bitter-sweet pills of success and yea, frustration. Thus they can sympathise and, in part, identify with these mythical characters of yore. I wouldn't mind betting that Ian Anderson, when he was a lad, far from thundering down the bypass with a broken bottle of brown ale between his teeth, astride a smoking motorcycle of British manufacture, actually stood midst clouds of exhaust at the bus stop, clutching library books and wondering whether there were kippers for tea. But that doesn't stop him displaying an almost touching faith in the rocker ideal on this latest popular gramophone record."

"The story of Ray Lomas (our hero) is told in song and illustrated by an elaborate strip cartoon on the centrefold of the album, which has all the realism and impact of the strips that appeared in such fifties comics as *Lion* and *Eagle*. Ray is a rocker whose friends 'have gone straight'. Alone and bitter, solaced by memories of days when he was called The Big Dipper among female rockers and rode the trunk roads at excessive speeds, he enters a quiz show and wins a washing machine, an act that seems strangely out of character, but gives the hero a chance to taste the high life of London. He gets stood up by a dolly bird and meets an old beatnik whose reminiscences he finds oddly irritating. But he, too, falls prey to nostalgia and remembers when he was a leather-jacketed churl of the road. He ventures out on his trusty, rusty machine and, filled with aimless frustration, hurtles into a bend at 120mph."

"While recuperating in hospital, a new group sets a trend for leather gear and when he gets out, Ray finds a world full of rockers. For once he is ahead of the trend. Girls flock and pop managers seek him out. Stardom is just around the corner and Ray has swept under the chequered flag. It's a tidy, amusing story, but the music does not match the narrative, which dictates each twist and turn of the tongue, and is perforce delivered in sing-song, balladeer style. Apart from the tender 'From A Dead Beat To An Old Greaser' and 'The Chequered Flag', there are no outstanding songs to speak of, and, because of Ian's dominating role and the wordy nature of the compositions, the band do not impress any of their musical personality on proceedings."

"I long for the beat of Barriemore Barlow to break free, or the guitar of Martin Barre to swoop. Not that Ian hasn't taken considerable care with his lyrics, which have a curious matter-of-fact-ness — either gentle irony or an attempt to capture the plain speaking of the aforementioned rocker. For example, Ray grumbles sourly of the girl who stood him up: 'she's a warm fart at Christmas'. But on 'The Chequered Flag', which seems to refer to the motor cycle of life, from birth to death, Anderson gets positively poetic. It must be said that Ian avoids such tempting devices as motorcycle sound effects, or period, Shadows style guitar, and he is determined to fashion a thing of beauty that will appeal to the vast bulk of Tull fans. But I remain singularly unmoved by these plaintive laments and am drawn to the conclusion one is simply too ear-bashed to care."

Notably, Welch's reviews of Jethro Tull's albums had always been very up and down across the band's discography. For instance, he gave *Thick As A Brick* a glowing review in 1972 but was incredibly scathing towards *A Passion Play* in 1973. In response to the negative review, Anderson endeavoured to invite a journalist from said publication on tour because, according to *New Musical Express*, "he believed at least 10,000 people would avoid the set as a result of the criticism."

Despite Jethro Tull's overall reluctance to have members of the press join them on tour at all, Anderson considered that it was an opportunity to show what they could do, to address critique and to perhaps regain lost ground, although it ended up being one from the *New Musical Express*.

Anderson told the NME; "At this point in time my rebellious nature is brought forth in actually talking a large amount of common sense and telling a large amount of truth about a business which is full of hype and petty sort of stardom trips. From the highest rock star right down to the lowliest cub reporter on the *New Musical Excess*. Haha! I'm being glib and sort of rude, but you know what I mean. There's a lot of things going on that I find absolutely irrelevant to the music business."

The journalist who toured with Jethro Tull considered in the same feature that "musically the show is considerably more dazzling and entertaining. There's precision, professionalism, excitement and an emphasis more on the show content than any distracting visual extravaganza."

Regarding the album title, Anderson explained; "The title openly invites all sorts of attack on

January 26th 1977,
Chrysalis Records Office,
London.

145

the music contained therein, and I really don't mind because it was going to happen anyway. The first two or three interviews I did here yesterday in Spain were the first ones I'd done in two weeks, and the second or third, if not the first question, was: 'Are you too old to rock 'n' roll? Is that what you're saying in this record?' It's great. Everybody in the record company, from the office boy on, must have looked at the proofs for the album cover with dread, and probably thought when they saw the title; 'Oh Christ. He's really going to get some stick over this one.' Strangely, certainly in the British papers, they haven't done that number on the headline. I thought at least one of them would. It said, 'Not A Ray Of Light' instead. Which is very intelligent, very clever." (the journalist noted that Anderson said the latter sarcastically).

Speaking to *Circus* in August 1976 Anderson remarked; "My small act of rebellion at the moment is to go around talking some common sense and truth. I'm actually trying to upset the little game by saying for real what I feel and what I think about things. And it's actually going to turn a lot of people off. They don't want to hear someone like me. They don't even want to consider the fact that I know about, for instance, income tax. You're not supposed to know about these things. It's bad for your image, boy. But I'm tired of playing the PR game."

"Ian Anderson should stick to music, because he most definitely is not a storyteller," is how *Rolling Stone* saw things. "This is the muddled story of one Ray Lomas, 'the last of the old rockers', whose long hair and tight jeans mark him as a person whom time has passed by. After a series of events remarkable only for their lack of humour and originality, we leave the "hero" as he is about to become a pop star in his own right. So what? We can take comfort, though, in knowing that Anderson's technical prowess as a composer remains undiminished. The album abounds in breathtaking musical passages. The title cut, for one, is a textbook example of the use of dynamics and nuance in a rock song: instruments subtly creep in during the verses, with the slightest of musical nods to let us know they're there. The music builds with a tension which heightens a desperate theme, then erupts in the chorus. 'Quizz Kid' features, in addition to numerous startling changes in texture, several brief but pungent solos by guitarist Martin Barre, whose playing is exemplary throughout. Unfortunately, the power of these passages and several beautiful melodies is undercut by Anderson's stillborn vocals and lyrical verbosity. Though his attempts at pithiness generally yield nothing more invigorating than 'Clear your throat and pray for rain…' it seems fair to suggest that a little less conversation would have saved this album from its most embarrassing moments."

Under the heading of "An Old Concept Will Maybe Let You Down", *Sounds* opined; "On a quick perusal of the field I reckon Ian Anderson is the most articulate rocker I've ever encountered. In fact, hearing him talk is probably a pleasure more unalloyed than listening to his music which is unusual in that it all sounds very much the same and yet is also very inconsistent. By his own admission he writes two basic numbers: the fast one surging along with the whole band hitting it with their own individual sound and the slow one placing his witty and conversational voice upfront against acoustic guitar, flute and suchlike pretty and charming sounds (my favourites being the maybe unlikely choices from *War Child*, 'Ladies Of Leisure' (sic) and 'Back-Door Angels'). So I'm not griping about his new one fitting the formula. That is Ian Anderson and either you get some kicks out of it or you don't. But this time he never quite makes it to one of his goodies."

"Musically it really does seem to be the old routine, standard arrangements knocked off as if they were of no particular concern to him (i.e. they sound perfectly palatable but lack sparkle). Honourable exception is 'From A Dead Beat To An Old Greaser' where he sings slowly, reflective, melancholy, his own voice harmonising a high and low line over subdued guitars and violins. The melodies likewise don't seem to have been the focus of his attention — they are subservient to the words even more than usual. The only ones that stick in your head an hour later are 'From A Dead Beat', 'Bad-Eyed And Loveless' and 'The Chequered Flag (Dead Or Alive)'. Which means the words have got to be ultra-riveting for the album to make it. Well, this is some kinda concept album folks — telling the story of an old rocker called Ray Lomas who flips, smashes himself up and ends up so out-of-fashion he's a la mode and pulling all the birds who are young enough to be his daughters (and very probably are). Sentence by sentence Anderson comes up with the striking phrases at the same remarkable rate as ever."

"How's this for tightness in 'Taxi Grab': 'Nowhere to put your feet as the big store shoppers…'. That's where he really has expressed his care this time round. There's hardly a loose or ungainly word throughout. So coupled with okay music that should have made the album one of his best shouldn't it? Yeah, but then you come to the important question of what's it all about, Ian? My feeling is that the story, told in cartoon form on the gatefold, has been a self-imposed restriction. Basically it is far too inconsequential for the thoughts he has tried to wrap around it and it doesn't hang together until Ray the hero burns away on his death trip. His appearance on a TV quiz show and meeting with a society beauty ('Salamander') who ditches him are both trite and unlikely events and there's a feeling of strain as the songs strive to invest them with social significance."

"Then, well put together as 'Taxi Grab' is, the thinking behind it is the clichéd moan about the grime, hurry and noise of city living. Anderson usually talks to us on a much deeper level than that — and on *Too Old To Rock 'n' Roll* he only hits those depths of awareness, a kind of sympathetic irony, with 'From A Dead Beat' and 'The Chequered Flag'. Ray the hero's rejection of his old mate the dead beat was the only moment which had any dramatic impact on Mike Mansfield's TV video of the album (to be shown later in the summer). And the despairing, defiant chorus of the album's last track at last steps out of the effort to make rockers significant in some way that could never ring true and look at er, well, the human condition. The opening verse is about a motor racing hero: 'The young man's home; dry as a bone…' In the later verses the same chorus is taken up by an old man and a still-born child — it's grim, rough and loving. The rest of the album is interesting but somehow you feel he'd lost track of where he was at."

The *New Musical Express* commented; "Where do you start unravelling Ian Anderson's latest concept agony? The problem is that Anderson's yarn can be interpreted in basically two different ways. Firstly, as exactly that: a yarn, or a piece of entertaining fiction, based on the ancient fable of rags to riches. Old greaser hits the telly screen, goes through the weirds of being famous, becomes disillusioned with London, returns home, almost kills himself in a motor bike accident, recovers, and the Once Upon A Time ending is he becomes famous and popular and loved. I'll explain later. Or, and possibly this has more credence, the yarn is merely a superficial gloss over some pretty solid woodwork. Strip the story line away and you'll experience some profound observations. Filed under The Pain Of Being A Star, Anderson draws an analogy between his own role (which it obviously is) with that of the old rocker who wins Telly Quiz Game and becomes public property. And in this context the weirds become more significant, the disillusionment and return home (to reappraise his early roots) more pertinent. The ending is then far from being happily optimistic, but instead forebodingly euphoric. A modern tragedy, if you like."

"You've heard the story before, perhaps read between the same lines, and such a generalisation obviously makes the album sound trite. But it isn't. When you get into it you'll discover it's exceptionally clever. But first back to those important basics. *Too Old To Rock 'n' Roll: Too Young To Die* it's called, and the story begins in the cartoon strip on the sleeve gatefold. The central character is an old greaser called Ray Lomas who can't accept or adopt the changing modes of fashion. But, for some reason unexplained, he enters and wins the TV quiz ('Quizz Kid'), is asked to return the next week, and so checks into a Kensington hotel, getting his first experience of London ('Crazed Institution'). He meets a desirable trendy ('Salamander') who's seen him on the box, and he steals a cab ('Taxi Grab') so they can hit a party together. But 'Salamander' has second thoughts — 'I bet he's well hung… but I couldn't make it with a working class lout like him' — and she dumps him in a pub to wait for her. Here he meets and talks with another has-been ('From A Dead Beat To An Old Greaser')."

"But when Sal's ninety minutes late for their meeting Ray bitterly realises he's been stood-up ('Bad-Eyed And Loveless') and so returns home the next day where he fondly remembers his past glory ('Big Dipper'). Then he leaves home on his motorbike, crashes, and finds himself in hospital ('Too Old To Rock 'n' Roll: Too Young To Die'). Healed in body, he comes out also healed in mind, and discovers the latest teen rage to be a group of Lomas look-alikes. Once again he's in fashion and able to pull chicks ('Pied Piper'). The story ends with him winning in the rat-race ('Chequered Flag') and receiving a cable telling him to phone a record company who're interested in recording him. Continued next week — Ray Lomas becomes a pop star! But don't cry with happiness, the sad cycle is merely restarting. So now do you get it?"

The review continued; "The story of Ray Lomas is probably the biggest red herring in popular music. Discard the cartoon, turn your attention to the songs and there unravel the real meaning of the album. Perhaps it's all Anderson paranoia, or maybe just his dry humoured sense of cynicism, but with what probably amounts to his most imaginative lyrical excellence Anderson's pulled off something quite unique: The classic Rock 'n' Roll Joke. And the first clue's in 'Quizz Kid', which aside from a brief snatch of the title track presumably to establish the thematic core, opens the set. 'May your answers not be wrong… Come back next week!' Who asks the questions in the rock world? Who treats it as a silly game? How many artistes don't come back next week? Answers on a £5 note, please."

"Basically Anderson is, to an extent, with tracks like 'Salamander', 'Taxi Grab', 'Pied Piper' and 'Big Dipper', romanticising from within the rock biz; the paradox being, of course, that the superficial sneer humming through the lyrics (and going back to the Great Press vs. Tull and vice versa controversy — hence the lyric quote) only partly hides his awareness of the realities that exist within the business. Which he makes obvious with 'Crazed Institution': 'And you can ring a crown of roses around your cranium…'."

"And perhaps, just perhaps, the title track is really a crystallisation of Anderson's thoughts on the subject, using the image of the old rocker merely to represent himself: how he falls from critical favour for unreasonable reasons as he sees it (*A Passion Play*) but with the power to return for similarly unreasonable reasons. 'The old rocker wore his hair too long, wore his trouser cuffs

February 1977, Hammersmith Odeon.

February 1977, Hammersmith Odeon.

February 1977, Hammersmith Odeon.

February 1977, Hammersmith Odeon.

February 1977, Hammersmith Odeon.

February 1977, Hammersmith Odeon.

February 1977, Hammersmith Odeon.

© Steve Emberton

too tight…'. The casualty of fickle fashion fads, eh? Ironically though, Tull's reaffirmation of their strength (*War Child*, but particularly *Minstrel In The Gallery*) was obviously a determined effort: working to achieve recognition. And similarly this album has the lyrical depth, which we've already covered, but a musical one too. The songs have simple structures and rely in the main on Anderson's vocal, acoustic guitar and flute, with the band lending unobtrusive musical support — Martin Barre excelling himself on guitar — to what are mainly excellent melodies. 'From A Dead Beat To An Old Greaser' and 'The Chequered Flag' are the highlights, while the band numbers 'Big Dipper' and 'Taxi Grab' are aggressively chaotic, which of course may be the whole point. Symbolisms of revolution and all that jazz. The surprise track of the album, in much the same way as 'Cold Wind To Valhalla' was on *Minstrel*, is the blues lament 'Bad-Eyed And Loveless', where Anderson uses sexual metaphor in much the same way as Bessie Smith did: 'I'm self-raising and I flower in her company. Give me no sugar without her cream'."

"But the punch line to Anderson's Rock 'n' Roll Joke is the final track, 'The Chequered Flag', which reveals his absurd sense of the theatric. And the question which posed itself was: Is this Anderson's epitaph? Is this his last album? After all, the tracks are full of mockery, cynicism, bitterness, disillusionment and, we should quickly note, a sense of humour normally present in a person who rationally appreciates his own position and is able to turn the joke in on himself. 'The deaf composer completes his final score…'. Conceptual agony and submission, or astute hilarity and remission? The answer is too personal for me to answer for you. And anyway, I'm still not sure."

Regarding Tull's back catalogue thus far, Anderson observed; "I can look back chronologically and I do actually think overall that each one is better than the last for different reasons that are important to me. To me, each one avoids some of the pitfalls of the one before. I think our fans weigh every album up with some consideration, it may not be to his taste. But it's something new, and at least it guarantees a change from what went before, an attempt to keep moving on. I suppose the story of my life is that I keep moving on, from one hotel to the next, but I always have a base to return to, both geographically and musically. In terms of recognisable tags, the base is closer to blues and folk music and it's particularly English. I don't owe very much to America apart from a liking for the fairly early urban American blues."

Although Adam Faith was unavailable, it didn't stop Jethro Tull from adding their own theatrics to how they performed their new songs. "On their current European tour, Tull have been testing a new stage act that includes a large section of the new album, *Too Old To Rock 'n' Roll: Too Young To Die*, another conceptual work that has brought some derisory cries from the critics," said *Melody Maker*. "The album, the story of an old rocker learning to come to grips with the changing times, was originally conceived by Anderson as a musical for Adam Faith. When he found that Faith was already involved in another stage presentation, Anderson decided to make it a Tull album, though seven of the songs, on his own admission, were not written specially for the band."

The theatrics weren't at the expense of the music though. Martin Barre explained; "Every day is different now. We're taking old songs off into new directions — developing them from one day to another. I think Ian's songs are getting very strong — very concise… We were the first group to do the weird visual things on stage. But people aren't surprised any more, that's why we're getting away from it now. It's the music really that they're paying to hear — so it's got to come down to the music — and you've got to have a quality sound."

Of course, the ergonomics of how things would work on stage always had to be taken into account. Barriemore Barlow said; "There are very few halls designed to accommodate rock music. We find ourselves in America playing in *ice rinks*! Personally, I think you have to be in a hall for more than one day so you can work at the sound. But it's economically not viable. So we have to do the best we can under the circumstances. I personally look forward to the day when the public realise that and the poor guy sitting at the back of a 20,000 seat hall no longer thinks — 'Christ, this is no good. I've paid my eight dollars and it's not bloody worth it. I can see five figures about two inches high and the sound is nothing like the album.' I would like to see the day when bands decide to play at a maximum capacity auditorium — say 5,000 seats — and play four nights."

In early May 1976, Tull embarked on a tour consisting of thirteen concerts in eight countries. It meant that they didn't get back to Britain until the end of the month. It was reported in *Circus* in August 1976; "The last but one of their short thirteen date European tour through eight countries, and we find Jethro Tull playing a 5,000 seat auditorium on the outskirts of Barcelona, Spain. Their opening piece is the adventurously complex and powerfully electric 'Thick As A Brick'. In his traditional role as the lewd, leery jester, Ian Anderson dominates at the front of the band. This is an important string of dates for Tull. It's their first set of live appearances in over a year and the in concert introduction of their new bassist, John Glascock, who joined their ranks last November. And it is also an act which features a lot of their new album, *Too Old To Rock 'n' Roll: Too Young To Die*. On keyboards John Evans wears a white pilot's suit, shoulder flashes too. Glascock could have fallen from the French aristocracy, flamboyantly ornamented as he is in a wide-brimmed red hat, a flared white blouse and bright red trousers. Sombrely, Martin Barre, on guitar, displays his natty but conservative tan corduroy trousers and waistcoat, while Barriemore Barlow is content to sit behind a blue Perspex double Ludwig. And on the extreme right of the stage behind various synthesisers and string machines, almost as an impartial observer, sits David Palmer, the man responsible for the string arrangements on Tull records since the early days."

"Sound is superb and the band extraordinarily ambitious, at one point working through the complexity of Beethoven's Ninth. There's precision, professionalism, excitement and an emphasis more on the show's content than any distracting visual extravaganza. The only humorous insertions are Anderson's frequent use of a baby pram to store his acoustic and flute, David Palmer strolling onstage in a monk's habit and, during 'Quizz Kid', Anderson tossing domestic appliances from the back of a trolley. But even without the theatrical elaboration the set works magnificently. Anderson sings well, and strives perhaps to be the only visually important enhancement to the music: his wild man posture, the displays of vulgarity, the flute continually thrust phallically between his legs, are balanced by his appearances as the mild, serious musician diligently working out lines on acoustic or flute. Let there be no doubt, he is Jethro Tull."

During the June of 1976, Tull didn't tour. It was probably something of a welcomed break for the band considering what their tour schedule had looked like overall. Barriemore Barlow commented; "I can't remember when we've had so long a spell off the road. Last year we toured for nine months of the year and I got down to about eight and a half stone. It proved a little too much for me."

It wasn't long before the band were back on the road again. The performance at New York's Shea Stadium was reviewed in *Sounds* in August 1976; "Perhaps Deep Purple, who were once rated the world's loudest group, could have won a battle against the LaGuardia Airport runway which neatly bordered Shea Stadium. At the peak of rush hour flights on a Friday evening, Jethro Tull didn't have a chance. Shea is normally a baseball stadium, capacity 55,000, and even with Tull's specially bulky outdoor sound system, it hardly constituted an ideal venue. For one thing, it took a bold leap of imagination to actually see anything resembling human beings at the several-hundred foot distance from the stage. For some others, almost everything below ninety decibels was drowned out by the jet paths, and, as you can probably guess from Britain's many mud-filled festivals, it steadily rained on all but the few enclosed seating areas. Add circumstances together, and the bands themselves seemed to take on their physical surroundings in performance, mediocrity of setwork matching the greyness on the field."

Following comments on the support acts who played for over an hour, the journalist continued, "Tull's show was preceded by another hour-long set change. Grand gestures introduced the almost full house to 'Tullavision', a group of large projection screens which made it possible for everyone to see at least one part of the stage action in close-up. Of course, ninety percent of the camera time was focused upon Ian Anderson, well-clothed in a neat, multi-colourful dancer's costume. The rest of Tull played with brilliant complexity, defying my belief that no one could sound discernible notes in such a large place, but they might have been hidden behind the stage for all we got to see of their musicianship. Only when Anderson played his one-legged flute trills, introduced a song via acoustic guitar, or physically left the stage, was any instrumental work illustrated. Anderson gave the audience the clever, warble-voiced madman they had waited four hours to see. He introduced 'Too Old To Rock 'n' Roll' pushing a baby carriage, and, growling, menaced his way through 'Aqualung'. Much of the set was fairly new; none of it was introduced, and songs had the uncanny way of blending into one another. Mostly, they began in quiet; always, they crashed into full force with great energy, Anderson careening around the stage bug-eyed, mugging for the camera. And that bothered me most — the use of long distance concert giving as a lucrative live show substitute. To pay the ten dollars for a slightly more personal *Top Of The Pops*? The choice may soon no longer be yours to make."

When asked by BBC Radio in 1979 if there was hope for *Too Old To Rock 'n' Roll: Too Young To Die* being worked into a stage show at a later date, Anderson was adamant that the idea was no longer viable or relevant: "I don't think so, because punk rock has really said it all. There's no point in bringing out something of this sort which would attempt to delineate the cyclic nature of music and fashion because punk rock has demonstrated that; at least to those of us who are too old to be punk rockers it has, because we know that music and fashion and behaviour has been through this cycle before. I started off that way, the equivalent of today's punk rocker, only back then we were doing rock 'n' roll and blues and rhythm 'n' blues. Musically there's not a dissimilarity between the two styles or indeed the modes of dress and the manner of behaviour. I mean I didn't actually spit on people at the Marquee when I began, but, you know, certainly insulted them a fair amount. So, no, I don't think there's any point now. As a document, it has been superseded by the reality of the new cycle of progressive music."

Anderson generally passed positive comment on the emergence of punk music in the late seventies. He told *Sounds* in June 1977; "I heard the Sex Pistols song on the radio the other day and what little I could make out of the lyrics, at least I heard some aggressive, nasty sounding English voices and I thought 'That's refreshing,' at least they're not listening to that mind-boggling top forty pseudo-American Epsom that you hear all the time on British radio. I'll give the Sex Pistols a listen, if they're singing in their own natural street voices. Just for that alone I would listen to them... It's also really worth the effort to sing in your own voice because it's the voice you use on the streets when you shout, it's that voice you use and you should damn well sing with it in a rock/punk/blues group, whatever, instead of copying the Americans. I'm tired of copying the Americans; I grew up with the musical heritage of copying the Americans, and I'm fed up with copying them. I've actually made it, been successful, made money, sold a lot of records, by *not* copying the Americans, by going there and doing something that they see as peculiarly quaint and English — they probably laugh at me. I mean I'm not even English, I'm Scottish, but anything for a laugh."

Equally though, he was quoted in *Creem* in June 1978; "It's a shame that the punk rock thing is so laden with the fact that it's very derivative musically of things that you and I are familiar with — the rock, the riffs, the beat. We've all heard and experienced it probably twice already. Punk rock is just another time for the same old tried and tested elementary rock riff, same old electric guitar, same old drumkit set up the same old way. And it's so class-ridden, 'the music of the working class'. The great thing when I came in was that it was classless. It was great back then. People did cross the borders of style and class. But the punk thing is a working-class thing and so you only get someone hyphen something following punk out of a terrible mixed-up rebellious thing."

Anderson told *Melody Maker*; "Perhaps one of the great limitations of rock music is that it is either temporary or a stultifying musical form, that you either have a couple of years of really progressive, progressing music in your particular framework and then you quit and forget it, or you end up doing the same thing over and over. You do it as well as you can, but eventually it's just going to turn you into a machine. That's why it really annoys me when people say Jethro Tull are a programmed sort of a group, because — less than any other group that has been going as long as we have that I can think of — we don't operate that way. At least we do get out with every album and do something that's gonna confound the critics. Nobody else does that. They're shit scared of the critics. I mean, I like to get good reviews as much as anybody, but if I have to play a certain music in order to please a critic in order to get a good review, I would be better employed in being a music writer than being a music player."

Perhaps in an attempt to illustrate his point, Anderson passed comment on one of Jethro Tull's older songs, describing 'Locomotive Breath' as "a very repetitive, rhythmic thing but in all honesty, I don't think it's a great song. The lyrics are all right and the basic rhythm and mood is all right, but I wouldn't write a song like that today because I would require something more sophisticated because I am more sophisticated. Sophistication is something that happens to anybody who begins their career as a I artist. Take Frank Zappa. Each of his albums has an identity of its own. You like some and you don't like some of the others, but each one is different. And thank Christ for Frank Zappa who is, for me, the only thing that's come out of America, apart from Captain Beefheart at his best or worst, that means a light to me."

By 1976, Anderson advocated that Jethro Tull were something of an underground band on the basis that they weren't reliant on the public relations machine that many other bands at the time were. Not only that, but Jethro Tull hadn't been big in the singles charts in the years prior. Elaborating on his position, Anderson commented; "The only time we ever left the underground, I think, was in England, the time when lots of people left and became distinctly overground on a commercial level. There was a time when bands like Jethro Tull and The Nice and Fleetwood Mac appeared on *Top Of The Pops* and improved the media for a while. And people like John Peel helped by playing people a little bit of music they otherwise would not have heard, including, for that matter, Jethro Tull in the early days. People like John Peel changed the media for a little while."

"Unfortunately, the media benefited from that change and asserted even more authority and have now rather excluded people like John Peel and Bob Harris from a position of power. In saying this I know I'm being a little bit down on the media but I do think that the BBC is now as bad as it was, as narrow-minded as it was, when I first came into this melee. It was terrible then. It's terrible now, but there was a little point in time where I think it got better. But it ain't now. It's the men with the big cigars again. There's not a decent manager in the business. If you had a group you could not, at this point in time, find them a manager that was worth an iota. You couldn't do it. I know. I tried. Not for me, but for other people. That's one reason why young groups are finding it difficult to establish themselves."

In terms of where Jethro Tull stood commercially, *Melody Maker* opined; "Even the ultra-confident, self-assured Anderson would have to admit that the popularity of Jethro Tull in Britain has been on the wane. While Led Zeppelin and the Rolling Stones were shooting into the chart on advance sales, Tull have had to content themselves with scratching the lower regions and be happy they've even done that. In the States and in Europe, they're bigger than ever. They're on a par with the Stones and Zeppelin in the States. Ian Anderson prophesied to the *Melody Maker* six months ago that Jethro Tull would enjoy a resurgence of popularity in Britain in 1976 — that they would become bigger than ever before — that they would pick up lots of new, younger fans. Five months into the new year, the signs of this happening are about as clear as London on a foggy night."

Anderson said; "We still get gold albums every year, you know. I mean, they are all gold albums and a few of them are platinum now. I don't think I'm worried that people don't rush out and buy them all at the same time. I think I'm glad if the fact that they don't jump straight into the chart illustrates cautiousness on the part of the public, and I'm very pleased for the public because they're not wasting their money by just rushing out and buying something, then finding they don't like it and complaining about it. I suppose our record sales have not been as good world-wide as Zeppelin or Floyd, but the Pink Floyd records get played as musical wallpaper muzak, for parties and easy listening. I don't think anyone could ever say that Jethro Tull music is put on as background music for parties. That's the last thing I would ever want. I'd much rather people sat down and listened to it than have it played while people sit round and talk about football."

"It would certainly be true to say we've lost ground but I think, also, we haven't been represented in Britain terribly well. I don't think we've been presented in any way at all. I think we've just continued to exist and make token appearances as far as the public is concerned. It's only since I've been back these last few months that there's been any relationship at all between the radio stations and Jethro Tull."

Anderson told *New Musical Express* in June '76; "There are some of us who, believe it or not, have a basic respect for what being a muso's all about. Like, I'm glad to be working — although we enjoy the hotels and we enjoy travelling first class, and who the hell wouldn't? There is that basic ingrained sort of thing: Glad to be treading the boards, having a dressing room, I'm very grateful for all that."

A 1976 press released stated that "fortunately, the thrill hasn't gone for Jethro Tull. They may have ten consecutive gold albums, astronomical attendance figures, and the tax nightmares that signify you've made it several times over — but they never lose sight of their obligation to their audience, and they believe they still have a way to go in cultivating new followers. They entered the pop music arena as innovators, and it is purely by extending the limits of each successive stage show and album that they have kept that vital faith with their admirers. With international record sales in excess of ten million, Ian Anderson still has to make it on his own terms."

Although *Too Old To Rock 'n' Roll: Too Young To Die* wasn't one of Jethro Tull's most successful albums commercially, things were about to take off for the band in a big way with their 1977 album, *Songs From The Wood*.

Songs From The Wood marked the beginning of what was a surge in popularity for Jethro Tull. It got to number thirteen in the UK and to number eight in the US. The singles released from the album were indicative of this. David Palmer told *Sounds* in January 1976; "This next single just might do it in Britain. Jethro Tull could be a brand new group."

'The Whistler' was released as a single in the US where it got to number fifty-nine in May 1977. Prior to that, released as a 1976 Christmas single, 'Ring Out, Solstice Bells' got to number twenty-eight in the UK. It was included on an EP containing three songs, the others being 'Pan Dance' and 'March The Mad Scientist'.

By this point in their tenure, Jethro Tull were certainly still keen to flirt with the singles market. Anderson told *Sounds* in January 1976; "At the back of the old fiendish brain there lurks something in me that wants to go on *Top Of The Pops*. I don't know why. I think I'll do it again. Have a hit single."

He was quoted in *Record Mirror* in February 1977; "Maybe singles could be a way of increasing our audience, getting hit singles again could be a viable proposition. We have another single planned, 'The Whistler'. The lyrics are a bit heavy for radio, it's a more serious single. I'll get in the studio and re-do it at the end of the tour. If you do a more serious single, you don't get on the radio playlist. The Radio One play list — and all the commercial stations run similar lists. It's like having to do an audition every time you bring out a record. All they want is the same old predictable stuff. People like me became so disillusioned we stopped doing singles for a long time. Others who are less concerned with artistic ideology compromise to the playlist requirements. What do you get? Two-hundred records a week that are boring and repetitive. Personally, I'd like to hear much more variety on the radio. I think they could be more generous to our sort of material. Now FM radio in the States — British radio stations could take an example from that. They're not what you'd call underground radio, they play a lot of album tracks and cover a wider format of music. But AM radio over there is worse than Radio One, strictly top forty stuff."

In November 1976, *New Musical Express* rated 'Ring Out, Solstice Bells' as Christmas EP of the week. They reviewed it as follows: "Ian Anderson apparently feels we might celebrate the Winter Solstice on December 22nd (sic) instead of Christmas, although that might prove less than fun. Imagine opening your packets of socks and underpants three days before everyone else. Joyless, that. Still, Anderson has a thing about Christmas. His delightful parody of 'Once In Royal David's City' is one of the tracks on this EP, but for all its charm 'Christmas Song' perhaps offers an unnecessarily sour view of the festivities. It is, nonetheless, a Tull milestone that deserved re-

The myth of Christmas begins with the winter solstice.

The new Jethro Tull E.P.
Remembering another England.
An England of mists, of long barrows and of legend. Of Druids, stone circles and pagan ceremony.
An England where the shortest day of the year, the winter solstice, was a major festival in the pre-Christian calendar.
And an England where much later, with the advent of Christianity, the time of the solstice was adopted to celebrate the birth of Christ.
The title track of the new Tull E.P. 'Ring Out, Solstice Bells' pays tribute to these ancient origins of the Christmas festival.

And the other three tracks speak of the changing seasons, Christmas as it is now, and finally a musical celebration of the Great God Pan, (he of the cloven feet and magic pipes).
The record comes in an illustrated sleeve depicting a "well known Druid" surrounded by the paraphernalia of his trade.
And at 75p it's well worth celebrating.
The new Jethro Tull E.P. Four tracks in all, three new recordings, plus Christmas song.

Chrysalis Records & Tapes

Ring Out, Solstice Bells. Christmas song. March the Mad Scientist. Pan dance.

release. The title track is the one that will get the promotional push, however, and that's a little less satisfying. Anderson has resolutely refused to compromise his creative instincts over the years, but 'Ring Out, Solstice Bells' seems a touch too fussy and complicated in its arrangement to cut it as a seasonal singalong. It's interesting to note, in the meantime, that there's been no loss of inspiration when you compare Tull's early work with their latest output, whatever the consensus view of the band among critics."

Tull's performance of 'Ring Out, Solstice Bells' on *Top Of The Pops* might not have even happened if it wasn't for some frantic last minute organisation. *New Musical Express* reported in December 1976; "The hassles some bands subject themselves to in order to appear on *Top Of The Pops* astonishes even us. Take for example the other Wednesday, when the TOTP bosses summoned famous pop group Jethro Tull before them to play their new record 'Ring Out, Solstice Bells' on the programme that very same day. The people at the Tull office were delighted, until they realised they'd mislaid three members, including leader Ian Anderson. Superstar Ian (well, so he tells us) was shopping in Oxford Street. Guitarist Martin Barre was driving up to London from Wales, and drummer Barriemore Barlow was attending his uncle's funeral in Birmingham."

"As we all know, an appearance on TOTP guarantees an immediate increase in record sales, so up at the Tull office the scramble button was pressed. A distress call for Martin Barre to phone the office was broadcast by Capital Radio and luckily he heard it. Barrie Barlow was located by telephone after the office had phoned every Barlow in the Brum area. But Ian Anderson was still adrift and failed to respond to tannoyed calls in every major department store in Oxford Street. Where on earth was the man? Eventually, after Tull's accountant's wife heard the Capital distress call and telephoned her husband, who had just been with Anderson, he was located in a boutique. A hurried recording session was arranged to lay down a backing track, and with only minutes to spare all members of Jethro Tull made it to the TOTP studios. The band, you might hazily recall, used to be termed "progressive" and "underground" so why such panic to get them on the grisly Pops nightmare? Answered A. Spokesman, 'Well, it's a good number to do'. We'll take their word for that."

Melody Maker reported in December 1976; "Jethro Tull return to the British concert stage early next year, playing their first tour in over two years. And the band's new album, *Songs From The Wood*, will be in the shops at the start of the tour."

To which Anderson commented; "The songs are related to my environment. I'm not a gentleman farmer, exactly, but I do lead a fairly rustic life among the foxes and badgers and pheasants. I also want to dispel the post-hippie syndrome which says everything's groovy and psychedelic about the countryside. In fact, it's a very cruel place, and I've been studying the ecology of country life. The songs are a result of this — you can call it funky British rock music, not rock 'n' roll. I suppose I'm the first medieval punk… We've not been able to do a major British tour so we're concentrating on the sort of halls which any group of our level should be proud to play. If there's one country in the world where you have to play for the troops, it's Britain — it's no good doing London, Manchester and Birmingham and expecting thousands of fans to travel. All those giant shows as status symbols are a thing of the past. There should be no need for anyone to prove they're bigger than Elton John or Led Zeppelin anymore. We're growing up!"

Back on the road at the start of '77, when Tull played to a full capacity crowd of 4,500 at Detroit's Masonic Auditorium on 19th January 1977, their setlist was as follows:

Wond'ring Aloud
Skating Away On The Thin Ice Of The New Day
Jack-In-The-Green
Songs From The Wood
Velvet Green
Hunting Girl
Thick As A Brick, Part I
To Cry You A Song
Bourée
Living In The Past
A New Day Yesterday
Minstrel In The Gallery
Too Old To Rock 'n' Roll: Too Young To Die
Aqualung
Cross-Eyed Mary
Wind-Up
Locomotive Breath
Back-Door Angels

Their performance was reviewed in a local paper: "The minstrel was Ian Anderson, showman extraordinaire, and the gallery was Detroit's Masonic Auditorium as Jethro Tull performed two shows last Wednesday and Thursday. Anderson, sporting hair and beard shorter than in years past, walked into the spotlight with his guitar to sing 'Wond'ring Aloud'. He was dressed in a vest and bowler, which he tapped against his head in a very vaudevillian manner. Ian was his old self throughout the night, using his flute as a prop and prancing about wildly. Anderson was joined by the rest of the group for 'Skating Away'… The band previewed four selections from their newest album, as yet untitled. Anderson has turned to old English heritage and music for inspiration. 'Jack-In-The-Green', for instance, was a melodic tune about a mythical character. 'Songs From The Wood', described as a 'celebration of music' by Anderson, employs unique old English harmonies in its vocals. It started out very light and turned into heavy metal as Barre unleashed his guitar. A kilted Barlow pulled on a medieval drumkit for 'Velvet Green', a very strange and ancient sounding composition. 'Hunting Girl' was a mediocre tale of a young lass who likes to use her riding crop."

"The newer songs were interspersed between the Tull favourites. They played 'Thick As A Brick' which Anderson said critics had called 'their standby'. Jethro Tull is a very tight stage band, a quality acquired through intense rehearsal. The rendition of 'Thick As A Brick' really showed the expert interplay among the musicians during an instrumental. A medley of older hits were very well structured. It started with 'To Cry You A Song' and 'New Day Yesterday'. At that point, Anderson played a flute solo incorporating the holiday tunes 'Comfort And Joy', 'Bourée' and a display of gasping intonation. The others then played an instrumental version of 'Living In The Past' and brought the medley to a full circle with a return to 'New Day Yesterday'. An instrumental lead-in to 'Minstrel In The Gallery' featured a riff stolen from the second movement of Beethoven's Ninth Symphony. They also played 'Too Old To Rock 'n' Roll' with Palmer supplying a marvellous fifties sax solo."

"*Aqualung*, Tull's first concept album as well as their most successful, comprised the remainder of the show. They played the title track and 'Cross-Eyed Mary' before leaving the stage. Martin Barre, an expert but underrated guitarist, returned alone for a solo. He began with a bit of classical Bach, but it didn't get any reaction from Detroit's rock orientated crowd. So he turned on his power boost and cranked out some very fluid high energy licks using speedy triplets and the heavy metal sound of feedback. For encores, the band played 'Wind-Up' and 'Locomotive Breath'. At the end Anderson was left alone to serenade the audience goodbye with 'Back-Door Angels' as the spotlight closed on his face. 'See you at your place,' he said, tipped his hat and the madman dashed offstage, leaving the audience content after nearly two and a half hours of excellent Jethro Tull."

There was much excitement surrounding the band's return to the UK. The journalist who reported in the *Aberdeen Evening Express* in February 1977 let on that he wasn't a massive fan of the band, but nevertheless gave a review that was reflective of what the audience got out of the performance: "Some time last year Ian Anderson devised a concept album called *Too Old To Rock 'n' Roll: Too Young To Die*. Last night he and the rest of Jethro Tull succeeded in telling a nearly capacity audience at Aberdeen's Capitol Cinema that this was no reflection on the band. It's over two years since Tull toured in this country and a lot longer since they visited Aberdeen. The band travelled north for a full day's rehearsal on Monday and prepared again yesterday before the concert. They wanted to get it right for their first British night in twenty-seven months. Anderson and band chose wisely when they decided to begin the tour here, for they evoked tremendous response from their followers."

"Surprisingly, Tull's opening was rather low-key instead of one of the immediately recognisable rockers. They opted for 'Skating Away On The Thin Ice Of The New Day' and 'Jack-In-The-Green', a song from the forthcoming album. On both these, Anderson's vocal was a tad underplayed. The power began to flow during the *Thick As A Brick* selection. The show was loud in many parts but more importantly, the sound was clear. Although Anderson's dress was not quite so bizarre as it has been in the past, the onstage antics were every bit as maniacal. There is his gentle side, however, and this was particularly evident on cuts from the new *Songs From The Wood* album. I found 'Too Old To Rock 'n' Roll: Too Young To Die' the most enjoyable number but I hasten to add I find Tull's music generally anti-climatic and difficult to respond to. 'Minstrel In The Gallery' and 'Aqualung' finished the set but the crowd brought the band back twice."

The following night's gig was reviewed in *New Musical Express*; "The scene for the latest round of Jethro Tull v The Music Press is a sellout concert at the Glasgow Apollo. Enter the press man, specially selected for his dislike of Ian Anderson; he's been thinking up insults all week. Roll the pre-recorded tapes — sounds like something The Nice rejected — and on comes Ian Anderson. Hells bells, he's had his hair cut! He looks almost neat. He's wearing a red bowler, a cream suit, the bottom half of which is the familiar breeches, and a red waistcoat. He starts off into 'Wond'ring Aloud' on acoustic guitar as the rest of the band file on one by one, bizarrely dressed as usual, and join in. The shadowy sixth member on pipe organ is later identified as David Palmer of the London College of Somethingorother. At the end of the number, Ian Anderson has his first go at his critics, and after a diversion for 'Skating Away' from *War Child*, a song from the new LP: 'Everyone will tell you it's really shit. It's 'Jack-In-The-Green'.' Unfortunately they were right — it is really shit. 'Our critics tell us this is something of a standby,' Anderson announces before a long version of some of *Thick As A Brick*, then into 'Songs From The Wood', a hopelessly contrived mock madrigal."

"After 'To Cry You A Song' Anderson goes off and the band take on the world for a long instrumental. Back comes Ian to lead on flute through snatches of classical music, 'Bourée', 'Driving Song' and 'Living In The Past' (greeted with deserved acclaim) and others from happier days. Another number from the justly-slated new LP is preceded by all the old kilt jokes strung together. Ho Hum. It's 'Velvet Green'. Isn't it rare to be taking the air? Putting on airs, you mean. The village squire bit fails flat on its face — a pity, because there's the basis of a really good song in there. Another new song, 'Hunting Girl': 'You'll hate it.' It's accompanied by limp SM jokes and Anderson hitting John Glascock with a riding crop. Next comes another dig at the music press. 'I seem to have acquired a reputation for hating the music press, as it likes to call itself.' A biting attack! That really showed 'em. But just to show he doesn't harbour grudges, this next one is dedicated to CW of MM — 'Too Old To Rock 'n' Roll: Too Young To Die'."

The review continued, "The rest of the show consists of an excerpt from *Passion Play*, *Minstrel In The Gallery* and *Aqualung*. 'Wind-Up' and 'Locomotive Breath' (superb) are the encores. During the latter, two big white balloons bearing £ signs, which have been attached to the back curtain without explanation during the whole show, are thrown out to the audience for bursting while the band play 'Land Of Hope And Glory'. A brief snatch of 'Back-Door Angels' and he's off. Another battle over, but the campaign goes on, and the Ian Anderson v The Music Press war shows no sign of being resolved."

"If you love Anderson, his shallow concepts and his infantile sexual innuendos, you'll wet yourself at this neat two hour show. But if you wish he'd drop all this contrived nonsense and just write songs again, real songs with feeling and spontaneity, you'll just have to wait and hope. I'll join you. This idea of a band leader as a man with a vision is okay while the leader's eye is in, but consistent panning does suggest something is wrong. 'Aqualung' isn't really Jethro Tull's finest hour — it's no less contrived a concept than any that followed it, it's just that the fine music obscured this rather than carried it off. I'd go back even further for the best Jethro Tull, before concepts."

"Perhaps it is all in the past, but it was first class stuff, and now I'm not prepared to settle for anything less. A word of praise for the excellent lights, and now let's hear it for the band. They were great. What a fine guitarist Martin Barre is: his talents are being wasted. Barrie Barlow is a good, solid rock drummer, and John Evan has come on by leaps and bounds (but less of the Upper Class Twit Of The Year act please). But the top notch is reserved for John Glascock on bass, who put heart and soul into his fine, fine work. I could have listened to him all night. I'd like to see a Jethro Tull Without Ian Anderson tour. That would really sort out the sheep from the goat."

Melody Maker reported in February 1977; "Life may be a long song, but staying in tune and on top of the shifting sands of the music scene has been achieved by few of the bands who surfaced in the late sixties alongside Jethro Tull. Tull have remained a vital force due to successive line-up changes and skilful musical experiments conducted by the band's mainstay, Ian Anderson. The long lay-off from touring in Britain, and Anderson's subsequent transformation from his wild and unkempt image of the past to the rural pose of the present, has produced some disappointing albums, but has seemingly not lessened the band's popularity. Saturday night's show at Manchester's Apollo Theatre had sold out so quickly that a second one the night before had been hastily added and that, too, was packed to the roof."

"Absence has obviously made the demand to see them live even greater. It was a two hour set, well-timed and cleverly thought out. Anderson bounced onto the stage, taking much of the audience by surprise in his country squire's outfit and his simple greeting of 'hello, boys and girls.' Accompanying himself on guitar, he launched into the whimsical 'Wond'ring Aloud', and then 'Skating Away On The Thin Ice Of The New Day', before the band had even appeared. He was clearly enjoying himself, and, despite his laryngitis, he sounded in good form. The rest of the concert was a tour de force of Tull's extensive catalogue. They included four songs from *Aqualung*, four from the new one *Songs From The Wood*, and a couple from *Benefit* and *Stand Up*. But, apart from a twenty-minute selection from *Thick As A Brick*, there was only passing reference to the conceptual epics like *War Child* and *Passion Play*, over which Anderson fell foul of the music press."

"Despite his constant sniping at the critics, he seems to have returned to the more structured and commercial sound of Jethro Tull of the early seventies, as those same critics have advised. Hence the heavy emphasis on *Aqualung*, still Tull's best-selling album, and the more attractive medieval arrangements of the new album. All the familiar traits of a Tull performance were there. Anderson cavorted around the stage, maintaining a constant rapport with the audience as he switched from acoustic guitar to flute, which he still plays standing on one leg. The band were also given room to display their talent, but are unable to take any of the limelight off their musical architect, and remain only as a competent vehicle for Anderson's performance. But all in all, it was an impressive return. They did end up with 'Locomotive Breath', but the contrast and vitality of the set dispelled

October 9th 1978, Madison Square Garden, New York.

my pre-concert impression that they were just living in the past (which, incidentally, they didn't sing)."

Sounds reviewed the Newcastle gig in February; "You know how supergroups are supposed to open the show with the 1812 Overture complete with real facsimile nineteenth-century Muscovite cannon and a battalion of the Green Howards rented for the day to pose as Napoleon's army (all marching on their stomachs for authenticity)? Or if that's felt to be a little tasteless perhaps just a *Ben-Hur* chariot race round the aisles? Well, the lights came up on the City Hall stage and Ian Anderson strode on alone with no special effects, no scenery bar the amps and drumkit, stared 2,500 people in the eye (for his gaze is always directed at you like the bottoms in Cezanne's nude Baigneuses) with the roguish glint which hints at Fagin, Captain Hook and the Lincolnshire Poacher, and unleashed an earthquake of applause that would have done credit to the San Andreas Fault."

"Anderson was magnificent. I can't remember when I last saw such crowd rapport generated. They whistled, shouted ('Where's your codpiece?') and roared ('Ah that new Indian restaurant? Yes, I sympathise,' said Anderson), sang all the words in the quiet verses of old favourites, and were vibrant with reaction to every move — particularly the first time he took up the flute and perched on one leg, left foot against right knee. His chat was as dazzling and dirty as ever. And I've hardly mentioned the music till now because it really was a secondary pleasure. But it was about as good as Tull music can be on stage."

"His classics 'Aqualung' and 'Thick As A Brick' (the fourth number and a standing ovation) really threw the switch. They are so nakedly heavy between the more delicate flute and acoustic passages. Four Songs From The Wood made it past the oldies and it seemed to perk up the band to be playing them though Anderson gave some credence to the Tull-go-Steeleye-Span lobby by describing 'Jack-In-The-Green', about a sprite-like protector of England's verdant pastures, as 'typical folkie bullshit'. Anyway, the title track won over the doubters of this country cuteness with a lovely acapella vocal erupting into get-down rock that even outweighed 'Brick'."

"My own favourites from *War Child* were interesting: 'Skating Away' was all light and airy beauty but 'Back-Door Angels' suffered from Anderson's razzmatazz and was pretty but not touching as on the record. All round, that was entertainment and proved that Anderson isn't too old to rock 'n' roll — but you have to add 'yet' and he knows it. The olde Englishe stuff seems to be a pleasant diversion rather than a whole new direction and he's got to find one sometime. The rather stereotyped pattern of all Tull's work was wearing thin after nearly two hours. So try this on for size. I see him as a kind of rock Lennie Bruce, talking more, playing less, getting more serious and more funny both, bouncing off hecklers, insulting them, hitting the audience where they live on subjects like sex and politics which he already flirts with. Between raps the music would be more wild, the lyrics more pointed. He's committed to entertainment and it's great to receive that, but I'm sure that a pyrotechnic mind like his has even more to offer."

The Newcastle show was also reviewed in *National Rock Star*; "Ian Anderson walked on under a battery of ultraviolets to massive applause. 'Here's a song my mother taught me,' was the brief introduction to 'Wond'ring Aloud'. The rest of the band took their places as required in the song's build-up. Newcomer David Palmer looked the part in concert pianist tie and tails. Anderson introduced him as 'trained at Trinity College of Music but saw the light.' The wit is as sharp as ever. But his over-publicised sensitivity to press criticism after the *Passion Play* saga will become further mis-proportioned on this tour if his references to journalists continue to be as frequent as they were here. 'The next number is one from our new album which in spite of what you read in the press is marvellous,' was one of at least four such remarks during the night."

"'Jack-In-The-Green' was the first of four cuts from *Songs From The Wood* that the band performed. The title track was followed by two medleys — a précis of *Thick As A Brick* side one and a superb sequence starting with Anderson offstage for an anonymous instrumental, returning for 'New Day Yesterday' complete with classic Anderson flute solo — eyes popping, leg up, mucus flying and snatch breaths providing a rhythm. The hits kept on coming: 'Bourée', 'Living In The Past', more from *Thick As A Brick*. 'Aqualung' closed the set, but they came back to do 'Back-Door Angels' and 'Wind-Up' and back yet again for 'Locomotive Breath'. You know how it feels: You come home on cloud nine after seeing one of your all time fave bands, head straight for the LP pile itching to start the show all over again only to find the recorded article sounds positively tame. I knew I'd been to a good gig."

Sounds reviewed the final show of three that took place at Hammersmith; "It's strange, but up until Sunday night at the Hammersmith Odeon, Jethro Tull had been an anonymous quantity in my musical catalogue. I might have bought the odd single but apart from that, their progress has gone over my ears, so to speak. Like, say, the Moody Blues, Tull seem to have gotten into their own personal niche and their performance, music and audiences remain insular to the rest of the music world. They move at their pace ignoring progress and an immense army of fans follow. There's something of an intimate atmosphere at Tull's shows, it's like everyone's come down to see an old friend. I felt left out."

October 9th 1978, Madison Square Garden, New York.

October 9th 1978, Madison Square Garden, New York.

October 9th 1978, Madison Square Garden, New York.

October 9th 1978, Madison Square Garden, New York.

October 9th 1978, Madison Square Garden, New York.

October 9th 1978, Madison Square Garden, New York.

"Being unfamiliar with most of the material, it was difficult to appreciate what was going on, whether it was a good or bad version of 'Too Old To Rock 'n' Roll: To Young To Die'. The only thing I know was I was impressed and want to hear more. These guys ain't as boring as most journalists think. Ian Anderson is a sparkling showman and the band are a remarkable collection of musicians. Their sound is more distinct than formularised, you can only describe their music as being Tull, it goes under many guises. Many traditional styles are twisted, transmogrified to accommodate new weird time changes. They have the rare ability of transforming a melodic song into a complex almost barbarian workout and then back to melody again."

"While Anderson adopts the pose of a drunken poacher from another era, the band, under the guise of equally insane eccentrics, bounce about the stage as if they were cheering a toast at some seventeenth century debauched blowout. And there's no way one can get bored, with Anderson's crazy mannerisms. Those taut features going into a proverbial carnival of grimaces, his eyeballs protrude as if they're trying to escape from their sockets while his limber torso dances about the stage as if possessed by the spirit of the bass pedal. The whole band approach their duties with maximum confidence, sometimes a bit too slick. The tightness of the material doesn't allow for any adventurous blowing and Anderson's onstage persona seems larger than life at times in the intimate jam-packed confines of the Odeon. But they do have an endearing quality which makes them one of the few mega star quantities that hold any genuine communication with audiences. Turkeys they are not!"

It was reported in the *Hammersmith & Shepherd's Bush Gazette* in the same month; "Ian Anderson must be one of the most unpredictable figures in British rock. To tie in with the rural flavour of the new Jethro Tull album, *Songs From The Wood*, Anderson has now taken up the pose of an eccentric English squire, complete with boots, hat and riding crop. It was a characterisation that thoroughly entertained audiences at three sell-out concerts at the Hammersmith Odeon last week and provided a compelling link between the many and varied songs of the set. During their two-hour performance, Tull managed to run through a fair selection of their work to date from the early days through *Thick As A Brick* and *Aqualung* to the current album."

"From *Songs From The Wood*, the most effective numbers were the title track and 'Velvet Green', a gentle song which featured a variety of medieval percussion instruments. While Tull music may sound relatively subdued on record, it contains no small amount of dynamism live and is further strengthened by visuals — a superb light show and, of course, the very presence of Anderson, tremendous showman. Interest did tend to flag during two badly placed numbers mid-set which went on for a little too long and somewhat lessened the impact of what had gone before."

"However, no fatal damage was done, and the band worked up to a great finale followed by well-deserved encores during which balloons bearing £ signs were unleashed to the strains of 'Land Of Hope And Glory'. The highspot of the whole show, for me, was a lively rendition of 'Too Old To Rock 'n' Roll: Too Young To Die' which Anderson explained was not autobiographical as the rock press had thought fit to suggest. This was one of several side-swipes at an industry which it is claimed has often gone beyond the call of duty in its criticisms of the band. But at Hammersmith, Jethro Tull proved that despite such attacks, they can claim a staying power and following that many a band would be proud to own."

With *Songs From The Wood*, Jethro Tull went back to the folk roots of what their earlier sound had been all about, all whilst avoiding what had become the clichés of blues music. It's a particularly British-sounding album, but equally it is in no way traditional in terms of the academic interpretation of old folk songs. The overall mood on *Songs From The Wood* is reflective of the fact that Anderson had recently moved to live in the country. Not only was he living there, but he had taken on the responsibility of running a commercial farm. Having grown up in the country, Anderson was at home with his new surroundings having lived in London and in hotels for most of his adult life up to that point. In later years he considered that the stability of being in one place had a positive influence on the creation of *Songs From The Wood*. It also brought the band closer together musically in terms of how involved they were on the album. Anderson would often leave the studio in order to give the rest of Jethro Tull some space to work on their own ideas for the album. Morale and creativity was excellent for the band during this period.

Anderson told *Circus* in April 1977; "I want to produce an album which is different from anything we've done before. It'll be less blues and more of some particularly British hybrid form — more modal, more Celtic. I find the music I'm writing now embodies something of the very earliest musical tradition, an almost religious music of celebration. I want to try to evoke something a little more spiritual and emotional... I feel obliged to take risks with the music. I hope it'll be something people will immediately respond to, though, because it contains basic elements of rhythm and melodic simplicity and verbal imagery. I'd rather do the most unusual album of the year rather than necessarily the best selling one. It's time for a rather larger step into the unknown."

To which the journalist considered, "*Songs From The Wood*, Jethro Tull's latest Chrysalis release, is Anderson's bid to fulfil that stated aim. Always a Heavy Elizabethan band drawing more from the olde folke tradition than rhythm and blues, Jethro Tull have given the new LP an even more pronounced medieval flavouring than gaieties of the past. With Anderson's hedonistic lyrics, the set has the thematic aura of a collection of organic, sixteenth century pastorals. Jethro Tull's idiosyncratic and rarely imitated sound springs from the personality of Ian Anderson, whose whole adult life has been characterised by a streak of non-conformity."

Anderson opined; "Rock music seems to have gone as far as it can go, I mean it couldn't go any further without leaving its audience behind. I dunno, it's rather sad that it's gone back to its roots rather than continuing on perhaps a more simple level but still be original. But it just doesn't happen that way, it's gone back to the rock 'n' roll riffs where people parade an endless variety of Keith Moon drum breaks and 'scorching guitar chords'. They may do them very well, but they have been done before as well as could ever be done, which negates doing them again, in my mind. Perhaps it's me getting old."

In contrast to the rustic sounds, the album isn't without its heavier moments. Amongst the focus on folk roots, there was no absence of sparkle from Barre's electric guitar and Barlow's drumkit. It's immediately clear upon listening to the album that Ian Anderson was in a mellower mood than many had perhaps come to expect from Jethro Tull. Thematically there were no signs of the abrasiveness or sardonic social commentary that featured in some of their previous albums. Anderson advocated a few years after the album came out that it was clearly indicative of where he was in his life at the time of making it; He had settled down, bought a house, got married, and had a baby. Not necessarily in that order, but almost.

Circumstances were similar for the rest of the band as well. Not only that, but they had all settled down in Britain having accepted the fact that they couldn't be tax exiles forever. None of them wanted to live in Liechtenstein or the Bahamas or wherever else had been recommended to them by those in the know. Consequently, for everyone in the band, there was a sense of general acceptance and an enjoyment of their environment — not just in terms of living in the country, but in the sense of living in Britain as a whole.

Anderson told *Sounds* in May 1976; "I'm not prepared to go over to America for the sake of having an extra ten or twenty percent of my money, as opposed to paying it in tax… Sure, the tax is a lot of bread. But it isn't what they have you believe. That's the truth. The English people are being misinformed. They should be given the facts. People are actually starting to hate pop stars for making money and running away. Twenty-five percent of what people like me earn is still a lot of money. I earn as much as a bricklayer who works really hard. And that's a lot of money. That's about my level of income, and that's all I need to live comfortably."

And in *New Musical Express* in June he said; "There are many reasons why I stay in England, not the least important being loyalty. Silly as it may sound, trivial as it may sound, that comes up reasonably high on the list for me. I'm British, and for a while now I've been making a good living by playing British music. It's British Music!"

Regarding *Songs From The Wood*, Anderson explained to *Record Mirror* in February 1977; "This is the first album we've recorded in Britain for three years. We did it over a full three months — September, October, November. We all lived at home during this time and commuted to the studios. You're more relaxed if you can sleep in your own bed at night. And we were all able to take a day's holiday a week. Every album we do has a different motive. This one was done a song at a time. I told the band I had written all the material before we went into the studios. I hadn't. In fact the first song we cut, 'Solstice Bells', I wrote the same morning we recorded it. Thinking about it afterwards, I suggested to the record company it would make a commercial Christmas single. They waffled for a month before deciding to release it. It sold. In the week before Christmas it jumped from forty-two to twenty-eight. Then it died on Christmas Day. If the record company hadn't dithered so long, it would have been a bigger hit. It's interesting. I remember last spring I made a bet with a journalist that we would be on *Top Of The Pops* by the end of the year. I wonder if she remembers."

Songs From The Wood seems to have been written quite spontaneously overall if Anderson's comment to *National Rock Star* in February 1977 is anything to go by; "Some of the songs were written on the train. It was quite fun to work that way."

Songs From The Wood was a deliberate attempt on Tull's part to make an album that wasn't overtly socially critical whilst trying to maintain some of the musical roots that the group was known for embracing. There was a conscious effort to express a feeling of joy across all of the songs on the album. Even on 'Hunting Girl', the message behind the song was put across in a tongue-in-cheek way; with warmth and no vitriol — there is no social critique involved.

Anderson told *Creem* in June 1978; "I try to write songs that aren't too different from the way I live and so my songs have necessarily had to change, as I've grown away from having a working group sort of life. As the logic of success prevailed we made a commitment to going first class in the world and then it suddenly dawned that it's not on to sing as if we're sitting down there. We're not anymore. We're sitting up here. And we can't really sing about sitting up here because that's irrelevant to most people and sounds a bit cocky, so it became a little more abstract. Lyrically things became more abstract and started taking on weird and weighty connotations, which were amusing for a bit, amused me, but after a while you want to get back to the direct meaningful songs that are about something and actually deal in fairly accessible English. You're forced to think what is there to write about, what moves me, and that's what I write about now, whatever it is that's left."

A few years after *Songs From The Wood* had been released, Anderson advocated that the songs didn't have "lyrical bite" but also acknowledged that in the context of Jethro Tull's entire discography, the album had been more readily accepted on the basis that it was more accessible and more cheerful and relaxed. He told BBC Radio in 1979; "At the time that was the most important thing for me to go for: that truly did represent the way I was feeling at that particular point in time."

In the same interview, in reference to the 'Ring Out, Solstice Bells' single, Anderson noted that it was "completely irreverent really" on the basis that the band didn't celebrate the solstice and neither did they ring bells during it. Equally though, at the time, Anderson wanted to write a Christmas song and was determined to do one that wasn't centred on Christianity. He said; "I wanted to write a song about what Christmas really is all about, which is something way before that, before the Christians adopted the date. To try to put something of the joy of the original Christmas festivity into a song which is seemingly innocuous. But really the thought behind that is directed very much against the idea of the Christian Christmas festival."

Songs From The Wood signified the extent to which David Palmer was a vital part of the band. A fulltime member by that point, he contributed keyboards (piano, portative pipe organ and synthesisers) to the album. Prior to that, by Anderson's own admission, his services had merely been employed if they required an orchestration for a couple of violins and a cello. No longer did Anderson phone Palmer and send him a tape inviting him to prepare an arrangement and bring an orchestra to a session. By the time it came to making *Songs From The Wood*, Palmer was part of the rehearsal process — and the rest of the band became involved with the arranging process in that regard too.

With David Palmer more involved, it resulted in an increased use of synthesiser. Anderson told BBC Radio in 1979 that he preferred to use "the conventional, individual, man-played instruments: French horns, flutes, oboes, bassoons, violins, cellos and whatever else, than hear them attempted as a synthesised likeness, which I usually find lacking in spirit" but Palmer came in with broader ideas for how to utilise the synthesiser on the album. Rather than using it to imitate existing instruments, it was used to contribute effective sounds in its own right. As Anderson put it, "David's use of synthesisers is not to replace musicians, it's to try and come up with different sounds which, from the final emotional point of view, serve the same purpose." (It was from *Songs From The Wood* that the portative pipe organ started being used as part of the live shows).

The variety of songs on the album is derived from the fact the band worked so well together in the studio when making it. 'Hunting Girl' was a full group effort. They all utilised some of their ideas regarding the arrangement and the parts they played. It was very much a rehearsed piece prior to being recorded (with the exception of the flute and vocals, which Anderson put on afterwards). The band spent around three to four days rehearsing 'Hunting Girl' so that when it came to recording it, they were very familiar with the piece — note perfect straight away.

'Cup Of Wonder' sounds very much like a group piece but it actually started out as acoustic guitar, bass and drums played live on the backing track. Anderson told BBC Radio in 1979; "I felt that since the simple rhythmic essence of the thing had to be conveyed on that first backing track recording, I should play acoustic guitar with drums and bass; which is not very good because you have separation problems, and I have to go in a booth so the drums don't leak down my mic. Having arrived at a backing track which was right, then we add the different things around that; and in a song like 'Cup Of Wonder' there was very little rehearsal done. All that I did was rehearse with the bass player and the drummer. The other things were conceived afterwards — all I had was a vocal tune, a set of chords, and then worked out a bass and drums part."

The title track contains a lot of musical variety. It consists of a wide range of ideas — there's the a cappella vocal, the acoustic guitar bit (which was done separately) and lots of overdubs (the harmonies were worked out in the studio). The section where the group play as an ensemble was rehearsed away from the studio. Consequently, the band knew every note of what they were going to play but they had yet to know how their part would fit into the context of the song overall.

Anderson told BBC Radio in 1979; "For them, they were learning a piece of instrumental music; they didn't know what I was going to do. And all these things are fun. Sometimes they know nothing about a song until they arrive in the studio and we try and whip it together in a few hours before putting it down on tape. On other occasions it will be rehearsed for several days or a week or maybe over a two week period, odd days here and there until every possibility within the arrangement has been explored. What we finally put down on tape is the result of a lot of trial and error considering an accurate arrangement."

For the beginning of 'Pibroch (Cap In Hand)', Anderson played Barre a melody line on the flute and told him to go into the studio and play it on his guitar. Whilst Barre was doing this, he was unaware of what Anderson was doing in the control room with all the echo effects. Anderson explained; "I did everything with that tape to make it sound as if you had about twenty guitars playing — all slightly different, staggered intervals, playing this thing that was meant to evoke the same emotional thing as a set of bagpipes playing on a windy hill. I mean Martin standing out there thought he was playing a blues riff; had no idea. He then went for a cup of tea and came back, by which time I'd played around with the tapes and done this to it. It absolutely staggered him. He said, 'Absolutely fantastic, that!' Which I found was very amusing, and very creative also: it's employing someone's I involvement in something and then twisting it around and then throwing back something totally different as a result."

In later years, Barre recalled how for 'Pibroch (Cap In Hand)' he turned the amps up to full volume to record the introduction. For the melody, Anderson had lent Barre an album of bagpipe music and had advised him to take note of the melodies on it. Although he advocated that the bagpipes and guitar are worlds away form each other in terms of what can be done on them, Barre considered that the bagpipe music must have gone some of the way towards inspiring what he played.

So is *Songs From The Wood* a concept album? Anderson explained; "Even the title of the album was quite openly saying, 'look, here's a bunch of songs, and the only thing they have in common is that most of them were written on a train from High Wycombe to Marylebone.' If that's a concept, then it's a concept album again. Most of the songs on *Wood* were written for once when I was living in England as opposed to a hotel room."

Songs From The Wood was reviewed in *Record Mirror* in February 1977; "Welcome to CAMRA, the Campaign for Rustic Anthems, brought to your ears courtesy of ye olde Ian Anderson Band, otherwise known as Jethro Tull. CAMRA albums come out, on average, once a year, and are all too often compared to the classic *Aqualung* of several summers ago. This latest brew, as the label suggests, features a selection of songs with strong rural flavours. Jolly mandolins, the flute — the trademark of all CAMRA products — and Squire Anderson's vocals potter their way through a selection of rhymes and ditties. Bonus ingredients are their last special single brew 'Ring Out, Solstice Bells' and their next 'The Whistler.' When you hold this brew up to the light, you should be able to see through it with little trouble. It has a mellow taste as of autumn leaves tinged with rabbit stew. Over-indulgence can lead to a headache and other symptoms known collectively as a hangover (from the sixties?). Three pints of ordinary, please."

It was reviewed in *National Rock Star* in the same month; "If Robin Hood was still around today he'd be bopping to this lad. Songs like 'Jack-In-The-Green', 'Hunting Girl' and 'Velvet Green' would have him dancing in the fauna. Unlike a lot of Tull albums, this one is neither a concept nor an exercise in social comment. The aggression and bite which Ian Anderson usually lets flow out of his songs has been replaced by a neat package of nine songs linked by this back-to-nature theme, and a definite leaning towards the folk end of rock music. The return to simpler material — Anderson denies it is commercial — is maybe an attempt on his part to try and recapture some of the immediacy which got lost during the epic days which peaked on *A Passion Play*. The success of the single 'Ring Out, Solstice Bells' reinforces this idea, and as 'The Whistler' is the next single, and the most immediately attractive track on the album, the projected success of that plus the sell-out UK tour should boost sales of this album above any since *Passion Play*. Tull have fought a hard and bitter battle since then. This album hints strongly they are slowly winning."

New Musical Express reviewed the album in March; "Jethro Tull died on February 21st 1741, but try telling that to Ian Anderson. Mention the author of *An Essay On The Principles Of Tillage And Vegetation*, and what figure is conjured up? The maniacal, pirouetting flautist with the sort of leer that causes nice girls to stay home nights — Ian Anderson! The task now in hand is the latest Tull offering, currently revolving at thirty-three and a third revolutions — give or take an insurrection — on my turntable; it's one hell of a fine record. *Songs From The Wood* is a vindication of Anderson's uncompromising attitude towards Tull's music, and an album that demands they be considered as one of your first division British bands."

"The whole album is a celebration of an English way of life long since gong, not perhaps as it was, but how it should have been. With ruddy cheeked peasants wassailing away around the maypole knocking back the mead and waving jugged hare around in rustic abandon, while speculating on who made Marian, Anderson and his merry minstrels lead the dance with music of a timeless kind upon the lute and flute and nakers and tabor."

"What Anderson's done is immerse himself in traditional music and translate it into contemporary terms, utilising all the technology the seventies can muster, without losing the essence of the music. Apart from producing, singing, playing flute, guitar, mandolin and whistle, Anderson wrote every song, and it's a tribute to him that they have a traditional appeal, yet retain a freshness of their own. The title track is a great opener, with unaccompanied vocals ushering in flute and acoustic guitars before the rest of the band chip in, while Anderson — in fine voice throughout the album — sings his 'kitchen prose and gutter rhymes', promising 'Songs from the wood make you feel much better', the universal panacea."

"An example of what's good about this album can be found on 'Cup Of Wonder' — a track with 'classic' stamped all over it. Guitars, flute and piano blend into a tune that leaves you little alternative but to tap a foot in time. Despite the electric guitar — courtesy of Martin 'Rarely puts a foot wrong' Barre — there's a feeling that this is the sort of song sung on the eve of Agincourt. Anderson wheedles and cajoles as master of the revels as he sings the chorus of 'Pass the plate to ward off hunger...' and lets his voice trail off at the end of 'wonder', in a manner redolent of troubadours departing the Squire's candlelit dinner table. If music be the food of love — play on, and pass the bicarbonate of soda."

"A stately introduction, courtesy of keyboard wizard David Palmer and his portative organ, introduces 'Velvet Green'. A serene and pastoral piece, with Anderson offering the beguiling invitation to 'tell your mother you walked all night on velvet green' — must've been a hell of a party. The lamentably underrated single 'Ring Out, Solstice Bells' (which must be Chrysalis' new 'Gaudete', due for re-release every November) still sounds good, even with spring eructing. The bells themselves, chiming away at the end of the track, bring a Christmas card serenity to the song."

"'Pibroch', according to the dictionary, is a variation of a bagpipes tune. Well, there's a lot of variation, and precious little bagpipe. Unfortunately it's the longest track on the album and only really picks up about two-thirds of the way through the song, with Anderson playing the Pipes of Pan with great aplomb. But 'Fire At Midnight' is a good way to end, an effective postscript, about Ian writing a love song beside a dying fire at midnight — nice one. Despite the fact that my review copy was warped enough to register on the Richter scale, this album has been a constant joy."

Sounds commented; "If you play this album at 45rpm it sounds just like Steeleye Span. If you then change the speed control and spin it again it sounds just as much like Cat Stevens backed by Fairport Convention at the execution of *Babbacome Lee*. Yes, friends, Jethro Tull have revamped their old medieval image. In fact, if you believe the press kit that accompanies *Songs From The Wood*, this latest album marks Jethro Tull's 'return to the earth, and for that matter, their roots'. In fact, far from being a return to the roots, *Songs From The Wood* is in fact just one more in the line of "concept albums" that started, somewhat hesitantly, with *Aqualung*."

"In many respects it's as good as all the others. You come to expect a certain level of competence and expertise from Tull, even when they're substandard. There's less of Martin Barre's ferocious electric guitar on this album and many more acoustic instruments than usual, but the production and the playing is well over par. The unaccompanied voices and then the sweeping guitar on the title track are extremely attractive, while 'Ring Out, Solstice Bells' is every bit as strong as the best from Tull's early years. The rest offer the customary bait of strange tempo changes, rich tones and Anderson's trademark, his double-track and slightly vibrated vocal mix. But as a concept album in the great tradition of concept albums it has absolutely nothing to say. Admittedly Ian Anderson has always been rock's Herman Hesse, a schoolboy intellectual with a particularly florid and attractive style. Yet *Aqualung* did burst a blood vessel or two over urban insecurity, and *Thick As A Brick* upstaged the Sex Pistols by about five years."

The review continued, "One should not refuse Anderson some of the relevance and achievement he seems to think has been denied him. *Songs From The Wood* then uses as its framework that often highly nebulous music that passes for 'period' when considering the dark ages before widespread literacy. But with a distinctly medieval taste to it. If track titles like 'Cup Of Wonder', 'Jack-In-The-Green', 'The Whistler', 'Velvet Green', 'Pibroch (Cap In Hand)' and the Christmas single 'Ring Out, Solstice Bells' don't evoke the same romantic vision of a by-gone age as Jay Lee's cover paintograph, then spin the record and listen to the words and the music. Literary archetypes from pre-theatrical drama and local legend walk down the old straight track as Ian Anderson follows the keylines of old English balladry with instruments and tunes to suit."

"But unfortunately the whole affair sounds like the background music to TV's *Robin Hood*, the score of a movie like *Tom Jones* or perhaps the lowlife themes from *Barry Lyndon*. Shot in Technicolor through gauze they may be, but they mean little or nothing alone. Steeleye Span play the same game but they succeed because they have strong control over the authenticity of their material. And, at heart, Maddy P. and the boys are well aware that in its original form their music was never meant to be more than a form of community-based entertainment. But on this album Ian Anderson sounds even more soulful and intense than usual. Sometimes he sounds as cloying as Cat Stevens. But he seems to have nothing to say to justify the emotional weight he's throwing about. After the heavy leather bias of the last album *Too Old To Rock 'n' Roll: Too Young To Die* it is hard to see *Songs From The Wood* as more than just a well-prepared exercise in style. If Tommy Garrett and his *50 Guitars* can play Hawaiian and James Last can play the Beatles then Jethro Tull can turn to traditional folk. Maybe the next one will be Latin American in flavour."

When *Melody Maker* reviewed the album it was compared extensively to Jethro Tull's previous ones: "Here we go again. Loath as I am to raise the subject, and loath as Ian Anderson is to accept it, it is a simple fact of life that a little masterpiece called *Aqualung* was easily the most successful and forceful work recorded by Jethro Tull. It's been said before — and it will be again — that until Tull reach a height that is comparable to the scintillating pitch you-know-what touched, then everything they do will live in its shadow. *Songs From The Wood* could have been swallowed by this ominous shadow, were it not for the fact that although it comes nowhere near striking the same high, it does manage to sow seeds on which Tull can build and, in perhaps a couple of albums' time, reach this elusive climax again."

"Why the optimism? Well, although this is only a fairly good, occasionally very good and-once-brilliant album, it can be justifiably argued that *Songs From The Wood* is the first of a new-age Tull recording. It is definitely unlike anything they have recorded before. Perhaps Ian Anderson has decided to put his money where his often over-sized mouth is, and really attempt to vary the formula. The three albums he has made since his "comeback", *War Child*, *Minstrel In The Gallery* and *Too Old To Rock 'n' Roll: Too Young To Die*, are practically all negligible contributions to the Tull repertoire, although *Minstrel In The Gallery* holds its head above water in the long term by providing a couple of classics in the shape of 'Black Satin Dancer', 'One White Duck' and 'Mother England Reverie', as well as being vaguely reminiscent of the Tull of the *Aqualung* period we all wanted to hear."

"*Songs From The Wood* is more durable than its three predecessors, probably because Anderson and his band start fiddling adventurously with the formula, kicking it around and coming up with more experimental arrangements. As well as that, Anderson's vocal blends in much more with the arrangement than it has done. It really sounds as if it is part of the songs. But before going any further, I'll refer to the discrepancies which make it only a fairly good album. First, there's the hideous concept, because these really are songs from the wood, and their substance never has much bite or attack. And anyway, Ian Anderson as Robin Hood, or even as the country squire on the sleeve, doesn't appeal to me. That's really bland. Really boring."

The review continued, "Coming as this does, then, from the wood, it's relevant that much of the instrumental music on the album is very folk-orientated, with lutes, whistles and, of course, flutes. Tull's attempts, however, at scoring a folk symphony on 'Velvet Green' or just playing the dumb folkie on 'Jack-In-The-Green', where he sings incredibly in the style of Cat Stevens, and 'The Whistler', getting a good old-fashioned jig together, are shallow. That side of the material is just plain weak. The optimism on *Songs From The Wood* stems from four tracks: 'Cup Of Wonder', 'Hunting Girl', 'Fire At Midnight' and 'Pibroch (Cap In Hand)'. 'Pibroch' is easily the album's superlative cut, a gutsy Tull rocker with a haunting build-up. It opens with a grinding riff from Barre on the guitar and Evan on synthesiser, drops to a taunting Anderson vocal and creeps back in at various times, with the impact sharpened even more by Anderson's flute line."

"One of the sadder aspects of this album, in fact, is that Martin Barre is never set loose, which seems to me to be a sad waste of talent, although one of the better aspects of the tracks — and 'Pibroch' in particular — is the contribution of the band to the arrangements, especially keyboard players Evan and Palmer. 'Cup Of Wonder' and 'Hunting Girl', placed side by side on the album, are snappy, melodic Anderson compositions, and judging by the positive feel on the two, were recorded when the band were in a very enthusiastic mood. The acoustic guitar/flute riff on 'Cup Of Wonder' is neat, and 'Hunting Girl' is beautifully punctuated throughout by Barre's jabbing phrases and Glascock's busy bass. On almost every album, Anderson comes up with a lovely mellow tune. 'Fire At Midnight' is the one on this album. As a sticker on the sleeve will probably announce: Includes the hit single, 'Ring Out, Solstice Bells' — to which I'm totally indifferent. *Songs From The Wood* won't restore Tull's flagging prestige in Britain. Nor will it be seen as a real downer. Its place lies somewhere in-between those two poles — an offering from a band that displays new potential without fully realising it. File under "reasonably popular"."

Throughout September '77, Tull toured Australia. In an interview for Australian TV at the time, Anderson spoke positively of how the audience there seemed to perceive the band: "In every other country in the world the audience go bananas when I pick up the flute, which is a bit embarrassing. I mean, I'm a fairly shy sort of person I do get embarrassed easily. As soon as they start clapping and cheering you haven't even played it yet and that first note tends to be a wrong one, you know. But over here they don't do that, I mean it's just another instrument — I would have thought — to the Australians; which is rather gratifying. I enjoy playing the flute, but I've always been a little concerned that it had become a sort of a trademark. I've been playing guitar much longer than I've been playing flute. The flute has always been a sort of additional thing, and it's rather unfortunate in some ways that it has been expected of me to stand on one leg and play the flute."

By 1977, there were probably more than a few moments in which Jethro Tull were keen to move away from what was expected of them based on their earlier work. Anderson expanded upon this in *National Rock Star* in February 1977; "Having started the theatrical approach around *Thick As A Brick* we now feel a little guilty that it's taken the place of the musical guts with a lot of groups. We don't want that to happen to us. It shouldn't be predictable for one-hundred percent. We fulfil expectation for eighty percent of the time, and play around with them for the other twenty. That's why they come to see Jethro Tull. They want to be manipulated just a little bit. They like it to feel a little unpredictable. They don't know what I'm going to do, whether I'm going to give some journalist some stick, from the stage, or whether I'm going to be really nice, or not say anything, or do a lot of ballet that night, or whatever it is they think I do. I like to ad-lib. I really do enjoy doing it. I have my greatest heartbreaks on stage, and my greatest enjoyments. One night in three I can feel really awful, because I haven't done that thing I'm all about. I've gone back to the hotel and cried, frustration at somehow not being able to get things to happen. You have to weigh it up each night just why you're going out there, and the answers are so many and complicated that you never have the answer. I don't know why I do it. I'm going out there to find out why."

For the UK tour, they deliberately chose smaller venues because, as Anderson put it to the *Daily Mirror*, "we wanted to create a more intimate atmosphere which you can't do in large halls. On the other hand, one place I would love to play — and it really annoys me that I can't — is the Albert Hall. We had done five concerts there over a period of five years before they put a ban on us along with other rock acts. Acts which are considered more cultural are allowed. I can't understand why we can't be included among those. We never damage dressing rooms, we are never any trouble at concerts. The ban even extends to hotels. There are various ones throughout the world where we are not allowed — even though we are model guests. And it's all because of the behaviour of groups who have been there before us." The pains of being lumped in with the stereotypical rock and roll image of the time!

In the autumn of 1977, *Repeat — The Best Of Jethro Tull — Volume II* was released. It got to number ninety-four in the US. The album contained the previously unreleased track, 'Glory Road'.

Heavy Horses continued in a similar vein to *Songs From The Wood* and it further stabilised Tull's popularity. It got to number twenty in the UK, to number nineteen in the US and to number eighteen in Australia (it would seem that having toured the latter in 1977 was to the ongoing commercial benefit of the band).

The album was recorded in London in January 1978. Anderson was quoted in *Melody Maker* in May 1978; "Living in England helps keep you realistic and sane, and moderately well off. Obviously we are not stony broke and we pay a lot of tax, but I like the old adage of the jazz musicians — I'm just happy to be working. As long as there is a gig to play, why worry?" Anderson has often advocated that *Heavy Horses* was a darker album than *Songs From The Wood*. Still though, he was quoted in *Record Mirror* in the same month; "I'm always working and touring around the place. But I do like the fields and the countryside. I suppose that the latest album, *Heavy Horses* may be regarded as a par with *Songs From The Wood*."

The title track is reflective of the extent to which the album is concerned with pastoral subjects. Anderson considered at the time that the *Heavy Horses* album had "more bite" than their previous one on the basis that the band were playing even better. Considering that an album can be made in so many different ways; with extensive rehearsal before recording it or by building things up as a team in the studio, a lot of the content on *Heavy Horses* came about from spontaneity in the studio rather than planning too far ahead.

There were times when Anderson would just do the vocals and a guitar track and then leave the rest of the band to add things around it and other times where the band would go in and do something even before he had worked out what the lyrics were going to be. The intention was to avoid being formulaic. It was surely something that ensured that the songs had their own individuality and identity as a result of the variety of working methods embraced. Anderson told BBC Radio in 1979; "Obviously we tend to start work on certain songs in the studio and find out they're not going the right way and have to throw them out. I mean as usual we must have recorded twenty pieces, of which six or seven pieces on some tape lying around will never be dug out again, half-completed things."

Regarding the album's title, Anderson explained; "Heavy horses, as you may or may not know, is the term given to the very large working horses indigenous to this country: the Shire and the Suffolk and the Clydesdale, and the borrowed Percheron from France. I have a soft spot for horses. I don't ride them: I don't like sitting on top of them, but I make friends with them and I have a few at home. Not that sort of horse, but I suppose it's rather like — I shouldn't be saying this, it's silly to say — but it's a bit like an equestrian *Aqualung*, if you like, where the downtrodden creature that I'm singing about is the poor old heavy horse who used to be in his heyday as the all-round working animal, both in industry and of course in agriculture. And very nearly disappeared altogether but for a few breeders who took a delight in preserving the species, and now it is beginning to come back again as a working animal."

He told *Record Mirror* in May 1978; "Heavy horses are magnificent animals. It's impracticable to use them on farms these days because it's easier to fuel up a tractor and leap on the back. In manpower terms you've got to feed the horses and take a long time in mucking out the stables and preparing them for work. But of course to see them in a field pulling something is a wonderful feeling. But horses still have their uses. Take the Highland pony for instance. It's used for deer stalking in places where wheeled vehicles just can't go."

"I wrote that one while we were in America," he told the BBC, "and it's one of the rather long ones. There are two long songs on the album, and that's one of them. It has a mixture of several different styles and a degree of ups and downs and levels — what do they call it, dynamics or something. So that's the title track. One thing looking at the list of songs, now, is that they are all actually about something, which makes me happy, when I can actually see they are about something. The worst thing in the world is to find yourself writing a lyric which isn't really about anything at all; it's just an excuse for opening your mouth while the group make a funky, danceable, exciting, crowd-waving-their-arms sort of sound, which is pointless rock 'n' roll. Maybe some people would say it's not pointless and that it is in fact what rock 'n' roll is all about: unfortunately I do aspire to these higher pretensions and I must insist that it has to be about something. I mean Johnny Rotten sings about something, and in a very different way so do I."

A number of other songs on the album are also about animals — '...And The Mouse Police Never Sleeps', 'One Brown Mouse' and 'Rover'. Anderson told BBC Radio; "I always have a soft spot for my cats, because I love cats. What I do love about cats is cats that appear to just lie there and sleep and do nothing, but in fact they're extremely vicious, aggressive, nasty animals who tear heads off little mice and do all sorts of despicable things. And I call my cats at home — because they are salaried employees of mine, and they're there to keep mice away from the kitchen and kill rats and things, which they do; they find rats in the barn going after the horses' feet and that sort of thing. They dispatch them with all due alacrity, as David Palmer might say if he were here, I call them the 'mouse police'. That's my little name for them all, collectively; they're the mouse police, so I have a song called '...And The Mouse Police Never Sleeps', which is really about one of the cats in particular, called Mistletoe. '... And The Mouse Police Never Sleeps' is quite a good one."

"People always have this idea that nature is soft and sloppy and something even worse than hippies going on about love and peace. But it isn't at all. Nature, I mean most people can't face up to it; that's why we all live in towns and live in houses with central heating and want nice warm motorcars, because it's actually too tough for all of us. I'm just keen to point out that some of these things are a bit hairier than people imagine. Almost every morning I find some small, dismembered warm-blooded mammal."

"Mistletoe, he has a thing about the heads. He always eats the head and he crunches the skull and everything is gone, and he leaves the bottom half. Probably because it has the naughty parts and it puts him off a bit — his stomach turns just at that point — but he leaves these headless little furry mammals lying everywhere. That's pretty horrific stuff when you actually have to pick them up all over the place, and he brings them in, and the baby's in his pram, probably about to get a present from one of the cats — half a shrew, you know. So anyway it's all about that. It's actually quite a good song. I always say my songs are good songs, but this is actually a good one. It's well-written, there's some nice lines in it."

'Moths' is about the courtship of moths, but there's more to it than that. It is a love song where the insects are plausibly a vehicle through which the emotions of the song are communicated. Anderson got the idea for the moths dancing around the candle from a game invented by John le Carré for Seamus in *The Naive And Sentimental Lover*. The character played the game with Cassidy and Helen. It's a game set on a billiard table where a candle is put in the middle and each participant takes a turn. They have to drive a white ball around the candle — one full turn for one point. Anderson said, "It's a very good game and I've played it many times. I don't know whether it's a real game or whether le Carré made it up, but it's a good game, and I've even introduced that in America now — apparently it's the rage in Beverly Hills, playing 'moths'."

The 'Moths' single was reviewed in *Record Mirror* in April 1978; "Whitesmock haychewing-turningthesodcalfstroking-rockaboo (sic). A single from the soil, for dancing around the campfire, Anderson intones a story of awakening summer (c'mon get out of bed) and moths gathering around the flame. Reminds you of sunrises and sunsets in deepest Berkshire, the roll of the hills and the birds black against the sunlit sky. Hopping acoustic guitar playing that had left me flat on my back and then the old flute trademark. B side is the evergreen 'Life Is A Long Song' timely reissue of the hit single a few years back. Pass the flagon of cider."

'One Brown Mouse' was inspired by Robert Burns' 1785 poem, *To A Mouse*. Although Anderson hadn't read much of Burns' poetry, he considered what he had read to be heartfelt and thus appealing. He told *Circus* in June 1978; "I find the music I am writing now embodies something of the very earliest musical tradition, an almost religious music of celebration. I want to try to evoke something a little more spiritual and emotional."

'Rover' is actually about Anderson's dog, Lupus, but he deemed it more appropriate to title the song after a name that sounded more dog-like. Not deeming 'Fido' to have a good ring to it, he opted for 'Rover'. The song is essentially about the dog's desire to run away and copulate. Regarding his own dog, Lupus, Anderson said; "He can't unfortunately because we had a little amendment made to his, um, anatomy. We did that, unfortunately, because he did have this tendency to go off. He's a

SOON THE HEAVY HORSES WILL BE COMING HOME.

Heavy Horses is the new album from Jethro Tull. Just one album ago, the world discovered a new and different Ian Anderson. Still exhibiting his wonderfully wicked sense of humour "Songs From The Wood" also lovingly took a musical tour of the English countryside.

"Heavy Horses", dedicated to the Shires, Percherons, and Suffolks that were once the backbone of rural England, travels through the same pastoral country of today exploring even newer directions. Musically it's one of the best Tull albums, Ian Anderson's lyrics being as sharp and perceptive as ever.

Included on the album you'll find the single "Moths" which has "Life Is A Long Song" on the B side, and if you're lucky, you'll be able to see Jethro Tull on their forthcoming sold out UK tour.

In the meantime take a listen to the album. Heavy Horses is the one worth coming home to.

May 1st	Usher Hall	Edinburgh.
May 2nd	Apollo Theatre	Glasgow.
May 3rd & 4th	Apollo Theatre	Manchester.
May 5th	Odeon	Birmingham.
May 7th & 8th	Rainbow	London.
May 9th & 10th & 11th	Odeon, Hammersmith	London.

ALL SHOWS SOLD OUT EXCEPT 11TH MAY ODEON HAMMERSMITH

JETHRO TULL
HEAVY HORSES
CHR1175 Also available on cassette.

Chrysalis
Records & Tapes

sheepdog, and given that livestock is nearby he will attempt to herd them, and is liable to be shot for his pains — interfering with other people's beasties. I get very angry when he does this, of course, really furious with him. He's brought back in disgrace, covered in mud and whatever else. But he does have that basic free-ranging spirit which I am attempting to acknowledge and in a tacit way applaud in this song."

Of course, not all of the songs on *Heavy Horses* are about animals. 'No Lullaby' is something of an anti-lullaby that Anderson wrote for his son, James: "It always amuses me that whenever he opens his mouth in the middle of the night he's descended upon by a flock of nannies and mothers and animals rushing to quieten him down and soothe him, whereas, in fact, you've got everything in the world to scream and shout about — everything in the world to be terrified about. So this is a sort of anti-lullaby saying, if you want to scream and shout and make a fuss then go ahead, because there's plenty to be frightened of. And in terms of the music it certainly isn't like a lullaby either. It's a fairly aggressive piece, so if I start playing that at him he'll definitely get no sleep." In later years Martin Barre spoke of how on 'No Lullaby', he played a Hamer guitar through Marshall amps turned up to high volume.

Anderson wrote 'Journeyman' whilst he was travelling on a train. "I usually try to write at least one song on the train," he said. "The last train back from Marylebone, which usually contains your businessmen who've usually been out on an expenses dinner, or who have told the wife it was a business dinner, and they're lurching home rather drunk and rather late on the last train, and they've just realised they've got to get all these accounts sorted out by tomorrow. Eleven o'clock at night and their briefcases are open and they're still frantically trying to get things sorted out that they've got to hand in the next day when they go back. And I only mention Gerrards Cross in it once — because that always amuses me. It's just hilarious. I'm already on the train, and at Gerrards Cross the carriage fills with these people. And you're always sitting in the seat that one of them customarily occupies, and it's his seat, and you get daggers because the seat he has every day has been taken."

"I used to do a lot of travelling on trains and I find them good to write songs on. You can lock yourself away in a first class compartment and you don't feel silly about writing things down on pieces of paper. The rhythm of the train is quite stimulating as well."

By the time *Heavy Horses* came out, Tull's music had become less concerned with wanting to pass comment on the wrongs of the world. In 1979, *Stormwatch* would soon put paid to that. Besides, on a more subtle level, it could be said that the songs about animals on *Heavy Horses* are reflective of themes that can be related to in human terms — all of the animals that Anderson sings about on the album are very much personified.

As he told BBC Radio about the songs on *Heavy Horses* in 1979; "I'm singing about people as well. That's what I think makes them good songs. They're not just literal. As I explain them they might sound a bit banal, and who knows, they may sound a bit like that when you hear them, but for me, if they're worth anything — at least as far as the lyrics are concerned — it's because they do have other shades of meaning, which is what makes them good."

Anderson told *Melody Maker* in May 1978; "I'm not particularly interested in horses as such but I read an article about them and just the title — 'Heavy Horses' — suggested a song and conjured the necessary images. I don't own the horses on the album sleeve, I just borrowed them. Most of the heavy horses today are used for shows and demonstrations, but they aren't dying out, they're very much on the up as a breed. When I was a lad I remember our milk being delivered in Edinburgh by horses and that's only going back twenty years. They do say that horse-drawn deliveries will come back, where people have to stop every few doors. Some breweries still use them because it's more economical."

The first verse of 'Acres Wild' is about the beauty of the rural environment, but in the next verse it goes on to reference the city as being another facet of a similar landscape. Darryl Way, previously of Curved Air, contributed violin to both this song and the album's title track.

Regarding both *Heavy Horses* and *Songs From The Wood*, Anderson explained that the songs manage to avoid "the Americanisms of rock 'n' roll." He added that "they still have rock rhythms and rock tempos and some of the excitement of rock, but they don't use the American blues and jazz influences. They retain something more precious, I think, about our own heritage of music. You'll hear sounds which will pull you gently over the border to the north, and some sounds which will certainly pull you back again down south."

He told *Creem*; "Stylistically, I've always said that we can't be a heavy riff group because Led Zeppelin are the best in the world. We can't be a blues-influenced R&B rock and roll group because the Stones are the best in the world. We can't be a slightly sort of airy-fairy mystical sci-fi synthesising abstract freak-out group because Pink Floyd are the best in the world. And so what's left? And that's what we've always done. We've filled the gap. We've done what's left. That may partly explain our popularity and we've done it for the most part without the aid of gargantuan feats of PR and manipulating the daily press with scandal stories. And we still are one of the most popular groups in the world. There is no explanation. At the same time as being one of these top groups, we are somehow not. We are somehow different."

Creem commented; "Jethro Tull are different in their lack of flash, their lack of hype, their lack of parasites, their lack of personality — I can't even remember who else is in the band. Tull musicians don't encourage groupies and they aren't groupies themselves — no hanging out with the international rock jet set. Anderson, with his confidence and responsibilities and aloof efficiency, is a country squire of the most traditional sort. His conversation was studded with anti-Americanism (he likes Ian Dury for his cockney vowels, for example) and *Songs From The Wood*, the last Tull album, sounded pretty much like straight old country folk to me. Anderson defies any purist folkie leanings but he did describe the new album, *Heavy Horses*, as *Songs From The Wood* Part Two plus a bit more Jethro Tull, and his concern did seem to be that it not be heard as twee."

"But it is a British country record, celebrating shire horses and Anderson's dog and cats on a track called '…And The Mouse Police Never Sleeps'. Not twee, because not romantic and not hippie is Anderson's hope. It's about town and country, the former's dependence on and exploitation of the latter. I didn't hear it and probably never will. But when I left I touched my forelock. Anderson was very gracious and I started musing that if Tull's success is based, as Anderson at some point said, on 'a lucky coincidence', then there must be millions more potential country gentry wandering about Britain's pubs and clubs, guitars clutched in sticky hands, waiting for their lucky break. They're mostly disguised as punks at present." (Anderson was quoted on his opinion of Ian Dury in *Record Mirror* in May 1978; "He's been very clever in getting involved in the Stiff thing. I heard a song called 'My Old Man'. The lyrics were very good and you could identify with them. He's able to put across a very clear thought.").

Heavy Horses was reviewed in *Record Mirror* in April 1978; "Further rural ramblings from Ian Anderson and co. Tull are getting so much into the mediaeval folksy bit that the heavy guitar noises in 'No Lullaby' sound totally out of place: an unwelcome (and anachronistic) intrusion. It's all very different from the crazed "progressive" outfit I used to know and love. In those days, Ian Anderson was the one-legged tramp in the filthy raincoat: these days he appears to be undergoing an identity crisis. On the front of the sleeve, he's the healthy peasant living off the land: on the back he's become the decadent lord of the manor. Very strange. The album meanwhile is dedicated to horses of all shapes, sizes and breeds — a nice idea, but we might ask ourselves what's it got to do with rock 'n' roll? Well, the answer to that is of course, not a lot — but no matter, I like it anyway. Though I must admit, musically, it's little more than a re-run of *Songs From The Wood*. I found it a totally charming collection of songs, but as with all sequels, the charm has worn off a little on the repeat showing. Still, there's enough here of interest to warrant a listen or two — try out 'Moths', 'Acres Wild' or 'Weathercock'. God knows what they'll do next though — a third album on the same lines definitely *would* be too much."

It was reviewed in *Melody Maker* in the same month; "A long-time fan of Jethro Tull, I have recently become concerned by Ian Anderson's gradual decline. I'm painfully forced to compare Tull to an ageing dog: lots of bark but no bite. I remember praising *Minstrel In The Gallery* to the high heavens and remarking that after a rather bleak and unproductive period Tull were back on song again. Then came *Too Old To Rock 'n' Roll*, which was just a minor setback, and last year *Songs From The Wood*, a definite indication that Anderson wasn't interested in the uncompromising but still subtle rock that made the band renowned."

"And now comes *Heavy Horses*, and by its title alone you'd expect well, you know, a bit of rock 'n' roll. By rights, I should allow an artist of Anderson's calibre the option to move along whatever path he wishes. *Aqualung* is no more after all. It's finished, past and buried, so I suppose you've got to admire him for going on to fresh pastures, which is exactly what he has done. He has become obsessed with the countryside. *Heavy Horses* takes up where *Songs From The Wood* left off: a celebration of Mother Nature. An artist's music is a reflection of his surroundings, Philip Chevron tells me, and that is certainly the case here. Anderson has engulfed himself in the peace and quiet of his country home, his animals and his acres of land, and the result, not surprisingly, is music that is frequently timid and gentrified. Rock 'n' roll this ain't."

"That is a generalisation, and there are rare moments of inspiration on *Heavy Horses*, 'Acres Wild', 'No Lullaby', 'Journeyman' and the second segment of the title track which see Tull in a much better light, though most of them are touched by a gentle, folky mood that Anderson appears determined to maintain. This works sometimes, and Tull respond with a couple of beautifully orchestrated pieces, particularly on 'Acres Wild', 'Heavy Horses' and an otherwise wretched track, 'Rover', where the acoustics blend nicely. For those whose interest in Tull is confined to their raunchier aspects, there is but one track, 'No Lullaby', where Martin Barre is given his obligatory two minutes to get his guitar frustrations down on tape. It's an excellent track, powerfully aided by some funky drumming from Barrie Barlow."

"But what seems to make it successful is that the entire band have contributed and Anderson's influence does not hold sway. A pity the band didn't exercise the same resourcefulness on the rest of the album. But what makes *Heavy Horses* even more insignificant — I never thought I'd hear myself calling Jethro Tull insignificant — is the lyrical matter. A look over the track listing: '... And The Mouse Police Never Sleeps' (about cats); 'Rover' (a dog, although it could also be any manner of subjects) and 'Heavy Horses' (a hymn to horses and how one day they'll make a glorious return — the album is actually dedicated to a wide species of other 'indigenous working ponies and horses of Great Britain'). Anderson manages to break the deadlock only twice: on 'Journeyman', a sarcastic, witty observation of the commuter's daily travels, and 'No Lullaby', a rather frightening children's tale. The music is often quite endearing, but Tull's drabness is starting to frustrate me. *Heavy Horses*, with its log-fire, boy scout overtures, only compounds the felony. Of course, all of this will probably earn me a couple of nasty asides from Anderson on Tull's forthcoming British tour."

Chris Welch, who had often been the bane of Tull's existence, travelled to Germany to catch the band live for *Melody Maker* in May 1978; "Last week in Berlin I saw the band play two hours with more energy than a brace of new wavers for 7,000 fans who were still yelling for more, while the staff of the Deutschlandhalle were clocking off for the night... I enjoyed the concert even more than their recent Rainbow performance, although the acoustics of the Deutschlandhalle and the sheer size of the place made the band seem somewhat remote. Among the high spots were Martin Barre's beautifully constructed guitar solo on 'A New Day Yesterday', followed by Ian's surprise entry on flute which drew a roar of appreciation, and the guitar and drum outings on the unnamed instrumental sans Anderson. With songs from *Thick As A Brick* to *Heavy Horses*, the band performed a satisfying mixture of material old and new that adequately represented their ten-year output. As the strains of Eric Coates' 'Dam Busters March' boomed across the hall, I wondered somewhat nervously if the Germans might not object to this hint of nationalism, but mercifully the tune seemed unknown to them, and certainly to the young Americans present, who have probably never heard of Guy Gibson, Barnes Wallis or the bouncing bomb. The band like to play the theme as giant balloons bounce over the audience, and the three unleashed in Berlin survived several minutes of pummelling before exploding in a shower of chalk dust. At least they weren't filled with water. There was a great thunder of feet as the fans demanded and got their encore."

By this point in Jethro Tull's tenure, it seems that Anderson took a pragmatic approach towards reviews. "If I read something that is adversely critical of what Jethro Tull is doing, I like to be told in a fair amount of detail why. If someone says, 'this is a load of rubbish', I like at least to have the option of profiting by somebody else's opinion and finding out *where* I may have gone wrong."

Besides, by 1978 Jethro Tull were very much an established group. Anderson was quoted in *Melody Maker* in May 1978; "One of the reasons we don't have a support act on our tour is that we just can't find one that audiences will accept. I remember hearing 12,000 people booing Alex Harvey, who I like and had invited to tour with us. Of course he didn't help by telling them they were shit. It's happened to quite a few of the acts who have supported us. Captain Beefheart had a really hard time. But we only got our chance playing on shows with Yes and Led Zeppelin and I appreciated that. In the old days people wanted to hear all the groups. Now they only have the patience to hear the headliner."

"Livingstone Taylor came on stage to play one of our shows and had hardly played a single chord on his guitar before they were throwing bottles and cans and booing. Within thirty seconds he was hit on the head and knocked down and had to be carried off. He was in tears in the dressing room because they wouldn't listen to his music, and I was too. In a rage I promised him I'd go out and tell the audience what absolute bastards they were and rushed back to the stage. And when I stepped out — what happened? 23,000 people cheered me as if nothing had happened. What could I do or say? I just zipped up and played for them. But I didn't understand them. If we put on a support now, the audience would stay in the bar until we came on, and the poor group would have to play to a quarter-full house. I just can't explain the kids' behaviour. Livingstone Taylor was totally destroyed and I've never seen him again. If we were a new group supporting Led Zeppelin today, they'd probably do the same to us, and I find that very disappointing. How will new acts get their chance?"

It was reported in *The Birmingham Post* on 5th May 1978 that less than just twenty-four hours before they were due to appear, Tull had needed to cancel their appearance at Birmingham's Odeon Theatre. According to the report it was on account of doctor's orders due to John Glascock having sustained a hand injury. Of course, the details of this were kept brief and may or may not allude to the realities of the overall health struggles that Glascock may have been experiencing at the time.

As well as *Heavy Horses*, 1978 was the year in which Jethro Tull released *Bursting Out*. Whilst their 1972 *Living In The Past* album included two live songs, *Bursting Out* was the band's first full live album. Phenomenal considering how long they had been going for by that point, especially seeing that they had often been keen to assert that they saw themselves as more of a live band overall. *Bursting Out* was recorded on an eight-track recorder. Anderson sold it after the album was finished. The content on the album was recorded in the early summer of the year it was released. It got to number seventeen in the UK and to number twenty-one in the US.

Bursting Out was reviewed in *Record Mirror* in September 1978; "Why ten years on the road and fourteen albums had to go by before the release of a Jethro Tull live platter, totally eludes me. The more so since Tull are very much an on-stage group. *Bursting Out* was recorded on their recent European trek and features eighteen numbers including two new ones 'Quatrain' and 'Conundrum'. Classics like 'Too Old To Rock 'n' Roll: Too Young To Die', 'Thick As A Brick' and 'Minstrel In The Gallery' emerge with more force than in their studio versions. Ian Anderson's vocals are diamond sharp and clear as a bell, matching the excellence of his flute playing. From Martin Barre comes invigorating guitar work, notably on the encore numbers 'Aqualung' and 'Locomotive Breath', while the rest of the band are in splendid form. The atmosphere is agreeably light-hearted, with some amusing remarks as Anderson introduces the material. Primarily what makes this album vastly superior to previous Tull works is the raw sound it attains, replacing the former complexities. Had the band released a live cut before, then maybe the 'greatest hits' tag and the customary lengthy drum and flute solos of a double album, might have been avoided. Besides, single live albums are always more effective, and less heavy going. *Bursting Out* closes with a rendition of the 'Dam Busters March' more deadly than Sir Michael Redgrave's bouncing bombs in the RAF movie where it was first heard. With this riveting album, Jethro Tull are right on target."

It was reviewed in the *Aberdeen Evening Express* in October 1978; "Jethro Tull have at last brought out a live double which superbly captures their dynamic stage set. Production by Tull leader Ian Anderson himself is near perfect — and this set should prove once and for all that although Anderson is the frontman of the group, Tull are no one-man band. This collection goes back to the early Tull with 'Bourée', takes in the developing stages with 'Sweet Dream', has fan favourite 'Aqualung' — the concept LP title track, 'Thick As A Brick' and includes new folk orientated cuts such as 'Songs From The Wood' and 'One Brown Mouse' from the latest studio album, *Heavy Horses*. And it ends on a high note with the showstopper of all rock showstoppers — 'Locomotive Breath'. Add to this the atmosphere of the crowd, the earthy humour of Anderson and the sheer all-round musicianship and *Bursting Out* is certainly one for the Tull fan — even if you already have all the tracks on previous albums." (Note how even though Anderson was adamant to exemplify that *Aqualung* was not intended to be a concept album, it was still considered as such by many people — even years later!).

Circus commented in November 1978; "*Bursting Out* bears convincing testimony. Drawing on material from 1969's *Stand Up* ('A New Day Yesterday') through 1978's *Heavy Horses*, Tull's first-ever live set is an animated documentary of their stage show, running the stylistic gamut from the quiet classicality of 'Bourée' to the heavy-metal huff and puff of 'Locomotive Breath' and the modal Scottish folk forms of 'No Lullaby' and 'Hunting Girl'. Anderson describes the album as 'a summation, a suitable point for saying 'this is it' to date. And it puts a little bit of pressure on us. It forces us into the next move'."

Prior to its release, Anderson said; "It will be our first "live" album although there was a bit of "live" stuff on the *Living In The Past* album. This will be a double album of properly constructed music. It's interesting that it's not only our tenth anniversary but it's also one for Yes and Black Sabbath... There does seem a desperation for new music and new heroes, not only among the groups but in terms of those who document what goes on, i.e. the writers and critics. And those who have been part of the shaping of today's music must come under the heading of — what is it they call us? Boring old farts, or dinosaurs or whatever."

The critics' comments were probably of little value in view of how in demand Jethro Tull were in 1978. *Record Mirror* opined; "Jethro Tull are ten years old and there's no wane in their popularity as they embark on another lengthy tour." And yet the band still perhaps felt the need to defy expectations. Anderson was quoted in the same feature; "I think we were the first band to talk to the audience. I mean we'd go on stage and laugh and clown around. After all these years it's still fun, but we haven't played the perfect gig, there have been many satisfying gigs but all the time we're still searching for perfection... Jethro Tull music has always been very eclectic, we never set out to be deliberately commercial. If I listen to the charts today then it seems that a lot of singles are just derivative of all the other singles. I prefer something that will stimulate and educate me. The feeling seems to me that if you're going to make it then you've got to wear a certain pair of ex-army trousers and look like everybody else. The media is really using its power to force people into that situation."

Across the entire first decade of their tenure, Jethro Tull were certainly a hardworking band. "For ten years now I haven't had weekends off or a chance to go down to the pub for a drink or sit and watch the telly," Anderson explained to *Melody Maker* in May 1978. "We wouldn't have missed the success of the group obviously, but nearly all of us in the group can say we only have one friend apart from each other, which is pretty poor in terms of ten years of getting around meeting people. I have never really made any friendships within music. There are lots of people we know but somehow not the sort of people you would ring up if you had a night off."

Overall though, things were looking good. "Most people who know me and the rest of the group the longest, all say we have changed remarkably little and we are still here doing the same gigs! And that fills people with a kind of dread about what the real bitter truth is about why we do it. Either we are true showbiz professionals and say the show must go on, or else we must need the money, or else we are so locked up in our own little world we just go on doing it until we have heart attacks on stage. The truth of the matter is — we are always trying to do a better gig than we did last year. We change the arrangements, we still do old songs and we try new stuff. There is no-one more surprised than me that we are still doing this. Really. By the end of 1969 I felt I had done what I wanted to do and that was it. We played the world and had fairly impressive record success and I thought then: 'Well, that's it, there's nothing more to do'."

"Music was far more individual then and I think people were prepared to listen to broader ideas… I'm not in it for the money anymore you know, my accountant might advise me to invest in a grocery business and make money that way. I'm touring because I enjoy it — maybe it's true to say it's a feeling that gets in your blood. We've lost fans and gained them by the changes in our music so our audience are never just a sterile mass. It's always seemed to be a word of mouth thing with us. We've never had to rely on heavy press coverage. People would come to see us and tell their friends."

With 1978 being such a big year, they had to work hard to prepare their newer songs for the stage. Martin Barre was quoted in *Melody Maker* in the May of that year; "We had to re-learn the album, because after you've done a studio album it's such a relief of pressure you go away and forget about it. When you come back to play it on stage you have to re-learn your part. Psychologically you always feel under-rehearsed on tour, because of the pressure. The first shows are always nerve-wracking, but it's good in a way, for the adrenalin. That first show was unbelievable, so nerve-wracking. We were up in Scotland and couldn't believe we'd go out and play the thing right, without it all grinding to a halt. We change a lot of the instruments around from the album to stage, so there's a lot of relearning anyway. We put one major instrumental bit into this show to feature the guitar and drums, when Ian wasn't on stage. We've done guitar and drum solos for years, but we wanted to change it for this show, and we just about got that right the day before the tour was due to start."

Tull made history by being the first band to broadcast a live show globally via satellite. In October 1978, their performance at Madison Square Gardens was shown all over the world on what was referred to as Tullivision. Tony Williams played bass on account of the fact that John Glascock was seriously ill by this point. Williams covered the entire tour of the US for that very reason.

Melody Maker reported on 16th September 1978; "Jethro Tull are set to perform in front of the biggest rock audience ever when they play at New York's Madison Square Garden on Monday, October 9th. The 20,000 people in the stadium will be joined by an estimated 400 million around the world when the show is televised live by BBC's *Old Grey Whistle Test* and transmitted in stereo simultaneously on radio. Tull's gig is the first rock concert ever to be televised live from America and, as well as being seen in Britain, it is being broadcast to most of Europe, Australia, Brazil, and America itself. Other countries will show recordings of the concert. Each country's TV network is buying the broadcasting rights from Chrysalis, Tull's record company, who are producing the show."

"It goes out in Britain as an *Old Grey Whistle Test* special on BBC Two at 11:15pm, at the same time as a radio broadcast as part of the *John Peel Show* on Radio One. It is repeated on BBC Two on October 14th at 5:55pm. The broadcast is a forty-five-minute excerpt from Tull's concert and will feature the band's best known material. The Madison Square Garden concert is part of a six-week American tour by the group which starts on October 1st and includes four nights at the New York venue. To coincide with the tour, the band are releasing their first live album, a double called *Bursting Out*, due to be released on September 29th. Recorded during their recent European tour, it contains eighteen songs with a total playing time of an hour and a half. All the band's best-known songs are included as well as two new ones: 'Quatrain', written by guitarist Martin Barre, and 'Conundrum' by Barre and drummer Barriemore Barlow."

Chris Welch reported in *Melody Maker* in October 1978 on what he had witnessed of the rehearsals and the main performance; "Fire crackers and steel bolts nearly aborted an historic satellite broadcast. On Sunday night a lunatic minority pelted Ian Anderson with missiles during Jethro Tull's opening night at Madison Square Garden in New York. Anderson came off stage in a black rage and threatened to pull out of the transatlantic TV hook-up, ignoring the elaborate preparations and publicity build-up. 'If it happened again during the show, I would just have to say what I thought of the audience, and I don't want my parents to hear me swearing on TV,' said Ian, who took an hour to calm down. 'The tragedy is that most of the kids on Sunday didn't know what was happening and enjoyed the show. But I didn't think we played well and I was just miming to my own songs. I was being hit from above and behind by steel bolts and if people come supplied with missiles like that to hurt me, then I just feel like saying 'Fuck you, I'm taking the dollars and going. And for me that is a complete betrayal of what Jethro Tull is all about. I actually do believe in those songs that I go out and sing, the songs from the albums mean a lot to me, and I want to give the best possible show and play the best music. But when this happens, just once in a while, then it destroys everything and I get really angry'."

"Sunday's show was virtually a dress-rehearsal for Monday night's telecast via the communications satellite, and necessitated the band preparing a new running order. A bad stage sound combined with the missile-throwing from fans behind the stage, and fire crackers from the auditorium, made the band tense and edgy. For the majority, the first show was a huge success; flaring gas lighters, thunderous applause and the obvious fanaticism of a 20,000 capacity crowd of new generation Tull freaks made it an impressive demonstration of the group's power and appeal after ten years on the road. But the tension and strain on Anderson was obvious, with the knowledge that an estimated potential audience of 400,000,000 TV viewers would be seeing the band with every possibility of a serious incident on stage. Anderson is an intelligent, witty and sensitive man, whose family life is as important to him as his role as an eccentric rock hero, and he does not enjoy being set up as a target for crazies, who perhaps see him as a fairground freak and fair game for attack."

"In the event the Monday — Columbus Day — concert and satellite transmission went off without a hitch. As the seconds ticked away in the control room at Madison Square Garden, the real stars of the hour, Tom Corcoran, BBC TV director of *The Old Grey Whistle Test* and his assistant, Rosa Rudnicka, kissed, lit cigarettes and emitted audible sighs of relief. The word came back from England: 'Sound and vision were great.' As OGWT producer Mike Appleton said: 'It was just like doing a show from the Odeon, Hammersmith.' The real significance of the whole exercise, nerves and tantrums aside, was that this could be the start of a whole new concept of rock promotion, where special shows are televised all around the world, helping to cut down the vast cost of touring. But even the Tull hook-up cost in the region of fifty-thousand dollars, with only the hope that losses will be recouped by selling video tapes of the show to other countries."

It was reported in *Circus* in November 1978; "Ever wonder, when the lights go up, how all that equipment got there? Behind the seven-week Jethro Tull/Uriah Heep tour, which runs through mid-November, is a logistics effort every bit the equal of the musical performances themselves. The plan calls for trucks (Ryder Rentals) to move from city to city, criss-crossing the country no less than ten times, for a total mileage of 12,406. Each move is plotted according to a timetable outlined in advance, calculated, for the British group's convenience, in European sequence, where 11pm is noted as 23:00 hours. For Tull's live television transmission to Europe from Madison Square Garden in New York on October 9th, the schedule called for a Tull sound check at 14:30 to 15:15 hours, a Heep setup at 15:15 to 16:00, doors opening at 16:00, a set change at 17:30, and Tull on stage at 18:00. While some ticket holders will wonder about or gripe at the seemingly long delays waiting for concerts to start, the clock-like precision of the workers behind the scenes makes it possible for tons of equipment and literally hundreds of people to have it all together."

When *Bursting Out* was reviewed in the *Burton Observer & Chronicle* in October 1978, it was suggested that the large scale broadcast would be excellent for the sales of Jethro Tull records: "It is hard to believe that *Bursting Out* is the first live album the band has made. Tull are one of the most popular live bands in the world and as there are so many live recordings on the market it seems high time that Tull was among them. The album, a double, is just what you would have expected complete with far too many verbal introductions and too much clapping and stomping. But at least Ian Anderson is fairly entertaining in his spiel and there are some genuinely exciting tracks among the onslaught of feedback and stage gimmicks. *Bursting Out* does manage to catch all the essential ingredients of Tull live and, after the recent Madison Square Garden extravaganza, there can be no doubt of sales prospect."

So who were Jethro Tull's audience by 1978? Anderson was quoted in *Creem* in the June of that year; "I've really no idea who they are and I've really no idea what they like about us. I posed this question on the last tour in America, particularly at the end of last year's tour, because the audience was so overwhelmingly young again. There was this incredible element of fifteen and sixteen-year-old kids there, who would have been seven or eight when we started and I don't know why they're there because why aren't they supporting the trendy up-and-comings? Why aren't they supporting their own heroes instead of latching on to the heroes of the generation before them? I don't know the answer. I find it distinctively worrying. I'm very gratified that they're there and people say I should be really pleased because this is your audience for the next five or ten years — you've actually broken that age barrier, they're yours. But I still find it worrying."

"I find it worrying because why weren't the Sex Pistols doing it already? Why aren't all the other groups who've had a go and haven't made it? In America particularly, and on the world stage, there still seems to be this handful of groups and most of them are British. It's your problem as a sociologist and it's my problem only in that I feel some responsibility for the fact that they're there, perhaps getting beaten up or mugged on their way home. That's the only way it worries me, because I can't really probe into the whys and wherefores of who they are and the reasons they like Jethro Tull. I don't know."

In *Circus* in November 1978 Anderson said; "Suddenly we've lost the older age group to their domesticity, their mortgages, their family cars, and half a swimming pool average. But it's left a free space for a much younger audience to come in and surprisingly they do. I've queried as to why they come to see Jethro Tull, why they don't want to find their own younger groups to follow. And the only explanation that makes any sense is that, like the Stones or The Who, Jethro Tull has a certain reputation, a mystique that's transcended the generation gap."

In contrast to where Jethro Tull were at with things by 1978, it's fascinating to consider what could have been. It was reported in *Circus* in November 1978; "A proud native Scotsman, the Edinburgh-born Anderson made his first move in 1968 when he formed Jethro Tull from the ruins of the John Evan Band in Blackpool, where he did some semi-pro gigging and listened to a lot of Rolling Stones. In London, Jethro Tull slipped easily into the amorphous blues-jazz-rock scene with Anderson garnering the bulk of attention for his Fagin-like dress and one-legged choreography. One producer at the time even had the brainstorm of slotting Anderson into a group called Chocolate Covered Rain alongside Nicky Hopkins and a young, flashy guitarist named Ritchie Blackmore. Ian understandably passed (he snickers at the thought now) but has since seen a number of faces pass through Tull while piling up a fortune in gold and platinum for records like *Benefit* and *Aqualung*."

The validity of information regarding Chocolate Covered Rain is questionable, bearing in mind that Ritchie Blackmore had just started Deep Purple — with significant financial backing — around that time. It's possible that there was an idea to do a session, especially if Derek Lawrence was the producer that is referred to; Blackmore and keyboard player Jon Lord did one or two sessions for Lawrence around this time.

As the decade was drawing to a conclusion, Tull started another US tour in April '79. *The Billings Gazette* reported on the show on the 8th April at The Metra; "Ian Anderson pranced across the Metra stage crashing cymbals, shaking tambourines and twirling his flute Sunday night in Jethro Tull's first appearance in Billings. Jethro Tull isn't your run of the mill rock band. One minute, Anderson sounds like he's in a Victorian parlour singing an old English aire and the next he and the band are hurling full-blown rock and roll. That was all in the same song — 'Heavy Horses'. There was a touch of baroque in 'One Brown Mouse', dedicated to Robert Burns 'who would have written this song given half the chance,' Anderson said. Here the band sounded like a group of medieval minstrels deep in Sherwood Forest would have sounded if they'd had electricity. Representing *Aqualung* was 'My God' with an excellent version of 'God Rest Ye Merry Gentlemen' thrown in on the side. Another English band, UK, started the concert with an interesting but interminable set. The three piece band at times sounded more like a full rock orchestra, thanks to a synthesiser and a good drummer. The guitar player was hardly noticeable. The songs were long and dynamic with endless instrumentals. An impatient audience, largely confined to assigned seats, was not extremely enthusiastic. But when Anderson pranced on stage like the Pied Piper the pace picked up and didn't let go through the Jethro Tull performance... Concert goers who came with cameras and tape recorders had to make a trip back to the car. A deputy explaining the situation to a photographer said it was one of the conditions in Jethro Tull's contract."

Between the end of the tour in May and before the next one in October, there was the little matter of the final studio album of the decade. Although *Stormwatch* was a successful album, it would signify the point at which things were about to change for the band. Thematically the album offers a commentary on a range of environmental issues (dwindling oil supplies, fear of nuclear disaster and energy shortages), as was picked up on in the majority of reviews relating to it. The songs aren't too stylistically different to Tull's 1977 and 1978 albums although it is often the case that those two are perhaps the more widely remembered. *Stormwatch* is less pastoral in its themes but the folk rock feel is certainly still there.

Besides, in Anderson's opinion; "I have very little time for the academic approach to folk music, but we all possess a folk, racial memory, an emotional response. It happens to me when I hear the pipes. It strikes a responsive chord, and I try to recreate music of a similar style without being authentic."

Even though *Stormwatch* is less focussed on pastoral themes, it is understandable as to how many still consider it to be closely linked to *Heavy Horses* and indeed *Songs From The Wood*. Throughout all of them, there appears to be something of a commentary on what it is for humans to claim possession of land and resources to use for their own means. Anderson told *Record Mirror* in May 1978; "As soon as you start putting fences around land and using it for your own use then you have to take a hand in maintaining the balance."

He was quoted in the *Newcastle Evening Chronicle* in October 1979 regarding *Stormwatch*; "The songs on the album have a theme running through them. I think that some sort of thread is needed — something that holds them together. There are a few exceptions but generally if a song doesn't fit then it's thrown out. I'm saying on the album — if I'm saying anything — that people should be aware of the temporary nature of the environment. I dare say that it won't change that much in our lifetime, but it's as sure as hell changed in the past, and it's going to change in the future. As a farmer, I'm aware that just half a degree temperature change annually makes a lot of difference and we suffer those kinds of change, or more, in between eleven or fifteen year cycles. I'm very much aware of those sort of long term weather trends. It would take only fifty years if we stopped mending the roads and tilling the fields and tending to gardens for everything to revert to its wild state — it's a constant slog against nature. Man has become very good at keeping things under control but a lot of dreadful things have been perpetrated along the way — the raping and scarring of the land is hideous in some areas."

"One hopes people are becoming a little more sensitive about it. I think I'm an anachronism at this time because I try and write lyrics that mean something — I try to avoid most of the clichés of pop music lyrics. I know that sounds awfully snobby but I think that most of the lyrics you hear are so much rubbish and they make very poor reading when you write them out — and they make very poor thinking about when you try to analyse them. There aren't that many people whose lyrics I could pretend to like."

All of the songs on *Stormwatch* were written by Anderson with the exception of 'Elegy' which was written by David Palmer. The album got to number twenty-seven in the UK and to number twenty-two in the US.

Although punk and new wave had been well on the way in 1977, by 1979 it was even more the case that Jethro Tull's music was perhaps overlooked in favour of what was happening in the mainstream of popular music. Still though, New York's *Daily News* reported 11th October 1979; "The late sixties, when rock was forging into its heavy-metal period, Jethro Tull emerged as a finely tuned pop omnibus fuelled by the flute and imagination of Ian Anderson. A dozen years later, after ten hit albums that reflect an upward spiral of sophistication and, creative verve, Tull's idiom remains one of the definitive forces in rock... As evidenced by the recent release of *Stormwatch*, the English quintet's fastest-selling LP of their career (including the classic *Aqualung*), and two sold-out concerts scheduled to begin tonight at Madison Square Garden."

Cash Box reviewed *Stormwatch* in September 1979; "This week's FM Analysis section logs in *Stormwatch* as the second most added album nationally. Considering the near timid nature of AOR radio, this auspicious airplay debut has to be more than just a sentimental gesture on the part of programmers over the age of thirty. Again, as always, it's in the grooves — Ian Anderson and crew have cooked up a veritable bitch's brew of potent, well, Tullian rock 'n' roll which places the band light years ahead of lesser pretenders."

Record World reviewed the album the following month; "The rock artist who made the flute a legitimate and very popular instrument of pop music presents yet another recording with his particular, and now famous, flute style. 'North Sea Oil' is pure Tull. The vocals, flute and timeliness are all there, but set against today's horizon of the energy crisis."

The same month, the *Aberdeen Evening Express* added; "This latest Tull album should please everybody. Well, Ian Anderson and the band try to anyway. There are flashes of the early Tull but somewhat a disappointing familiarity in some of the numbers, which sounds straight out of *War Child* or *Thick As A Brick*. *Stormwatch* could be regarded as something of a concept album. But Tull fans will love it and the critics — who always slag their albums these days — should also be happy. The rest of the band are far more active. 'Flying Dutchman' could become another classic, in the mould of 'Aqualung' and 'Orion' and 'Dun Ringill' are two other superb tracks."

So is *Stormwatch* a concept album? Not necessarily! Anderson was quoted in the *Liverpool Echo* in October 1979; "I try to stay away from making an album too thematic or too likely to be tagged a concept album, which I think is a meaningless term."

The *Daily Mirror* reviewed the 'North Sea Oil' single in September '79; "You love or loathe Jethro Tull. If you like their music, you'll like this track from new album, *Stormwatch*."

The single was also reviewed in the *Lichfield Mercury* in October; "Jethro Tull may or may not strike it rich with 'North Sea Oil', a single which takes some listening to before you can decide whether you really like it or not. On the other side is the more pleasing, yet mournful instrumental, 'Elegy'. Both tracks are taken from Tull's current album *Stormwatch*, which should do better."

In the same month, the *Newcastle Evening Chronicle* asserted that *Stormwatch* "stands up strongly to any critical scrutiny."

Cash Box reviewed 'Home', the follow-up single, in October; "With Tull's new *Stormwatch* LP already gaining heavy sales and FM play, this single, a short delicate number which features Ian Anderson's spectral lyrics, will introduce the veteran rock unit to fanciers of light rock. An engaging mix of strings and crying lead guitar is perfect for the pastoral theme. This will catch pop programmers by surprise."

In the same month, *Record World* referred to 'Home' as "a sensitive ballad" and "a quiet, moving tune for AOR and Tull fans."

Commencing their final North American tour of the decade in Toronto in October, the following month *The Tampa Bay Times* reported; "The key to Jethro Tull's long-standing popularity has always been simple — don't mess with success. A combination of acoustic, old English folk ballads and boisterous rockers unique to Tull are blended to make up the majority of the band's fifteen albums. The same formula usually holds true for the band's live performances as it plays mostly established hits from the past. Although Tull strayed somewhat from their usual format Saturday night at the Lakeland Civic Centre they were nonetheless engaging. On stage for a concert sold out three weeks prior, Ian Anderson and company were impeccable as they performed a show in two acts."

"Dedicating the first act of their ninety minute show exclusively to Tull's latest release *Stormwatch*, the band came across sounding far more aggressive, with a rougher edge than is apparent on the album. Martin Barre, one of rock's most underrated guitarists, took the forefront musically with searing leads as flute player Anderson, always the focal point, pranced theatrically about, often leaping onto two small annexes jutting out from the stage into the audience, but playing little flute. In past shows, Tull has been satisfied to incorporate material from new albums with more familiar hits throughout. Putting all new work up front is a gamble for a less talented ensemble. If the audience is not receptive at the outset, the group runs the risk of losing them for good. But Tull pulled it off without a hitch as it worked its way visually as well as musically through five offerings from the icy-sea flavoured *Stormwatch*."

"This act featured Anderson's vocal prowess on the eerie rocker 'Orion' and acoustic shanty 'Dun Ringill', along with Barre's consistently incisive lead guitar work. Mock snow fell on the band members during 'Dun Ringill' as two characters attired in white insulated cold protection suits and a huge polar bear made their presence known to further the *Stormwatch* theme."

"Act two… Ian Anderson takes flute in hand for some rapid-fire playing that has become Jethro Tull's trademark. Described as 'a demented flamingo', 'a mad dog Fagin' and a 'deranged dance master', twirling his flute as if it was a baton and cutting down the ship's rigging that had flanked the group setting the stage for the *Stormwatch* sequence. While the young adult audience of approximately 12,000 apparently enjoyed the show's first half, the loudest, most rambunctious ovations were saved for the old favourites that were to come. 'Aqualung', Tull's 1971 classic, penned by Anderson's wife Jennie, kicked off the transition. That was followed by other impressively performed title cuts including a condensed but superb version of 'Thick As A Brick', 'Too Old To Rock 'n' Roll', 'Songs From The Wood', and 'Minstrel In the Gallery'."

"But Tull's finest work was turned in on sensational, rock-out versions of 'Cross-Eyed Mary' and 'Locomotive Breath', both from the *Aqualung* album. Barriemore Barlow on drums and new bassist Dave Pegg, late of Fairport Convention, did a fine job of keeping up Tull's complex rhythms all evening as pianist John Evan and David Palmer on organ and synthesiser deftly worked up the intricate melodies. Barre and Anderson, of course, had firm control of the leads on guitar and flute respectively when not combining acoustic guitar talents on the lighter numbers. Show opener UK had little success with its Emerson, Lake and Palmer cloned technology rock. The British trio's only highlight was the nimble-fingered staccato violin work of Eddie Jobson, but even that device seemed trite after a while."

The *St Louis Post Dispatch* reported on 9th November 1979; "If British rock bands Jethro Tull and UK were booked together to complement each other, it was a good idea. Because they did. The styles were completely different. Still, the Checkerdome crowd last night really appreciated both. It was the usual creative dramatics for Ian Anderson on vocals and flute, and the rest of Jethro Tull. They were dressed in medieval costumes, or so it seemed. Because part of the time a Sherlock Holmes hat or two could be seen as well as a variety of items undefinable. The sunglasses were not an affectation; Anderson recently was hit in the eye at a concert when one of his fans threw something on stage, and it was obvious he was having some difficulty throughout the performance."

"From the *Stormwatch* album, Tull opened with 'Dark Ages', a song in which it sounded as if Anderson was singing through a reverberator. Most of the songs had that reverb effect. Then there was the mellower 'Home', the vigorous 'Orion' and finally two acoustic numbers, the title song and 'Flying Dutchman'. At the climax of 'Flying Dutchman' Anderson emerged with a cutlass to strike the rope holding up the ladders to end that section of the show. There were a number of occasions in which Anderson left the stage to tend to his eyes."

Why did Anderson need to tend to his eyes? It was asserted in *Cash Box*; "The stage and costumes for Jethro Tull's performance at Madison Square Garden were designed as lavishly as the production and arrangements of the group's latest Chrysalis album, *Stormwatch*. At a time when new artists are characterised by pop at its most elemental, Tull's uniqueness lies in the group's highly developed, almost classical sense of modes and harmonies. After eleven years of performing, the group proved it could still pack Madison Square Garden with what appeared to be a new generation of enthusiastic fans. But the enthusiasm, which manifested itself with raised flutes, banners and portraits of group leader Ian Anderson, has its consequences."

"During the course of a new song, 'Dark Ages', a rose was thrown at Anderson, and as was later reported its thorn scarred his eye. But Anderson demonstrated his professionalism by finishing the show without further mention, though the next night's performance had to be cancelled. The show was an ingratiating blend of old and new. The lyrics to 'Something's On The Move' evoked the Cream's 'Tales Of Brave Ulysses' with its surreal images of a dazzling woman, while the group's classic 'Aqualung' featured a blistering drum solo by Barriemore Barlow. For 'Bourée' and 'Fat Man', Anderson used tape loops to set up tasteful harmonies with himself. With full audience participation, the group closed with 'Thick As A Brick'. The group encored with 'Too Old To Rock 'n' Roll' followed by 'Cross-Eyed Mary', which was highlighted by a fiery exchange of riffs between Anderson and longtime Tull guitarist Martin Barre. For the group's second encore, Barre delivered 'Minstrel In The Gallery', which included a highly percussive guitar solo. Meanwhile, Anderson, who had been hiding behind stage monitors, suddenly reappeared and hurled two giant balloons into the audience which burst upon contact, leaving befuddled onlookers showered with white talc. It was a finale that offered ample evidence of why the group recently won an award as one of Madison Square Garden's top attractions."

On the day of the penultimate show of the tour, and indeed the decade, John Glascock passed away. He had played bass for some of the tracks ('Orion', 'Flying Dutchman' and 'Elegy') but due to his declining health, Anderson did the rest. It was reported in New York's *Daily News* in October 1979; "Tull was stopped cold in the recording studio last year when bassist John Glascock had to quit the band after unsuccessful heart surgery. *Stormwatch* was only halfway completed at the time: With no bass player readily available, a month of studio time passed by without any work, and forced the cancellation of scheduled British and European tours. Finally, Anderson took matters into his own hands, strapping on a bass guitar and finishing the final four cuts himself."

To which Anderson was quoted, "This last album was fought with great difficulty. It turned out quite good, actually, and I think we put forth some tasty tidbits. We weren't concerned with making statements, we're still painting pictures, but it was quite a spirited sojourn."

Martin Barre said to *Melody Maker* in October 1979; "Well — sad story. John got an infection in his teeth, which turned into a blood infection and got to a heart valve — he had a heart murmur, anyway. It was straight into hospital and an operation to replace the valve — he ended up with a bit of pig in him. What he'd been through had upset his whole metabolism, so he couldn't take the strain of going away with us. Tony Williams, a friend of Barry's (Barriemore Barlow) from Blackpool, did the tour while John was in hospital for three months. This year we completed an album's worth of material, and then we went away to America — and when we got back, we listened to it again and it wasn't there at all. There was nothing in it. So we all decided to start again. We were all going through quite a lot of pressure, anyway, and it was worse for John, not being in one-hundred percent condition."

Anderson explained to the *Newcastle Evening Chronicle* in October 1979; "The only answer was for us to let him have the proper period of time off that he really needed... I'm not particularly proud, mind you, of my bass playing. On the other hand, I certainly don't think that it would have been any better if we'd got in a bass player on a session basis and said to him 'Here's the music, here are the chords, now play.' It would have been weird creating some faceless person who would have never played with us again. I actually enjoyed the experience very much, playing on an intimate basis with Barrie Barlow and Martin Barre. The drummer, bass player and guitarist have a close musical relationship. Normally I'm way out in front — my flute lines are twittery things way above everything else, and acoustic guitar is so quiet. It was like meeting two people you know very well on completely different footing. I think it worked — it's tight and punchy."

1979 was also the year that some of Jethro Tull had the opportunity to contribute to some local theatre. It was reported in *Melody Maker* in the February of that year; "Ian has written with David Palmer and Martin Barre an evocation of Scotland called 'The Water's Edge' which deals with the myths and legends of that ancient Kingdom including the Loch Ness monster and various silkies, sea beasties, warts, mermaids and shubunkins." The ballet, *Underground Rumours*, premiered at Glasgow's Theatre Royal on 7th March.

Dave Pegg explained to *Melody Maker* in October 1979; "I come into the story around July, when Ian phoned me up several times while I was working with Fairport, who were gigging incredibly hard because we were knocking it on the head after a long time — about as long as Tull. We had the usual bills to pay off... What I wanted to do was produce records, which is every musician's dream. I produced Ralph McTell's last album, *Slide Away The Screen*, which I really enjoyed doing."

Upon being asked if he knew Anderson prior to being invited to join Jethro Tull, Pegg was quoted in the same feature; "No, but I was very aware of the band, obviously because they'd made a lot of albums, been going for a long time, and Fairport had worked with them in the past on tour in the States. In 1970 there was a bill on at the Fillmore West, which was like one of the havens of rock 'n' roll."

Anderson told New York's *Daily News*; "I never met Dave until he played for the band. He heard we needed a bass player and called us up. It's working out rather well because Dave has similar folk and traditional musical leanings to mine. He's given us new life as a touring band."

Barre told *Melody Maker* the same month; "We considered every kind of bass player imaginable — in theory, I'd be wary of choosing someone who's "folk" — or, say, a "jazz" player, because I don't know anything of either. It just has to be the right person."

On Pegg, Anderson speaking to the *Newcastle Evening Chronicle* said; "He fits in so well — the same sense of humour and the same personality as the rest of the group. Same sort of background and age — old."

Despite a change of line-up, the working rapport within Jethro Tull continued to function as an established one. Anderson was at the forefront of things but it didn't seem to be to the detriment of morale — possibly quite the opposite in fact. Barre opined; "When anyone works with Ian, Ian dominates. He's a very strong person, a very strong musician, with strong musical roots and direction. I couldn't write songs with him, 'cos he would dominate and I would sit back. It's a shame, that — but it's good, because it works."

Pegg added; "Ian writes all the lyrics and is the centre of attention on stage. But apart from that, in terms of organisation he's better equipped than any of the people who run offices like these we're sitting in today. In terms of business — the whole thing comes down to business — he's taken control and coped with the music business to the extent where he can almost run the band — period."

Being in Jethro Tull was an exciting new venture for Pegg. "I've had to really work," he said. "They work much harder than any band I've been involved in. I've done more in the last month, doing rehearsals, than I've done for about the last four years. I like that. I'd like to sit back and think about it too, but it's going to be a long time before I can do that."

Despite the tragedy of Glascock's passing, there was a sense of optimism within Jethro Tull overall. Martin Barre had gone on record as having said; "I think it's a good time to be joining the band. The first three years we were trying to make it, then we had made it, and for another three years we were riding the tidal wave in America. We've gone through a stage of relaxing a bit, necessarily; you can't go in top gear for ten years. We're beginning another stage where we're going to be much stronger. In the last two or three years there's been a lot of pressure: from England that you're going to be ignored if you don't do something really good, but not because of musical reasons. In America it is for musical reasons; over the last two years the standard of rock musicians has got staggering, incredible."

It was reported in *Musicians Only* in December 1979; "San Francisco — Jethro Tull completed a successful seven week tour of America at Oakland Coliseum here after a series of disasters ending in the news of the death of an ex-member of the band. John Glascock, twenty-eight-year-old bass guitarist who played on their latest album *Stormwatch*, died in London and the news reached the band just before their final US concert. Glascock, who left the band last year, had undergone open heart surgery and had left the band because of his medical condition. But he never fully recovered. News of his death shattered Tull leader Ian Anderson and other members of the band Martin Barre, Barriemore Barlow and John Evan who were particularly close to Glascock. The tragedy completed a Tull tour marked by sell-out concerts but bad incidents. Anderson was badly injured in his right eye by the stem of a rose thrown by a well-meaning fan at Madison Square Garden, New York. This resulted in hospital treatment and postponed concerts. Later in the tour Ian suffered a sprained ligament and during a thorough physical check-up was told he had a heart murmur. 'I will have a proper check in Britain but I do know it's a heart valve and I'm glad to say not the heart proper. I'm beginning to think there's something wrong with American tours for us — the last time we came here I returned home to another funeral, that of my father. Now, it's news of John Glascock's death.' There will be a BBC TV documentary on Tull in January, and a British and European tour is planned for the spring."

Despite how established Jethro Tull had become by the end of the decade, their strength was in working within their capabilities rather than trying to push too far outside of them. Considering the weight of their discography by that point, it is certainly something that had gone in their favour. Anderson was quoted in *Grooves* in December 1979; "What I play, I can play convincingly and well, but I'm limited in that I can't use the whole range of the instrument and its different voicings. Basically, I play with two sounds and have a limited ability in a limited number of keys. If there's too many sharps and flats in it, I'm lost. My flute playing is either in D, E, A, G or F. You won't find me playing anything in any other key besides set phrases. I can't play anything that's fairly free or improvised other than these keys."

He told New York's *Daily News* in October 1979; "I don't think it would be wise to compose rock music that comes from too lofty a place. We've found that if you place too many demands on an audience, they're liable to walk out on you... Over the years, we've been able to give our music more depth by adding nuances and subtleties, and as a result, there's a lot less holes in our music, less things we're ashamed of. But it has been a blessed relief for us that we don't feel the need to challenge our musical style. Taking chances makes the chances of failure too grand. I have a strong sense of self-preservation."

A change of direction was certainly on the horizon. Clive Walter — an English accountant who handled Anderson's affairs at the time said; "They recorded more songs than they need, and the ones that get used will depend on things like running order and such. The songs I've heard sound great. Before he went into the studio, Ian publicly announced his intention of producing a more rock 'n' roll-oriented album this time. He was talking about leaving the English countryside and the songs about woodland animals, and perhaps getting back to something more reminiscent of the old stuff. I do know he intends to feature the new album very strongly in the new American stage show."

In early 1980, Jethro Tull embarked on another tour of the US. It wasn't long after that Barriemore Barlow announced that he would be leaving the band. *Stormwatch* was also the last album to include John Evan and David Palmer. After leaving the band, they went on to form the short-lived group, Tallis. Palmer had actually set the foundations for Tallis whilst he was still in Jethro Tull. The band was named after the musician, Thomas Tallis. Palmer arranged versions of Pachelbel's Canon and Gigue in D utilising synthesisers, bass guitar and drums. The tracks were recorded at Maison Rouge in 1977 with John Glascock and Barrie Barlow. The acoustic guitar was played by Robert Foster — a pupil of Palmer's from when he had held a teaching post at Trinity College.

Disappointingly for Tallis and for the fans of the musicians involved, Chrysalis decided to pass on releasing the tracks as a single. It was in 1980 that John Evan came on board following Jethro Tull's line-up change. Although Tallis began recording an album, once again the band struggled to get the support of a record label behind them and consequently the project was put on the backburner.

In April 1980, *Melody Maker* reviewed the show that took place at London's Hammersmith Odeon on 11th of that month. The five nights that Jethro Tull played there (10th-14th) would be the last of the live performances by the Anderson / Barre / Barlow / Evan / Palmer team; "Such a storm! Such a season of wonder! In this sun-stroked spring, the old masters are coming out again and making most (not all) of those children, who have recently been masquerading as rock stars, understand how much they still have to learn. Thus, after Genesis, nights of delight from Jethro Tull at Hammersmith. Ian Anderson, leader, in his thirties — looking wickedly like Errol Flynn almost looked in those Spanish Main movies — leaping and declaiming around the stage with his zany companions, while producing music of splendour."

"How to tell the story briefly? To begin — Tull's sheer humour, fun, spirit. It is, as Anderson cavorts, as keyboards man John Evan beams loonily in his Ruritanian Admiral's finery and as seagulls erupt on the set, like a cross between Monty Python, Hellza Poppin and the Crazy Gang. But (do I hear?) wherein lies the music? Consider, say, Anderson's statement that Tull play "English rock." He is so triumphantly right. There are passages in his last album, *Stormwatch*, when the dark lyricism of guitars, piano and pipe-organ suggest he is the street man's Elgar. At times, the keyboard counterpoint reminds me of Byrd. Yet there's so much more. The folk element grows strong in 'Heavy Horses' (Anderson's superb anthem to Clydesdales) or 'Songs From The Wood'. Since bassist Dave Pegg joined the band, the reels flow more thickly."

"On Friday, Tull played Henry VIII's hit, 'Pastime With Good Company'. Anderson must guest at the *Schools' Prom* one day. Yet even this only adumbrates Tull's mastery. Anderson sings, of course, but also offers a flute extravaganza spanning a mad Roland Kirk voice-over and smooth jazzy Herbie Mann. Martin Barre's lead guitar is stunning, while the twin keyboards (Evan and David Palmer) and Barriemore Barlow's powerful drumming round out this world-class band. They played, unbroken, for two hours ten minutes. For the last half-hour the audience was standing, not menacingly, but laughing, clapping, drinking in the joy, Anderson seemingly amidst them. He began his encores with 'Too Old To Rock 'n' Roll' (which you never are, unless atrophied): 'Too Young To Die'. The oldies sang along. As Don Black so cannily said, in *Tell Me On A Sunday*: 'You only act your age if that's the age you want to be.' Glorious Jethro Tull." (*Schools' Prom* was a version of *The Proms* made for a younger audience. Genesis had played three nights at the Hammersmith Odeon — 27th-29th March 1980).

One of Tull's Hammersmith shows was also reviewed in *Record Mirror* in April 1980; "Come rain or snow. Come punk, mod, or pork pie hat, they'll be there. The tireless campaigners and unsung heroes of a whole generation. Jethro Tull are die hard ancient mariners, charting their steady course through unsteady seas frequented by the press pirates anxious to make a quick killing. But they've avoided all the broadsides, booming back with album after album and stage shows that almost defy description. Ian Anderson has the best stage act since Moses parted the Red Sea. A man whose every move stuns and captures your attention and whose sheer vitality could fill the entire London underground."

"Tull's Hammersmith set was a glorious homecoming. Anderson emerged modestly in Scottish cap and long-flowing robe peering mischievously about the stage like some moustache twirling villain from a very old film. Much of the first half of the set relied on Tull's latest album *Stormwatch* and live and loosened up it had some epic moments — especially during the quieter segments, by god, it made you proud to be British. But soft 'Jack-In-The-Green' this way came, with Anderson armed with his guitar perched on a stool. But as usual, the real gut wrenching moment of the concert was 'Thick As A Brick', tranquil melodies before a hard sprint through the finish line. The song was the ideal counterpoint to the rumblings and sweat of 'Heavy Horses' and Anderson's flute solo where he proved he has the capacity of a blacksmith's bellows at full tilt. This review isn't too over the top is it?"

As ever, Jethro Tull's approach to working to please a crowd is one that went in their favour. In October 1979, Anderson had told the *Newcastle Evening Chronicle*; "In our tour — we'll reach the UK early next year — we'll be featuring the new album in the set, most of it in fact. It'll be nice to dress up the work and present it as a whole, rather than playing another 'best of Jethro Tull' tour. If it works well and pleases the audience and the musicians performing it, then we'll continue. If not, we'll stop after a couple of nights and revert to a safer way of doing it."

1980 was the year in which Ian Anderson set to work on what was originally going to be a solo album. Dave Pegg and Martin Barre were already scheduled to play on it. Eddie Jobson was invited to play keyboards due to his strong reputation having already worked with Curved Air, Roxy Music and Frank Zappa. Jobson had already toured with his band, UK as Jethro Tull's support act. Mark Craney was brought in to play drums. The working title of the album was *A*, purely because of how the tape boxes of recorded material had been labelled.

Anderson was persuaded by Chrysalis to release the album under the name of Jethro Tull rather than take on the risk of trying to market it as a solo project. As a result, the line-up on the album was put forward to the press as the new line-up of Jethro Tull. Not only was the line-up different but as was the case with many groups who had been prolific in the seventies, the challenge to move into the new sound of the eighties was one that couldn't be ignored. As a result, *A* was a move away from what many considered to be Jethro Tull's familiar sound. The folk influence was reduced in favour of something more electronic-sounding. *A* was recorded quickly — predominantly across a period of just a few weeks. It got to number twenty-five in the UK and to number thirty in the US.

Although a new era for Jethro Tull was clearly dawning, there was certainly something to build on to carry them through the rest of the eighties and beyond.

Ian Anderson on his estate on the Isle of Skye.

Discography
Albums

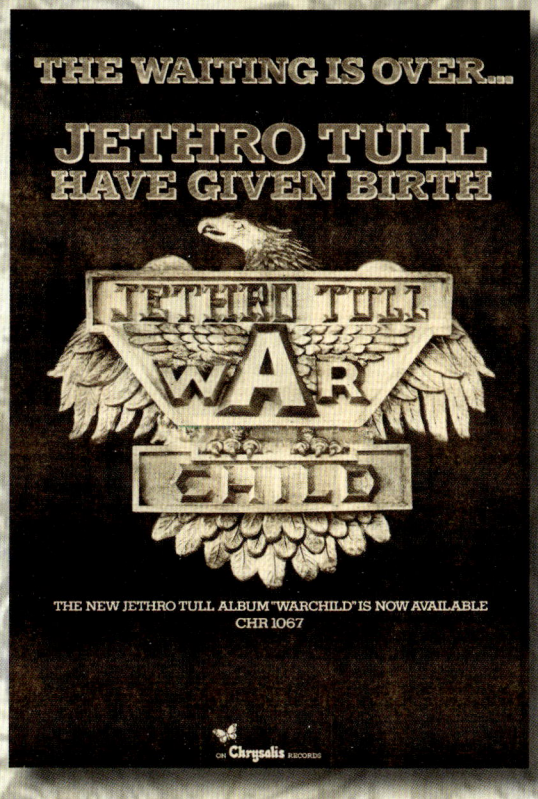

This Was (1968)

Personnel

Ian Anderson — lead vocals (all except track 4), flute, mouth organ, claghorn, piano
Mick Abrahams — lead vocals (track 4), co-lead vocals (track 2), backing vocals, electric guitar, nine-string guitar
Glenn Cornick — bass guitar
Clive Bunker — drums, percussion, hooter, charm bracelet
David Palmer — French horn and orchestral arrangements

Terry Ellis — producer
Victor Gamm — engineer

Tracks

Side One
1. My Sunday Feeling (3:43)
2. Some Day The Sun Won't Shine For You (2:49)
3. Beggar's Farm (4:19)
4. Move On Alone (1:58)
5. Serenade To A Cuckoo (6:07)

Side Two
6. Dharma For One (4:15)
7. It's Breaking Me Up (5:04)
8. Cat's Squirrel (5:42)
9. A Song For Jeffrey (3:22)
10. Round (1:03)

Stand Up (1969)

Personnel

Ian Anderson — vocals, flute, acoustic guitar, Hammond organ, piano, mandolin, balalaika, mouth organ, production
Martin Barre — electric guitar, additional flute (on tracks 2 and 9)
Glenn Cornick — bass guitar (all tracks but 5 and 7)
Clive Bunker — drums, percussion

Terry Ellis — production, cover concept
Andy Johns — engineer, bass guitar (on track 5)
David Palmer — string arrangements and conductor (on track 9)
John Williams — cover concept
James Grashow — cover art

Tracks

Side One
1. A New Day Yesterday (4:10)
2. Jeffrey Goes To Leicester Square (2:12)
3. Bourée (3:46)
4. Back To The Family (3:48)
5. Look Into The Sun (4:20)

Side Two
6. Nothing Is Easy (4:25)
7. Fat Man (2:52)
8. We Used To Know (4:00)
9. Reasons For Waiting (4:05)
10. For A Thousand Mothers (4:13)

Benefit (1970)

Personnel

Ian Anderson — vocals, acoustic guitar, electric guitar (uncredited), flute, balalaika, keyboards, production
Martin Barre — electric guitar
Glenn Cornick — bass guitar, Hammond organ (uncredited)
Clive Bunker — drums, percussion
John Evan — piano, organ

David Palmer — orchestral arrangements
Robin Black — engineer
Terry Ellis — cover design, executive producer
Ruan O'Lochlainn — cover design, photography

Tracks

Side One
1. With You There To Help Me (6:15)
2. Nothing To Say (5:10)
3. Alive And Well And Living In (2:43)
4. Son (2:48)
5. For Michael Collins, Jeffrey And Me (3:47)

Side Two
6. To Cry You A Song (6:09)
7. A Time For Everything? (2:42)
8. Inside (3:38)
9. Play In Time (3:44)
10. Sossity; You're A Woman (4:31)

Aqualung (1971)

Personnel

Ian Anderson — lead vocals, acoustic guitar, flute, production
Martin Barre — electric guitar, descant recorder
Jeffrey Hammond (as Jeffrey Hammond-Hammond) — backing vocals (track 4), bass guitar, alto recorder, odd voices
John Evan — piano, organ, Mellotron
Clive Bunker — drums and percussion

Glenn Cornick — bass guitar (he played with the band at rehearsals for the album in June 1970, some of which may also have been recording sessions — particularly early versions of My God and Wond'ring Aloud — he is not credited on the album though)
John Burns — recording engineer
David Palmer — orchestral arrangements and conducting
Burton Silverman — album artwork
Terry Ellis — executive producer

Tracks

Side One
1. Aqualung (6:34)
2. Cross-Eyed Mary (4:06)
3. Cheap Day Return (1:21)
4. Mother Goose (3:51)
5. Wond'ring Aloud (1:53)
6. Up To Me (3:15)

Side Two
1. My God (7:08)
2. Hymn 43 (3:14)
3. Slipstream (1:13)
4. Locomotive Breath (4:23)
5. Wind-Up (6:01)

Thick As A Brick (1972)

Personnel

Ian Anderson — vocals, acoustic guitar, flute, violin, trumpet, saxophone
Martin Barre — electric guitar, lute
John Evan — piano, organ, harpsichord
Jeffrey Hammond (as Jeffrey Hammond-Hammond) — bass guitar, spoken word
Barriemore Barlow — drums, percussion, timpani

David Palmer — orchestral arrangements
Terry Ellis — executive producer
Robin Black — engineer

Tracks

Side One
1. Thick As A Brick, Part I (22:40)

Side Two
2. Thick As A Brick, Part II (21:06)

A Passion Play (1973)

Personnel

Ian Anderson — lead vocals, flute, acoustic guitar, soprano and sopranino saxophone
Martin Barre — electric guitar
John Evan — backing vocals, piano, organ, synthesizer
Jeffrey Hammond — bass guitar, spoken word (on The Story Of The Hare Who Lost His Spectacles)
Barriemore Barlow — drums, percussion, timpani, glockenspiel, marimba

David Palmer — orchestral arrangements
Robin Black — sound engineer
Terry Ellis — producer
Brian Ward — photography

Tracks

Side One
1. A Passion Play, part I
I. Act 1: Ronnie Pilgrim's Funeral — a winter's morning in the cemetery
    I. Lifebeats (1:14)
    II. Prelude (2:14)
    III. The Silver Cord (4:29)
    IV. Re-Assuring Tune (1:11)
II. "Act 2: The Memory Bank — a small but comfortable theatre with a cinema-screen (the next morning)
    I. Memory Bank (4:20)
    II. Best Friends (1:58)
    III. Critique Oblique (4:38)
    IV. Forest Dance #1 (1:35)
III. Interlude: The Story of the Hare Who Lost His Spectacles
    I. The Story of the Hare Who Lost His Spectacles (1:30)

Side Two
2. A Passion Play, part II
I. Interlude: The Story of the Hare Who Lost His Spectacles
    I. The Story of the Hare Who Lost His Spectacles (2:48)
II. Act 3: The business office of G. Oddie & Son (two days later)
    I. Forest Dance #2 (1:12)
    II. The Foot Of Our Stairs (4:18)
    III. Overseer Overture (4:00)
III. Act 4: Magus Perdé's drawing room at midnight
I. Flight From Lucifer (3:58)
II. 10:08 To Paddington (1:04)
III. Magus Perdé (3:55)
IV. Epilogue (0:43)

War Child (1974)

Personnel

Ian Anderson — vocals, flute, acoustic guitar, saxophone
Martin Barre — electric guitar, Spanish guitar
John Evan — piano, organ, synthesizers, accordion
Jeffrey Hammond — bass guitar, string bass
Barriemore Barlow — drums, percussion

David Palmer — orchestral arrangements
Robin Black — sound engineer
Terry Ellis — executive producer

Tracks

Side One
1. War Child (4:35)
2. Queen And Country (3:00)
3. Ladies (3:17)
4. Back-Door Angels (5:30)
5. Sealion (3:37)

Side Two
6. Skating Away On The Thin Ice Of The New Day (4:09)
7. Bungle In The Jungle (3:35)
8. Only Solitaire (1:38)
9. The Third Hoorah (4:49)
10. Two Fingers (5:11)

Minstrel In The Gallery (1975)

Personnel

Ian Anderson — vocals, flute, acoustic guitar
Martin Barre — electric guitar
John Evan — piano, organ
Jeffrey Hammond — bass guitar, string bass
Barriemore Barlow — drums, percussion

David Palmer — string quintet arrangements and conducting
Rita Eddowes, Elizabeth Edwards, Patrick Halling and Bridget Procter — violin
Katharine Tullborn — cello
Brian Ward — photographs
Ron Kriss and J.E. Garnett — front cover, based on a print by Joseph Nash
Robin Black — sound engineering

Tracks

Side One
1. Minstrel In The Gallery (8:13)
2. Cold Wind To Valhalla (4:19)
3. Black Satin Dancer (6:52)
4. Requiem (3:45)

Side Two
5. One White Duck / 010 = Nothing At All (4:37)
6. Baker St Muse (16:39)
    a) Pig-Me And The Whore
    b) Nice Little Tune
    c) Crash-Barrier Waltzer
    d) Mother England Reverie
7. Grace (0:37)

Too Old To Rock 'n' Roll: Too Young To Die (1976)

Personnel

Ian Anderson — lead vocals, acoustic guitar, flute, harmonica, additional electric guitar and percussion
Martin Barre — electric guitar
John Evan — piano, keyboards
John Glascock — backing vocals, bass guitar
Barriemore Barlow — drums, percussion
David Palmer — saxophone (on track 5), piano (on track 11)
Maddy Prior — backing vocals (on track 8)
Angela Allen — backing vocals (on tracks 2 and 7)
Orchestrations by Dee Palmer. Orchestra conducted by Dee Palmer.

Robin Black — sound engineer
Michael Farrell — cover design, illustrations
David Gibbons — design, illustrations

Tracks

Side One
1. Quizz Kid (5:09)
2. Crazed Institution (4:48)
3. Salamander (2:51)
4. Taxi Grab (3:54)
5. From A Dead Beat To An Old Greaser (4:09)

Side Two
6. Bad-Eyed And Loveless (2:12)
7. Big Dipper (3:35)
8. Too Old To Rock 'n' Roll: Too Young To Die (5:44)
9. Pied Piper (4:32)
10. The Chequered Flag (Dead Or Alive) (5:32)

Songs From The Wood (1977)

Personnel

Ian Anderson — lead vocals, flute, acoustic guitar, mandolin, cymbals, whistles; all instruments (on track 2)
Martin Barre — electric guitar, lute
John Glascock — backing vocals, bass guitar
John Evan — piano, organ, synthesisers
David Palmer — piano, portative pipe organ, synthesisers
Barriemore Barlow — drums, percussion, marimba, glockenspiel, bells, nakers, tabor

Robin Black — sound engineering
Thing Moss and Trevor White — assistant engineers
Keith Howard — wood-cutter
Jay L. Lee — front cover painting
Shirt Sleeve Studio — back cover

Tracks

Side One
1. Songs From The Wood (4:52)
2. Jack-In-The-Green (2:27)
3. Cup Of Wonder (4:30)
4. Hunting Girl (5:11)
5. Ring Out, Solstice Bells (3:43)

Side Two
6. Velvet Green (6:03)
7. The Whistler (3:30)
8. Pibroch (Cap In Hand) (8:35)
9. Fire At Midnight (2:26)

Heavy Horses (1978)

Personnel

Ian Anderson — lead vocals, flute, acoustic guitar, additional electric guitar, mandolin
Martin Barre — electric guitar
John Glascock — backing vocals, bass guitar
John Evan — piano, organ
David Palmer — keyboards, portative pipe organ, orchestral arrangements
Barriemore Barlow — drums, percussion

Darryl Way — violin (on track 2 and track 8)
Shona Anderson — photography
Robin Black — sound engineer
James Cotier — photography

Tracks

Side One
1. ...And The Mouse Police Never Sleeps (3:11)
2. Acres Wild (3:22)
3. No Lullaby (7:55)
4. Moths (3:24)
5. Journeyman (3:55)

Side Two
6. Rover (4:17)
7. One Brown Mouse (3:21)
8. Heavy Horses (8:58)
9. Weathercock (4:02)

Stormwatch (1979)

Personnel

Ian Anderson — vocals, flute, acoustic guitar, bass guitar (on tracks 1 and 3-8)
Martin Barre — electric guitar, classical guitar, mandolin
John Glascock — bass guitar (on tracks 2, 9 and 10)
John Evan — piano, organ
David Palmer — synthesisers, portable organ and orchestral arrangements
Barriemore Barlow — drums, percussion

Francis Wilson — spoken word (on tracks 1 and 8)
Robin Black — sound engineer
David Jackson — artwork
Peter Wragg — art direction

Tracks

Side One
1. North Sea Oil (3:12)
2. Orion (3:58)
3. Home (2:46)
4. Dark Ages (9:13)
5. Warm Sporran (3:33)

Side Two
6. Something's On The Move (4:27)
7. Old Ghosts (4:23)
8. Dun Ringill (2:41)
9. Flying Dutchman (7:46)
10. Elegy (3:38)

The first tour with John Glascock.
Tampa Stadium, Florida, USA,
31st July 1976.

© Philip Buonpastore / Alamy Stock Photo

Tour Dates

Please be aware that the following list may not be exhaustive. Conflicting accounts exist of Jethro Tull's tour dates. Consequently, the list here is derived from corroboration of information from posters, ticket stubs and reviews. For the avoidance of doubt, dates are listed in day-month-year format

1967

Performing as The John Evan Smash were Ian Anderson on vocals, Barrie Barlow on drums, John Evan on organ, Glenn Cornick on bass, Chick Murray on guitar, Tony Wilkinson on baritone sax and Neil Valentine on tenor sax.

It is a strong likelihood that more gigs took place in 1967 but owing to the fact that the band were yet to have their commercial breakthrough, the recording of such data was less prolific.

04.02.67 The Union Rowing Club, Sunderland, UK
19.06.67 The Marquee Club, London, UK
30.06.67 The Nottingham Boat Club, Nottingham, UK
04.07.67 The Didsbury College Hall, Manchester, UK
28.07.67 The Southbank Jazz Club, Grimsby, UK
30.07.67 The Top Twenty Club, Oldham, UK
04.08.67 The Marquee Club, London, UK (cancelled due to transport failure)
21.10.67 The Beachcomber Club, Luton, UK

November 1967 saw the first incarnation of Jethro Tull with Ian Anderson on vocals/harmonica/flute, Mick Abrahams on guitar, Glenn Cornick on bass and Clive Bunker on drums.

14.12.67 The Marquee Club, London, UK

1968

16.01.68 The Marquee Club, London, UK
19.01.68 The Marquee Club, London, UK
02.02.68 The Marquee Club, London, UK
05.02.68 The Speakeasy, London, UK
09.02.68 The Marquee Club, London, UK
16.02.68 The Marquee Club, London, UK
26.02.68 The Cromwellian, London, UK
28.02.68 The Falmer House University Of Sussex, Brighton, UK
07.03.68 The Metro Club, Birmingham, UK
08.03.68 The Argus Butterfly, Newcastle, UK
15.03.68 The Marquee Club, London, UK
18.03.68 The Star Hotel, Croydon, UK
29.03.68 The Marquee Club, London, UK
06.04.68 Magic Village, Manchester, UK
11.04.68 The Railway Hotel, Bishops Stortford, UK
12.04.68 The Candlelight Club, Scarborough, UK
13.04.68 The Cat Balou Club, Grantham, UK
14.04.68 Britannia Rowing Club, Nottingham, UK
15.04.68 The Marquee Club, London, UK
16.04.68 The Fishmongers Arms, Wood Green, London, UK
18.04.68 The Railway Hotel, Bishops Stortford, UK
22.04.68 The Star Hotel, Croydon, UK
23.04.68 The Marquee Club, London, UK
03.05.68 The Marquee Club, London, UK
05.05.68 The Queens Stagg Hounds, Ascot, UK
17.05.68 The Marquee Club, London, UK
20.05.68 The Nags Head, London, UK
24.05.68 The Nags Head, High Wycombe, UK
25.05.68 Bluesville '68 - The Farmers Inn, Bradford, UK
26.05.68 ?, Coventry, UK
29.05.68 The Hub Club, Marlow, UK
30.05.68 ?, Hull, UK
31.05.68 The Marquee Club, London, UK
14.06.68 The Marquee Club, London, UK
15.06.68 Klooks Kleek, West Hampstead, UK
18.06.68 Klooks Kleek, West Hampstead, UK
21.06.68 The Candlelight Club, Scarborough, UK
26.06.68 Sheffield University, Sheffield, UK

28.06.68 The Marquee Club, London, UK (first show)
28.06.68 The Marquee Club, London, UK (second show)
29.06.68 Hyde Park, London, UK
05.07.68 The Marquee Club, London, UK
11.07.68 The Railway Hotel, Wealdstone, UK
17.07.68 The Toby Jug, Tolworth, UK
19.07.68 The Marquee Club, London, UK
20.07.68 The Magic Village, Manchester, UK
26.07.68 The Marquee Club, London, UK
02.08.68 (Bluesville '68) Hornsey Wood Tavern Manor House, London, UK
04.08.68 Mothers, Birmingham, UK
09.08.68 The Marquee Club, London, UK
11.08.68 The Sunbury Jazz & Blues Festival, Kempton Park, UK
16.08.68 The Candlelight Club, Scarborough, UK
21.08.68 Mothers, Birmingham, UK
23.08.68 The Marquee Club, London, UK
24.08.68 The Marquee Club, London, UK (first show)
24.08.68 The Marquee Club, London, UK (second show)
27.08.68 Blaises Club, London, UK
28.08.68 The Country Club NW3, London, UK
29.08.68 The Railway Hotel, Wealdstone, UK
03.09.68 The Marquee Club, London, UK
05.09.68 The Metro Club, Birmingham, UK
06.09.68 The Grand Hotel, Felixstowe, UK
07.09.68 The Magic Village, Manchester, UK
09.09.68 The Nags Head, Battersea, London, UK
20.09.68 The Marquee Club, London, UK
21.09.68 Mothers, Birmingham, UK
23.09.68 Edmonton Cooks Ferry Inn, London, UK (early show)
23.09.68 The Black Bull Blues Club, London, UK (late show)
29.09.68 The Croydon Gala, Croydon, UK
05.10.68 Brondby Pop Club, Copenhagen, Denmark
06.10.68 The Star Club, Copenhagen, Denmark
11.10.68 The Marquee Club, London, UK
13.10.68 The Leofric Hotel, Coventry, UK
15.10.68 The Royal Albert Hall, London, UK
16.10.68 The Toby Jug, Tolworth, UK
22.10.68 The Fishmongers Arms, Wood Green, London, UK
24.10.68 The Red Lion Hotel, Leytonstone, UK
26.10.68 The London College Of Printing, London, UK
29.10.68 The Crown Hotel, Birmingham, UK
01.11.68 The California Ballroom, Dunstable, UK
02.11.68 University College, London, UK
02.11.68 Chalk Farm Roundhouse, London, UK
05.11.68 Klooks Kleek, West Hampstead, UK
09.11.68 Town Hall, Glastonbury, UK
13.11.68 The Velvet Underground Club, Chesterfield, UK
15.11.68 The Hornsey Wood Tavern, London, UK
23.11.68 Magic Village, Manchester, UK
24.11.68 Mothers, Birmingham, UK
26.11.68 The Marquee Club, London, UK
29.11.68 The Vandyke Club, Plymouth, UK
30.11.68 School Of Economics, London, UK

For around two weeks, the members of Jethro Tull were Ian Anderson, Tony Iommi, Glenn Cornick and Clive Bunker.

12.12.68 The Rolling Stones Rock 'n' Roll Circus, London, UK
20.12.68 The Marquee Club, London, UK (cancelled)

By December 1968, Jethro Tull were Ian Anderson, Martin Barre, Glenn Cornick and Clive Bunker. The band continued with this line-up until April 1970.

30.12.68 The Winter Gardens, Penzance, UK
31.12.68 Mothers, Birmingham, UK (cancelled)

1969

02.01.69 The Winter Gardens, Penzance, UK
03.01.69 The Ritz, Bournemouth, UK
04.01.69 The Vandyke Club, Plymouth, UK
05.01.69 The Boat Club, Nottingham, UK
07.01.69 Bath Pavilion, Bath, UK
08.01.69 The Toby Jug, Tolworth, UK
09.01.69 The Koncerthaus, Stockholm, Sweden (first show)
09.01.69 The Koncerthaus, Stockholm, Sweden (second show)
10.01.69 Falconer Theatre, Copenhagen, Denmark (first show)
10.01.69 Falconer Theatre, Copenhagen, Denmark (second show)
11.01.69 Norwich Gala, Norwich, UK
12.01.69 Redcar Jazz Club, Redcar, UK
14.01.69 The Speakeasy Club, London, UK
15.01.69 Keele University, Keele, UK
16.01.69 The Lafayette Club, Wolverhampton, UK
18.01.69 Manchester University, Manchester, UK
24.01.69 The Fillmore East, New York, USA
25.01.69 The Fillmore East, New York, USA
31.01.69 The Grande Ballroom, Detroit, USA
01.02.69 The Grande Ballroom, Detroit, USA
02.02.69 The Grande Ballroom, Detroit, USA
07.02.69 The Kinetic Playground, Chicago, USA
08.02.69 The Kinetic Playground, Chicago, USA
09.02.69 The Labor Temple, Minneapolis, USA
13.02.69 The Boston Tea Party, Boston, USA
14.02.69 The Boston Tea Party, Boston, USA
15.02.69 The Boston Tea Party, Boston, USA
16.02.69 The State University Of New York, Stoney Brook, USA
20.02.69 The Stone Balloon, New Haven, USA (first show)
20.02.69 The Stone Balloon, New Haven, USA (second show)
21.02.69 The Stone Balloon, New Haven, USA (first show)
21.02.69 The Stone Balloon, New Haven, USA (second show)
22.02.69 The Stone Balloon, New Haven, USA (first show)
22.02.69 The Stone Balloon, New Haven, USA (second show)
23.02.69 The Stone Balloon, New Haven, USA (first show)
23.02.69 The Stone Balloon, New Haven, USA (second show)
28.02.69 The Worcester Memorial Auditorium, Worcester, USA
01.03.69 The Alexandria Roller Rink, Alexandria, USA
02.03.69 The Symphony Hall, Boston, USA (cancelled)
07.03.69 The Eagles Ballroom, Seattle, USA
08.03.69 The Eagles Ballroom, Seattle, USA
09.03.69 The Eagles Ballroom, Seattle, USA
13.03.69 The Fillmore West, San Francisco, USA
14.03.69 The Fillmore West, San Francisco, USA
15.03.69 The Fillmore West, San Francisco, USA
16.03.69 The Fillmore West, San Francisco, USA
21.03.69 The Rose Palace, Pasadena, USA
22.03.69 The Rose Palace, Pasadena, USA
23.03.69 The Sound Factory, Sacramento, USA
28.03.69 The Aquarius Theatre, Phoenix, USA
29.03.69 The Aquarius Theatre, Phoenix, USA
31.03.69 The Aquarius Theatre, Los Angeles, USA
05.04.69 The Electric Theatre, Pittsburgh, USA
06.04.69 The 13th Hour, Evansville, USA
07.04.69 The Grande Ballroom, Detroit, USA
08.04.69 The Grande Ballroom, Detroit, USA
09.04.69 The Boston Tea Party, Boston, USA
11.04.69 The Fillmore East, New York, USA
03.05.69 The Leas Cliff Hall, Folkestone, UK
06.05.69 The Free Trade Hall, Manchester, UK
07.05.69 The Palais Des Sportes, Paris, France

08.05.69 The Royal Albert Hall, London, UK
09.05.69 The Colston Hall, Bristol, UK
11.05.69 The Redcar Jazz Club, Redcar, UK
13.05.69 The Guildhall, Portsmouth, UK
14.05.69 The City Hall, Newcastle, UK
15.05.69 The Town Hall, Birmingham, UK
17.05.69 The Gala Ballroom, Norwich, UK
23.05.69 Grosmont Wood Barn, Abergaveney, UK
24.05.69 Walsall Common Equestrian Centre, Coventry, UK
28.05.69 The National Stadium, Dublin, Ireland
29.05.69 The Ulster Hall, Belfast, Ireland
30.05.69 ?, Cork, Ireland
31.05.69 The Winter Garden Pavilion, Weston-Super-Mare, UK
03.06.69 The Cherry Tree (Bluesville '69), Welwyn Garden City, UK
04.06.69 The Sherwood Rooms, Nottingham, UK
05.06.69 The Assembly Hall, Worthing, UK
06.06.69 The Vandyke Club, Plymouth, UK
07.06.69 The Roundhouse, Dagenham, UK
09.06.69 ?, Cambridge, UK
12.06.69 The Locarno, Hull, UK
13.06.69 The Bay Hotel, Sunderland, UK
14.06.69 The Winter Garden, Malvern, UK
15.06.69 The Lafayette Club, Wolverhampton, UK
17.06.69 The Town Hall, Middlesbrough, UK
21.06.69 The Newport Pop Festival, Devonshire Downs, USA
24.06.69 The Cobo Hall, Detroit, USA
28.06.69 The Miami Jazz Festival, Miami, USA
03.07.69 The Fillmore East, New York, USA
04.07.69 The Newport Jazz Festival, Newport, USA
05.07.69 The Randall's Island Pop Festival, New York, USA
11.07.69 The Laurel Pop Festival, Laurel Springs, USA
12.07.69 The Newport Jazz Festival, Philadelphia, USA
15.07.69 The Revolution, Monticello, USA
16.07.69 The Revolution, Monticello, USA
17.07.69 The Revolution, Monticello, USA
18.07.69 The Kinetic Playground, Chicago, USA
19.07.69 The Kinetic Playground, Chicago, USA
22.07.69 The Stony Brook University, Stony Brook, USA
23.07.69 The Boston Tea Party, Boston, USA
24.07.69 The Boston Tea Party, Boston, USA
25.07.69 The Boston Tea Party, Boston, USA
26.07.69 The Newport Jazz Festival, Brunswick, USA
28.07.69 Central Park, New York, USA
01.08.69 The Fairgrounds Arena, Santa Barbara, USA
02.08.69 The Eagles Ballroom, Seattle, USA
03.08.69 The Eagles Ballroom, Seattle, USA
08.08.69 The Swing Auditorium, San Bernardino, USA
09.08.69 The Convention Centre, Anaheim, USA
10.08.69 San Diego Sports Arena, San Diego, USA
12.08.69 The Fillmore West, San Francisco, USA
13.08.69 The Fillmore West, San Francisco, USA (cancelled)
14.08.69 The Fillmore West, San Francisco, USA
15.08.69 The Hemisfair Arena, San Antonio, USA
16.08.69 The Catacombs, Houston, USA
07.09.69 The Amsterdam Concertgebouw, Amsterdam, Holland

19.09.69 — 23.09.69 Lyceum Theatre, London, UK (tour rehearsals)

25.09.69 City Hall, Newcastle, UK
26.09.69 The Usher Hall, Edinburgh, UK
27.09.69 The National Stadium, Dublin, Ireland
29.09.69 The Ulster Hall, Belfast, Ireland
01.10.69 The Royal Albert Hall, London, UK

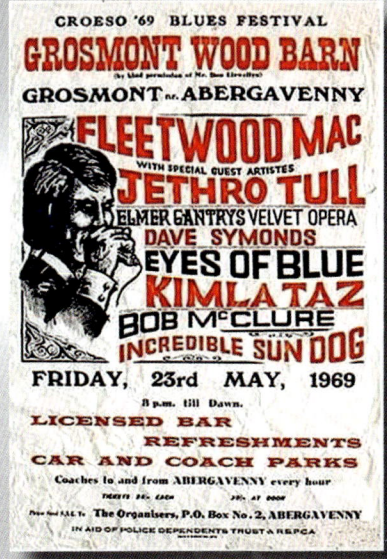

02.10.69 The Free Trade Hall, Manchester, UK
03.10.69 The Brighton Dome, Brighton, UK
06.10.69 The City Hall, Hull, UK
07.10.69 The Town Hall, Leeds, UK
08.10.69 The Town Hall, Birmingham, UK
10.10.69 The Concertgebouw, Amsterdam, Holland
11.10.69 The Town Hall, Antwerp, Belgium
12.10.69 The Olympia, Paris, France
15.10.69 The City Hall, Sheffield, UK
19.10.69 The Rex Cinema, Cambridge, UK
20.10.69 The Guildhall, Southampton, UK
21.10.69 The Colston Hall, Bristol, UK
23.10.69 The De Montfort Hall, Leicester, UK
25.10.69 The Guildhall, Plymouth, UK
26.10.69 The Town Hall, Oxford, UK
29.10.69 The St Andrews Hall, Norwich, UK
14.11.69 The Baldwin Gym Drew University, Madison, USA
15.11.69 ?, Hartford, USA
20.11.69 The Fillmore West, San Francisco, USA
21.11.69 The Fillmore West, San Francisco, USA
22.11.69 The Fillmore West, San Francisco, USA
23.11.69 The Fillmore West, San Francisco, USA
26.11.69 The Civic Auditorium, Santa Monica, USA (first show at 8pm)
26.11.69 The Civic Auditorium, Santa Monica, USA (second show at midnight)
27.11.69 The Community Concourse, San Diego, USA
28.11.69 The Riviera Theatre, Detroit, USA
29.11.69 The Riviera Theatre, Detroit, USA
30.11.69 The Spectrum, Philadelphia, USA
05.12.69 The Fillmore East, New York, USA (first show)
05.12.69 The Fillmore East, New York, USA (second show)
06.12.69 The Fillmore East, New York, USA (first show)
06.12.69 The Fillmore East, New York, USA (second show)
07.12.69 The University Of Massachusetts, Amherst, USA
08.12.69 The Boston Tea Party, Boston, USA
09.12.69 The Boston Tea Party, Boston, USA
10.12.69 The Soldiers & Sailors Auditorium, Kansas City, USA
11.12.69 The Houston Music Hall, Houston, USA (first show)
11.12.69 The Houston Music Hall, Houston, USA (second show)
12.12.69 The Municipal Auditorium, San Antonio, USA (first show)
12.12.69 The Municipal Auditorium, San Antonio, USA (second show)
13.12.69 ?, Austin, USA
14.12.69 The Aragon Ballroom, Chicago, USA

1970

16.01.70 The Fyns Forum, Odense, Denmark
17.01.70 The K.B. Hallen, Copenhagen, Denmark
19.01.70 Kulttuuritalo, Helsinki, Finland
20.01.70 The Kunglinga Tennishallen, Stockholm, Sweden
21.01.70 The Konserthuset, Gothenburg, Sweden
22.01.70 The Olympen, Lund, Sweden
21.02.70 The Jarhunderthalle, Frankfurt, Germany (first show)
21.02.70 The Jarhunderthalle, Frankfurt, Germany (second show)

By April, Jethro Tull were Ian Anderson, Martin Barre, Glenn Cornick, Clive Bunker and John Evan. The band continued with this line-up until December 1970.

05.04.70 ?, Nuremberg, Germany (first show)
05.04.70 ?, Nuremberg, Germany (second show)
07.04.70 The Musikhalle, Hamburg, Germany (first show)
07.04.70 The Musikhalle, Hamburg, Germany (second show)

10.04.70 The Lyceum, London, UK (tour rehearsal)

17.04.70 The Mammoth Gardens, Denver, USA
18.04.70 The Mammoth Gardens, Denver, USA
19.04.70 The Long Beach Arena, Long Beach, USA
22.04.70 The Santa Barbara Bowl, Santa Barbara, USA
24.04.70 The Swing Auditorium, San Bernardino, USA
25.04.70 The Convention Hall, San Diego, USA
26.04.70 The County Fairgrounds, Santa Clara, USA
28.04.70 The Civic Auditorium, Honolulu, USA
30.04.70 The Fillmore West, San Francisco, USA
01.05.70 The Fillmore West, San Francisco, USA
02.05.70 The Fillmore West, San Francisco, USA
03.05.70 The San Fernando College, Devonshire Downs, USA
07.05.70 The Sports Arena, Tucson, USA
08.05.70 The Phoenix High School Gym, Phoenix, USA
09.05.70 The Ice Palace, Las Vegas, USA
10.05.70 Washington University Field House, St Louis, USA
13.05.70 The State Fair Music Hall, Dallas, USA
14.05.70 The Houston Music Hall, Houston, USA
16.05.70 The Miami University, Miami, USA
17.05.70 The Hilton Convention Centre, Cape Kennedy, USA
20.05.70 The Bushnell Auditorium, Hartford, USA
21.05.70 The Fillmore East, New York, USA
22.05.70 The Fillmore East, New York, USA
23.05.70 The Fillmore East, New York, USA
24.05.70 The Autostade, Montreal, Canada
28.05.70 Selby Stadium, Wesleyan University, Delaware, USA
29.05.70 The East Town Theatre, Detroit, USA
30.05.70 The East Town Theatre, Detroit, USA
31.05.70 ?, Minneapolis, USA
05.06.70 The Aragon Ballroom, Chicago, USA
06.06.70 The Allen Theatre, Cleveland, USA
03.07.70 The Long Island University, Southampton, USA
07.07.70 The Tanglewood Festival, Tanglewood, USA
08.07.70 The Spectrum, Philadelphia, USA
10.07.70 The Boston Tea Party, Boston, USA
11.07.70 The Boston Tea Party, Boston, USA
13.07.70 The Shady Grove Music Fair, Shady Grove, USA
14.07.70 The Eastown Theatre, Detroit, USA
15.07.70 The Aragon Ballroom, Chicago, USA
16.07.70 The Spectrum, Philadelphia, USA
17.07.70 The Randall's Island Festival, New York, USA
18.07.70 The New Orleans Warehouse, New Orleans, USA

22.07.70 The Municipal Auditorium, West Palm Beach, USA
24.07.70 The Curtis Hixon Hall, Tampa, USA
25.07.70 Miami Beach Convention Hall, Miami Beach, USA
26.07.70 The Jacksonville Coliseum, Jacksonville, USA
27.07.70 The Music Fair, Westbury, USA
28.07.70 The Capitol Theatre, Port Chester, USA
01.08.70 The Powder Ridge Ski Area, Middlefield, USA (cancelled)
03.08.70 Central Park, New York, USA
05.08.70 The Fillmore East, New York, USA
06.08.70 The Fillmore East, New York, USA
07.08.70 The Strawberry Fields Festival, Mosport Park, Canada
09.08.70 Goose Lake Park Music Festival, Jackson, USA
10.08.70 The Red Rocks Amphitheatre Morrison, USA
11.08.70 The P.N.E. Coliseum, Vancouver, Canada
15.08.70 The Majestic, Lake Geneva, USA
16.08.70 The Aragon Ballroom, Chicago, USA
17.08.70 ?, Bluffs, USA
30.08.70 The Isle Of Wight Festival, Isle Of Wight, UK
23.09.70 The City Hall, Sheffield, UK
24.09.70 Nottingham, The Albert Hall, UK
25.09.70 The Town Hall, Birmingham, UK (first show)
25.09.70 The Town Hall, Birmingham, UK (second show)
27.09.70 The City Hall, Newcastle, UK
28.09.70 The De Montfort Hall, Leicester, UK
30.09.70 The Aberdeen Music Hall, Aberdeen, UK
01.10.70 The Caird Hall, Dundee, UK
02.10.70 The Playhouse Cinema, Glasgow, UK
03.10.70 The Free Trade Hall, Manchester, UK
04.10.70 The Colston Hall, Bristol, UK
09.10.70 The Guildhall, Southampton, UK
10.10.70 The Olympia, Paris, France
13.10.70 The Royal Albert Hall, London, UK
16.10.70 The Memorial Auditorium, Sacramento, USA
17.10.70 The Berkeley Community Theatre, Berkeley, USA
18.10.70 The Los Angeles Forum, Inglewood, USA
19.10.70 The Anaheim Convention Centre, Anaheim, USA
20.10.70 The Coliseum, Phoenix, USA
22.10.70 The Swing Auditorium, San Bernardino, USA
23.10.70 The Oregon State University, Corvallis, USA
24.10.70 The Seattle Arena, Seattle, USA
28.10.70 The Eastown Theatre, Detroit, USA
30.10.70 The Civic Arena, Pittsburgh, USA
31.10.70 The War Memorial Auditorium, Syracuse, USA
01.11.70 The Mosque, Richmond, USA
03.11.70 Comerford Paramount Theatre, Wilkes-Barre, USA (first show)
03.11.70 Comerford Paramount Theatre, Wilkes-Barre, USA (second show)
04.11.70 Carnegie Hall, New York, USA
05.11.70 The Rhode Island Auditorium, Providence, USA
06.11.70 St Anselms College, Manchester, USA
07.11.70 Michigan State University, Lansing, USA
08.11.70 The Kiel Opera House, St Louis, USA (first show)
08.11.70 The Kiel Opera House, St Louis, USA (second show)
09.11.70 The Ohio Theatre, Columbus, USA
10.11.70 The Baldwin-Wallace College Gym, Berea, USA
11.11.70 The St Lawrence University, Canton, USA
12.11.70 The War Memorial Auditorium, Buffalo, USA
13.11.70 The Union College, Schenectady, USA
14.11.70 The War Memorial Auditorium, Rochester, USA
15.11.70 The State University Of New York, Plattsburg, USA

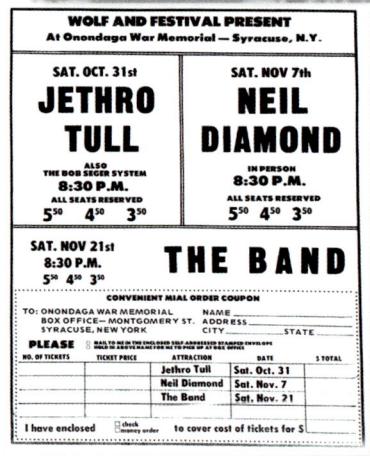

1971

By January 1971, Jethro Tull were Ian Anderson, Martin Barre, Clive Bunker, John Evan and Jeffrey Hammond-Hammond. The band continued with this line-up until May 1971.

07.01.71 The Fyns Forum, Odense, Denmark
08.01.71 The Marselisborg Hallen, Arhaus, Denmark
09.01.71 The K.B. Hallen, Copenhagen, Denmark
10.01.71 The Konsertuset, Gothenburg, Sweden
11.01.71 The Njardhallen, Oslo, Norway
12.01.71 The Konsertuset, Bergen, Norway
14.01.71 The Konserthus Stockholm, Sweden
15.01.71 The Tivoli Konsertsal, Copenhagen, Denmark
16.01.71 The Holstebro, Holsted, Denmark
17.01.71 The Musichalle, Hamberg, Germany
18.01.71 The Rheinhalle, Düsseldorf, Germany
19.01.71 The Sporthalle Boblingen, Stuttgart, Germany
20.01.71 The Meistersinger Halle, Nurnberg, Germany
21.01.71 The Konzerthaus, Vienna, Austria
22.01.71 The Deutsches Museum, Munich, Germany (first show)
22.01.71 The Deutsches Museum, Munich, Germany (second show)
23.01.71 The Kongresshalle, Frankfurt, Germany
24.01.71 The Deutschlandhalle, Berlin, Germany
25.01.71 The Stadthalle, Wolfsburg, Germany
26.01.71 Munsterlandhalle, Munster, Germany
27.01.71 The Westfalenhalle, Dortmund, Germany
28.01.71 The Stadthalle, Heidelberg, Germany
29.01.71 The Stadthalle, Freiburg, Germany
30.01.71 The Altes Casino, Montreux, Switzerland
01.02.71 The Teatro Smeraldo, Milan, Italy
02.02.71 The Teatro Brangaccio, Rome, Italy (first show)
02.02.71 The Teatro Brangaccio, Rome, Italy (second show)
26.02.71 The Gaumont State Theatre, London, UK (first show)
26.02.71 The Gaumont State Theatre, London, UK (second show)
28.02.71 The Gaumont State Theatre, London, UK (first show)
28.02.71 The Gaumont State Theatre, London, UK (second show)
03.03.71 The Dome, Brighton, UK
05.03.71 The Winter Gardens, Bournemouth, UK
07.03.71 The Guildhall, Plymouth, UK (first show)
07.03.71 The Guildhall, Plymouth, UK (second show)
11.03.71 The Town Hall, Leeds, UK
12.03.71 The Victoria Guildhall, Stoke on Trent, UK
13.03.71 The Mountford Hall, Liverpool, UK (first show)
13.03.71 The Mountford Hall, Liverpool, UK (second show)
14.03.71 The Opera House, Blackpool, UK
19.03.71 The Empire Theatre, Edinburgh, UK
20.03.71 The Empire Theatre, Sunderland, UK (first show)
20.03.71 The Empire Theatre, Sunderland, UK (second show)
01.04.71 The Tyrone Guthrie Theatre, Minneapolis, USA (first show)
01.04.71 The Tyrone Guthrie Theatre, Minneapolis, USA (second show)
02.04.71 The Civic Opera House, Chicago, USA
03.04.71 The Kiel Convention Hall, St Louis, USA
04.04.71 The Civic Centre, Baltimore, USA
05.04.71 The Fillmore East, New York, USA (first show)
05.04.71 The Fillmore East, New York, USA (second show)
06.04.71 The Fillmore East, New York, USA (first show)
06.04.71 The Fillmore East, New York, USA (second show)
10.04.71 The Cincinnati Gardens, Cincinnati, USA
13.04.71 The Municipal Auditorium, Atlanta, USA
14.04.71 The Uihlein, Milwaukee, USA (first show)
14.04.71 The Uihlein, Milwaukee, USA (second show)
16.04.71 Pirates World Park, Dania, USA
17.04.71 Pirates World Park, Dania, USA

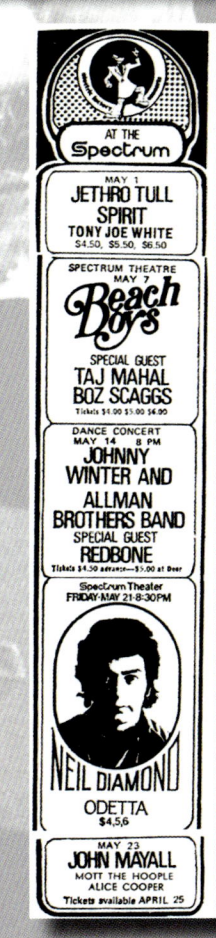

18.04.71 The Civic Centre, Roanoke, USA
20.04.71 The State Fairground Coliseum, Detroit, USA
22.04.71 The Robertson Memorial Field House, Peoria, USA
24.04.71 The Monmouth College, West Long Beach, USA
25.04.71 The New York State University, Stony Brook, USA
26.04.71 The C.W. Post College Dome, Greenville, USA
27.04.71 The Capitol Theatre, Port Chester, USA (first show)
27.04.71 The Capitol Theatre, Port Chester, USA (second show)
29.04.71 The New York State University, Delhi, USA
01.05.71 The Philadelphia Spectrum, Philadelphia, USA
02.05.71 The Kutztown University Hall, Kutztown, USA
04.05.71 The Fillmore East, New York, USA (first show)
04.05.71 The Fillmore East, New York, USA (second show)
05.05.71 The Fillmore East, New York, USA (first show)
05.05.71 The Fillmore East, New York, USA (second show)

From May 1971, Jethro Tull were Ian Anderson, Martin Barre, John Evan, Jeffrey Hammond-Hammond and Barriemore Barlow. The band continued with this line-up until December 1975.

09.06.71 The Salt Palace, Salt Lake City, USA
10.06.71 The Red Rocks Amphitheatre, Morrison, USA
11.06.71 The Civic Auditorium, Albuquerque, USA
12.06.71 The Hic Arena, Albuquerque, USA
16.06.71 The San Diego Convention Centre, San Diego, USA
17.06.71 The San Diego Convention Centre, San Diego, USA
18.06.71 The Los Angeles Forum, Los Angeles, USA
19.06.71 The Anaheim Convention Centre, Anaheim, USA
20.06.71 The Berkeley Community Theatre, Berkeley, USA
24.06.71 The Gardens, Edmonton, Canada
25.06.71 The Pacific Coliseum, Vancouver, Canada
26.06.71 The Seattle Coliseum, Seattle, USA
27.06.71 Memorial Auditorium, Sacramento, USA
29.06.71 The Kansas City Auditorium, Kansas City, USA
30.06.71 The Oklahoma City State Fairgrounds, Oklahoma City, USA
01.07.71 The Municipal Auditorium, San Antonio, USA
02.07.71 The Dallas Memorial Auditorium, Dallas, USA
03.07.71 The Sam Houston Coliseum, Houston, USA
04.07.71 The Warehouse, New Orleans, USA
05.07.71 The National Guard Armoury, Indianapolis, USA
07.07.71 The Sports Stadium, Orlando, USA
08.07.71 The Casino Ballroom, Hampton Beach, USA
09.07.71 The Wildwood Convention Centre, Wildwood, USA
10.07.71 The Ashbury Park Convention Centre, Ashbury Park, USA
11.07.71 The Alexandria Roller Rink, Alexandria, USA
14.07.71 The Fox Theatre, Hackensack, USA
15.07.71 The Bayfront Centre, St Petersburg, USA
16.07.71 The Civic Centre, Jacksonville, USA
17.07.71 The Coliseum, Charlotte, USA
18.07.71 Madison Square Garden, New York, USA
19.07.71 The Civic Centre, Springfield, USA
21.07.71 The Civic Arena, Pittsburgh, USA
22.07.71 The Jenison Field House University, East Lansing, USA
23.07.71 The St John Veterans Arena, Columbus, USA
24.07.71 The Hara Arena, Dayton, USA
25.07.71 The Sports Arena, Ohio, USA
26.07.71 The Chicago Amphitheatre, Chicago, USA
27.07.71 The University Assembly Hall, Champaign, USA
28.07.71 The New Haven Arena, New Haven, USA
29.07.71 The Exposition Centre, Portland, USA
30.10.71 The Rochester War Memorial, Rochester, USA
31.10.71 The Harper College, Binghamton, USA
01.11.71 The Memorial Auditorium, Buffalo, USA
03.11.71 The Lowell Technical College, Lowell, USA

05.11.71 The W & M College Field House, Williamsburg, USA
06.11.71 The Carmichael Auditorium, North Carolina University, Chapel Hill, USA
07.11.71 The East Carolina University Coliseum, Greenville, USA
08.11.71 The Coliseum, Greensboro, USA
09.11.71 The Bradley University Field House, Peoria, USA
10.11.71 The Ima Sports Arena, Flint, USA
11.11.71 The Mid South Coliseum, Memphis, USA
12.11.71 The Louisville Convention Centre, Louisville, USA
13.11.71 The Cleveland Public Hall, Cleveland, USA
14.11.71 The Civic Centre, Baltimore, USA
15.11.71 The Boston Tea Gardens, Boston, USA
16.11.71 The Palace Theatre, Albany, USA
18.11.71 Madison Square Garden, New York, USA

1972

06.01.72 The Holstelbrohallen, Holstelbro, Denmark
07.01.72 The Fyns Forum, Odense, Denmark
08.01.72 The KB Hallen, Copenhagen, Denmark (first show)
08.01.72 The KB Hallen, Copenhagen, Denmark (second show)
09.01.72 The Konserthuset, Gothenburg, Sweden
10.01.72 The Konserthuset, Oslo, Norway
11.01.72 The Konserthus, Stockholm, Sweden
14.01.72 Lund University Akademiska Foreningen, Lund, Sweden
15.01.72 The Tivoli Konsertsal, Copenhagen, Denmark
16.01.72 The Tivoli Konsertsal, Copenhagen, Denmark
17.01.72 The Munsterlandhalle, Munster, Germany
18.01.72 The Deutchlandhalle, Berlin, Germany
19.01.72 The Musikhalle Grosser Saal, Hamburg, Germany
20.01.72 The Hansahalle, Lubeck, Germany
21.01.72 The Grugahalle, Essen, Germany
22.01.72 The Stadthalle, Offenbach, Germany
23.01.72 The Meistersingerhalle, Nurnburg, Germany
24.01.72 The Konserthaus, Vienna, Austria
25.01.72 The Meistersingerhalle, Nurnburg, Germany (cancelled)
26.01.72 The Frederich-Ebert Halle, Ludwigshafen, Germany
27.01.72 The Niedersachsenhalle, Hannover, Germany
28.01.72 The Oberheinhalle, Offenburg, Germany
29.01.72 The Hallenstadion, Zurich, Switzerland
30.01.72 The Festhalle, Berne, Switzerland
31.01.72 ?, Milan, Italy
01.02.72 The Palasport, Rome, Italy
02.02.72 Palazzo Dello Sport, Bologna, Italy (first show at 17:30)
02.02.72 Palazzo Dello Sport, Bologna, Italy (second show at 21:00)
03.02.72 The Bocciodromo Ovest, or 05be, The Palazzo Dello Sport, Italy
04.02.72 Palazzo Dello Sport, Varese, Italy
05.02.72 Palazzo Dello Sport, Novaro, Italy
06.02.72 ?, Paris, France
11.02.72 The De Doelen, Rotterdam, Holland
12.02.72 The Concertgebouw, Amsterdam, Holland
02.03.72 The Guildhall, Portsmouth, UK
03.03.72 The Abc Cinema, Exeter, UK
04.03.72 The Guildhall, Plymouth, UK
05.03.72 The Colston Hall, Bristol, UK
06.03.72 The Town Hall, Birmingham, UK
07.03.72 The City Hall, Newcastle, UK
08.03.72 The University Central Hall, York, UK
10.03.72 The Winter Gardens, Bournemouth, UK
11.03.72 The City Hall, Sheffield, UK
13.03.72 The St Andrews Hall, Norwich, UK
14.03.72 The De Montfort Hall, Leicester, UK
15.03.72 The St Georges Hall, Bradford, UK

16.03.72 The Victoria Hall, Stoke on Trent, UK
17.03.72 The Abc Cinema, Stockton, UK
19.03.72 The Civic Hall, Wolverhampton, UK
20.03.72 The Town Hall, Oxford, UK
21.03.72 The Royal Albert Hall, London, UK
22.03.72 The Royal Albert Hall, London, UK
24.03.72 The Empire Theatre, Edinburgh, UK
25.03.72 The Caird Hall, Dundee, UK
26.03.72 The Playhouse Cinema, Glasgow, UK
27.03.72 The Liverpool Stadium, Liverpool, UK
28.03.72 The Free Trade Hall, Manchester, UK
29.03.72 The Royal Albert Hall, London, UK
14.04.72 The Forum, Montreal, Canada
15.04.72 The Varden Hall, Cornell University, Ithaca, USA
16.04.72 The War Memorial Auditorium, Syracuse, USA
17.04.72 Capitol Plaza Convention Centre, Frankfort, USA
18.04.72 The High School Hall, Lorain, USA
19.04.72 Cumberland County Auditorium, Fayetteville, USA
20.04.72 The Dorton Arena, Raleigh, USA
21.04.72 The University of Alabama, Tuscaloosa, USA
22.04.72 The Norfolk Scope, Norfolk, USA
23.04.72 The Salem Valley Civic Centre, Salem, USA
24.04.72 The Memorial Hall Bowling Green State University, Bowling Green, USA
25.04.72 The West Virginia University Hall, Morgantown, USA
26.04.72 The Tech University Hall, Blacksburg, USA
27.04.72 The Municipal Auditorium, Atlanta, USA
28.04.72 University of Georgia Coliseum, Athens, USA
29.04.72 The Auditorium, West Palm Beach, USA
30.04.72 The Marine Stadium, Miami Beach, USA
01.05.72 The Municipal Auditorium, New Orleans, USA
02.05.72 The Coliseum, Indianapolis, USA
03.05.72 The Dane County Coliseum, Madison, USA
04.05.72 The Southern Illinois University, Carbondale, USA
05.05.72 The Kiel Convention Hall, St Louis, USA
06.05.72 The Stokely Athletic Centre, Knoxville, USA
07.05.72 The Stadium Amphitheatre, Chicago, USA
08.05.72 The Cobo Hall, Detroit, USA
09.05.72 The Gardens, Cincinnati, USA
10.05.72 The Sports Centre, Hershey, USA
11.05.72 The Spectrum, Philadelphia, USA
12.05.72 The Tea Gardens, Boston, USA
13.05.72 The Nassau Veterans Coliseum, Uniondale, USA
14.05.72 The Nassau Veterans Coliseum, Uniondale, USA
02.06.72 The Quebec Coliseum, Quebec, Canada
03.06.72 The Civic Centre, Ottawa, Canada
04.06.72 The Maple Leaf Gardens, Toronto, Canada
06.06.72 The Milwaukee Arena, Milwaukee, USA
07.06.72 ?, Duluth, USA
08.06.72 The Gardens, Edmonton, Canada
09.06.72 The Stampede Corral, Calgary, Canada
10.06.72 The Pacific Coliseum, Vancouver, Canada
11.06.72 Seattle Centre Coliseum, Seattle, USA
12.06.72 The Memorial Coliseum, Portland, USA
14.06.72 Oklahoma City State Fairgrounds, Oklahoma City, USA
15.06.72 The Municipal Auditorium, Kansas City, USA
16.06.72 The Coliseum, Oakland, USA
17.06.72 The Convention Centre, Las Vegas, USA
18.06.72 The Dallas Memorial Coliseum, Dallas, USA
19.06.72 The Sam Houston Coliseum, Houston, USA
20.06.72 The Convention Centre Arena, San Antonio, USA
21.06.72 ?, El Paso, USA
22.06.72 ?, Albuquerque, USA
23.06.72 The Forum, Los Angeles, USA

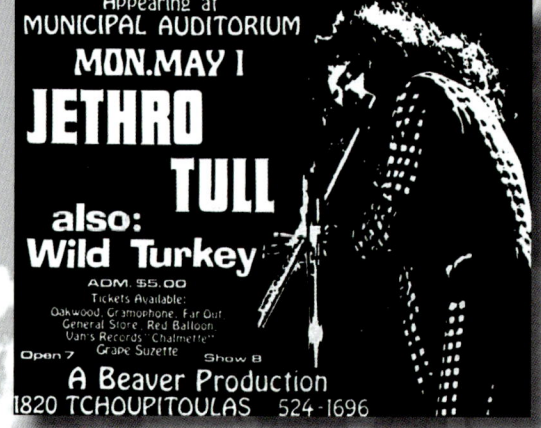

24.06.72 The Forum, Los Angeles, USA
25.06.72 The San Diego Sports Arena, San Diego, USA
26.06.72 The Community Centre Arena, Tucson, USA
27.06.72 ?, Phoenix, USA
28.06.72 The Salt Palace, Salt Lake City, USA
29.06.72 The Denver Coliseum, Denver, USA
30.06.72 The Denver Coliseum, Denver, USA
01.07.72 The Hic Arena, Honolulu, USA
05.07.72 The Town Hall, Auckland, New Zealand
07.07.72 The Festival Hall, Melbourne, Australia
08.07.72 The Apollo Stadium, Adelaide, Australia
09.07.72 The Festival Hall, Melbourne, Australia
11.07.72 The Horden Pavilion, Sydney, Australia
12.07.72 The Horden Pavilion, Sydney, Australia
13.07.72 The Horden Pavilion, Sydney, Australia
14.07.72 The Festival Hall, Brisbane, Australia
15.07.72 The Koseinenkin Kaikan, Tokyo, Japan
16.07.72 The Budokan, Tokyo, Japan
17.07.72 The Kouseinemkin Kaikan Dai Hall, Osaka, Japan
13.10.72 The Buffalo Memorial Auditorium, Buffalo, USA
14.10.72 The Rochester War Memorial, Rochester USA
15.10.72 The Bangor Auditorium, Bangor, USA
16.10.72 The Springfield Civic Centre, Springfield, USA
17.10.72 The Civic Arena, Pittsburgh, USA
18.10.72 The Civic Centre, Charleston, USA
19.10.72 The South Carolina Coliseum, Columbia, USA
21.10.72 The Cleveland Public Hall, Cleveland, USA
22.10.72 The Mid-South Coliseum, Memphis, USA
23.10.72 The Barton Coliseum, Little Rock USA
24.10.72 The Municipal Auditorium, Nashville, USA
25.10.72 The Louisville Convention Centre, Louisville, USA
26.10.72 West Kentucky University, Diddle Arena, Bowling Green, USA
27.10.72 The Mississippi Coliseum, Jackson, USA
28.10.72 The Louisiana State University, Baton Rouge, USA
29.10.72 The Macon Coliseum, Macon, USA
30.10.72 The Spectrum, Philadelphia, USA
31.10.72 The Spectrum, Philadelphia, USA
01.11.72 The Boston Gardens, Boston, USA
02.11.72 The Boston Gardens, Boston, USA
03.11.72 The Bayfront Centre, St Petersburg, USA
04.11.72 The Convention Hall, Miami Beach, USA
05.11.72 The Jacksonville Coliseum, Jacksonville, USA
06.11.72 The Civic Centre Arena, Savannah, USA
07.11.72 The Allen County Memorial Coliseum, Fort Wayne, USA
08.11.72 The Detroit Cobo Hall, Detroit, USA
09.11.72 The Detroit Cobo Hall, Detroit, USA
10.11.72 The Chicago Stadium, Chicago, USA
11.11.72 The Chicago Stadium, Chicago, USA
12.11.72 The Baltimore Civic Centre, Baltimore, USA
13.11.72 The Madison Square Garden, New York, USA
07.12.72 The Convocation Centre, Athens, USA
08.12.72 The Madison Square Garden, New York, USA

1973

29.01.73 The Stadthalle, Vienna, Austria
02.02.73 The Festhalle, Frankfurt, Germany
04.02.73 The Hallenstadion, Zurich, Switzerland
02.03.73 ?, Gothenburg, Sweden
04.03.73 The Brondby Hallen, Copenhagen, Denmark
06.03.73 The Congress Centrum Halle, Hamburg Germany
07.03.73 The Congress Centrum Halle, Hamburg Germany
08.03.73 The Munsterlandhalle, Munster, Germany
09.03.73 The Philipshalle, Düsseldorf, Germany
11.03.73 The Deutschlandhalle, Berlin, Germany
13.03.73 The Olympiahalle, Munich, Germany
15.03.73 The Palasport, Vicenza, Italy
16.03.73 The Palazzo Dello Sport, Rome, Italy
18.03.73 The Palasport, Bologna, Italy
19.03.73 The Palasport, Bologna, Italy
20.03.73 ?, Milan, Italy
26.03.73 The Phillipshalle, Düsseldorf, Germany
28.03.73 Empire Pool Wembley, London, UK (postponed)
29.03.73 Empire Pool Wembley, London, UK (postponed)
04.05.73 The Roberts Stadium, Evansville, USA
05.05.73 The Clemson University Coliseum, Clemson, USA
07.05.73 The War Memorial, Johnstown, USA
09.05.73 The Millet Hall, Miami University, Oxford, USA
11.05.73 The Scope, Norfolk, USA
13.05.73 The Civic Coliseum, Knoxville, USA
14.05.73 The Louisville Convention Centre, Louisville, USA
15.05.73 The Jenison Field House, East Lansing, USA
16.05.73 The Hershey Park Arena, Hershey, USA
17.05.73 The Hofstra University, Hempstead, USA
18.05.73 The Richmond Coliseum, Richmond, USA
19.05.73 The Coliseum, Greensboro, USA
20.05.73 The Omni, Atlanta, USA
21.05.73 The Municipal Auditorium, Nashville, USA
22.05.73 The Indiana Convention Expo Centre, Indianapolis, USA
23.05.73 The Kiel Convention Hall, St Louis, USA
24.05.73 The Kiel Convention Hall, St Louis, USA
24.05.73 The Assembly Centre, Tulsa, USA
29.05.73 The Memorial Auditorium, Kitchener, Canada
30.05.73 The Maple Leaf Gardens, Toronto, Canada
31.05.73 The Civic Centre Lansdowne Arena, Ottawa, Canada
01.06.73 The Coliseum, Quebec City, Canada
02.06.73 The Forum, Montreal, Canada
22.06.73 The Empire Pool Wembley, London, UK
23.06.73 The Empire Pool Wembley, London, UK
30.06.73 The War Memorial Auditorium, Syracuse, USA
01.07.73 The Memorial Auditorium, Buffalo, USA
03.07.73 The Metropolitan Sports Centre Arena, Minneapolis, USA
04.07.73 The Municipal Auditorium, Kansas City, USA
07.07.73 The Berkeley Community Theatre, Berkeley, USA
08.07.73 ?, Albuquerque, USA
09.07.73 The Denver Coliseum, Denver, USA
10.07.73 The State Fair Arena, Oklahoma City, USA
12.07.73 The Convention Centre Auditorium, Dallas, USA
13.07.73 The Convention Centre Arena, San Antonio, USA
14.07.73 Sam Houston Coliseum, Houston, USA (postponed until 1st August)
15.07.73 Sam Houston Coliseum, Houston, USA
16.07.73 Tarrant County Convention Centre, Fort Worth, USA
18.07.73 The Los Angeles Forum, Inglewood, USA
19.07.73 The San Diego Sports Arena, San Diego, USA
20.07.73 The Los Angeles Forum, Inglewood, USA
21.07.73 The Los Angeles Forum, Inglewood, USA

22.07.73 The Los Angeles Forum, Inglewood, USA
23.07.73 The Oakland Coliseum, Oakland, USA
24.07.73 The Pacific Coliseum, Vancouver, Canada
25.07.73 The Seattle Coliseum, Seattle, USA
26.07.73 The Seattle Coliseum, Seattle, USA
27.07.73 The Seattle Coliseum, Seattle, USA
28.07.73 The Memorial Coliseum, Portland, USA
30.07.73 The Salt Palace, Salt Lake City, USA
01.08.73 Sam Houston Coliseum, Houston, USA (rescheduled from 14th July)
26.08.73 The Civic Centre, Baltimore, USA
27.08.73 The Civic Centre, Baltimore, USA
28.08.73 The Madison Square Gardens, New York, USA
29.08.73 The Madison Square Gardens, New York, USA
30.08.73 The Providence Civic Centre, Providence, USA
31.08.73 The Nassau Coliseum, Uniondale, USA
01.09.73 The Nassau Coliseum, Uniondale, USA
03.09.73 The Dane County Coliseum, Madison, USA
04.09.73 The Chicago Stadium, Chicago, USA
05.09.73 The Chicago Stadium, Chicago, USA
06.09.73 The Detroit Cobo Hall, Detroit, USA
08.09.73 The Cleveland Public Hall, Cleveland, USA
09.09.73 The Cleveland Public Hall, Cleveland, USA
10.09.73 The War Memorial Auditorium, Rochester, USA
11.09.73 The Pittsburgh Civic Arena, Pittsburgh, USA
12.09.73 The Pittsburgh Civic Arena, Pittsburgh, USA (cancelled)
13.09.73 The Detroit Cobo Hall, Detroit, USA
14.09.73 The Detroit Cobo Hall, Detroit, USA
15.09.73 The Milwaukee Arena, Milwaukee, USA
17.09.73 The Hirsch Coliseum, Shreveport, USA
18.09.73 The Municipal Auditorium, New Orleans, USA
19.09.73 The Municipal Auditorium, New Orleans, USA
20.09.73 The Municipal Auditorium, Mobile, USA
21.09.73 The Coliseum, Jacksonville, USA
22.09.73 The Bayfront Centre, St Petersburg, USA
23.09.73 The Jai Alai Fronton, Miami, USA
24.09.73 The Jai Alai Fronton, Miami, USA
26.09.73 The Civic Centre Coliseum, Roanoke, USA
27.09.73 The Springfield Civic Centre, Springfield, USA
28.09.73 The Boston Tea Gardens, Boston, USA
29.09.73 The Boston Tea Gardens, Boston, USA

1974

25.07.74 The Centennial Hall, Adelaide, Australia
28.07.74 The Festival Hall, Melbourne, Australia
29.07.74 The Festival Hall, Melbourne, Australia
30.07.74 The Sydney Opera House, Sydney, Australia
31.07.74 The Sydney Opera House, Sydney, Australia
01.08.74 The Festival Hall, Brisbane, Australia
02.08.74 The Festival Hall, Brisbane, Australia
03.08.74 The Hordern Pavilion, Sydney, Australia
04.08.74 The Hordern Pavilion, Sydney, Australia
05.08.74 The Hordern Pavilion, Sydney, Australia
10.08.74 The Civic Theatre, Auckland, New Zealand
11.08.74 The Civic Theatre, Auckland, New Zealand
12.08.74 The Town Stage Hall, Christchurch, New Zealand
13.08.74 The Town Stage Hall, Christchurch, New Zealand
17.08.74 The Kosei Nenkin Kaikan, Tokyo, Japan
18.08.74 The Nagoya City Koukaido, Nagoya, Japan
19.08.74 The Nagoya City Koukaido, Kyoto, Japan
21.08.74 The Kaikan Dai Hall, Osaka, Japan
23.08.74 The NHK Hall, Tokyo, Japan

1974 Japan Tour Programme

24.08.74 The NHK Hall, Tokyo, Japan
25.08.74 The NHK Hall, Tokyo, Japan
26.08.74 The NHK Hall, Tokyo, Japan
28.08.74 The NHK Hall, Tokyo, Japan
12.10.74 The Ahoy Hall, Rotterdam, Holland
13.10.74 The Voorst National, Brussels, Belgium
14.10.74 The Voorst National, Brussels, Belgium
16.10.74 The Palais Des Sportes, Grenoble, France
17.10.74 The Palais Des Sportes, Grenoble, France
18.10.74 ?, Marseille, France
19.10.74 The Parc Des Expositions, Colmar, France
23.10.74 The Pabellon De Desportes, Madrid, Spain
24.10.74 The Pabellon De Desportes, Madrid, Spain
25.10.74 The Pabellon De Desportes, Madrid, Spain
09.11.74 The Usher Hall, Edinburgh, UK
10.11.74 The Usher Hall, Edinburgh, UK
11.11.74 The Apollo Theatre, Glasgow, UK
12.11.74 The Apollo Theatre, Glasgow, UK
13.11.74 The Odeon, Newcastle, UK
14.11.74 The Rainbow Theatre, London, UK
15.11.74 The Rainbow Theatre, London, UK
16.11.74 The Rainbow Theatre, London, UK
17.11.74 The Rainbow Theatre, London, UK
18.11.74 The Colston Hall, Bristol, UK
19.11.74 The Odeon, Birmingham, UK
20.11.74 The Odeon, Birmingham, UK
21.11.74 The Empire Theatre, Liverpool, UK
22.11.74 The Opera House, Manchester, UK
23.11.74 The Opera House, Manchester, UK
24.11.74 The New Theatre, Oxford, UK
25.11.74 The Capitol Theatre, Cardiff, UK
26.11.74 The Guildhall, Portsmouth, UK (cancelled but replaced with a date at Southampton)
26.11.74 The Gaumont Theatre, Southampton, UK
30.11.74 The Scandinavium, Gothenburg, Sweden
01.12.74 ?, Malmo, Sweden
02.12.74 The Olympen, Lund, Sweden
04.12.74 The Falkonerteatret, Copenhagen, Denmark
05.12.74 The Falkonerteatret, Copenhagen, Denmark

1975

17.01.75 The Asheville Civic Centre, Asheville, USA
19.01.75 The Memorial Coliseum, Tuscaloosa, USA
20.01.75 The Atlanta Omni, Atlanta, USA
21.01.75 The Mid South Coliseum, Memphis, USA
22.01.75,The City State Fairgrounds, Oklahoma City, USA
23.01.75 The Convention Centre Arena, Fort Worth, USA
24.01.75 Hemisfair Convention Centre Arena, San Antonio, USA
26.01.75 The Assembly Centre, Tulsa, USA
27.01.75 The Pershing Auditorium, Lincoln, USA
28.01.75 The Kemper Arena, Kansas City, USA
29.01.75 The Arena, St Louis, USA
31.01.75 The San Diego Sports Arena, San Diego, USA
01.02.75 The San Diego Sports Arena, San Diego, USA
02.02.75 The Selland Arena, Fresno, USA
03.02.75 The Los Angeles Forum, Inglewood, USA
04.02.75 The Los Angeles Forum, Inglewood, USA
05.02.75 The Community Centre Arena, Tuscon, USA
06.02.75 El Paso Civic Centre, El Paso, USA
08.02.75 The Los Angeles Forum, Inglewood, USA
09.02.75 The Los Angeles Forum, Inglewood, USA
10.02.75 The Los Angeles Forum, Inglewood, USA
16.02.75 Dane County Coliseum, Madison, USA

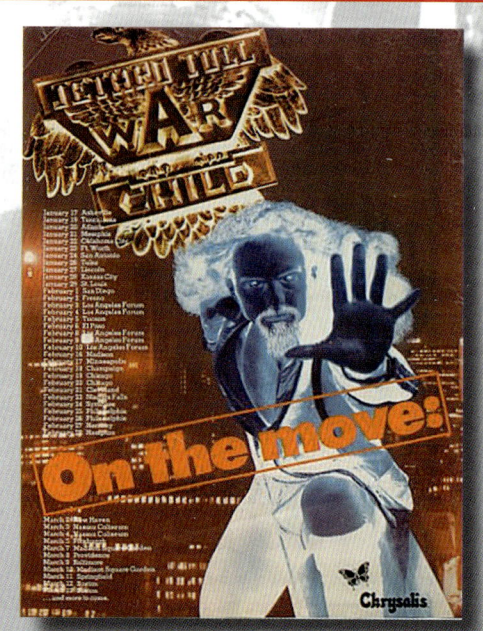

17.02.75 The Metropolitan Sports Centre, Minneapolis, USA
18.02.75 The Assembly Hall Illinois University, Champaign, USA
19.02.75 The Chicago Stadium, Chicago, USA
20.02.75 The Chicago Stadium, Chicago, USA
21.02.75 The Richfield Coliseum, Cleveland, USA
23.02.75 The International Convention Centre, Niagara Falls USA
24.02.75 The War Memorial Centre, Syracuse, USA
25.02.75 The Spectrum, Philadelphia, USA
26.02.75 The Spectrum, Philadelphia, USA
27.02.75 The Hershey Park Arena, Hershey, USA
28.02.75 The Hampton Roads Coliseum, Hampton Roads, USA
02.03.75 The Veterans Memorial Coliseum, New Haven, USA
03.03.75 The Nassau Coliseum, Uniondale, USA
04.03.75 The Nassau Coliseum, Uniondale, USA
05.03.75 The Civic Arena, Pittsburgh, USA
06.03.75 The Spectrum, Philadelphia, USA
07.03.75 The Madison Square Garden, New York, USA
08.03.75 The Providence Civic Centre, Providence, USA
09.03.75 The Baltimore Civic Centre, Baltimore, USA
10.03.75 The Madison Square Garden, New York, USA
11.03.75 The Springfield Civic Centre, Springfield, USA
12.03.75 The Boston Tea Gardens, Boston, USA
13.03.75 The Boston Tea Gardens, Boston, USA
30.03.75 The Deutschlandhalle, Berlin, Germany
01.04.75 The Ostseehalle, Kiel, Germany
05.04.75 The Festhalle, Frankfurt, Germany
07.04.75 Cologne, The Sporthalle, Germany
08.04.75 The Grugahalle, Essen, Germany
09.04.75 The Schwarzwaldhalle, Karlsruhe, Germany
10.04.75 The Freidrich-Ebert-Halle, Ludwigshafen, Germany
11.04.75 The Festhalle, Frankfurt, Germany
14.04.75 The Hala Pionir, Beograd, Yugoslavia
15.04.75 The Hala Tivoli, Ljubljana, Yugoslavia
16.04.75 The Dom Sportova, Zagreb, Yugoslavia
17.04.75 The Wienstadthalle, Vienna, Austria
18.04.75 The Olympiahalle, Munich, Germany
20.04.75 The Hallenstadion, Zurich, Switzerland
29.06.75 The Congress Centrum Hall, Hamburg, Germany
30.06.75 The Munsterlandhalle, Munster, Germany
01.07.75 The Munsterlandhalle, Munster, Germany
02.07.75 The Phillipshalle, Düsseldorf, Germany
03.07.75 The Boblingen Sportshalle, Boblingen, Germany
05.07.75 The Palais Des Sportes, Paris, France
24.07.75 Pacific National Exhibition Coliseum, Vancouver, Canada
26.07.75 The Memorial Coliseum, Portland, USA
27.07.75 The Seattle Coliseum, Seattle, USA
28.07.75 The Oakland Coliseum, Oakland, USA
30.07.75 The Salt Palace, Salt Lake City, USA
01.08.75 The Dallas Convention Centre, Dallas, USA
02.08.75 The Sam Houston Coliseum, Houston, USA
03.08.75 The Madison Square Garden, New York, USA
06.08.75 The Nashville Municipal Auditorium, Nashville, USA
07.08.75 The Boutwell Auditorium, Birmingham, USA
09.08.75 The Coliseum, Greensboro, USA
11.08.75 The Gardens, Louisville, USA
12.08.75 The Civic Centre, Charleston, USA
13.08.75 The Richmond Coliseum, Richmond, USA
14.08.75 The Memorial Auditorium, Chattanooga, USA
15.08.75 The Civic Centre Coliseum, Roanoke, USA
16.08.75 The Coliseum, Charlotte, USA
17.08.75 The Coliseum, Macon, USA
18.08.75 The Von Braun Civic Centre, Huntsville, USA
19.08.75 The Carolina Coliseum, Columbia, USA
20.08.75 The Civic Coliseum, Knoxville, USA
21.08.75 The Freedom Hall Civic Centre, Johnson City, USA
23.08.75 The Mississippi Coliseum, Jackson, USA

24.08.75 The Municipal Auditorium, Mobile, USA
25.08.75 The Coliseum, Jacksonville, USA
27.08.75 The Bayfront Centre, St Petersburg, USA
28.08.75 The Jai Alai Fronton, Miami, USA
29.08.75 The Jai Alai Fronton, Miami, USA
30.08.75 The Civic Centre Arena, Lakeland, USA
26.09.75 The War Memorial Auditorium, Buffalo, USA
27.09.75 The War Memorial Auditorium, Buffalo, USA
29.09.75 The Montreal Forum, Montreal, Canada
01.10.75 The Capitol Centre, Largo, USA
02.10.75 Broome County Veterans Memorial Arena, Binghamton, USA
04.10.75 The Riverfront Coliseum, Cincinnati, USA
05.10.75 The Detroit Cobo Hall, Detroit, USA
06.10.75 The Detroit Cobo Hall, Detroit, USA
07.10.75 The Maple Leaf Gardens, Toronto, Canada
08.10.75 The Wings Stadium, Kalamazoo, USA
09.10.75 The Detroit Cobo Hall, Detroit, USA
12.10.75 The Jenisen Field House, East Lansing, USA
13.10.75 The Des Moines Veterans Stadium, Des Moines, USA
15.10.75 The Magaw Hall, Evanston, USA
16.10.75 The Evans Field House, DeKalb, USA
17.10.75 The Indiana State University, Terre Haute, USA
18.10.75 The Kansas State University, Manhattan, USA
19.10.75 Joliet High School Gym, Joliet, USA
21.10.75 Horton Field House, Illinois State University, Normal, USA
22.10.75 The Sports Arena, Toledo, USA
23.10.75 The Lafayette College Hall, Easton, USA
24.10.75 The Kent State University, Kent, USA
26.10.7 The University Of Iowa, Iowa City, USA
27.10.75 The Milwaukee Arena, Milwaukee, USA
28.10.75 The Dane County Coliseum, Madison, USA
29.10.75 ?, Omaha, USA
30.10.75 The Fairgrounds Coliseum, Columbus, USA
31.10.75 The Indiana University Assembly Hall, Bloomington, USA
01.11.75 The University Of Notre Dame, South Bend, USA
02.11.75 Purdue University Hall, West Lafayette, USA
03.11.75 The St John Arena, Columbus, USA

By December 1975, Jethro Tull were Ian Anderson, Martin Barre, John Evan, Barriemore Barlow and John Glascock. This line-up would continue until May 1976.

1976

From May 1976 to August 1979, Jethro Tull were Ian Anderson, Martin Barre, John Evan, Barriemore Barlow, David Palmer and John Glascock (with Tony Williams filling in for when Glascock was ill).

01.05.76 The Vorst National, Brussels, Belgium
03.05.76 The Pavillion De Paris, Paris, France
05.05.76 The Ahoy Hall, Rotterdam, Holland
08.05.76 The Konserthuset, Stockholm, Sweden
09.05.76 The Konserthuset, Stockholm, Sweden
10.05.76 The Tivoli Konsertsal, Copenhagen, Denmark
12.05.76 The Congress Centrum Halle, Hamburg, Germany
14.05.76 Festhalle, Frankfurt, Germany
15.05.76 The Olympiahalle, Munich, Germany
16.05.76 The Hallenstadion, Zurich, Switzerland
18.05.76 The Pabellon Del Juventas De Barcelona, Barcelona, Spain
20.05.76 The Pabellon Deportivo, Madrid, Spain
15.07.76 The Providence Civic Centre, Providence, USA
16.07.76 Colt Park, Hartford, USA
18.07.76 The Capital Centre, Washington DC, USA
19.07.76 The Spectrum, Philadelphia, USA
21.07.76 The Boston Tea Garden, Boston, USA

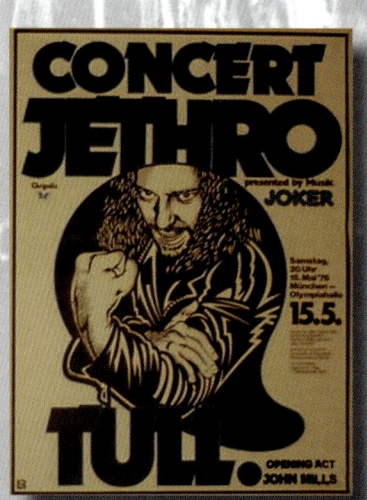

23.07.76 The Shea Stadium, New York, USA
25.07.76 The Pontiac Stadium, Detroit, USA
26.07.76 The Civic Arena, Pittsburgh, USA
27.07.76 The Market Square Arena, Indianapolis, USA
28.07.76 The Louisville Convention Centre, Louisville, USA
29.07.76 The Omni, Atlanta, USA
31.07.76 The Tampa Stadium, Florida, USA
03.08.76 The Richfield Coliseum, Cleveland, USA
04.08.76 The Riverfront Coliseum, Cincinnati, USA
05.08.76 The Chicago Stadium, Chicago, USA
06.08.76 The Chicago Stadium, Chicago, USA
07.08.76 The Kiel Auditorium, St Louis, USA
08.08.76 The Arrowhead Stadium, Kansas, USA
09.08.76 The Assembly Centre, Tulsa, USA
10.08.76 The Moody Coliseum, Dallas, USA
12.08.76 The McNichols Arena, Denver, USA
13.08.76 The Salt Palace, Salt Lake City, USA
15.08.76 The Los Angeles Memorial Coliseum, Los Angeles, USA
16.08.76 The Balboa Stadium, San Diego, USA
18.08.76 The Oakland Coliseum, Oakland, USA
20.08.76 The Memorial Coliseum, Portland, USA
21.08.76 The Seattle Coliseum, Seattle, USA
23.08.76 The Northland Coliseum, Edmonton, Canada
25.08.76 The Calgary Stampede Corral, Calgary, Canada

1977

14.01.77 The Pasadena Civic Auditorium, Pasadena, USA
15.01.77 The Pasadena Civic Auditorium, Pasadena, USA
16.01.77 The Dorothy Chandler Pavilion, LA, USA
19.01.77 The Masonic Auditorium, Detroit, USA
20.01.77 The Masonic Auditorium, Detroit, USA
22.01.77 The Radio City Music Hall, New York, USA
23.01.77 The Radio City Music Hall, New York, USA
01.02.77 The Capitol Theatre, Aberdeen, UK
02.02.77 The Apollo Theatre, Glasgow, UK
03.02.77 The Newcastle City Hall, Newcastle, UK
04.02.77 The Manchester Apollo, Manchester, UK
05.02.77 The Manchester Apollo, Manchester, UK
06.02.77 The Birmingham Odeon, Birmingham, UK
07.02.77 The Empire Theatre, Liverpool, UK
09.02.77 The Gaumont Theatre, Southampton, UK
11.02.77 The Hammersmith Odeon, London, UK
12.02.77 The Hammersmith Odeon, London, UK
13.02.77 The Hammersmith Odeon, London, UK
14.02.77 The Colston Hall, Bristol, UK
23.02.77 The San Diego Sports Arena, San Diego, USA (cancelled but rescheduled for 8th April)
25.02.77 The Anaheim Convention Centre, Anaheim, USA
01.03.77 The Oakland Coliseum, Oakland, USA
03.03.77 The Seattle Coliseum, Seattle, USA
04.03.77 The University Of Oregon, Eugene, USA
05.03.77 The Washington State University, Pullman, USA
06.03.77 The University Of Montana, Missoula, USA
08.03.77 The McNichols Arena, Denver, USA
09.03.77 Omaha City Auditorium Arena, Omaha, USA
10.03.77 The University Of Missouri, Columbia, USA
11.03.77 The Riverfront Coliseum, Cincinnati, USA
12.03.77 The North Western Illinois University, Evanston, USA
13.03.77 The Kiel Auditorium, St Louis, USA
14.03.77 The Municipal Auditorium, Nashville, USA
15.03.77 The Mid-South Coliseum, Memphis, USA
16.03.77 Louisville Gardens Convention Centre, Louisville, USA
17.03.77 The Chicago Stadium, Chicago, USA
18.03.77 The Bradley University Field House, Peoria, USA
19.03.77 St John's Arena, Colombo, USA
21.03.77 The Detroit Cobo Hall, Detroit, USA
22.03.77 The Detroit Cobo Hall, Detroit, USA
23.03.77 The Richfield Coliseum, Cleveland, USA
24.03.77 The Maple Leaf Gardens, Toronto, Canada
25.03.77 The Montreal Forum, Montreal, Canada
26.03.77 The Ottawa Civic Centre, Ottawa, Canada
28.03.77 The Boston Tea Gardens, Boston, USA
29.03.77 The Buffalo War Memorial Auditorium, Buffalo, USA
30.03.77 The Syracuse War Memorial, Syracuse, USA
31.03.77 The Veterans Memorial Coliseum, New Haven, USA
01.04.77 The Veterans Memorial Coliseum, New Haven, USA
06.04.77 The Anaheim Convention Centre, Anaheim, USA
07.04.77 The Anaheim Convention Centre, Anaheim, USA
08.04.77 The San Diego Sports Arena, San Diego, USA
09.04.77 The Long Beach Arena, Long Beach, USA
10.04.77 The Aladdin Theatre, Las Vegas, USA
16.04.77 The Messecentrum, Nurnberg, Germany
17.04.77 The Olympiahalle, Munich, Germany
18.04.77 The Festhalle, Frankfurt, Germany
19.04.77 The Eilenfriedehalle, Hannover, Germany
20.04.77 The Sporthalle, Collogne, Germany
21.04.77 The Grugahalle, Essen, Germany

22.04.77 The Stadthalle, Bremen, Germany
23.04.77 The Deutschlandhalle, Berlin, Germany
24.05.77 The Konserthuset, Stockholm, Sweden
25.05.77 The Scandinavium, Gothenburg, Sweden
27.05.77 The Falkonerteatret, Copenhagen, Denmark
29.05.77 The Congress Centrum Halle, Hamburg, Germany
30.05.77 The Saarlandhalle, Saarbrucken, Germany
31.05.77 The Palais Des Congress, Paris, France
02.06.77 The Ahoy Hall, Rotterdam, Holland
03.06.77 The Voorst National, Brussels, Belgium
05.06.77 The St Jacob Stadium, Basal, Switzerland
06.06.77 ?, Innsbruck, Austria
07.06.77 The Sporthalle, Linz, Austria
08.06.77 The Stadthalle, Vienna, Austria
04.09.77 The Perth Entertainment Centre, Perth, Australia
05.09.77 The Perth Entertainment Centre, Perth, Australia
06.09.77 The Apollo Stadium, Adelaide, Australia
08.09.77 The Festival Hall, Melbourne, Australia
09.09.77 The Festival Hall, Melbourne, Australia
10.09.77 The Festival Hall, Melbourne, Australia
11.09.77 The Festival Hall, Melbourne, Australia
12.09.77 The Festival Hall, Melbourne, Australia
14.09.77 The Hordern Pavilion, Sydney, Australia
15.09.77 The Hordern Pavilion, Sydney, Australia
17.09.77 The Festival Hall, Brisbane, Australia
19.09.77 The Hordern Pavilion, Sydney, Australia
20.09.77 The Hordern Pavilion, Sydney, Australia
04.11.77 The Jai Alai Fronton, Miami, USA
05.11.77 The Jai Alai Fronton, Miami, USA
06.11.77 The Bayfront Centre, St Petersburg, USA
07.11.77 The Atlanta Omni, Atlanta USA
08.11.77 The Municipal Auditorium, New Orleans, USA
09.11.77 The Sam Houston Coliseum, Houston, USA
10.11.77 The Dallas Convention Centre Arena, Dallas, USA
11.11.77 The Dallas Convention Centre Arena, Dallas, USA
12.11.77 The City Fairgrounds, Oklahoma, USA
13.11.77 The Municipal Auditorium, Kansas, USA
14.11.77 The Milwaukee Arena, Milwaukee, USA
15.11.77 The Civic Centre, St Paul, USA
16.11.77 The Dane County Coliseum, Madison, USA
18.11.77 The Springfield Civic Centre, Springfield, USA
19.11.77 The Springfield Civic Centre, Springfield, USA
20.11.77 The Nassau Coliseum, Uniondale, USA
21.11.77 The Capital Centre, Washington, DC, USA
22.11.77 The Hampton Coliseum, Norfolk, USA
23.11.77 The Greensboro Coliseum, Greensboro, USA
24.11.77 The Rupp Arena, Lexington, USA
25.11.77 The Hara Arena, Dayton, USA
27.11.77 The Civic Centre, Portland, USA
28.11.77 The Civic Centre, Hartford, USA
29.11.77 The Madison Square Garden, New York, USA
30.11.77 The Madison Square Garden, New York, USA
01.12.77 The War Memorial Auditorium, Rochester, USA
02.12.77 ?, Wilmington, USA
03.12.77 The Broome County Veterans Memorial Arena,
         Binghamton, USA
04.12.77 The Providence Civic Centre, Providence, USA
05.12.77 The Philadelphia Spectrum, Philadelphia, USA
06.12.77 The Boston Tea Gardens, Boston, USA

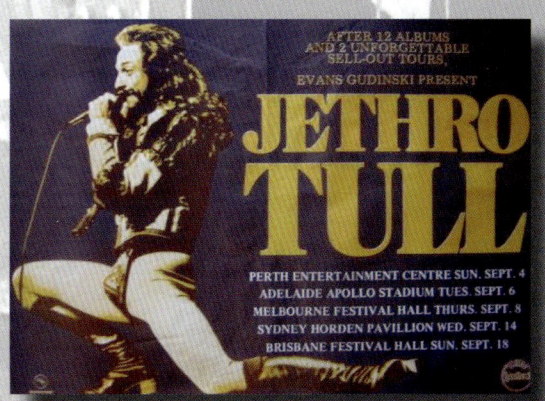

1978

01.05.78 The Usher Hall, Edinburgh, UK
02.05.78 The Apollo Centre, Glasgow, UK
03.05.78 The Apollo Theatre, Manchester, UK
04.05.78 The Apollo Theatre, Manchester, UK
05.05.78 The Odeon Theatre, Birmingham, UK
07.05.78 The Rainbow Theatre, London, UK
08.05.78 The Rainbow Theatre, London, UK
09.05.78 The Hammersmith Odeon, London, UK
10.05.78 The Hammersmith Odeon, London, UK
11.05.78 The Hammersmith Odeon, London, UK
13.05.78 The Congresgebouw, The Hague, Holland
14.05.78 The Voorst National, Brussels, Belgium
15.05.78 The Sporthalle, Cologne, Germany
16.05.78 The Stadthalle, Bremerhaven, Germany
17.05.78 The Munsterlandhalle, Munster, Germany
18.05.78 The Deutschlandhalle, Berlin, Germany
20.05.78 The Grugahalle, Essen, Germany
21.05.78 The Frederich Eberthalle, Ludwigshafen, Germany
22.05.78 The Frederich Eberthalle, Ludwigshafen, Germany
23.05.78 The Sporthalle, Boblingen, Germany
25.05.78 Palais Des Congres, Strasbourg, France
26.05.78 The Saarlandhalle, Saarbrucken, Germany
27.05.78 The Olympiahalle, Munich, Germany
28.05.78 The Festhalle, Berne, Switzerland
29.05.78 The Walter Kubel Halle, Russelheim, Germany
30.05.78 The Walter Kubel Halle, Russelheim, Germany
31.05.78 The Kuppelsalle, Hannover, Germany
02.06.78 The Ostseehalle, Kiel, Germany
04.06.78 The Odeon, Birmingham, UK
05.06.78 The Apollo Theatre, Manchester, UK
01.10.78 The Hampton Roads Coliseum, Hampton USA
02.10.78 The Capital Centre, Largo, USA
03.10.78 The Philadelphia Spectrum, Philadelphia, USA
04.10.78 The Philadelphia Spectrum, Philadelphia, USA
06.10.78 The Boston Tea Gardens, Boston, USA
07.10.78 The Boston Tea Gardens, Boston, USA
08.10.78 Madison Square Garden, New York, USA
09.10.78 Madison Square Garden, New York, USA
11.10.78 Madison Square Garden, New York, USA
12.10.78 The Providence Civic Centre, Providence, USA
13.10.78 The Montreal Forum, Montreal, Canada
15.10.78 The Maple Leaf Gardens, Toronto, Canada
16.10.78 The War Memorial Auditorium, Buffalo, USA
17.10.78 The Detroit Cobo Hall, Detroit, USA
18.10.78 The Detroit Cobo Hall, Detroit, USA
19.10.78 The Checkerdome, St Louis, USA
20.10.78 The Mid South Coliseum, Memphis, USA
21.10.78 The Werner Von Braun Civic Centre, Huntsville, USA
23.10.78 The Chicago Stadium, Chicago, USA
24.10.78 The Sports Arena, Toledo, USA
25.10.78 The Riverfront Coliseum, Cincinnati, USA
26.10.78 The Pittsburgh Civic Arena, Pittsburgh, USA
27.10.78 The Richfield Coliseum, Cleveland, USA
28.10.78 The Wings Stadium, Kalamazoo, USA
30.10.78 The Veterans Memorial Coliseum, New Haven, USA
31.10.78 The Veterans Memorial Coliseum, New Haven, USA
01.11.78 The Onondaga County War Memorial, Syracuse, USA
02.11.78 The War Memorial Auditorium, Rochester, USA
07.11.78 The McNichols Arena, Denver, USA
08.11.78 The Salt Palace Arena, Salt Lake City, USA
09.11.78 The Centennial Coliseum, Reno, USA

10.11.78 The Aladdin Theatre, Las Vegas, USA
12.11.78 The Oakland Stadium, Oakland, USA
13.11.78 The Inglewood Forum, Los Angeles, USA
14.11.78 The Inglewood Forum, Los Angeles, USA
15.11.78 The Long Beach Arena, Long Beach, USA
16.11.78 The Long Beach Arena, Long Beach, USA
17.11.78 The Long Beach Arena, Long Beach, USA

1979

01.04.79 The El Paso County Coliseum, Albuquerque, USA
02.04.79 The Tempe Activity Centre, Tempe, USA
03.04.79 The Sports Arena, San Diego, USA
04.04.79 The Selland Arena, Fresno, USA
06.04.79 The Dee Events Centre, Ogden, USA
07.04.79 The Mini Dome, Pocatello, USA
08.04.79 The Metra, Billings, USA
10.04.79 The Seattle Coliseum, Seattle, USA
11.04.79 The Pacific Coliseum, Vancouver, USA
12.04.79 The Memorial Coliseum, Portland, USA
14.04.79 The Northlands Coliseum, Edmonton, Canada
15.04.79 The Stampede Corral, Calgary, Canada

17.04.79 The Met Centre, St Paul, USA
18.04.79 The University Of North Iowa Unidome, Cedar Falls, USA
19.04.79 The Milwaukee Arena, Milwaukee, USA
20.04.79 The Dane County Coliseum, Madison, USA
21.04.79 The Bob Devaney Centre, Lincoln, USA
23.04.79 The Kemper Arena, Kansas City, USA
24.04.79 The Kansas Coliseum, Wichita, USA
25.04.79 The Myriad, Oklahoma, USA
26.04.79 The Lubbock Coliseum, Lubbock, USA
28.04.79 The Sam Houston Coliseum, Houston, USA
29.04.79 The Sam Houston Coliseum, Houston, USA
30.04.79 The County Convention Centre Arena, Fort Worth, USA
01.05.79 The San Antonio Convention Centre, San Antonio, USA

From August 1979 through to June 1980, Jethro Tull were Ian Anderson. Martin Barre, John Evan, Barrimore Barlow, David Palmer and Dave Pegg.

05.10.79 The Maple Leaf Gardens, Toronto, Canada
06.10.79 The Quebec Coliseum, Quebec, Canada
07.10.79 The Montreal Forum, Montreal, Canada
09.10.79 The New Haven Coliseum, New Haven, USA
10.10.79 The New Haven Coliseum, New Haven, USA
11.10.79 The Madison Square Garden, New York, USA
12.10.79 The Madison Square Garden, New York, USA
14.10.79 The Providence Civic Centre, Providence, USA
(rescheduled from the 13th due to Anderson having been hit in the eye with a rose on the 12th)
16.10.79 The Philadelphia Spectrum, Philadelphia, USA
17.10.79 The Philadelphia Spectrum, Philadelphia, USA
18.10.79 The Capital Centre, Washington DC, USA
19.10.79 The Civic Centre, Portland, USA
20.10.79 Community War Memorial, Rochester, USA
21.10.79 The Boston Tea Gardens, Boston, USA
22.10.79 The Nassau Coliseum, Uniondale, USA
24.10.79 Olympia Stadium, Detroit, USA
25.10.79 The Civic Arena, Pittsburgh, USA
26.10.79 The Richfield Coliseum, Cleveland, USA
27.10.79 The Riverfront Coliseum, Cincinnati, USA
29.10.79 The Chicago Stadium, Chicago, USA
30.10.79 The Municipal Auditorium, Nashville, USA
31.10.79 The Mid-South Coliseum, Memphis, USA
01.11.79 The Atlanta Omni, Atlanta, USA
02.11.79 The Coliseum, Jacksonville, USA
03.11.79 The Lakeland Civic Centre, Lakeland, USA
04.11.79 The Hollywood Sportatorium, Miami, USA
05.11.79 The Hollywood Sportatorium, Miami, USA
06.11.79 The Jefferson Civic Centre Arena, Birmingham, USA
07.11.79 The South Illinois University Arena, Carbondale, USA
08.11.79 The Checkerdome, St Louis, USA
09.11.79 The Omaha Civic Auditorium Arena, Omaha, USA
10.11.79 The McNichols Arena, Denver, USA
12.11.79 The Aladdin Theatre, Las Vegas, USA
13.11.79 The Long Beach Arena, Long Beach, USA
14.11.79 The Long Beach Arena, Long Beach, USA
15.11.79 The Long Beach Arena, Long Beach, USA
16.11.79 The Civic Auditorium, Santa Monica, USA
17.11.79 The San Diego Sports Arena, San Diego, USA
18.11.79 The Oakland Coliseum, Oakland, USA